Fritz Forkel
Bahrain
1983

Library of Arabic Linguistics

The reasons behind the establishment of this Series on Arabic linguistics are manifold.

First: Arabic linguistics is developing into an increasingly interesting and important subject within the broad field of modern linguistic studies. The subject is now fully recognized in the Universities of the Arabic speaking world and in international linguistic circles, as a subject of great theoretical and descriptive interest and importance.

Second: Arabic linguistics is reaching a mature stage in its development benefiting from both the early Arabic linguistic scholarship and modern techniques of general linguistics and related disciplines.

Third: The scope of this discipline is wide and varied, covering diverse areas such as Arabic phonetics, phonology and grammar, Arabic psycholinguistics, Arabic dialectology, Arabic lexicography and lexicology, Arabic sociolinguistics, teaching and learning of Arabic as a first, second, or foreign language, communications, semiotics, terminology, translation, machine translation, Arabic computational linguistics, history of Arabic linguistics, etc.

Viewed against this background, Arabic linguistics may be defined as: the scientific investigation and study of the Arabic language in all its aspects. This embraces the descriptive, comparative and historical aspects of the language. It also concerns itself with the classical form as well as the modern and contemporary standard forms and its dialects. Moreover, it attempts to study the language in the appropriate regional, social and cultural settings.

It is hoped that the Series will devote itself to all issues of Arabic linguistics in all its manifestations both on the theoretical and applied levels. The results of these studies will also be of use in the field of linguistics in general, as well as related subjects.

Although a number of works have appeared independently or within Series, yet there is no platform designed specifically for this subject. This Series is being started to fill this gap in the linguistic field. It will be devoted to Monographs written in either English or Arabic, or both, for the benefit of wider circles of readership.

All these reasons justify the establishment of a new forum which is devoted to all areas of Arabic linguistic studies. It is also hoped that this Series will be of interest not only to students and researchers in Arabic linguistics but also to students and scholars of other disciplines who are looking for information of both theoretical, practical or pragmatic interest.

The Series Editor

Language and linguistic origins in Baḥrain

Library of Arabic Linguistics

Series editor
Muhammad Hasan Bakalla
King Saud University, Riyadh, Kingdom of Saudi Arabia

Advisory editorial board
Peter F. Abboud *University of Texas at Austin*
M. H. Abdulaziz *University of Nairobi*
Yousif El-Khalifa Abu Bakr *University of Khartoum*
Salih J. Altoma *Indiana University*
Arne Ambros *University of Vienna*
El Said M. Badawi *American University in Cairo*
Michael G. Carter *University of Sydney*
Ahmad al-Dhubaib *King Saud University* (formerly, University of Riyadh)
Martin Forstner *Johannes Gutenberg University at Mainz*
Bruce Ingham *University of London*
Otto Jastrow *University of Erlangen-Nurnberg*
Raja T. Nasr *University College of Beirut*
C. H. M. Versteegh *Catholic University at Nijmegen*
Bougslaw R. Zagorski *University of Warsaw*

Mahdi Abdalla Al-Tajir

Language and linguistic origins in Baḥrain

The Baḥārnah dialect of Arabic

Monograph No. 5

Kegan Paul International

London, Boston and Melbourne
1982

First published in 1982
by Kegan Paul International Ltd
39 Store Street, London WC1E 7DD,
9 Park Street, Boston, Mass. 02108, USA, and
296 Beaconsfield Parade, Middle Park,
Melbourne, 3206, Australia
Printed in Great Britain by
The Thetford Press Ltd, Thetford, Norfolk

ISBN 0-7103-0024-7

In memory of my beloved parents

Editor's note

Dialectology is the systematic study of dialect: its origin, history, procedures, methods, notions and concepts. This study concerns itself with findings about dialect singly or in groups. These are studied in various ways: synchronically, diachronically, historically or comparatively. They can also be studied geographically, socially, folkloristically and according to various sociological variables and continua. Early (or traditional) dialect studies placed emphasis on rural dialects. More recent works, however, have concentrated on urban dialects.

Dialects are said to be 'the various different forms of the same language'. Thus the word for 'fish' in Modern Standard Arabic and Meccan Arabic is *samak*, but in Baḥraini *simač*. These variants are considered forms of the same language, i.e. Arabic. In other words, the term *dialect* covers any combination of observable variable features of a language, involving bundles of geographical or social isoglosses.

Over the past two decades or so a great deal of research has been undertaken on the use of language in a social context and interest in this field has grown rapidly. Dialectology is considered a branch of sociolinguistics today, since it has become more seriously concerned with the study of language in society. It deals with, among other things, the diagnosis of social dialects, social or religious groups. It also includes discussion of data collection and analysis. This trend is exemplified by J. K. Chambers and Peter Trudgill's recent book *Dialectology*, published in the Series of Cambridge Textbooks in Linguistics, Cambridge University Press, London, etc., 1980.

The present book falls within the boundaries of sociolinguistic framework, particularly applied to the Arabic dialects of Baḥrain. It discusses these dialects in terms of their linguistic levels indicating the various factors which have influenced them. Evidence from history and genealogy is brought forward to explain the variations and differences which already exist in the dialects under investigation. Statistical data are incorporated to show the diffusion of the population of Baḥrain and the distribution of the speakers of its dialects.

Editor's note

Linguistic research on Baḥrain is still in its infancy despite the fact that it was once an important region. Two works have been published quite recently. The first is a research paper by Clive Holes entitled 'Phonological Variation in Baḥraini Arabic: the [*j*] and [*y*] allophones of [*j*]', published in *Zeitschrift für Arabische Linguistik (ZAL)*, Volume 4, Wiesbaden, 1980. In 1981 he completed his doctoral dissertation on the sociological aspects of Baḥraini Arabic. The second is a book in Arabic by Dr Abdul Aziz Matar entitled *Phonological Study of the Baḥraini Dialects*, published by ᶜAyn Shams University Press, Cairo 1980. In this work Dr Matar discusses certain phonological variations of Baḥraini dialects both descriptively and comparatively. More recently also T. Prochazka has compared the dialects of Baḥrain with the dialect of al-Ristāq in *ZAL*, Volume 6, 1981.

The main body of Dr Al-Tajir's book is essentially a synchronic analysis of the Baḥārnah dialect of Arabic. Comparative data is also included to illustrate the close relationship between the local dialects on the one hand and certain Arabic dialects of the Arabian Peninsula on the other. Two main groups of Baḥraini dialects are analysed. They are: (1) the indigenous Baḥārnah dialect and to a somewhat lesser extent (2) the ᶜAnazi dialect of Baḥrain. The book consists of an Introduction and six parts. Part I gives a detailed analysis of the origins of the Baḥārnah Arabs. It also includes an historical survey of the region. Parts II-IV treat the phonology, morphology and syntax of the Baḥārnah dialect respectively. Part V is a lexical analysis of Baḥraini Arabic which also includes an analysis of loan words from Persian, English and Hindustani. Part VI presents a comparative study of the Baḥraini dialects and the dialects of the Arabian Peninsula.

Three points should be noted about the present study. First it aims to determine the linguistic origins of the population of Baḥrain. The author shows the influences of southern, northern and central Arabian dialects on Baḥraini dialects. The author lays particular stress on evidence demonstrating that Baḥrain is linguistically an integral part of the Arabian Peninsula and that it is not a dialect produced by outside influences. Secondly the author points to the existence of many of the present dialectal features of Baḥrain, in early Arabic dialects as shown by early Arab linguists. These include the phenomena of *imālah*, *kaškašah*, *ᶜan ᶜanah* and various other phonological alternations. Similarly he points to morphological, syntactic and lexical links with Ancient Arabian dialects. Finally he provides maps and tables illustrating the distribution of different dialectal features in Baḥrain as well as other parts of the Arabian Peninsula.

The present book is the first systematic and comprehensive analysis of the dialects of Baḥrain. It is based on extensive field work and is therefore a significant contribution to our linguistic knowledge of a region which is becoming increasingly more important in the world today.

The author was born in 1940. He received his secondary schooling in Baḥrain. In 1961 he joined al-Saᶜīdiyya Secondary School, Cairo, where he obtained his Secondary Certificate. In 1965 he received his B.A. in English literature from Cairo University. He then joined the Department of Education in Baḥrain. In 1967 he obtained a Post-Graduate Diploma in English Studies at the University of Leeds, England.

During September 1973, he represented the Department of Education at the Conference on the Teaching of Foreign Languages in the Arab World, held under the auspices of the Arab Organization for Education, Culture and Science. In the summer of 1979 he obtained his Ph.D. in Semitic Studies from the University of Leeds. His doctoral dissertation was entitled 'A Critical and Comparative Study of the Baḥārnah Dialect of Arabic as Spoken in Present-Day Baḥrain'.

Dr Al-Tajir contributed a paper entitled 'Notes on the Places and Tribes of the Ancient Region of al-Baḥrain and the Island of ?Awāl', to the Seminar for Arabian Studies held at the University of Cambridge in July 1979.

He obtained an M.A. in Area Studies from the School of Oriental and African Studies, University of London in 1980 and is at present reading history at the same School.

M. H. Bakalla
Series Editor
King Saud University
(formerly *University of Riyadh*)

Contents

PREFACE xxiii
TRANSCRIPTION AND TRANSLITERATION xxv
ABBREVIATIONS xxvii
INTRODUCTION 1
Field Work and the Informants 2
Tape recordings and Transcriptions 3
Arrangement of the Material 3
The Schools and the Emergence of Pan-Arabic 'koine' Forms 3
  The earliest missionary schools 4
  The Hidāya School 4
  Traditional Baḥārnah schools 4
  The BAPCO School at Zallāq 4
  The Urdu School 4
  The first batch of expatriate Arab teachers 4
New Items pertaining to Agriculture 5
The Media 5
Non-Local Element in the Population 6
  The local Arabs of Baḥrain 7
  The Huwalah Arabs 7
  The Baḥārnah Arabs 7
Geographical Distribution of the Baḥārnah 8
Linguistic Contact between local and nonlocal elements 9
  Situation in the villages 10
Previous Studies of East Arabian speech 10
  The Baḥrain Petroleum Company and Arabic studies 10
  Further publications on east Arabian speech 11
Local View on Current Spoken Arabic 12
Notes 13

PART I: SECTION (A) 15

THE ANCIENT REGION OF AL-BAḤRAIN 15

Baḥrain and ᶜUmān 16

?Awāl Island and the Region of al-Baḥrain 16

The Early Settlers 16

The Emergence of ᶜAbd al-Qais Tribes 16

- The descendants of ᶜIjl ibn ᶜAmr ibn Wadīᶜah ibn Lukayz 18
- The descendants of Hinb ibn Afṣa ibn Duᶜmiyy 18
- The descendants of Shann ibn Afṣa of ᶜAbd al-Qais 18
- The descendants of an-Nimr ibn Qāsiṭ ibn Hinb ibn Afṣa Duᶜmiyy ibn Jadīlah 19

On the Early Inhabitants of the Island of ?Awāl 19

Diverse Arab Elements in Contemporary Baḥrain 23

- Āl-Khalīfah the ruling house of Baḥrain 23
- The early inhabitants of the island of ?Awāl (a recapitulation) 24
- The early inhabitants of Samāhīj 24
- The inhabitants of Bani Jamrah village 24
- 1783 and after 25

PART I: SECTION (B) 27

NOTES ON THE GEOGRAPHY OF THE ISLANDS OF BAḤRAIN 27

The Significance of the Islands 27

- Geographical 27
- Economic 28
  - The old pearling industry 28
  - The coming of oil and the diversification of resources 28

Historical Survey of the Islands 28

- The Phoenicians 28
- Pre-Islamic and early Islamic Baḥrain 28
- Baḥrain under the Umayyad dynasty 29
- Baḥrain under the ᶜAbbāsids 29
- Baḥrain under Ṣāḥib az-Zanj 29
- The Carmathians in the region of al-Baḥrain (899–1060 A.D. app.) 29
- Abu al-Bahlūl al-ᶜAwwām, independent chief of ?Awāl 29
- Baḥrain in the twelfth century A.D. and after 30
- Baḥrain under the Portuguese 1521–1602 30
- The arrival of the ᶜUtūb, 1783 and after 30

The Emergence of Shīᶜism in the region 33

Notes 34

PART II: THE PHONOLOGY OF THE BAḤĀRNAH DIALECT 40
The Consonants 41
The plosives: The *hamza* or the glottal stop 41
Elision of the glottal stop 42
The plosive *b* 43
The plosive *t* 43
The emphatic *ṭ* 43
The plosive *d* 43
Devoicing of *d* to *t* 43
The emphatic *ḍ* 44
The plosive *k* 44
Affrication of *k* to *č* 44
k remains stable 45
The occurrence of *č* in loan-words 46
The plosive *q* 46
The fronting of *q* 47
Realization of *q* as *k* 47
The occurrence of *q* as *ġ* in A 48
The affrication of *g* to *j* in B 48
The occurrence of *g* in A 49
The occurrence of *g* < *q* as *j* in A 49
j > *g* in B 50
Realization of *j* as *y* 50
The velarized *ḷ* 50
The liquid *r* 51
The fricatives: the guttural *ġ* 52
The guttural *x* 52
The guttural *h* 52
The fricative *w* 52
The fricatives *f* and *ṯ* 52
The fricative *ḏ* 53
The fricative *s* 53
The fricative *z* 53
The nasal *n* 53
Assimilation of consonants 54
Contractions 54
The Vowel System 55
The front vowel *a* 56
The anaptyctic *a* 56
Front *a* > back *ɑ* 57
Word-final *imāla* 57
The front vowel *i* 59
The *u* variant of *i* 59
The prosthetic vowel *i* 61

The anaptyctic vowel *i* 61
The back vowel *u* 62
The occurrence of the long vowels: Long *ii* 63
Long *ee* 63
Long *aa* 63
Back vowel *αα* 64
Long *oo* 64
Long *uu* 65
Diphthongs 65
Consonant Clusters 66
Gemination or Duplication of a Consonant 67
The Syllabic Structure of Certain Nominal and Verbal Forms 67
Stress in B 68
Notes 69

PART III: THE MORPHOLOGY OF THE BAḤĀRNAH DIALECT 70

The Strong Verb 72
The simple verb: The perfect 72
The imperfect 72
The imperative 74
Some common forms of the perfect, imperfect and imperative 74
Derived themes 74
The Weak Verb 75
The *hamzated* verb: verbs with initial *hamza* 75
Verb medial *hamza* 76
Verb final *hamza* 76
Verb initial *w* 77
Derived themes 77
Verb initial *y* 77
Derived themes 78
Hollow verbs 78
Derived themes 78
Defective verbs 78
Doubly weak verbs 80
Geminate Verbs 80
The Passive Verb 81
Hamzated forms of the passive verb 81
Hollow verbs as passive forms 82
Defective verbs as passive forms 82
Geminate verbs as passive forms 82
Quadriliteral Verb 82
Derived Themes 82

Active and Passive Participles 83
Active participles as verbs 84
Some common forms of the active participles 84
The Nominal Patterns 85
The formation of nouns and adjectives by suffixes:
The singular 86
The dual 86
The sound plural 86
The diminutive 87
Collectives 87
The verbal nouns: derived themes 88
Common forms of nouns and verbal nouns in B 89
The broken plural 91
Common patterns of the broken plural in B 92
Tanwīn (nunation): An archaic feature preserved in B 94
The construct state 95
The comparison of adjectives 95
The Numerals 96
The cardinals one to ten 96
The numerals from three to nine 97
The cardinals eleven to nineteen 97
The numerals twenty to ninety 97
Numbers above a hundred 98
The ordinals one to ten 98
The Personal Pronouns 98
The pronominal suffixes 99
The particle *iyya* + pronominal suffixes 100
The reflexive pronouns *nafs* and *ruuḥ* 100
maal and *maalat* as possessive pronouns 100
Demonstrative pronouns 101
The demonstrative of place 102
The demonstratives in liaison with pronominal suffixes 102
The relative pronoun *?illi* 102
Particles 102
Prepositions 102
Adverbial particles 103
Conjunctions 105
Interjections 105
Interrogative particles 106
Notes 106

PART IV: SOME SYNTACTIC FEATURES 108

The Verb
The perfect 108

The imperfect 109
The use of the imperfect verb *iji* (for about, since) as an adverbial particle 110
The imperative 110
The active participle 111
The employment of participles to indicate past or future time 111
The passive verb 111
Subject-verb concord 112
Interrogation 112
Negation of verbs 114
Double negation 114
The Noun 115
The indefinite noun 115
Definite and indefinite concord 115
Gender and number concord 116
Adjectives of colour 117
Negation of the nominal sentence 118
Negated forms of the personal pronouns 118
Sentence Structure 119
The nominal sentence 119
The verbal sentence 119
The effect of emphasis on positional variations 120
The sequential order: adj. + noun 120
The adjective *xo(o)š* (good, excellent) 120
The particle *weeš* 120
The particle *kill/e* 120
Demonstratives 121
Near objects 121
Remote objects 121
Demonstratives in liaison with pronominal suffixes 122
The particle *-iyya* 122
Conditional sentences 123
Relative clauses 125
Temporal clauses 126
Notes 127

PART V: LEXICAL FEATURES 128

Section A 128
Specimens of two-word collocates 128
Specimens of common verbal forms 129
Specimens of localisms 129
Some common proverbial expressions 130
Classical Arabic items in B 131
Pan-Arabic koine forms in current speech 131

Comparative lexis: specimens of regional variations 132
Specimens of inter-dialectal variations: rural and urban forms of B 132
Section B
Notes on English loan-words 133
Notes on Hindustani loan-words 134
Notes on Persian loan-words and place names 134
Further notes on Persian and Hindustani loan-words 135
Arabicized forms in current circulation in the area 135
Specimens of borrowings from English 135
Specimens of borrowings from Hindustani (Urdu) 136
Specimens of borrowings from Persian 137
Specimens of borrowings from Turkish 138
Section C
Specimens of specialized lexis: items pertaining to *l-izraa*ᶜ*a* (gardening) 138
Items from the text of an interview with a date planter 139
Specimens from the nautical vocabulary of a local *baḥḥaar* (seaman) 139
Specimens from a weaver's specialized vocabulary 140
Specialized lexis: folk-medicine 140
Notes 141

PART VI: COMPARATIVE ANALYSIS 143

Phonology 143
The plosives 143
Affrication of *k* 145
2 f.s. *-k* > *-s* 146
Devoicing of *q* to *k* in rural B 147
q > *ġ* in A 148
ġ > *q* in A 148
The affrication of *q* in A 148
Palatalization of *j* 149
Velar *ḷ* 149
The fricatives 150
The occurrence of *ṯ* as *f* in B 150
The occurrence of *-n* in 2 f.s. and 2 c.pl. in B 151
Imāla in B 152
Diphthongs 153
Morphology 154
Verbal forms 154
The imperfect preformative *y-* 155
The terminations *-inne* and *-tinne* 156

FaMaaMiiL for FaMMaaLuun	157
?aFMaL > FaMaL in A	157
Tanwīn	157
-^{c}*aš* and ^{c}*ašar*	157
Personal pronouns	158
Demonstratives	158
The occurrence of a series of short syllables in B	159
The effect of gutturals on the syllable structure in A	159
Lexis	160
Notes on comparative lexis	160
Distribution of comparative data: Phonological features	163
Morphological features	164
Summary and Conclusion	165
Notes	168
APPENDICES AND TEXTS	174
Distribution by Nationalities	174
Increase by Nationalities	174
Distribution by Religion	175
Distribution of Non-Muslims	175
Distribution by Towns and Villages	175
Census of Dwelling Houses	176
Total Population of Major Civil Divisions by Urban/Rural Residents, Sex and Nationality, 1971	177
Specimens from Baḥārnah Texts	178
The Informants and their Villages	195
BIBLIOGRAPHY	200
GENERAL INDEX	205
INDEX OF LEXICAL ITEMS	207

ARABIC SECTION

EDITOR'S NOTE	1
PREFACE BY THE AUTHOR	8
GLOSSARY OF LINGUISTIC TERMS: ENGLISH-ARABIC	30

Illustrations

Plates — between pages 100 and 101

A Baḥārnah villager
A Baḥārnah gardener displaying his tools
Ḥajji ^{c}Ali ^{c}Abdalla Nijim at his ground-loom in Bani Jamrah
A fisherman in the process of finishing a wire trap
Fishermen from the village of Dirāz
Traditional houses of Baḥrain
Other traditional houses (of Baḥrain)

Maps

Map I	Baḥrain in relation to the rest of the area	213
Map II	Old place names mentioned by Medieval Arabic sources	214
Map III	Geographical distribution of tribes in ancient Baḥrain	215
Map IV	Geographical distribution of speech-communities in A and B	216
Map V	The realization of 2 f.s. *-k* as *-š*	217
Map VI	Distribution of the affrication of *k*, *g* into *č*, *ǧ*	218
Map VII	The realization of *q* as *ġ*	219
Map VIII	Distribution of dental *ṯ* > labio-dental *f*	220
Map IX	The occurrence of the pronominal suffixes: *-č*, *-čem*, *-hem*	221
Map X	The traditional industries of Baḥrain: Geographical distribution	222

Preface

The present study notes the existence, in contemporary Baḥrain, of two distinct dialect-groups, viz. (a) the Baḥārnah speech-community (b) the ^{c}Anazi speech community.

Nowadays, common cultural ties as well as shared linguistic features are factors, among others, that unite the members in each group. Historically, speakers in group (a) are largely descendants of the early ^{c}Abd al-Qais tribes of eastern Arabia, whereas those that constitute group (b) are descended from diverse peninsular Arab tribes many of whom came to Baḥrain in the wake of the ^{c}Anazi take-over of 1783.

The study attempts to describe, in analytical as well as historical terms the Baḥārnah speech-forms; also it attempts, to some degree, inter-and cross-dialectal comparisons and relates its findings to the dialects prevailing in the adjoining areas. It is a synchronic as well as diachronic account of the phonology, morphology, syntax, and lexis of the Baḥārnah dialect of Arabic. The approach followed throughout is in line with the one employed by linguists interested in the Arabic dialects of the region. In addition, the study devotes attention to the examination of the origins of the speakers in both communities, especially the Baḥārnah Arabs of Baḥrain whose tribal descent has been somewhat misrepresented.

Some of the findings of the study are:

(a) In many respects, the Baḥārnah speech-forms, which constitute an older stratum in east Arabian speech, tie in closely with early east and south Arabian Arabic, and less so with north Arabian.

(b) On the other hand, the ^{c}Anazi speech-forms of Baḥrain show clear resemblance to central and north Arabian peninsular Arabic, and hence represent the eastern dimension of north Arabian speech.

(c) Circulation in current Baḥārnah Arabic of a large number of classical and archaic forms.

(d) The presence in Baḥārnah speech of quite a number of localisms which deviate from the established usage elsewhere in the area, therefore deserve to be noticed.

Since I committed myself to the present study, I have incurred obligations of gratitude to many people. I am greatly indebted to all those who helped, one way or another, particularly my informants, males and females who have furnished me with the basic material without which such a dialect survey would have been impossible. Their positive attitude, coupled with the courtesy and patience which they exhibited during the recording sessions, has greatly facilitated my field work. Except for my female informants, whose names, at their own request, are not disclosed, names of my male informants are provided on separate lists.

My sincere thanks go to Mr. Anwar al-Dirāzi, who not only assisted me on several field work sessions, but also arranged for interviews, especially with female Dirāzi speakers. My thanks are also due to Mr. H. A. al-Madani and my cousins Mrs. Bāqir and Sa^{c}īd al-Tājir, who were all of great help while conducting field work in Baḥrain, particularly Mr. Sa^{c}īd who later helped in verifying some of the information recorded on previous occasions. I would like also to thank Mr. ^{c}Abdul Raḥmān ^{c}Abdalla of Baḥrain Radio, who kindly carried out, on my behalf, the tape-recordings of certain old plays produced for Baḥrain Radio in Muḥarraqi dialect; and to Mr. Aḥmad al-^{c}Urayfi of the Drama and Arts Section of the Ministry of Information who helped in arranging some of my earlier interviews.

My thanks also go to Mulla ^{c}Aṭiyyah, a religious personality from the village of Bani Jamrah, and to his brother Ḥajji Ḥusain, and Ḥajji ^{c}Ali ^{c}Abdalla Nijim of the same village for granting me long interviews. I am also grateful to my cousin Muḥammad Ḥasan al-Tājir of Abū Sēbi^{c} village for arranging meetings with the local people of the same village, all of whom were extremely helpful. My thanks are also due to Mr. ^{c}Abdul Jalīl ^{c}Ali al-Ṣaffār for furnishing me with the relevant issues of *al-Mawāqif* weekly, viz. those which included the texts of interviews with the well-known Baḥrāni scholar, Mr. Ibrāhīm al-^{c}Urayyiḍ.

I should like also to thank my brother-in-law Mr. ^{c}Ali al-Tājir, for answering my various early queries, and perhaps even more for providing me with a photocopy of Chapter I – Part V of his late father's unpublished work *^{c}Uqūd al-Āl fi Tārikh Jazā?ir ?Uwāl,* to the existence of which attention was drawn in 1968 by R.B. Serjeant in a footnote to his article "Fisher-Folk and Fish-Traps in al-Baḥrain", *BSOAS,* vol. XXXI, 1968. The chapter made available to me deals with the physical and human geography of the Baḥārnah villages.

I should like to express my deep gratitude to Dr. B.S.J. Isserlin, Head of the Department of Semitic Studies for his guidance and encouragement throughout, to Mr. S.F. Sanderson, Head of the Institute of Folklore, Leeds University, and Mr. A.E. Green, from the same Institute for their kind assistance, and to Professor T.M. Johnstone of the London School of Oriental and African Studies, who was kind enough to place his great first-hand knowledge of the linguistic features of the Gulf area at my disposition and who in addition looked through most parts of the present work and gave me the benefit of criticism and advice.

I am also grateful to the staff of the following libraries:
The Brotherton Library at Leeds University
The School of Oriental and African Studies main library
The British Library, Main and Oriental rooms, OPL section
India Office Library
Public Records Office
Royal Geographical Society Library.

Finally, I am also grateful to the Al-Tājir Establishments and I should like to express my deep gratitude to my brother-in-law, Mr. M.M. al-Tājir, for his firm moral and material support, without which this work might not have materialized. I should also like to thank him for occasionally correcting me on various points relating to the Baḥārnah Arabs of Baḥrain, whose language is the main theme of this study.

M.A. al-Tajir

Transcription and transliteration

Phonetic Transcription

Below are the symbols employed throughout the study to represent the consonantal sound-units of the Baharnah dialect of Arabic. Free variants or alternative realizations are shown in parenthesis.

?		*z*		*k*	(*č*)
b	(*p*)	*s*	(*ṣ*)	*g*	
t		*š*		*l*	
ṯ	(*f*)	*ṣ*		*m*	
j	(*y*), (*g*)	*ḍ*		*n*	
č		*ṭ*		*h*	
ḥ		*ẓ*	(*ḍ*)	*w*	
x		c		*y*	
d		*ġ*			
ḏ		*f*			
r		*q*	(*g*), (*k*), (*j*)		

Notes:

The vowels are broadly described *a, α, e* < *ee, i, o* < *oo* and *u*. Their longer equivalents are *aa, αα, ee, ii, oo, uu*. The above distinctions were found adequate to the aims laid down for this study as it also helps avoid typographical complications. Vocalic lengthening or shortening, brought about as a result of elision or affixation, are discussed under the appropriate sections. Emphatic consonants are distinguished by the placing of a dot under the consonant as in the ^{c}Anazi form *buṣal,* "onion".

Partial realization of a consonant is indicated by a small circle placed under the consonant as in: *^{c}alašaaŋ̥,* "for, so that".

A vowel in parenthesis such as *ma(a)* "not" is, broadly speaking, indicative of the occurrence of both long and short forms. Often parentheses are also used to indicate prosthetic vowels. Final *e* < *a*, known as *imāla* is in effect, an allophonic variant of *a* in B.

For typographical convenience, allophonic variants such as front *a* and back *α*, short and long forms are, throughout this study, transcribed *a* and *aa*, except where the distinction between the two is discussed.

Note also, that in connected speech, word-final vowel is in liaison with the initial consonant of the item following it and word-final consonant is in liaison with the initial vowel of following item, as in: *?il‿ġurfa š-šargiyye* "the eastern room" and *daak‿il-yoom* "that day".

Transliteration

Except for slight modifications, the following symbols, such as normally used by Orientalists, have also been employed for transliteration purposes: e.g.

th	*dh*	*ḍ*	c	?
ḥ	*sh*	*ṭ*	*gh*	
kh	*ṣ*	*ẓ*	*q*	

In transliterated forms, vowel length is indicated by a dash over the letter as in: *ḥalāyil*, "native islanders from the rural areas."

Names of places quoted in this study generally conform to the official spelling, without regard to what would be their correct phonetic transcription.

Abbreviations

(a) Works Referred to by Abbreviated Titles:

Abbreviated form	Author	Full title
CDB	H. Blanc	*Communal Dialects in Baghdad*
EADS	T.M. Johnstone	*Eastern Arabian Dialect Studies*
Ein arabischer Dialect	Carl Reinhardt	*Ein arabischer Dialekt gesprochen in ^{c}Oman und Zanzibar*
Études	J. Cantineau	*Etudes sur quelques parlers de nomades arabes d'orient*
GCASP	G.R. Driver	*A Grammar of the Colloquial Arabic of Syria and Palestine*
al-Ibdāl	Abū al-Ṭayyib	*Kitāb al-Ibdāl*
al-I^{c}rāb	Ibn Jinnī	*Sirr Ṣinā^{c}at al-I^{c}rāb*
al-Kitāb	Sībawaihi	*Kitāb Sībawaihi*
L'Arabo Parlato	E. Rossi	*L'Arabo Parlato a Ṣan^{c}ā*
Lexicon	E.W. Lane	*Arabic-English Lexicon*
Lisān	Ibn Manẓūr	*Lisān al-^{c}Arab*
MDA	H. Blanc	*Mesopotamian Dialect of Arabic*
WGAL	W. Wright	*A Grammar of the Arabic Language*
al-Muzhir	al-Suyūṭi	*al-Muzhir fī ^{c}Ulūm al-Lughah*
ODA	A.S.G. Jayakar	*The ^{c}Omānee Dialect of Arabic*

(b) Journals and Series:

AIEO	*Annales de l'Institut d'Études Orientales d'Alger*
BASOR	*The Bulletin of the American School of Oriental Research*
BSOAS	*The Bulletin of the School of Oriental and African Studies*, London
EI	*Encyclopaedia of Islam*
JAOS	*Journal of the American Oriental Society*, Newhaven
JRAS	*Journal of the Royal Asiatic Society*
JRCAS	*Journal of the Royal Central Asian Society*
JRGS	*Journal of the Royal Geographical Society*
JRSA	*Journal of the Royal Society of Arts*
JSS	*Journal of Semitic Studies*
MEJ	*Middle East Journal*, London
MMA	*Majallat Majam^{c} al-Lughah al-^{c}Arabiyyah*, Cairo

(c) Other abbreviations and symbols:

A	^{c}Anazi dialect or speech of Bahrain
act. part.	active participle
adj.	adjective
anap.	anaptyctic vowel
app.	approximately

assim.	assimilation
B	Baḥārnah dialect or speech of Baḥrain
c.	common gender
cf.	compare
con.	consonant
f. or fem.	feminine
fig.	figurative
fin.	final
imp.	imperative
imperf.	imperfect
inf.	informant
init.	initial
IOR	India Office Records
lib.	liberal (ly)
lit.	literal (ly)
lit. Ar.	Literary Arabic
m. or masc.	masculine
MDA	Mesopotamian dialect area
med.	medial
n.	noun
N.A.	North Arabian (dialects)
p.	person
parag.	paragraph
pass. part.	passive participle
perf.	perfect
pl.	plural
prep.	preposition
pron.	pronoun
pron. suff.	pronominal suffix
pros.	prosthetic vowel
ref.	reference
s. or sing.	singular
v.	vowel
v.n.	verbal noun
vd.	voiced
vl.	voiceless

The sign < means arising or derived from

The sign > means becoming or realized as

Introduction

The aim of the present work is (a) to produce a descriptive study of Baḥārnah Arabic, one of the native dialects of eastern Arabia, and (b) to give a comparative account of the inter-dialectal forms therein.

As this study is one of the earliest on Baḥārnah speech-forms, I have had to rely, chiefly, on the basic data collected from my informants. Other than Jayakar and Reinhardt's works on ^{c}Umāni Arabic, followed in 1967 by T.M. Johnstone's *EADS*, which is mainly a study of the ^{c}Anazi dialects of the area, no other systematic study of relevance to pre- ^{c}Anazi east Arabian speech has been undertaken. Had such a study been attempted, particularly for Qaṭīfi and Ḥasāwi speech-forms, it would have been of great comparative value.

The Baḥārnah Arabs of Baḥrain, whose language is the subject of this study, concentrate mainly in the northern green belt which subsumes a series of closely adjoining settlements, extending from Jufayr and Manāmah to Dirāz, continuing mid-southwards to a few scattered villages culminating in Dār Chulayb (also: Kulayb), in addition to the islands of Sitrah and Nabīh Ṣāliḥ, and a sparse Baḥārnah presence on some of the old villages of Muḥarraq island (see Map IV (Appendices) on the speech-communities A and B).

However, in contemporary Baḥrain, two major dialect communities, each characterized by certain common cultural links, can be observed. Nevertheless, mutual intelligibility among the speakers of both dialects is maintained without difficulty. These two speech-communities are: (1) The Baḥārnah, native islanders, who dwell largely in the rural areas of Baḥrain and to a lesser degree in Manāmah, the capital, and are entirely of the Shī ^{c}i sect of Islam. (2) The other speech-community whom we will, though somewhat reluctantly, and for linguistic reasons only, call ^{c}Anazi, because, except for Āl-Khalīfah, the ruling house of Baḥrain, who also form a substantial minority within this community and are descendants of the ^{c}Anazi tribes of central and northern Arabia, the rest of the speakers in this community, constituting a substantial majority, are descended from diverse peninsular Arab tribes. Their immediate ancestors established themselves on the islands during and after the ^{c}Anazi take-over of 1783. Generally speaking, members of this speech-community show strong traces of central and northern peninsular Arabic, and belong predominantly to the Sunni sect of Islam.

Hereafter and throughout we will be referring to all the members of group (2) as ^{c}Anazi speakers for the reasons explained above. Accordingly, the term ^{c}Anazi, as employed here, designates the Āl-Khalīfah take-over of the islands in 1783 from the Bushire Arabs who were in possession of them and who owed their allegiance to Persia. Hence, the terms pre- ^{c}Anazi, i.e., before 1783 and post- ^{c}Anazi, i.e., after 1783; consequently, the Baḥārnah speech-forms, like ^{c}Umāni, or for that matter Qaṭīfi and Ḥasāwi are pre- ^{c}Anazi because these constitute an older and native stratum of east Arabian speech.

As regards the tribal descent of the speakers in both communities, adequate ethnological data is provided in Part I, Section (A) of this work. Meanwhile, we should note:
(a) that the Baḥārnah, as certain medieval Arab sources reveal, are largely descendants of early ^{c}Abd al-Qais tribes, who controlled the eastern region of peninsular Arabia and the island of ?Uwāl in pre-Islamic times.[1]
(b) that the ^{c}Anazi speakers, viz. the ruling family of Baḥrain, are descendants of the multitudinous ^{c}Anazi tribes whose original homelands were in central and northern Arabia, prior to their settlement in Kuwait, Zubārah, etc., and eventually Baḥrain.[2]

By reason of the geographical, cultural, and tribal divergences mentioned above, diverse linguistic features for each of the two dialect-groups are bound to exist. Although this study focuses mainly on Baḥārnah speech-forms, comparable forms such as found in ^{c}Anazi Arabic of Baḥrain are, to some extent, taken into consideration. Contrastive analysis of the salient features of these two dialects will be of great synchronic as well as diachronic value, knowing that in view of east Arabian speech, the linguistic strata of B is older than A.

Field Work and the Informants

Field work for the present study was conducted on two separate missions carried out during November and December of 1976 and again, in the same period, in 1977. As regards the main island, it was found that the distances separating certain villages from others are not remote enough to warrant their seclusion for any specific field work. Therefore, field work was restricted to the areas where a sizeable and long established Baḥārnah community was found. The basic linguistic data obtained from around thirty informants, mostly males, form the main corpus of this study. The criteria for the selection of informants were generally based on these principles:
(a) that the informant should be an elderly person, preferably with little or no formal schooling
(b) that for a living he should pursue a traditional trade or craft.

Accordingly, the majority of my informants are elderly people; retired gardeners or date planters, fisher folk, weavers, potters, and the owner of a local laboratory for the extraction of folk medicines. A few are employees of the Baḥrain Petroleum Company, a painter, a carpenter, and the operator of an artesian well installed in a date garden.

My female informants come from Manāmah, Abū Ṣēbi ^{c} and Dirāz. These have provided me with considerable material mostly of a folkloristic nature, some of which I have excluded from the present work. It remains to be said that the peculiarities of female speech, especially in rural areas of the Baḥārnah community call for further attention.

Being a Baḥrāni myself, I occasionally acted as my own informant. Listed below are the names of the villages involved in this study:

(1) Abū Ṣēbi ^{c}	(2) ^{c}Āli	(3) Bani Jamrah
(4) Damistān	(5) Dirāz	(6) ^{c}Ēn Dār
(7) Jid Ḥafṣ	(8) Karrānah	(9) Budayyi ^{c}
(10) Mhazza (Sitrah island)		(11) Markubān (Sitrah)
(12) Shahrakkān.		

Finally, my data on ^{c}Anazi speech-forms come from informants from the village of Budayyi^{c}. Often, I had to check on the ^{c}Anazi forms of Baḥrain with Baḥraini colleagues studying at the Institute of Education, Leeds University.

For the location of the Baḥārnah villages and the geographical areas they occupy, a copy of a detailed map produced by the India Office and surveyed under the direction of

Lieutenant Colonel F.B. Longe, Surveyor General of India, Seasons 1904–1905 is appended.

Tape Recordings and Transcriptions

The basic material was recorded on tapes, which were then transcribed phonetically on paper. The symbols used for transcriptions were mainly such as those employed by Orientalists. All the tapes were transcribed regardless of the material they contained. Material such as pertaining to folk-lore was only used for whatever relevance it had to this work.

The terminology employed for linguistic analysis, corresponds throughout to that normally used by linguists interested in Arabic dialect studies.

Arrangement of the Material

The material is divided into six parts. Part I (Section A) treats of the pre-Islamic tribes of Baḥrain, their descendants in the area, and to some extent, traces the origins of the contemporary Arab population of Baḥrain. This was necessitated mainly by the inadequacy of the ethnological data, particularly in respect of the origins of the Baḥārnah of Baḥrain, prevailing in the literature on the area. In addition, a historical survey of Baḥrain is provided in Section B of the same part.

Part II is devoted to the phonology of the Baḥārnah dialect. Characteristic phonological features and dialectal peculiarities are discussed in this part. Inter-dialectal comparisons, where considered necessary because of regional variations etc. are made; and to some degree the Baḥārnah forms which diverge from their ᶜAnazi counterforms are also considered. Definitions of local terms and occasional diachronic remarks on certain features are made. At the start of each part, a brief account of the findings and the topics discussed is given.

In Part III of the study the morphology of B is examined. Here, again, a descriptive analysis of the basic nominal and verbal forms is made. Comparisons especially in those areas where no marked differences are observed, are held to a minimum. Again, characteristic features and peculiarities are sorted out and commented upon.

Part IV examines syntactical features of this dialect. It investigates the syntactic behaviour of certain verbs, the concepts of past, present, and future. In addition, it examines interrogation, negation, definite and indefinite concord, gender and number of nouns and adjectives, plus the special features of verbal and nominal constructions. An analysis of comparable features of the syntax of A and B is also attempted.

Part V deals with lexis, which is examined under three sections:

Section A sets out specimens of noun-adjective collocates, localisms, classical and archaic Arabic forms, pan-Arabic "koine" forms, and some account of comparative data in A and B.

Section B deals with borrowings—mainly from Persian, English and Hindustani.

Section C looks into the special registers of language such as pertaining to traditional activities.

Part VI deals with the comparative data, viz. the special features of ᶜAnazi and Baḥārnah speech-forms, together with the peculiarities of rural and urban B. The comparative data is also examined in relation to other dialects in the area, and a brief historical account of the striking features in A and B is attempted.

The Schools and the Emergence of Pan-Arabic "koine" Forms

The occurrence of a large number of koine forms in current speech is to a large extent the result of expansion in education and the spread of the media among the population. A brief look at the old, traditional system and the new western-style schooling will surely help us to understand the impact of educational developments on the verbal behaviour of the people.

Prior to 1921, there were no public schools in the modern sense of the word. Teaching or religious edification of young children was the job of the *m ᶜallim* "traditional teacher" or *m ᶜalme* "female counterpart of the former", *kuttāb* "lit. literate persons", *maṭāwᶜa*[3] "teachers of the Koran" and sometimes even *malāli "Shīᶜi*, religious preachers". All these were well versed in Qur'anic and religious matters. Their main job, as parents demanded, was to enable the young to learn basic Qur'anic *suras*, i.e., chapters, and to say their prayers by heart.

The earliest missionary schools

R.B. Winder in a well-informed article,[4] observes that the first western-style schools in Baḥrain were founded by the Arabian Mission, an independent group which began its operations in Baḥrain in 1892 and which was "adopted" by the Dutch Reformed Church in America in 1894.[5]

In 1905, Winder adds, the school moved from Mr. and Mrs. S. Zwemer's house into 'The Memorial School and Chapel".

In 1940, the Roman Catholic Sacred Heart School was opened in Manāmah.

The Hidāya School

1921 marks the inception of what may be called systematic schooling in Baḥrain. In that year, the Hidāya Boys' Primary School was established on Muḥarraq island. Shaikh Ḥāfiẓ Wahba, who was later to become the Sa ᶜūdi Ambassador to Great Britain, served for a couple of years as the headmaster of the Hidāya School.

Traditional Baḥārnah Schools

The *Shīᶜah* Arabs of Baḥrain had their own traditional schools. In 1927 *al-Madrasah al-ᶜAlawiyyah* was founded in the village-town of al-Khamīs; and in the following year the Jaᶜfariyyah School, on the lines of the former, was established in Manāmah. The teaching of Qur?ān, prayers, arithmetic and Arabic, took precedence in school syllabus over anything else.

The BAPCO School at Zallāq

In November 1948, the Baḥrain Petroleum Company (BAPCO) opened a small school at Zallāq. The school provided local BAPCO employees with a four-month course in basic English. With the expansion in BAPCO operations, a new school built in ᶜAwāli in October 1949, replaced the one at Zallāq.

The Urdu School

The Urdu School, founded, financed, and administered largely by the Pakistani community on the island, was established in 1956.

The first batch of expatriate Arab teachers

In 1926, that is in the wake of the Syrian uprising of 1925 against the French, a few Syrians joined the teaching staff of Baḥrain's Primary schools.

In 1931 the Official Department of Education was founded. Earlier there had been a local committee in charge of the administrative and pedagogical affairs of schools.

In 1944, in response to a demand by the Baḥrain Government, the first Egyptian mission was despatched to teach literary and scientific subjects.

With the increase in the number of students, who according to recent official estimates number more than one fifth of the total population (boys and girls) the tendency to employ "koine" forms has gained momentum. Alongside this process, a tendency to employ correct pronunciation, and therefore to reintroduce Arabic inter-dentals *ṯ, ḏ, ẓ,* hitherto only partially preserved, can be noted.

The bulk of the above developments not only affected the traditional system of religious education but also helped in the shaping of new linguistic attitudes. Certain dialectal forms were dropped in favour of their pan-Arabic "koine" forms. With the rise in national feelings, a tendency to shun borrowings and to favour their literary Arabic equivalents, has begun to show itself, especially among the young literates. The examples appearing below are indicative of the changes noted above:

Dialectal forms		Pan-Arabic forms
m ^{c}allim	"traditional school"	*midrase*
bilbile	"tap"	*ḥanafiyye*
bulisiyye	"police"	*šurta*
tiksi	"taxi"	*sayyaarat ijra*
ruumaal	"handkerchief"	*mandiil*
zinjufra[6]	"vest"	*faanile*
juuti	"shoe"	*ḥiḏaa ?*
baakeet	"packet"	*^{c}ulbe*
gawaaṭi	"tins" (food)	*mu ^{c}allabaat*
beeb	"pipe"	*?unbuub*
da ^{c}me	"accident"	*ḥaadiṯ*
diira	"village or village-town"	*qarye*
^{c}aks	"photograph"	*ṣuura*
ġurb	"foreigners, strangers"	*?ajaanib*
buusṭa	"post-office"	*bariid*

New Items Pertaining to Agriculture

Since the start of the Government's Experimental Garden at Budayyi^{c} village-town, a range of new lexical items has gained currency. Local gardeners came to acquire new vocabulary from visiting experts; these items were not part of a date-planters repertoire of vocabulary. Cf:

qarnaabiiṭ	"cauliflowers"	*karneešan*	"carnation" (flowers)
malfuuf	"cabbage"	*alyandar*	"oleanders"
šawandar	"white beet"	*samaad keemaawi*	"chemical fertilizer"

Borrowings, such as names of materials, for which no "koine" forms were coined yet, have remained stable in local speech. Cf:

bleewuud	"plywood"	*blaastiik*	"plastic"
farmeeka	"Formica"	*azbestus*	"asbestos"

The Media

On 4 November 1940, a broadcasting station, on the lines of the British Near-East Broadcasting Station in Cyprus (i.e., *?Iḏā ^{c}at ash-Sharq al-Adnā*) was founded at Ḥūrah Telegraphic Office. However, the present Baḥrain Radio in the Māḥūz area was created in the summer of 1955.

Besides, we should not neglect the impact of local T.V. stations on shaping the verbal behaviour of the people, especially in view of its appearance in the area for over twenty years now.

In 1943–1944, a public library with generous donations from the British Council, was opened in Manāmah.

Non-Local Element in the Population

The expatriate population of Baḥrain is officially estimated at not less than one quarter of the total population. The latest figures for non-Baḥrainis, available here in Britain, are those of the 1971 population census which puts these at 37,885 non-Baḥrainis out of a total population of 216,078.[7] This figure has increased largely ever since.

Among the expatriate population, the Iranians, most of whom are naturalized citizens, figure more than any other single nationality. Many of these are involved in small businesses. They are mainly of the *Shī ᶜi* sect of Islam and speak Persian and Arabic.

Indians, Pakistanis and Baluchis, constitute the second largest section of the expatriate community on the islands. Among the first two are doctors who have been practising medicine for many years. Others pursue clerical jobs such as banking, insurance, clearance. A few Indian merchants of long standing are also engaged in vital businesses such as imports and agencies.

With the expansion in construction work and industry, many new workers, chiefly from the Indian sub-continent, have obtained work permits in Baḥrain. A parallel increase in the European and American community of Baḥrain has also taken place.

The table below illustrates the total figures for local and non-local elements from 1941 to 1971.[8]

Nationality	1941	1950	1959	1965	1971
Baḥraini	74,040	91,179	118,734	143,814	178,193
Non-Baḥraini	15,930	18,471	24,401	38,389	37,885
Total	89,970	109,650	143,137	182,203	216,078

The ratio of Baḥrainis to non-Baḥrainis above, marks a steady progress from 1941 to 1965. From 1965 to 1971 the graph remained more or less stable. As noted above, the non-Baḥraini element in the population today, has surely escalated owing to the import of foreign labour for ambitious economic developments the country is presently witnessing.

However, the non-Baḥrainis, as referred to in the Statistical Abstract (1941–1971) are:[9]

Persians: the larger section of these are naturalized Baḥrainis; they are *Shī ᶜi* Moslems.
Indians: Christians and Hindu
Pakistanis: Moslems
Baluchis: Moslems
plus Americans and Britons
Non-Baḥraini Arabs: Egyptians, Palestinians, Gulf Arabs, Syrians, and Lebanese.

As regards Britons, Americans, Europeans, Asians, no precise figures of their current numbers are available, but the fact is that they increase and decrease according to the demands of economic development in Baḥrain.

The Local Arabs of Baḥrain

Local Arabs constitute over two-thirds of the total population of Baḥrain today. Among the *Sunni* Arabs of Baḥrain are many influential families, such as Āl-Khalīfah, the ruling house of Baḥrain, Al-Quṣaibi and Al-Zayyāni and some other descendants of peninsular Arabs who settled in the islands chiefly during and after 1783. However, overall harmony prevails among the cultured élite of the country, a large number of whom are officials of the State and belong to different sectarian communities.

Among the prominent Arab families of Muḥarraq and Ḥidd are: Āl-Bin ^{c}Ali, Āl-Jalāhimah, Āl-Ma^{c}āwidah, Āl-Muslim, Āl-Manāni^{c}ah, Āl-Bu Falāsah, Āl-Muqlah, Āl-Sādah. Some of these have members living in Manāmah or Rafā^{c}.

The Āl-Khalīfah, the rulers, are of the Māliki branch of Islam, many other Arabs are of the Ḥanbali and Shāfi ^{c}i divisions.

The Huwalah Arabs

A brief account of the Huwalah[10] Arabs is given in Part I (Section–B, p. *60*) of this study. It is generally accepted that the Huwalah, who are mainly of the *Shāfi ^{c}i* division of Islam, are descendants of Arab tribes which once inhabited the coastal regions of Southern Iran. They have been influenced by Persian culture and to some degree by Persian blood. Although they revel in thinking of themselves as belonging to Arab Stock, among themselves they still communicate through the medium of *Bastaki*, a variety of Persian in use in the southern region of Bastak. One of their Shaikhs held the Baḥrain islands during 1753.

Lorimer emphasized their economic importance when he wrote in 1915:

"The Huwalah are the most numerous community of *Sunnis*, but they are all townsmen living by trade and without solidarity among themselves; consequently, they are unimportant, except commercially."[11]

In an article which appeared in early 1970, Frank Stoakes gave this account of their origins:

"Hawali (different spelling of the same) are *Sunni* Persians of allegedly Arab origin."[12]

However, M.G. Rumaiḥi, a contemporary writer on Gulf affairs, regards them of Arab descent when he writes:

"Huwala ..... applies in the Gulf to people of Arab origin who emigrated from the Arab mainland to Persia and came back again."[13]

The Baḥārnah Arabs:

Throughout the twentieth century writers who have dealt with the origins of the Baḥārnah have often unknowingly, ascribed conflicting origins to them. Lorimer wrote:

"The Baḥārnah are generally stated to have come into existence by the conversion of certain Arab tribes, including one called the Bani Rabī ^{c}ah to *Shi ^{c}ism* about 300 years ago; this is the local Muslim tradition. Some European writers on the other hand have manifested an inclination to regard the bulk of the Baḥārinah as an aboriginal tribe conquered by the Arabs."[14]

That the Baḥārnah are descendants of ^{c}Abd al-Qais tribes of Eastern Arabia, a branch of Rabī^{c}ah, is attested by a number of Medieval Arab sources as well as by local tradition, but that their conversion to *Shī ^{c}ism* occurred, as Lorimer stated above, 300 years ago, is far from being so. As a matter of fact,ᶜAbd al-Qais tribes converted to Shīᶜism since 36 A.H. when they supported ᶜAli's right-the fourth Caliph-to the Caliphate and fought on his side first in the battle of al-Jamal in the year 36 A.H. and later in the battle of Ṣiffīn.[15]

Misinformed accounts of the Baḥārnah origins, some fairly old, some recent, are unwittingly cited from time to time. Specimens of quite a few of these are adduced below:

Dr. Paul Harrison (1924) referred to them as "that semi-Persian community known as Baḥārnah."[16] A. Faroughy (1951), accounting for the Baḥārnah classified their race as "Persians."[17]

H.H. Hansen, who was a member of the Danish Archaeological Expedition to Baḥrain and who lived for a couple of months in the Baḥārnah village of Sār near ᶜĀli, wrote in 1966:

"The villagers constitute the older layer of the population. They themselves emphasize that they are not Arabs like the ruler, his family, and the town people. They call themselves Baḥārna."[18]

As a matter of fact, besides its well known ethnic designation, the term Arab to Baḥārnah villagers once connoted more specially the influx in 1783 and after of peninsular Najdi and Qaṭari Arabs into Baḥrain. In saying they are not Arabs like the ruler or his family, but Baḥārnah or *Ḥalāyil* (another term they employ to describe themselves, from Arabic *ḥalāʔil* i.e., lawful possessions but also owners), they are not denying their Arab origin, they are simply distinguishing between themselves being native islanders and therefore, in their own view, the lawful owners of the lands of which they had been dispossessed, as against the non-native tribesmen who established their supremacy during late 18th-century onwards. It is in this context that the above use of the term ought to be viewed, though such a usage is now a relic of the past rarely heard among the younger generation.

R.B. Serjeant, wrote in 1968:

'The *Shīᶜah* of al-Baḥrain, called al-Baḥārinah, form about half the population . . . It has been supposed, though proof is not yet forthcoming, that they descended from converts from the original population of Christians (Arameans?) Jews and Majus . . . inhabiting the island . . at the time of the Arab conquest."[19]

The above account, as the writer correctly indicates, is based on speculation; moreover the conflicting origins he ascribes to the Baḥārnah is not supported by evidence or references.

Finally, a well-researched account is given by the *Encyclopaedia of Islam:*

"The *Shīᶜis* appear to be descendants of early inhabitants of the area, and there seems to be no justification for the hypothesis that they are of Persian origin. A good number of the *Sunnis* of al-Baḥrain are Arabs or the descendants of Arabs once resident on the Persian Coast, such are known as Huwalah."[20]

Geographical Distribution of the Baḥārnah

As this study is chiefly concerned with the Baḥārnah dialect of Arabic, some account of their numbers and villages is, perhaps, necessary to our understanding of the area and its people.

Lorimer, writing around 1915 informs us of 104 villages with a population of 38,275 out of a grand total of 99,075.[21] According to official censuses of 1941, 1950, 1965, and 1971, these are the figures for the geographical distribution of the population:[22]

Geographical Distribution of the Population

Towns and Villages	1941 Jan.	1950 Mar.	1959 May	1965 Feb.	1971 Apr.
Manāma	27,835	39,648	61,726	79,098	89,728
Muḥarraq & Ḥidd	21,439	25,577	36,742	46,373	49,387
ᶜAwāli	1,532	3,846	3,123	2,097	988
Other towns and villages	39,164	40,579	41,544	54,635	76,712
Total	89,970	109,650	143,135	182,203	216,815

The figures given for towns and villages, in the last entry in the table above, give some idea of the Baḥārnah rural population, though these figures also include non-Baḥārnah villages and towns.

Note that the official commentary on the results of the 1941 census tells of strong rumours such as the introduction of taxation, conscription, etc., which circulated among the rural community at the time of the population count. Therefore, the figures obtained were not completely reliable because many Baḥārnah villagers abstained from recording their names during the population count of 1941.

Some writers, however, estimated the Baḥārnah islanders at over 80% of the total population.[23] As regards the Baḥārnah now living in the adjacent Gulf States or certain coastal towns of Iran, these are the descendants of those who left the country on several occasions in the past, chiefly:

(1) During Muscaṭi occupation on several occasions, i.e., around 1718, and during 1800–1801.
(2) During early ᶜAnazi rule, i.e., from 1783 onwards.
(3) During Wahhābi control of the islands between 1803–1811.
(4) During the influx in 1845, and after, of the Dawāsir tribes into Baḥrain and their settlement in Zallāq and Budayyiᶜ and the subsequent tension this created, culminating in the attacks in 1923 on Baḥārnah villages.

It is worth noting here, perhaps, that a few Baḥārnah accompanied by their families settled in Bombay in the early twenties, since relations between them and their early ᶜAnazi rulers were not always happy. These families had to send their children to Indian schools where the medium of instruction was either Urdu, Persian, or English. While in Bombay, some Baḥārnah Ṭawāwīsh, i.e., pearl dealers, became bilingual. They picked up Hindustani, the medium of daily communication among the heterogeneous population of that place. They communicated with their Hindu counterparts through this medium with a surprisingly great degree of mutual intelligibility.[24] These Baḥārnah returned to Baḥrain mainly after the introduction of the cultured pearls to international markets, and the subsequent decline of *iṭwāshe* in the whole Gulf.

Linguistic Contact between Local and Non-Local Elements

Perhaps Manāmah, the principal city of Baḥrain, provides at present the most apt meeting ground for linguistic interaction between the local and the expatriate elements of the population. Among the non-Baḥrainis, Indians and Pakistanis rank highest in number. Some of these are owners of small restaurants where Indian and Pakistani cuisine is relished by local Arabs. Indian culinary skill is just one aspect; the main market in Manāmah is full of Indians who regularly come into day to day contact with the local inhabitants. Such linguistic contacts are of long standing, therefore it is not surprising to find a number of Indian words recurring in local speech, though not as copiously now as the case was in the recent past.

Banks, insurance companies and other agencies all constitute areas of linguistic contact between the locals and their foreign work-mates. For about five decades, English has been the language of communication among the employees of BAPCO. A similar situation also obtains, though to a lesser extent, in Aluminium Baḥrain (ALBA).

Situation in the Villages

Normally, rural communities are least affected by alien linguistic influences. It is to be noticed, however, that a large number of borrowings are found in rural forms of B; this is due to the fact that a majority of BAPCO employees are Baḥārnah villagers who picked up, at their place of work, certain English words relating to domestic or office tools and gadgets, names of building materials, etc. However, the spread of schools in rural areas has created a tendency to replace foreign words with their pan-Arabic "koine" forms.

Previous Studies of East-Arabian Speech

The earliest mention of the occurrence of foreign words in Baḥraini speech is contained in the account by W.G. Palgrave, who writing in the second half of the nineteenth century, refers to local people discussing politics in Manāmah coffee houses. He lists these words as occurring in their conversations:

Ingleez for "English", *Fransees* for "French", *Muscop* for "Russians".[25]

Rev. S. Zwemer, writing in 1889, notes the high frequency of Indian words circulating in local Arabic. He also tells of considerable immigration from the Persian coast, viz. Lingah and Bushire, as a result of which Persian became, after Arabic, in copious use in certain quarters of Manāmah.[26]

The two works referred to above offer only observations made by people engaged in spheres of activities other than language.

Also, in 1889, one of the earliest studies on east Arabian speech was published, viz. "The ᶜOmanee Dialect of Arabic".[27] This study comprises two parts describing, in general terms, the peculiarities of ᶜUmāni Arabic. Part II of the study focuses, mainly, on ᶜUmāni lexis. This work is of great comparative value, because of the large number of lexical items, the author lists, in Part II; items which pertain to pre-ᶜAnazi eastern Arabic.

In 1894, C. Reinhardt published his book *Ein arabischer Dialekt gesprochen in ᶜUmān und Zanzibār* which is a systematic study of the Bani Kharūṣ dialect of ᶜUmān. In the foreword to the book Reinhardt states that the dialect in question is that which is spoken by the upper-classes including the Court. He professes that his data was acquired from informants in Zanzibār, particularly an informant by the name of ᶜAbdalla who introduced his newly arriving countrymen to Reinhardt there. However, when he was in Muscaṭ, he adds, his travel plans were aborted by intrigues at the Court.

Both Jayakar and Reinhardt's data provide an adequate picture of ᶜUmāni speech in the Muscaṭ and Jabal al-Akhḍar areas.

The Baḥrain Petroleum Company (BAPCO) and Arabic Studies

Around 1952 a section, viz. Arabic Studies, was created by BAPCO. Better communication between the local and non-local employees of the Company was among the practical considerations that led to the establishment of this section. However, a Persian employee of BAPCO, Mr. Fayḍi, was appointed in charge of the section. Four years later Mr. Alec Gordon succeeded as head of the section. And shortly afterwards, a *Handbook of the Spoken Arabic of Baḥrain,* with a view to the communicative needs of the expatriate employees of BAPCO, was published. The chief aim was to familiarize them with a functional knowledge of local Arabic. The material for the *Handbook* consisted of basic vocabulary, structure, and expressions of courtesy and civilities, etc. However, owing to the success of the course, the section has remained open ever since it was created.[28]

On the other hand, to increase the communicative skills of local employees and to expand their technical lexis, English classes, on the lines of the above section, were organized. A *Handbook* for this course was also produced. It contained technical lexis pertaining to specific job requirements such as: *span-ər* "spanner", *valv* "valve", *hōz* "hose" etc. The fact that the above courses were governed by practical considerations contributed greatly to their success.

Further publications on east Arabian speech

In 1961 and 1964, two articles were published on the Dōsiri dialect of Kuwait.[29] The former is a preliminary study of certain linguistic aspects of the dialect in question, whereas the latter is a closer examination of the same. Preliminary examination of this dialect, the author notes, showed some resemblance in its structure and vocabulary to Najdi Arabic. Closer investigation revealed traces of ᶜAjmi influence, especially on the phonology of the Dōsiri dialect of Kuwait. In the second article, however, the writer concludes that although "the Dōsiri dialect of Kuwait does not share all the distinguishing features of the Najdi group, the parent dialect does belong to the south-central type of Najdi dialect."

In 1964, Sheikh Jalāl al-Ḥanafi's *Muᶜjam al-Alfāẓ al-Kuwaitiyya,* a glossary of Kuwaiti lexis, was published. Colloquial Kuwaiti, the author writes, like other colloquials of Iraq and the Arab world, draws its vocabulary from different languages; a number of Kuwaiti words are borrowings from Hindustani, English, Turkish, and Persian, including this latter's sub-branches, viz. Lāristāni, Khonji, Bastaki, and Garāshi dialects, and perhaps Portuguese and Dutch. Having studied Kuwaiti vocabulary, al-Ḥanafi concludes that the colloquial of Kuwait shows apparent affinity with the dialects of Baṣrah and Zubayr.

Also in 1964, T.M. Johnstone and J. Muir published their article *"Some Nautical Terms in Kuwaiti Dialect of Arabic".*[30] This work is a systematic compilation of indigenous and foreign terms such as found in the nautical register of Kuwaiti lexis. In their preliminary remarks the writers state:

> 'The Portuguese profoundly affected ship-building techniques in the Persian Gulf and this has left distinct traces in the local nautical vocabulary. Furthermore, there is little doubt that the most important of the Portuguese terms quoted were in use at the time of the explorations. Some of them, however, must have come to the Persian Gulf later from India."

To facilitate the reader's job and to attract his interest, supplementary drawings showing the items and their corresponding words are also provided.

In 1967, however, Johnstone, produced his major book on the post-ᶜAnazi dialects of the area, viz. *Eastern Arabian Dialect Studies* (*EADS*). This was one of the earliest attempts at a scientific study, i.e., descriptive and analytical, of the spoken Gulf Arabic. *EADS* has laid the basis for modern dialect studies in the area and it remains a source book for language learners as well as course planners.[31]

In 1969, a publication of Kuwait University, viz. Dr. A. Matar's work entitled *Khaṣā ʔiṣ al-Lahjah al-Kuwaitiyyah* appeared. This book as the title indicates is a study of the characteristic features of the Kuwaiti dialect of Arabic. Accounting for his aims, the author states that dialect studies are meant to serve and enrich Arabic language. The outcome of such studies, he adds, can add to our understanding of Arabic, past and present. He describes his approach to Kuwaiti dialect as "an integrated, descriptive and historical account."

In 1970, another book by the same author came out, *Min ʔAsrār al-Lahjah al-Kuwaitiyyah,* which is a further study of Kuwaiti dialect based on descriptive and historical principles. In the main, the above two works are comprehensive accounts of the similarities or deviations of Kuwaiti Arabic as compared with literary Arabic.

The above two works were followed by *Ẓawāhir Nādirah fi Lahajāt al-Khalīj al-ᶜArabi* by the same author. This last work as the title suggests sets out, briefly, the peculiarities of contemporary Gulf Arabic including those present in the Baḥārnah speech-forms. The approach followed in this last work, is again, like the previous ones, based on historical principles.

In 1973, the monograph *Lexical Expansion due to Technical Change* was published by Indiana University.[32] This study, as the author states, examines how new referents, characteristic of an industrial society, are superimposed upon a non-industrial speech-community, in this case the latter being settled, coastal Arabs of al-Aḥsāʔ. This work sets out to show how the lexical repertoire of a language was enlarged to include technical concepts. The author writes: "...no attempt is made to describe the Arabic of the region, in the linguistic sense, other than to the degree necessary to account adequately for the forms presented to illustrate the phenomena. Accordingly, lexis takes precedence over morphology and phonology."

The author, who was in the employment of the Arabian American Oil Company (Aramco) Education Division from 1945 to 1949, gives this definition of Ḥasāwi speakers: "The term (i.e. the Baḥārnah) as generally used, coincides approximately with the Arabic-speaking *Shi ᶜite* population of Baḥrain and the adjoining Arabian mainland, a group more or less united not only in religious and cultural tradition but also in certain speech-tendencies and, to the eye, in racial stock."

In 1975, *A Basic Course in Gulf Arabic* appeared.[33] This book as the title suggests is designed for foreign students wishing to learn Gulf Arabic. Its teaching material is based on the principles of the structural approach which advocates extensive classroom drilling. The language material of the book shows a careful process of selection indicative of the writer's close interest in the Arabic spoken in the Gulf area. The book is divided into 42 units each comprising (i) text (ii) translation (iii) vocabulary (iv) grammar (v) drills. The author's definition of Gulf Arabic runs: " . . . it is the language used in informal situations by the educated indigenous populations of the United Arab Emirates."

Local View on Current Spoken Arabic

In an interview with a local weekly, Mr. Ibrāhīm al-ᶜUrayyiḍ, a leading scholar (ex-speaker of the Constitutional Assembly, 1972), has summed up his views on spoken Arabic in the area. He seems to differentiate between two modes of usage: the written, being a vehicle for literary appreciation, and the spoken, being an effective means of daily interaction. In his view, written forms remain captive of norms and rules; but the spoken forms are more spontaneous and therefore more telling. By aiming at literary norms, as correct modes of usage to be imitated, we seem to neglect, Mr. al- ᶜUrayyiḍ observes, so many developments that have affected the spoken-forms. Languages do not remain static, therefore usage is subject to change and development. Rigid rules and norms such as those appearing in grammar books are mainly written by and for foreign learners of Arabic. The Arab child uses his language correctly before being exposed to any form of formal instruction.[34]

One might add, the notion of correctness in language is related to usage rather than conformity to pre-set norms.

NOTES:

1. These sources are cited in Part I of this study.
2. For their tribal descent, see al-Nabhāni, *al-Tuḥfah* (2nd ed.) (Cairo) pp. 116–117; also H.R.P. Dickson, *Kuwait and Her Neighbours*, ch. III, p. 87.
3. These were on the lines of their Wahhābi colleagues in Arabia.
4. *"Education in al-Baḥrayn".*
5. A.D. Dixey, in his article: "*In The Persian Gulf,* 1907", informs us that President Roosevelt was a member of the Reformed Church. See: *Church Missionary Review,* Edited by Rev. W.M. Thornton. No. 58. Oct. 1907, p. 614.
6. From Hindustani, ganji faraak.
7. *Statistical Abstract (1971), State of Baḥrain* – Ministry of Finance and National Economy. Available from SOAS; also OPL, section of the British Library.
8. See Appendices for the distribution of non-Baḥrainis according to nationalities in the two censuses of 1941 and 1950.
9. *Government of Baḥrain, Annual Report* (Oct. 1949–Nov. 1950) provides this commentary on the "Jewish Exodus" (1950) from Baḥrain: "The Jewish community in Baḥrain, which numbered in the past about 300 persons, consisting of Jewish families who came originally from Iraq and Persia, was long established in the country. Most of the Jews traded in piece-goods and gold. They were, on the whole, quite law-abiding people. Many of them were Baḥrain subjects by birth or had obtained Baḥrain nationality. During 1369 A.H. about 29 families out of the 43 families who lived in Manāmah, left the country and went to Palestine, viz Israel. No pressure was put on them to leave Baḥrain, but apparently, they were attracted by the possibilities of life in Israel. It is understood that a number of the Baḥrain Jews after spending a short time in Israel much regretted that they had gone there and now desire to return to Baḥrain."
10. From the Arabic base-root, *ḥāla* "to change, transfer, hence: *taḥawwala*" he shifted to another place". In local usage, one of the connotations of the singular form: *hōli* is "somebody who is not clearly Arab".
11. *G azetteer,* p. 241.
12. *Social and Political Change in the Third World: Some Peculiarities of Oil-Producing Principalities of the Persian Gulf* in the Derek Hopwood (ed.): *The Arabian Peninsula,* p. 198.
13. See his celebrated work: *Baḥrain: Social and Political Change Since the first World War,* p. 34–footnot 33.
14. *Gazetteer,* p. 208.
15. For a full account of *ᶜAbd al-Qais* support for ᶜAli ibn Abi Ṭālib, see at-Ṭabari, *Tārīkh al-Rusul Wa al-Mulūk,* vol. IV, ed. M. Abu l-Faḍl Ibrāhīm (Cairo–1963), pp. 442–576; also al-Mas ᶜūdi, *Murūj,* ed. C. Pellat (Beirut, 1970), vol. III, pp. 114–115; and Ibn Khaldūn's history, *Min Kitāb al- ᶜIbar Wa Dīwān al-Mubtadaʔ Wal-Khabar,* vol. II, pp. ISO–9. For further account of ᶜAbd al-Qais, see: *Kitāb Khabar*

^{c}Abd al-Qais by Abu ^{c}Ubaydah Mu ^{c}ammar ibn al-Muthanna. Also: *Ashrāf ^{c}Abd al-Qais* by al-Madā?ini.

16. *The Arab at Home* (London, 1924), p. 92. Note that Harrison spent fourteen years as the representative in Arabia of the Trinity Reformed Church of Plainfield, N.J.
17. *The Baḥrain Islands 750–1951* (New York 1951), p. 19, table 5.
18. *'Problems of Contact and Change' Jahrbuch des Museums zur Volkerkunde zu Leipzig*, 23, 1966, pp. 82–94.
19. *"Fisher-Folk and Fish-Traps in al-Baḥrain"*, *BSOAS*, vol. XXXI (1968), pp. 486–514.
20. *EI*, G. Rentz and W.E. Mulligan, vol. I (1960), p. 941.
21. *Gazetteer*, p. 238.
22. *Statistical Abstract, State of Baḥrain*, 1971 (SOAS Library).
23. A. Faroughy, *The Baḥrain Islands* (1951), p. 18.
24. Among the earliest Baḥārnah *Ṭawāwīsh* who frequented or settled in Bombay were: Ḥajji Aḥmad bin Manṣūr; Ḥajji Muḥammad Jawād; Ḥajji Muḥammad bin ^{c}Īsa Āl-Ṭāha; Sayyid Ḥasan al- ^{c}Alawi; Sayyid Ni ^{c}me al- ^{c}Alawi; Ḥajji ^{c}Abdalla al-Tājir; Ḥajji Yūsuf al-Ṣāyigh; Ḥajji Aḥmad Shardan; Ḥajji Ja^{c}far Mandīl; and later, Manṣūr and Sālim al- ^{c}Urayyiḍ. These were all to become bilinguals in Bombay. Ḥajji Ja^{c}far ^{c}Abd al-Raḥīm, a philanthropic businessman from Muscaṭ, together with Ḥajji Yūsuf al-Ṣāyigh, a Dubai-Baḥārni, and Shaikh Muḥammad Ḥasan Najafi, an Iraqi religious figure and Masjid Imām (prayer leader) of the Khōjah community of Bombay, were among those who patronized the Baḥārnah community there, especially their religious occasions such as *Majālis-Muḥarram* (i.e., their *Muḥarram* gatherings). The two books, *al-Fakhri* and *al-Wafāt*, both of which are anthologies of *Shī^{c}i* religious literature, were repeatedly printed at the Jahrumi Zādeh Printing Press in Bombay.
25. *Narrative of a Year's Journey through Central and Eastern Arabia* (1883), ch. XIV, pp. 218–9.
26. *Arabia the Cradle of Islam* (1900), pp. 108–9.
27. Surgeon-Major A.S.G. Jayakar, *JRAS*, vol. XXI, part I, pp. 649–87, Part II, pp. 811–80.
28. Among the teaching staff, during the early sixties, were Ṭāha al-Dirāzi, Sayyid ^{c}Īsa and Sa^{c}īd al-Tājir, the latter being the only university graduate among them. The present head of the section is Mr. al-Dirāzi.
29. T.M. Johnstone, *"Some Characteristics of the Dōsiri Dialect of Arabic as Spoken in Kuwait"*, *BSOAS*, vol. XXIV, Part II, 1961. Also by the same author, *"Further Studies on the Dōsiri Dialect of Arabic as Spoken in Kuwait"*, *BSOAS*, vol. XXVII, Part I, 1964.
30. *BSOAS*, vol. XXVII, pp. 299–332.
31. The pre- ^{c}Anazi dialects of eastern Arabia are excluded from the above study.
32. The author of this work is B. Hunter Smeaton.
33. The author of this work is Dr. Ḥamdi Qafīsheh of Arizona University.
34. The texts of the interview which was conducted by Mr. Jalīl al-Ṣaffār appear in the issues 199 (17 Oct. 1977), 200 (24 Oct. 1977), 201 (28 Nov. 1977) of *al-Mawāqif*, weekly of Baḥrain.

Part 1

Section (A)

The ancient region of Al-Baḥrain[1]

In this section of Part I we intend to examine, mainly, three things:

(a) Medieval Arab accounts of the old region of al-Baḥrain, including the island of ?Awāl, i.e., present Baḥrain; particularly the earlier settlers in the area and the subsequent arrivals therein.

(b) The origins and tribal ancestry of the Baḥārnah Arabs, native islanders, whose language is the theme of this study.

(c) The component elements in the contemporary population of Baḥrain, viz. the ᶜUtub, the ruling house of Baḥrain today, in addition to other peninsular Arab elements who have established themselves on the islands during 1783 and after.[2] Here again we will rely, for their tribal ancestry, on Arab accounts.

Before we proceed any further, it is necessary to remember that medieval Arab sources treat the ancient region and its dependency, i.e., the island of ?Awāl, as one entity. Ethnic ties and shared history form the basis of their accounts.

Most Arab geographers place Baḥrain in the second clime (*?iqlīm*), whereas some assign it to the third. Yāqūt, writing in the thirteenth century A.D. renders the following account:

> "It is a general name for a region that occupies the coastal area on the Indian sea between Baṣra and ᶜUmān. It is said that al-Baḥrain is the metropolis of Hajar; it is also said that Hajar is the metropolis of al-Baḥrain. Some sources regarded it part of the Yemen and others treated it as a region by itself."

However, prior to Islam and after its advent, Baḥrain embraced the coastal line of Eastern Arabia, thereby subsuming al-Qaṭīf, al-Ahsā? and the island of ?Awāl.[3]

Medieval Arab sources also furnish us with some information regarding the distances from and to al-Baḥrain. We are told that between al-Baḥrain and Yemāma is a ten days' camel ride, between Hajar and Baṣra is fifteen days' ride and that it takes a month to reach ᶜUmān by the same means of transport.[4]

The main towns of the district of Hajar, cited in these sources are: al-Khaṭṭ, al-Qaṭīf, al-Āra, Hajar, Baynūnah, al-Zārah, Juwātha, al-Sābūr, Dārīn, al-Ghābah, al-Ṣafa, and al-Mushaqqar.

On the Naming of al-Baḥrain "The Two Seas"

Many explanations are put forward regarding the name al-Baḥrain. Some sources attribute the "two seas" to the existence of two strata of water, the upper film being salty and the lower sweet due to the existence of many underwater springs.

Others referred it to the river Tigris pouring sweet water into the salty sea of *Baḥr Fāris.*

However, a third explanation is adduced by Yāqūt who tells of the existence on the gateways of al-Aḥsā? of a large lake whose water is stagnant, coupled with "the green sea"[5] which is only ten farsangs from the villages of Hajar.

Baḥrain and ᶜUmān

Al-Qalqashandi,[6] writing in the fifteenth century A.D., includes ᶜUmān in al-Baḥrain proper, and so does al-Suwaidi in his *Sabā?ik adh-Dhahab fī Maᶜrifat Qabā?il al-ᶜArab,*[7] the latter work being the *Nihāyat al- Arab* of al-Qalqashandi rearranged with additional matter by Muḥammad Amīn al-Suwaidi.

?Awāl Island and the Region of al-Baḥrain

Although Yāqūt discusses the island of ?Awāl in a separate entry under the appropriate alphabetical order, yet he treats it as part of the old region. In his account of Baḥrain not only does he mention specific places on the island of ?Awāl but the inhabitants of those places as well. He describes the island as being situated in the vicinity of the region, famous for its date plantations and lime. He also adduces certain verses that tell of the "famous palm-trunks" of ?Awāl and the busy harbour, crowded with ships, indicative of a flourishing trade centre.

Al-Hamdāni writing in the tenth century A.D. informs us of two distinct ?Awāls.[8] One is in the Ḥijāz region, on the right side of al-Suwaydā?, a place by-passed by pilgrims from Egypt and al-Shām, and the other is the island of ?Awāl, which he says, contains all sorts of animals except lions.[9]

Another interesting account of ?Awāl, is given by al-Bakri who quotes al-Kalbi and some others. For them Ṣanᶜā?, the capital of the Yemen in olden times, was also called ?Awāl. It was then built by the Ethiopians. Having defeated the Ethiopians, the Persian monarch Wahraz named it Ṣanᶜā? and it has so remained ever since.[10]

As regards the significance of the name ?Awāl, we get two accounts. First Yāqūt, who observes that ?Awāl was an idol of Bakr ibn Wā?il, and second al-Masᶜūdi, who tells of "a kind of fish in the sea of Zanj called al-?Uwāl" which is, he adds, from four to five hundred cubits long.[11] The first interpretation is widely accepted to meet the case, for in pre-Islamic times the region of al-Baḥrain was peopled by ᶜAbd al-Qais, Bakr ibn Wā?il, and Tamīm.[12]

The Early Settlers

Al-Masᶜūdi states that Ṭasm and Jadīs, sons of Lā?udh ibn Iram ibn Sām ibn Nūḥ, were among the earliest settlers in the region of al-Baḥrain and Yemāma.[13]

Al-Ṭabari informs us of the descendants of ᶜImlīq, known as al-ᶜAmāliqah,[14] i.e., Amalekite, who dispersed all over the country including al-Baḥrain.[15]

The Emergence of ᶜAbd al-Qais Tribes[16]

Al-Bakri, accounting for the tribal wars, tells of the fighting among the B(ani) Rabīᶜah, in the wake of which the B. Yashkur of Rabīᶜah assumed leadership having defeated the Nimr branch of the same tribe. Hostilities among the B. Rabīᶜah resulted in the dispersion of its members. Lukayz and Shann ibn Afṣa of ᶜAbd al-Qais and their followers settled in al-Baḥrain and Hajar which was then populated by Iyād and al-Azd.[17] Having forced Iyād to evacuate al-Baḥrain, B. ᶜAbd al-Qais, the new masters, became the dominant tribe in the region. Thus, Jadhīmah of ᶜAbd al-Qais, occupied al-Khaṭṭ.[18] Shann ibn Afṣa of ᶜAbd al-Qais settled on the outskirts of al-Khaṭṭ and the region bordering al- ^{c}Iraq. Nukrah ibn Lukayz of ^{c}Abd al-Qais occupied al-Qaṭīf and its surroundings. ^{c}Āmir ibn al-Ḥārith of ^{c}Abd al-Qais and their allies settled in al-Jawf, al- ^{c}Uyūn, and al-Aḥsā? and B. Zākiah of ^{c}Abd al-Qais established kinship ties with the indigenous population of Hajar.[19]

Accounting for ^{c}Abd al-Qais, al-Qalqashandi, writing in the fifteenth century A.D. observes: "The homelands of ^{c}Abd al-Qais were in Tihāmah; when they came to al-Baḥrain it was peopled by Bakr ibn Wā?il, and Tamīm whose homelands these, i.e., ^{c}Abd al-Qais occupied. They are the B. ^{c}Abd al-Qais ibn Afṣa ibn Du ^{c}miyy ibn Jadīlah."[20]

Kaḥḥāla, quoting various medieval Arab sources, renders this account of ^{c}Abd al-Qais: "they supported ^{c}Ali ibn Abi Ṭālib in the events of 36 A.H."[21]

The illustration below, compiled from medieval Arab sources, is an attempt to reconstruct the genealogy of the B. ^{c}Abd al-Qais tribes of Eastern Arabia and the island of ?Awāl:

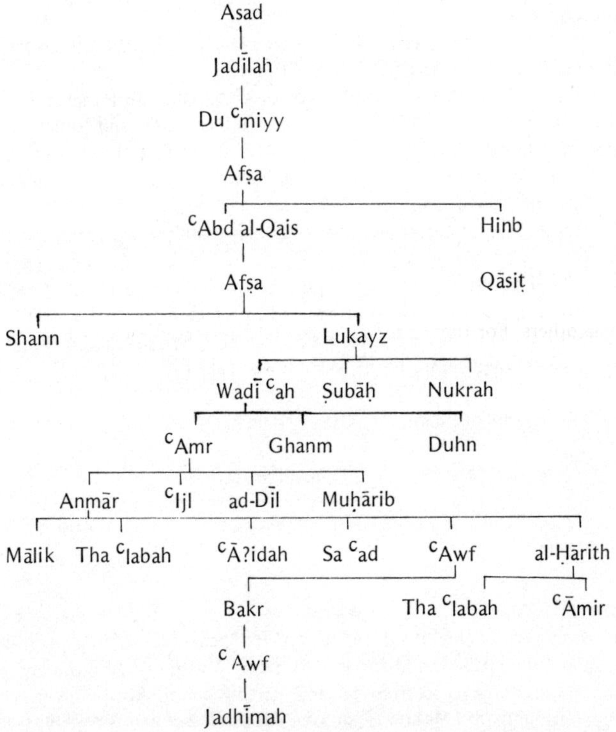

Notes:

A descendant of Jadhīmah ibn ^{c}Awf is Abū Ghiyāth (known as al-Jārūd) ibn Ḥanash ibn al-Mu ^{c}alla ibn Zayd ibn Ḥārithah ibn Mu ^{c}āwiyah ibn Tha ^{c}labah ibn Jadhīmah ibn ^{c}Awf ibn Anmār ibn ^{c}Amr ibn Wadī^{c}ah ibn Lukayz ibn Afṣa ibn ^{c}Abd al-Qais. He was an eminent Moslem, favoured by the Prophet, and the Caliphs Abū Bakr and ^{c}Umar. His descendants in al-Baṣrah are respectable and eminent people. Al-Mundhir, son of al-Jārūd, was the *wālī* (Governor) of Iṣṭakhr (in Persia) during the caliphate of ^{c}Ali ibn Abi Ṭālib (35–40 A.H. i.e., 656–661 A.D.) (see Ibn Ḥazm (384–456 A.H.), *Jamharat Ansāb al-^{c}Arab:* 296).

The Descendants of ^{c}Ijl ibn ^{c}Amr ibn Wadī^{c}ah ibn Lukayz

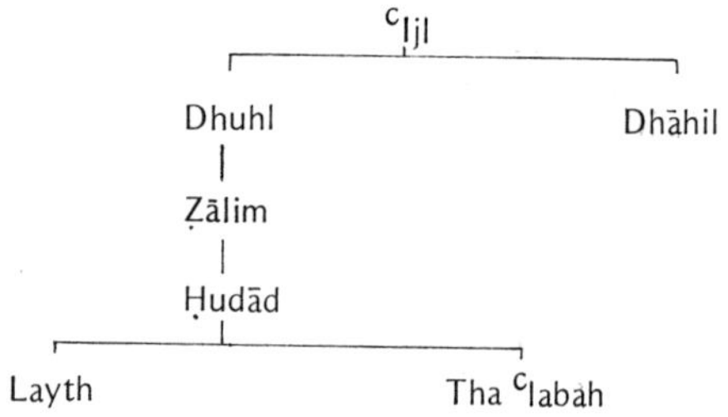

Notes:

The brief notes given below are concerned with ^{c}Abd al-Qais personalities particularly those who supported ^{c}Ali ibn Abi Ṭālib.

From B. Layth ibn Ḥudād descended ^{c}Abdalla ibn Raqabah uncle of Maṣqalah ibn Karib ibn Raqabah ibn Layth, who was the flag bearer and fought on ^{c}Ali's side in the battle of al-Jamal, in which he was killed. Also, from the B. Layth came Sayḥān, Ṣa^{c}ṣa^{c}ah, and Zayd, sons of Ṣōḥān ibn Ḥujr ibn al-Ḥārith ibn al-Hijris ibn Ṣabrah ibn al-Ḥidrijān ibn ^{c}Isās (see Ibn Ḥazm, *Jamharah:* 297).

Lorimer in his *Gazetteer,* under Baḥrain Island, p. 213, mentions:[22]

> "Rās Ḥayyān, 5 miles east of Jabal ad-Dukhkhan, carries an old and prominent building, said to have been erected as a memorial or as a tomb; this promontory is also known as Rās Ṣa^{c}ṣa^{c}ah [i.e, Ṣa^{c}ṣa^{c}ah ibn Ṣōḥān ibn Ḥujr, a follower and supporter of ^{c}Ali ibn Abi Ṭālib]."

The Descendants of Shann ibn Afṣa of ^{c}Abd al-Qais

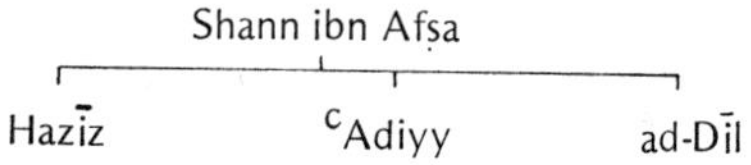

Notes:

Hazīz ibn Shann introduced the famous spears of al-Khaṭṭ. ^{c}Amr ibn al-Ju^{c}ayd ibn Ṣabrah ibn ad-Dīl ibn Shann ibn Afṣa ibn ^{c}Abd al-Qais, was the one who ordered ^{c}Abd al-Qais to proceed from Tihāmah to al-Baḥrain. Also, known as al-Afkal, his son al-Muthanna ibn Mukharribah was ^{c}Ali's follower and supporter (see *Jamharah:* 299).

The Descendants of Hinb ibn Afṣa ibn Du^{c}miyy

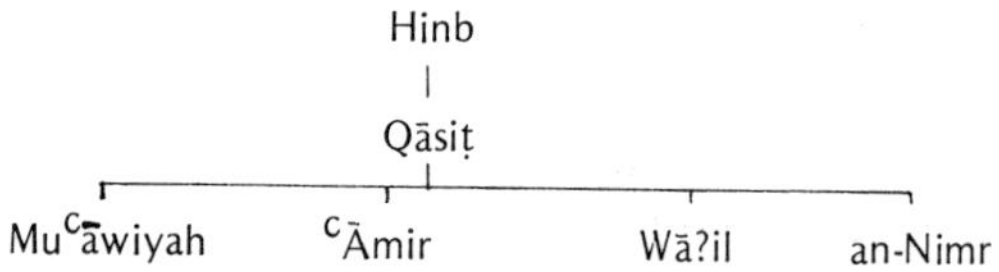

Notes:

ᶜĀmir ibn Qāsiṭ was also known as Ghofaylah. The descendants of Wā?il and an-Nimr were massacred by the Carmathians after 300 A.H. Other members of the same branch were absorbed by Arab tribes (see *Jamharah:* 300).

The Descendants of an-Nimr ibn Qāsiṭ ibn Hinb ibn Afṣa ibn Duᶜmiyy ibn Jadīlah

an-Nimr
- Taym Allāh
  - al-Khazraj
    - Saᶜd
      - ᶜĀmir aḍ-Ḍaḥyān
- Aws Manāt
- ᶜAbd Manāt
- Qāsiṭ

Notes:

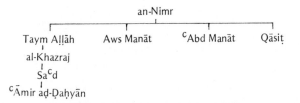

From an-Nimr branch descended Ṣuhayb ibn Sinān ibn Mālik ibn ᶜAbd ᶜAmr ibn ᶜAqīl ibn ᶜĀmir ibn Jandalah ibn Jadhīmah ibn Ka ᶜb ibn Sa ᶜd ibn Aslam ibn Aws Manāt ibn an-Nimr ibn Qāsiṭ, a favourite of the Prophet. Sinān ibn Mālik, father of Ṣuhayb, ruled over Abullah, on behalf of Kisra (see *Jahmhara:* 300).

From ᶜĀmir aḍ-Ḍaḥyān descended ᶜUqbah ibn Qais ibn al-Bishr ibn Hilāl ibn al-Bishr ibn Qais ibn Zuhayr ibn ᶜUqbah ibn Josham ibn Hilāl ibn Rabī ᶜah ibn Zayd Manāt ibn ᶜĀmir aḍ-Ḍaḥyān, leader of the apostate group of the B. Nimr, who was put to death by Khālid ibn al-Walīd in the battle of ᶜAyn at-Tamr (see *Jamharah:* 301).

Also from ᶜĀmir aḍ-Ḍaḥyān descended Nutaylah bint Janāb ibn Kolayb ibn Mālik ibn ᶜAmr ibn Zayd Manāt ibn ᶜĀmir aḍ-Ḍaḥyān, mother of al- ᶜAbbās ibn ᶜAbd al-Muttalib (see (*Jamharah:* 301).

Two ancient verses, composed by different Arab poets, tell of the dominance of two Arab tribes over the region of al-Baḥrain at different times. The first,[23] composed by Āl-As ᶜad, tells of some of the earlier settlers who left the Yemen after the burst of Ma?rib dam. It states clearly that al-Baḥrain was at one time held by al-Azd tribes. The other verse, by al-Akhnas ibn Shihāb al-Taghlibi confirms the dominance of Lukayz ibn Afṣa of ᶜAbd al-Qais, over the whole region.[24]

(1) Āl-As ᶜad: وأزدُلها البحران والسيفُ كله وأرض عمان بعد أرض المشقّر

(2) al-Taghlibi لكيزلها البحران والسيف كله وإن يَغشها بأس من الهند كارب

It should be noted, however, that the dominance of Lukayz of ᶜAbd al-Qais over the region of al-Baḥrain is attested by a number of Medieval Arab sources.

On the Early Inhabitants of the Island of ?Awāl

The island of ?Awāl, as it was known in pre-Islamic times, was part of the larger region called al-Baḥrain. Therefore, any account of that region in old Arab sources is taken to embrace both the island and the region facing it.

Due to the abundance of sweet water and date plantations, the island must have been, from earliest times, a haven for Arab tribes of the mainland who sought refuge in it at one time or another. As stated in the foregoing pages, the Iyād and al-Azd tribes, seem to be among the earliest settlers in the region. After them the B. ᶜAbd al-Qais of Rabī ᶜah, viz. Lukayz ibn Afṣa, ruled the region including the island of ?Awāl.

Al-Masᶜūdi, writing around the tenth century A.D., gives this account of the inhabitants of ?Awāl island.[25] Accounting for *Baḥr Fāris,* i.e., the Persian Gulf, he writes:

". . . another island is called the isle of ?Awāl; there live the B. Ma^{c}n, B. Mismār, and a great number of other Arabs."

Who are the B. Ma ^{c}n and B. Mismār? Al-Ṭabari informs us that the B. Ma ^{c}n are members of the al-Azd tribes who are also known as Bāhilah. He quotes Sharīk ibn ^{c}Ali Qīlah al-Ma ^{c}ni as saying[26] "that ^{c}Umar ibn Muslim of Taghlib ibn Wā?il, addressing the gathering of the B. Ma ^{c}n, used to say: "If we are not from the same stock as you are, then we are not Arabs."

It is noteworthy that the majority of the inhabitants of ^{c}Umān are of the Azd tribes, who are Qaḥṭānites. They are called Azd of ^{c}Umān to distinguish them from the Azd of Shanū?a, Azd of as-Sarāt, and Azd of Ghassān.

Based on the preceding information we come to the conclusion that the B. Ma ^{c}n of ?Awāl were most probably descendants of the Azd of ^{c}Umān rather than the rest of its branches.

Al-Nuwayri[27] accounting for B. Ma ^{c}n says: "Ma ^{c}n and Buḥtar are two sons of ^{c}Utūd. Every Ma ^{c}ni and Buḥtari is a descendant of either of these two. Thuwab, Wudd and Mālik are descendants of Ma ^{c}n bin ^{c}Utūd. Ghanm and Abu Ḥārithah are sons of Thuwab ibn Ma ^{c}n."

The following tree diagram illustrates the above point:

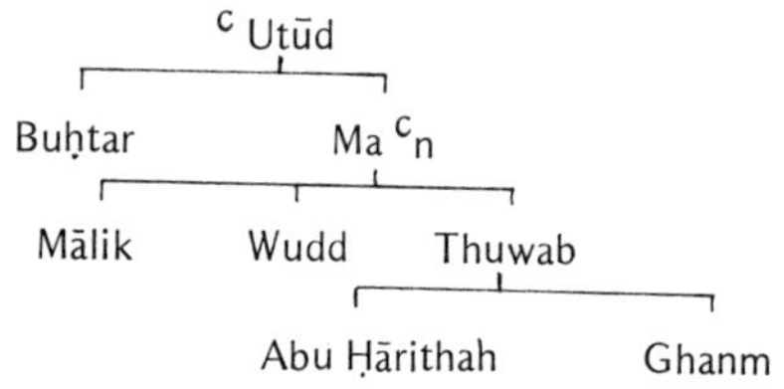

The other inhabitants of ?Awāl, mentioned by al-Mas^{c}ūdi, are the B. Mismār. Accounting for the *Carmathians* in the region of al-Baḥrain, he says that the B. Mismār of ^{c}Abd al-Qais were the influential inhabitants of al-Qaṭīf and that Abū Sa ^{c}īd al-Jannābi, the *Carmathian* chief, could subdue the cities of al-Baḥrain only after killing Abū Zakariyya al-Baḥrāni,[28] and that al-Qaṭīf surrendered only when ^{c}Ali ibn Mismār of ^{c}Abd al-Qais and his brothers were killed by al-Jannābi.[29] Al-Hamdāni observes that the B. Jadhīmah of ^{c}Abd al-Qais were among the influential inhabitants of al-Qaṭīf and that ibn Mismār was their chief.[30]

From the above account the following facts emerge:

(1) That the B. Ma^{c}n of ?Awāl island were descendants of the Azd of ^{c}Umān.

(2) That the B. Mismār of ?Awāl island had kinship ties with the B. Mismār of al-Qaṭīf, both of which are descended from Jadhīmah branch of ^{c}Abd al-Qais. The tree diagram, below, based on genealogical information such as found in Arab sources, shows where ^{c}Abd al-Qais and ^{c}Anazah tribes meet:

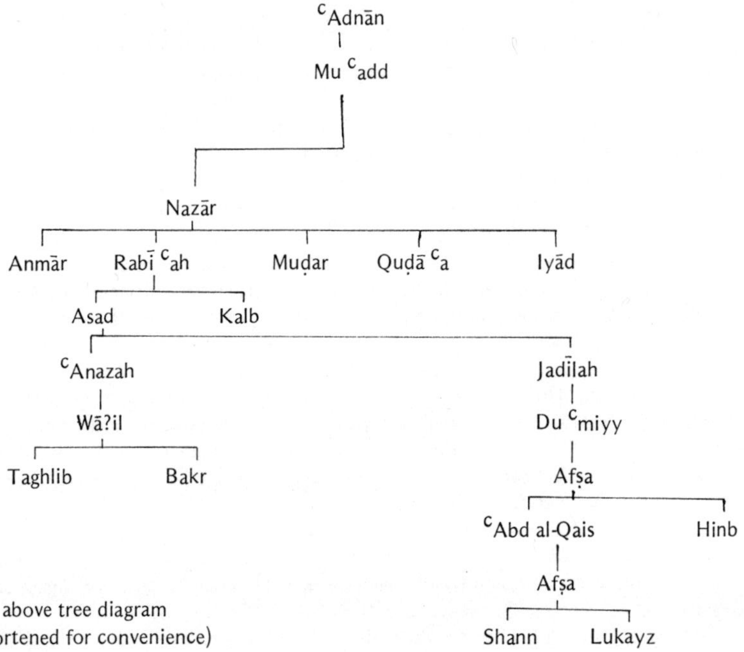

(The above tree diagram
is shortened for convenience)

Notes:

(1) For B. ^{c}Abd al-Qais see illustration pp. 17–19 above. Other subdivisions of ^{c}Abd al-Qais mentioned by al-Hamdāni, al-Bakri, or Yāqūt as occupants of a place or area are: B. Muḥārib, B. Salīm, B. ^{c}Āmir and their descendants: B. Khālid, al- ^{c}Amāyir, and finally, B. Jadhīmah.

(2) Note above that bani ^{c}Abd al-Qais meet with ^{c}Anazah in Asad from Rabī ^{c}ah.

The following list extracted from al-Hamdāni and Yāqūt, exhibits the names of the tribes which inhabited the towns and villages of the peninsular part of the ancient region from pre-Islamic times.

Hajar[31] meaning "village" in the language of Ḥimyar was inhabited by bani Muḥārib of ^{c}Abd al-Qais. It was also a pre-Islamic market place, named after Hajar bint Miknaf, a descendant of al-^{c}Amālīq, after whose husband, Muḥallam ibn ^{c}Abdalla, the river of Muḥallam was named.[32] Hajar, Yāqūt adds, was also employed to embrace Baḥrain proper.

Al- ^{c}Uqair was the homeland of Muḥārib of ^{c}Abd al-Qais.

Al-Aḥsā?, built and fortified by Abū Ṭāhir al-Jannābi, was the homeland of bani Tamīm.

Al-Khaṭṭ, the coastal town of the region, famous for its spears, was peopled by Jadhīmah of ^{c}Abd al-Qais.

Qaṭar, famous for its camels and wine, was part of the region.[33]

Juwātha, Yāqūt says, was the stronghold of ^{c}Abd al-Qais. After the death of al-Mundhir ibn Sāwa, whose death occurred shortly after that of the Prophet, B. Rabī ^{c}ah apostasized. It was in Juwātha that the Muslim defenders were beseiged and set free only when the Caliph Abu Bakr sent reinforcements under the command of al- ^{c}Alā? al-

Ḥaḍrami in the twelfth year of the Hijra. It is also stated that the first mosque to be built outside al-Madīnah was in Juwātha, and so was the first Friday prayer performed outside al-Madīnah;[34] and that the inhabitants of the region accepted Islam voluntarily and not forcibly.[35]

In their account of the region of al-Baḥrain, medieval Arab sources provide us with important information regarding the island of ?Awāl, part of the old region. A brief account of the earlier settlements and the tribes that inhabited them will be rendered here for the relevance such information may have to the tribal structure of the people in the area under question.

We will begin with *Sīf al-Baḥrain,* i.e., harbour of al-Baḥrain, a term employed to embrace both the harbour of ?Awāl as well as the eastern coastal line of the peninsular region facing it. In a specific reference to *Sīf-?Awāl,* Yāqūt tells us that this place was frequented by ships from India.

To Arab geographers, the contemporary island of Muḥarraq[36] was, in earlier times, known as Samāhīj. On the origins of the name Samāhīj, al-Bakri quoting others says: "Samāhīj is from Persian se (three) and māhi (fish) and hence, 'the three fish'."[37] The sound change final *i* < *y* of the Persian form māhi pronounced locally *-j* is a phonetic feature known as *ᶜajᶜajah,* and ascribed to Quḍāᶜah tribes as in the word Tamīmi (a person belonging to bani Tamīm tribes) realized Tamīmij.[38]

Writing about Samāhīj, which has survived in the name of a village on contemporary Muḥarraq island, al-Bakri informs us that this place was peopled by ᶜAbd al-Qais tribes.[39] Yāqūt also mentions an island by the name of Samāhīj situated between ᶜUmān and al-Baḥrain, a reference to the present island of Muḥarraq.[40]

Arad, we are told, is an island situated to the north-east of Baḥrain island.[41] It is stated that this place was the homeland of the ᶜAmāliqa who later came to be known as the Phoenicians.[42] However, Aryan's Aradus, corresponding to the above name, has since then survived as ᶜArād, a village in contemporary island of Muḥarraq.[43]

Al-Dār: Yāqūt quoting ibn Durayd in *al-Malāḥin* says "Dār is a popular place in al-Baḥrain."[44] Today al-Dār has survived as ᶜĒn Dār, a small village to the south-west of Jid Ḥafṣ. It has come to be known as ᶜĒn Dār after the natural pool there.

Al-Qulayᶜa, diminutive form of Arabic *qalᶜa* (fort) is also mentioned by Yāqūt being a place in Baḥrain peopled by ᶜAbd al-Qais tribes.[45] Al-Tājir in his aforesaid book provides us with this information about the place:[46] "Opposite to the village of al-Ḥūrah, north-east of ?Awāl island, there is an old construction amidst the sea known as al-Qulayᶜa which serves as a sign-post for passing ships."

Al-Ḥūrah: Yāqūt quoting al-Samᶜāni renders this account of Ḥuwārīn, corresponding to the present town of al-Ḥūrah: ". . . a village in Baḥrain reduced by Ziyād Ḥuwārīn, said to be Ziyād ibn ᶜUmar ibn al-Mundhir ibn ᶜAṣar, brother of Khilās ibn ᶜUmar, Ziyād was a theologian and a supporter of ᶜAli ibn Abi Ṭālib."[47]

Lāfith, Yāqūt writes, is an island in the sea of ᶜUmān between ᶜUmān and Hajar. It is also known as the island of bani Kāwān which was reduced by ᶜUthmān ibn Abi al- ᶜĀṣ al-Thaqafi during the caliphate of ᶜUmar ibn al-Khaṭṭāb. From this island he marched to Persia and conquered certain regions there. In this island there is a famous mosque in commemoration of ᶜUthmān ibn Abi al- ᶜĀṣ. This island was one of the most flourishing of the islands; it has villages, natural pools, and buildings.[48]

This island, al-Tājir writes, is also known as ?Ukul and Lāfith. Among its villages today is the one called Kāflān, which is mentioned by Ibn Ḥajar as Kāwān, the same as the one quoted by Yāqūt above.[49]

However, Yāqūt's account of the island of Lāfith or banī Kāwān, corresponds closely to the island of Nabīh Ṣālih in present-day Baḥrain. Its inhabitants are exclusively

Baḥārnah; the main natural pool known locally as as-Saffāḥiyya, the date plantations and the mosque, mentioned by Yāqūt, have all survived ever since, and Kāflān is among one of its villages today.

Al-Jufayr: Yāqūt mentions al-Jufayr, diminutive form of *al-jafr* (well) being a village in Baḥrain peopled by bani ᶜĀmir ibn ᶜAbd al-Qais.[50] This place has survived ever since and grown into an important town in contemporary Baḥrain. Accordingly, the present Baḥārnah Arabs of Jufayr are descendants of ᶜAbd al-Qais tribes.

Al-Sihlah, meaning "plain, low-land", is mentioned by ibn al-Faqīh as being one of the twenty-two villages of Baḥrain which he lists in *Kitāb al-Buldān.*[51] The inhabitants of these villages, he adds, including Al-Sihlah, are bani Muḥārib ibn Wadīᶜah of ᶜAbd al-Qais. This place has survived to this very day and is entirely inhabited by the Baḥārnah. Yāqūt also mentions the same place as being one of the villages in Baḥrain.[52]

Jaww, a village situated on the eastern coast of contemporary Bahrain, is mentioned by Yāqūt being as place on the coast of al-Baḥrain.[53]

Yāqūt also mentions Tarm, which he says was the old city of ?Awāl island in al-Baḥrain.[54] Perhaps this was the case before it was known as Manāmah. However, the present name Manāmah was first mentioned around the year 730 A.H., i.e., 1330 A.D. (app.) when Turān Shah of Hurmuz visited the island. It had been annexed by his predecessor Tahamtam the second of Hurmuz.[55]

Two similar place names found in eastern Arabia and the island of Baḥrain ought to be mentioned here. These names are perhaps relatively recent because no account of them is given by Arab geographers. They are Sūq al-Khamīs: market, until recently held every Thursday in the village of al-Khamīs in contemporary Baḥrain. Here, villagers used to sell their local crafts. Such a market, bearing the same name, is also found in al-Hufūf (al-Aḥsā?).[56] Al-Budayyiᶜ: once a Baḥārnah coastal village-town on the north-western tip of the island of Baḥrain, occupied around 1845 by the Dawāsir tribes of mainland Arabia, is also found in the northern part of al-Qaṭīf, near the island of al-Muslimiyya.[57]

From the preceding accounts of the area and its early inhabitants one can safely conclude that the occupants were of predominantly Arab origin.

Diverse Arab Elements in Contemporary Baḥrain

On the following pages we will attempt a reconstruction of the major elements in the present Arab population of Baḥrain, based on the data obtained from Arab sources, old and new. This will be followed by a similarly succinct account of the origins of the Baḥārnah Arabs of Baḥrain, the subject of this study.

Āl-Khalīfah, the Ruling House of Baḥrain

From ᶜAnazah descended some of the most influential ruling families of the area, such as Āl-Suᶜūd, Āl-Ṣubāḥ, Āl-Khalīfah. Āl-Khalīfah, whose original homelands were al-Aflāj in Najd, are the descendants of bani ᶜUtbah, an offshoot of Jumailah tribe which is a sub-division of ᶜAnazah.[58]

The Āl-Rumayḥi of Baḥrain are descendants of Thaᶜl ibn Sunbus.[59] Al-Qalqashandi renders this account of them:[60] "Banu Rumayḥ is an offshoot of al-Khazāᶜilah from Sunbus."

The Āl-Jalāhimah of Baḥrain, the present residents of Ḥālat Abu Māhir on Muḥarraq island, are descendants of bani ᶜUtbah.[61]

The Āl-Jasās and Āl-Marīs of Muḥarraq island are descendants of Āl-Mughīrah.[62]

The present inhabitants of al-Ḥidd on Muḥarraq island are Āl-Sādah and Āl-Bin ᶜAli.[63]

About 1845 the Dawāsir tribes came to Baḥrain and established themselves mainly in Zallāq and Budayyi^{c}.[64] Ibn Shihāb al-Maqarri, in his *Kitāb al-Ta ^{c}ārīf,* traces them back to a sub-division of al-Azd tribes, i.e, Qaḥṭānite Arabs of the Yemen. In *Nihāyat al-Arab fī Ma ^{c}rifat Ansāb al- ^{c}Arab,* they are said to be sons of al-Azāyid (plural of Azd) from bani Wadā ^{c}ah ibn ^{c}Umar ibn ^{c}Āmir, king of al-Sadd. Their homes were in ^{c}Umān, the region of al-Baḥrain, Iraq, and Najd. Their country was al-Wādi and al-Aflāj. They were nomads and settled.

Wahba, who was writing in the thirties, has this to say about Budayyi^{c}: "Its population is eight thousand, mostly Dawāsir tribes. A dispute between them and the Government of Baḥrain led to their departure from Baḥrain to Dammām in late 1922. However, after two years' time, and in the wake of conciliatory steps taken by the Government of Baḥrain, some of them came back."[65]

Writing about the places and people of Baḥrain, Wahba adds:[66]

"The inhabitants of ^{c}Askar are Āl-Bu ^{c}Aynayn.
The inhabitants of ^{c}Arād are Baḥārnah.
The inhabitants of ad-Deer are also Baḥārnah.
The inhabitants of al-Rafā ^{c} al-Gharbi are bani ^{c}Utbah.
The inhabitants of Galāli are al-Manāni ^{c}ah."

The Early Inhabitants of the Island of ?Awāl (a recapitulation)[67]

As stated by al-Mas ^{c}ūdi in *Murūj adh-Dhahab,* they are the bani Mismār of ^{c}Abd al-al-Qais, and the bani Ma ^{c}n, and some other Arab tribes.

As regards the bani Ma ^{c}n, the only reference to these which we know of, and which comes from a local source, is the mention by al-Tājir of the existence in the past of a village near ^{c}Āli known as ^{c}Āli Ma ^{c}n, the homeland of Shaikh Muḥammad bin ^{c}Abd al-al-Salām al-Ma ^{c}ni.[68]

Al-Sihlah was peopled by bani Muḥārib ibn Wadī ^{c}ah of ^{c}Abd al-Qais.

Al-Jufayr was peopled by bani ^{c}Āmir ibn ^{c}Abd al-Qais.

The Early Inhabitants of Samāhīj (i.e., present Muḥarraq)

As stated earlier, the island of Muḥarraq was known as Samāhīj, which has survived ever since in the name of a village on the same island. Al-Bakri mentions ^{c}Abd al-Qais being the inhabitants of Samāhīj. The present Baḥārnah community on Muḥarraq island, though sparse, comprises the descendants of those tribes. They are date planters, fishermen, and sail makers, though sail making is dwindling now. They are found in these villages: ad-Deer, al-Janameh, Rayyah, Samāhīj, al-Ḥillah, Galāli, ^{c}Arād.

The Inhabitants of Bani Jamrah Village

As the name of the village implies, and as far as local tradition is concerned, these are the descendants of an extinct Arab tribe called Jamrah or Jamarāt al- ^{c}Arab.[69]

Kaḥḥāla gives this account of al-Jamarāt:[70] "Al-Jamarāt, it is said, is an offshoot of Lakhm of Qaḥṭanite Arabs. They comprise, banu Dabba, banu ?Udd, banu al-Harith ibn Ka ^{c}b, banu Numayr ibn ^{c}Amir." Al-Mubarrad on the ancestry of the same tribe writes: "It is said that Jamarat al- ^{c}Arab are banu Numayr ibn ^{c}Amir ibn Sa^{c}sa ^{c}ah, and banu al-Harith ibn Ka ^{c}b ibn ^{c}Ulah ibn Jald, and banu Ḍabba ibn ?Udd ibn Ṭābikha, and banu ^{c}Abs ibn Baghīḍ ibn Rayth ibn Ghaṭafān."[71]

Finally, I would like to call attention to a place name, viz. Sitār al-Baḥrain, which means "veil, screen, protection, shelter, etc.". Yāqūt, accounting for this place, informs us that it comprised well over one hundred villages inhabited by bani Imra? il-Qays ibn Zayd Manāt and Ifnā? Sa ^{c}ad ibn Zayd Manāt, both of which are Tamīmi tribes.[72]

In another account, al-Hamdāni observes that Sitār al-Baḥrain is a place of gathering or call for the bani Tamīm of the mainland.[73]

The above place name should not be confused with the island of Sitrah, one of the islands in contemporary Baḥrain, nor with al-Sitār al-Aghbar, and al-Sitār al-Jābiri, both of which are three nights from al-Aḥsā?, on the mainland of peninsular Arabia.[74]

1783 and After

A document dated 7 October 1873 (Bushire) and signed by the local *munshi*, Abu al-Qāsim ibn ᶜAbbās, probably an official of the East India Company, renders this account of the leading Baḥārnah families at the time the document was written. It reads: "They are the Sādat [i.e., notables], Āl- ᶜUmrān, Āl-Mājid, Āl- ᶜAbd al-Ra?ūf . . ., each family is in possession of its lands; they are date-planters of the Shī ᶜi sect."[75] This early nineteenth century document, accounting for the ᶜUtūb, i.e., the ruling house of Baḥrain, and their allies provides this specific information:

Names of families	Sect	Habitation	Estimated number	Remarks
Āl-Bin ᶜAli	*Sunnee*	Is. of Muḥarraq	600	Divided into three sections, Ahl bin Laḥdān, Ahl bin Bishboogh. Divers. Headman, Sulṭān ibn Selāmah.
El-Sādeh	"	"	200	Divers
El-Menāne ᶜeh	"	"	350	Divers
El-Na ᶜaaem	"	"	100	Divers
El-Salālah	"	"	150	Divers
Bu Falāsah	"	"	170	Divers
El-Mudhāḥekeh	"	"	200	Divers
El-Lee ᶜānanah	"	"	100	Ship owners and traders
El-Mu ᶜāwideh	"	"	150	Ship owners and traders
Āl-Bu-Kawwārah	"	"	50	of Persian origin[76]
El-Jalāhemeh	"	"	80	Sailors and ship owners
El-Hooleh(Huwalah)	"	Manāma and Muḥarraq	2000	From Persian coast, divided into Kashkanāra, Āl-Gābendee. A sheikh of this tribe held Baḥrain in time of Nādir Shāh.
Āl-Simāheejee	*Shī ᶜah*	Manāma and Muḥarraq	300	Fishermen and divers
El-Ḥayaaycheh	"	"	80	Sail-makers
Āl-boo Romeyḥ	*Sunnee*	Jaw	300	Divers
Āl-boo ᶜAinein	"	ᶜAskar	250	Divers
El-Dawāsir	"	Western side of Manāma	300	Divers

El-Dhawāwdeh	"	near Portuguese fort	100	Divers
El-ᶜAmāier	"	Zallāq	100	Divers
El-Ḥusaynat	"	Ḥoorah	80	Divers
El-Ḥamādeh	*Shīᶜah*	Rās Rummān	220	Divers

The document ends with this remark: "The residue of the inhabitants are called el-Baḥārneh (i.e. people of Baḥrain). The above are nearly all modern family names and some are sub-branches of the al-ᶜUtūb."

Finally, Lorimer writing in the opening years of the twentieth century, gives this account of the leading Baḥārnah families:[77]

ᶜAnābirah	Āl-Mājid
ᶜAṣāfirah (Al-ᶜAṣfūr)	Āl-Muslim
ᶜAsakirah	Āl-Rafyah
Ghabārah	Āl-Raḥmah
Ḥadādīd	Āl-Bin Suwār

Further to the above, Lorimer adds, "besides numerous families of Saiyids who are now recognised as Baḥārinah."[78]

Section (B)

Notes on the geography of the islands of Baḥrain

Baḥrain, which was declared independent on 14 August 1971, consists of an archipelago of several small islands, the largest of which is called the Baḥrain island. It comprises: Manāmah,[79] the principal town and hence the centre for governmental activities; ᶜAwāli, the oil capital of Baḥrain and the residence, chiefly, for all European employees of the Baḥrain Petroleum Company.

The islands of Baḥrain, which have a total area of 255 square miles,[80] are only fifteen miles from the eastern coast of Saudi Arabia. The main island is about 30 miles in length and twelve in breadth.[81]

Along the northern shore there is a green belt of date plantations stretching, almost uninterrupted, from Manāmah to Bārbār, then from ᶜĀli to Buri, and from Damistān to Dār Chulaib.

The other two islands, significant in terms of magnitude and economic activity are Muḥarraq and Sitrah.[82]

Muḥarraq,[83] the second largest island of the archipelago, is the site of Baḥrain's international airport. Sitrah, the third most significant of the islands has a large jetty where tankers obtain their load of refined oil.

Rainfall is confined to the winter months, that is December to March. Drinking water is obtained from fresh-water springs, artesian wells, and fairly recently a desalination plant. This last development was brought about by the increase of alkali in natural sources, and also by the higher consumption of water. The abundance, however, of fresh-water springs, both offshore and on the mainland led to the existence, since earlier times, of a settled population, and hence the emergence, in the past, of a local civilization. It is believed that these springs receive their supply of water from the highlands of Najd which is the nearest locality with adequate rainfall.[84] Pearl divers and fishermen, however, are familiar with the location of these springs. Zwemer,[85] writing in 1899 informs us that "the natives lower a hollow, weighted bamboo through which the fresh water gushes out a few inches above sea-level."

During the hot season, i.e., from May to October, the temperature remains intolerably high. A local sea-breeze called *al-Bāriḥ*, alleviates the overall temperature, especially on coastal areas. *Shamāl*, which is a dry, northerly wind, prevails during winter and so does the *kōs*, a south-easterly wind.

The Significance of the Islands

Geographical

As early as the sixteenth century, European powers recognized the importance of

Baḥrain to trade routes linking Bombay to Baṣrah. The strategic position of the islands can be viewed in relation to the whole Gulf, once described as "one of the highways of the world, an important link in a chain of communication between East and West."[86]

Economic

The old pearling industry

The rich pearl fisheries of Baḥrain attracted several local and foreign powers to occupy the islands. The annual value of the pearls obtained in the first half of the nineteenth century is estimated at 1,000,000 to 1,200,000 German crowns, and the number of boats involved fifteen hundred.[87]

The coming of oil and the diversification of resources

Prior to 1932, the year oil was discovered in Baḥrain, date plantations and pearl fishing were the two pillars of economic activity in Baḥrain. Besides constituting the staple food of the islanders and their cattle, the date palm was put to many different uses. It provided palm leaves and fronds for making *barastaj* or *ᶜish-she* (local huts); its trunks were used as load-bearing lintels for old gypsum-built houses, and the *karab* (dried branch stumps) for cooking; and the leaves for basket and mat plaiting.

The Baḥrain Petroleum Company Limited (BAPCO), a subsidiary of the Standard Oil Company of California, commenced operations at the end of 1931 and oil was struck in May 1932. Production in 1934 averaged 902 barrels a day and in 1971 reached 75,000 barrels a day.[88] In March 1975, complete ownership of BAPCO operations was transferred to the Government of Baḥrain. In the last decade or so, an era of industrialization in line with the policy of diversification of economic resources has begun. Aluminium Baḥrain (ALBA) was established on 9 August 1968 and production began in May 1971.

A large dry-dock, financed by OAPEC countries, was started in November 1974.[89] This and other industrial projects have, however, entailed the import of a large foreign work force.

Historical Survey of the Islands

Many authorities have identified Dilmun, described in the Sumerian tablet "diluge" as "the place where the sun rises", "the abode of the blessed", with Baḥrain.[90] Others took it for ᶜUmān, and still a few others took it to be western Iran. However, in view of recent archaeological findings, some authorities are inclined to equate Dilmun or Tilmun of the Sumerian and Akkadian inscriptions with Baḥrain.[91]

The Phoenicians

Certain Arab and European sources have considered the Gulf as the original abode of the Phoenicians. It was thought, at one time, that the sepulchral tumuli at ᶜĀli were of Phoenician origin. However, lack of adequate evidence, and in view of recent archaeological finds, the above theory seems to have lost the wider currency it once had among the earlier excavators such as Theodore Bent, Captain Durand, and Prideaux.[92]

Pre-Islamic and Early Islamic Baḥrain

In pre-Islamic times, the region of al-Baḥrain formed part of the Persian kingdom. Local Christians, Magians, Jews, and pagan Arabs peopled the area. There is evidence of trade between ancient Persia and Baḥrain which was ruled by Ardashir in the Sasanian period (226–241 AD.), and later by Shahpur II (310–379 A.D.). Shahpur, enraged by Baḥraini raids, occupied the island in a bloody foray and it remained part of the Persian empire for the next three centuries.[93] The chief tribes of pre-Islamic Baḥrain were ᶜAbd al-Qais, Tamīm, and Bakr ibn Wāʔil.[94] Al-Mundhir ibn Sāwa ibn Zayd Manāt ibn Tamīm was governor on behalf of the Persians. In the eighth year of al-Hijra, the Prophet Muḥammad delegated al-ᶜAlāʔ al-Ḥaḍrami, an ally of the banu ᶜAbd Shams, to the region to call its people to Islam, which they did voluntarily.

On the death of the Prophet and during the caliphate of Abu Bakr, Arab tribes in the region, under the leadership of al-Ḥuṭam ibn Ḍubay ᶜa apostasized.

At-Ṭabari,[95] accounting for this period, observes that ᶜAbd al-Qais tribes of the region were persuaded by al-Jārūd ibn al-Mu ᶜalla, to return to Islam which they did, but Bakr ibn Wāʔil tribes remained in their apostasy. An expedition under the command of al-al- ᶜAlāʔ al-Ḥaḍrami, was sent against the renegades. This Islamic force was joined by al-Jārūd and his followers from the region. In the ensuing battle al-Ḥuṭam was killed and Islam was re-established.

Baḥrain under the Umayyad Dynasty

Muᶜāwiyah appointed his wāli in Baṣrah, Ziyād ibn Abīh, also wāli of ᶜUmān and Baḥrain. The island of ʔAwāl, at this time, was a refuge and a stronghold for ᶜAli's supporters, viz. ᶜAbd al-Qais.[96]

During the caliphate of ᶜAbd al-Malik, around 72 A.H. Abu Fudayk, a Kharijite, declared himself independent chief of the island. ᶜAbd al-Malik sent an army against him. Abu Fudayk was killed and the island was restored to bani Umayyah.

Baḥrain under the ᶜAbbasīds

In the year 151 A.H. Abu Ja ᶜfar al-Manṣūr sent an army against Sulaymān ibn Ḥakīm, then independent chief of the island. In the battle that followed, Sulaymān was killed and an ᶜAbbasid governor was appointed. Baḥrain remained under the ᶜAbbasids until 249 A.H. which marks the emergence of Ṣāḥib az-Zanj (Leader of the Blacks).[97]

Baḥrain under Ṣāḥib az-Zanj[98]

Ṣāḥib az-Zanj first appeared in Sāmirra, in Iraq around 249 A.H. Having first established himself in al-Aḥsāʔ, he later occupied the island of ʔAwāl and ruled it until 270 A.H. when he died. Once again the island was restored to the ᶜAbbasids who continued to rule the region until the time of the Caliph al-Muktafi, the year that witnessed the rise of the Carmathians.

The Carmathians in the region of al-Baḥrain (899–1060 A.D. app.)[99]

The Carmathian doctrine, first preached in al-Kūfah in 278 A.H. by Ḥamdān al-Ash ᶜath, better known as Qirmiṭ, soon spread in the region at the hands of al-Ḥasan ibn Bahrām, renowned as Abu Sa ᶜīd al-Jannābi.[100]

The Carmathian dream of a state materialized around 286 A.H. when al-Aḥsāʔ came under their rule and shortly afterwards ʔAwāl. Under the leadership of al-Jannābi clan, the Carmathians ruled over the region including the island of ʔAwāl from around 286 to 366 A.H.

Abu al-Bahlūl al- ᶜAwwām, independent chief of ʔAwāl

When the Carmathian power began to dwindle, al- ᶜAwwām ibn Muḥammad ibn Yūsuf az-Zajjāj declared himself independent chief of the island. At this time the ᶜUyūnis, Arab tribes of al-Aḥsāʔ, under their leader ᶜAbdalla al- ᶜUyūni, and also Yaḥya ibn al-ᶜAyyāsh of al-Qaṭīf, had already risen against the Carmathians. But the Carmathians were able to send an army against al-ᶜAwwām of ʔAwāl. In the battle that ensued, at a place called Kaskūs, the Carmathians met with defeat. Their defeat encouraged al-^{c}Ayyāsh to seize power and declare himself chief of al-Qaṭīf. Shortly afterwards, Yaḥya ibn al-^{c}Ayyāsh sent his son Zakariyya with an army to reduce ?Awāl, which he did. Zakariyya tried to take al-Aḥsā? but the ^{c}Uyūnis defeated him and this resulted in the occupation of al-Qaṭīf, Zakariyya's seat of government. Zakariyya fled to ?Awāl. ^{c}Abdalla al-^{c}Uyūni sent his son al-Faḍl with an army to reduce ?Awāl. In the battle that followed Zakariyya was killed and with it the ^{c}Ayyāsh rule over al-Khaṭṭ ended.

The ^{c}Uyūni rule over the region, including the island of ?Awāl lasted for about two hundred years.

Baḥrain in the 12th century A.D. and After

In the twelfth century Baḥrain is said to have become a tributary of Qais island. However, al-Idrīsi, the Arab geographer who visited the islands then, described its ruler as an independent chief, just and pious, and loved by his subjects. A description of Baḥrain in the thirteenth century is given by ibn al-Mujāwir who mentions that the people of Baḥrain Island are Arabs, and that there are three hundred and sixty villages in Baḥrain all of which profess the Shī^{c}i faith except one.[101]

About 1320, the Arab rulers of Hormuz conquered Baḥrain. Their influence diminished with the fall of Hormuz to the Portuguese in 1506.[102]

Baḥrain under the Portuguese 1521–1602.

The Portuguese occupation lasted from 1521–1602 with some interruptions in between. A rebellion against them took place in 1522 when the insurgents, acting on orders from their chief, Shaikh Ḥusain ibn Sa^{c}īd, attacked the Portuguese garrison on the island and had the commander of the garrison hanged on a date palm tree.[103]

About 1718, the islands were occupied, for a short time, by the Arabs of Muscaṭ. Lorimer writes, of this period, "the inhabitants temporarily forsook the islands and by this means the ^{c}Umāni occupation was brought to an end."[104]

Shortly afterwards, the Huwala Arabs,[105] under the leadership of Shaikh Jabbāra of Ṭāhiri, established themselves on the islands. It was at this time that the East India Company provided Nādir Shāh with ships to attack the Huwala of Baḥrain. The expedition was successful and Baḥrain became a dependency of Faris, viz. from 1736, i.e. during the reign of Nādir Shah to his successor Karīm Khān Zand (1756–1779).[106]

From 1753 to 1782, Shaikh Naṣr of Bushire and his family governed the islands.

In 1761, Niebuhr visited the islands and has this to say: "In this isle there were once three hundred and sixty towns and villages. At present it contains, beside the capital only sixty wretched villages. A long series of wars have ruined the others."[107]

The Arrival of the ^{c}Utūb, 1783 and After

Modern history of Baḥrain begins with the ^{c}Utbi occupation of the islands in 1783.[108] This year marks the end of the Bushire-Arab rule over the islands, and the start of peninsular Arab control. However, the name ^{c}Utūb, meaning "roamers or wanderers" is indicative of the vast journeys that these tribes had to undergo starting from their homelands in al-Aflāj, a region in Najd, down to Qaṭar, and then to Kuwait, and finally to Zubārah and Baḥrain. [109]

As regards the tribal ancestry of the ^{c}Utūb, an-Nabhāni informs us that the ^{c}Utūb are an offshoot of ^{c}Anazah, the multitudinous tribes of north Arabia.[110] In 1716, however, the ^{c}Utūb established themselves in the bani Khālid territory, a place later came to be known as Kuwait. Misunderstanding among themselves, inter alia, led Khalīfah, the Āl-Khalīfah chief, to move to Zubārah on the Qaṭari coast facing the island of Baḥrain in 1766.

In 1775, the year that also marks the start of the siege of Baṣrah by the Persians, direct relations between Kuwait and the British East India Company were established. [111]

Abu Ḥākimah, accounting for this period observes that East India Company officials were in favour of consolidating the ^{c}Utbi presence in the area, especially in the wake of the surrender of Baṣrah in 1776 to the Persians, and the implications of that surrender to British interests in the Gulf. Goods coming from India, destined for Aleppo, were now unloaded at Zubārah and Kuwait. Consequently, the appearance of the ^{c}Utūb of Kuwait and Zubārah as new rivals in Gulf trade aroused the jealousy of both the bani Ka^{c}b Arabs of the Persian littoral and also the Bushire Arabs who were then in possession of Baḥrain, and who until recently had benefited from British-India trade routes.

With the death in 1779 of Karīm Khān, the struggle for power in Persia began. Moreover, the Wahhābi threat to Zubārah, the seat of the Āl-Khalīfah rule, was more real now than any time in the past. Realizing this, in addition to having a foreknowledge of the Baḥārnah rivalries over leadership viz. between the Baḥārnah of Bilād al-Qadīm and Jid Ḥafṣ, the ^{c}Utūb and their allies from Āl-Muslim and bani Khālid, viz. Qaṭari tribes, invaded Baḥrain in 1783.[112]

However, from 1800 to 1801, the Imām of Muscaṭ was in possession of Baḥrain, and from 1803 to 1811 Baḥrain was under tight Wahhābi control. To avoid oppression and persecution many Baḥārnah fled the country to safer places such as al-Ḥijāz, Muḥammarah and Baṣrah. Lorimer, in this respect, informs us of the Baḥārnah immigration to Lingeh and other parts of the Gulf during the early ^{c}Anazi rule and again when the islands came under Muscaṭi and Wahhābi influence in the early 19th century.

In 1811, the Imām of Mascaṭ agreed to help Āl-Khalīfah regain the islands from the Wahhābis, provided they remained subservient to him.

In 1816, the Imām with the help of Bushire vessels undertook an armed expedition against Baḥrain. This was repulsed with the help of the Wahhābis.

In the early part of 1820, the rulers of Baḥrain agreed to pay a tribute of 30,000 dollars to the Imām of Muscaṭ. Shortly afterwards and in the same year, Baḥrain became a party to the General Treaty of Peace signed by all Arab chiefs of the Gulf. During the years 1853, 1861, and 1880, three treaty agreements with Britain were signed. A final treaty known as the Exclusive Agreement between Great Britain and the Shaikh of Baḥrain was concluded in 1892.

In 1900 a British Political Agency was established in Baḥrain. 1917 was a period of internal unrest. A report by Major Daly, Political Agent (1921–1926), describes the oppressive conditions to which the Baḥārnah were subjected during the autocratic chiefship of Shaikh ^{c}Īsa ibn ^{c}Ali. It runs:

"Forced labour, forced contributions of fowls, eggs, etc. and the commandeering of boats, animals for transport are of daily occurrence. Commandeering of transport and forced labour, both known as "Sukhrah" (i.e. Corvee) was originally a privilege of the ruler. It is now practised by every cadet of the family and by their Satellites, . . . and is a great hardship for the inhabitants."[113]

Owing to a number of incidents tension between the *Sunni* and the *Shī*^{c}*i* communities culminated in early May 1923, in an attack by the Dawāsir tribesmen on the Baḥārnah village of ^{c}Āli.

As a result, Lieut-Colonel S.G. Knox, who was then officiating as Political Resident, paid an epoch making visit to the islands. On May 26th., before a gathering of local notables, Knox announced the forced abdication of Shaikh ^{c}Īsa and the accession to the Chiefship of his eldest son Shaikh Ḥamad.

Shortly afterwards, ibn Sa^{c}ūd, in a letter to Knox, expressed concern over the deposition of Shaikh ^{c}Īsa and the deportation of his agent ^{c}Abdulla al-Quṣaibi from Baḥrain. In reply to the above letter and in justification of the strong measures the British Government had recently adopted in Baḥrain, Knox wrote:

"Shaikh ᶜĪsa's increasing age had made it impossible for him to exercise that vigilant supervision over affairs . . . and owing to this weakness, many (irresponsible) petty tyrants had been growing up in Baḥrain, chiefly irresponsible members of the Ālkhalīfah family and the Baḥārnah were grievously oppressed by them . . . there was no shadow of doubt that the Baḥārnah had valid grievances".[114]

Reassuring ibn Saᶜūd of the British intentions viz, the maintenance of Ālkhalīfah supremacy over the islands, Knox added:

"We firmly believe that the steps the British Government has been reluctantly forced to take will eventually conduce to the stability of the rule of the Ālkhalīfah family, will prevent foreign interference and preserve the essentially *Sunni* influence in the administration of the islands and the progress of all *Sunni* elements of the population."[115]

Unlike the twenties, the early thirties witnessed a new type of Baḥārnah leadership whose members were not only village headmen, as the case had been in the past, but also wealthy landowners who were better informed than their predecessors, and therefore more determined to pursue the Baḥārnah demand for equality of treatment with *Sunni* Arabs.

Realizing that the Baḥārnah constituted the native majority in the population of Baḥrain,[116] the eight leaders, acting on behalf of their fellow Baḥārnah, demanded political rights proportionate to their numbers.

An important event of late 1934 is the submission of what is known in British documents as 'The Baḥārnah Grievances of 1934.' A series of incidents in the Summer of 1934 motivated the demands embodied in the petition of 30.12. 1934 submitted to Shaikh Ḥamad the Ruler. Among other things, miscarriage of justice in recent court cases, discrimination against the Baḥārnah in job opportunities, lack of adequate Baḥārnah representation on various councils were among the main complaints raised in the above petition.

As the institutions which constituted Shaikh Ḥamad's administration were created with British knowledge and support, any call for reform was dommed to fall on deaf ears. The official response to the Baḥārnah demands was characterised by procrastination, vague promises and half-solutions culminating in the agitations of 1934.

Other than a stern warning from the P.A. to the eight leaders to be held responsible for the Baḥārnah actions, no positive steps were taken to meet their main demand, viz. proportionate political rights.

Realizing this marked transformation in British policy towards the Baḥārnah, by 1938 their leaders joined hands with their *Sunni* brethren and forwarded a joint demand for the formation of a Legislative Council.[117]

In February 1942, Shaikh Ḥamad died. He was succeeded by his son Shaikh Salmān ibn Ḥamad Āl-Khalīfah (1942–1961) whose reign is usually described as one of internal stability and harmony.

In 1950 (1369 A.H.) the Zubārah dispute between Qaṭar and Baḥrain was settled.[118]

From 1954 to 1956 Baḥrain witnessed a series of outbreaks of labour and student unrest culminating in demands for popular participation in government and the formation of trade unions. A committee of National Union (known earlier as the Higher Executive Committee) consisting of eight members forming the Executive Council was elected on 13 October 1954 in the Baḥārnah village of Sanābis. After two stormy years, i.e., from 13 October 1954 to November 1956, three members of the Executive Council were arrested and convicted of incitement to rebellion. On 28 December 1956 these three were exiled to St. Helena and with it the Committee ceased to exist.[119]

In 1961, on his father's death, Shaikh ᶜĪsa, the present ruler of Baḥrain took over.

In the years 1969–1970, the British informed all parties concerned with the Gulf of their decision to withdraw from the area including Baḥrain. Consequently, the old Persian claim to Baḥrain was renewed and in the wake of it the future status of Baḥrain was brought to the attention of the United Nations.

From 1 to 18 April 1970, a fact finding mission headed by the U.N. Secretary's personal emissary was involved in canvassing the public opinion in Baḥrain in regard to the future of the country. The mission found that the overwhelming majority of the people favoured an independent Arab State. on 14 August 1971, Baḥrain was as a result announced an independent sovereign State.[120]

On 20 June 1972, law No. 12, concerning the establishment of a Constitutional Assembly, was made public and in December 1973 the National Assembly was convened. The following two years witnessed a series of heated sessions.

On 26 August 1975, the National Assembly was officially dissolved. In the wake of it, constitutional rule, a long-standing public aspiration, has come to an end, giving way to a new era of relative stability and prosperity.

The Emergence of Shī^{c}ism in the Region

The emergence of *Shi^{c}ism* in al-Baḥrain is often, erroneously, associated with either the Carmathian movement or the Persian sway in the region. A closer look at the history of the old region seems to contradict such associations. In fact, the appearance of *Shī^{c}ism* in the area dates back to around 656–661 A.D., the years that mark ^{c}Ali ibn Abi Ṭālib's caliphate. First, let us examine the implications of the term *Shī^{c}ah* as described by *Lisān al-^{c}Arab* which defines it thus: "a group of people, united by one doctrine; or, the followers of a man, a leader, and the plural form is *Shiya^{c}*."

The *Shī^{c}ah* regard themselves as followers of ^{c}Ali ibn Abī Ṭālib, and the earliest of the *Shī^{c}ah* were those who sided with ^{c}Ali during the life of the Prophet and immediately after his death. *Al-Mu^{c}tazilah, al-Murji?ah,* and *al-Khawārij* are different schismatic groups.[121]

The first *Shī^{c}ah* to support ^{c}Ali's right to the caliphate were the bani Hāshim, bani ^{c}Abd al-Muṭṭalib, al-Zubayr ibn al-^{c}Awwām, plus some others from the *Muhājirīn* and *al-Anṣār.*[122]

Shī^{c}ism in the region dates back to the time of the Prophet when Abān ibn Sa^{c}īd al-^{c}Āṣ was appointed *wāli* (governor) of al-Baḥrain. He was a staunch follower of ^{c}Ali, and it was he who preached *Shī^{c}ism* in the region. He supported ^{c}Ali's right to the caliphate of Islam and enjoined the inhabitants to rally behind him.[123] ^{c}Abd al-Qais tribes, we are told, were among the first to support ^{c}Ali in the events of 36 A.H. (see supra, p. 8 top and also p. 13, note 15).

History also tells of other *wālis* of the region of al-Baḥrain who cultivated the same trend, established by Abān ibn Sa^{c}īd al-^{c}Āṣ. Among these were ^{c}Umar ibn Abī Salma, who was brought up by the Prophet, and Ma^{c}bad ibn al-^{c}Abbās, both supporters of ^{c}Ali.

Misinformed accounts of the *Shī^{c}ah* of al-Baḥrain were, more often, wittingly perpetuated by their rivals. These accounts found their way into a few European sources who ascribed a Persian origin to the Arabs of Baḥrain. Some such accounts went further to say that when the *Carmathians* fell into disfavour, their followers from the region repudiated the old doctrine and embraced the *Ja^{c}fari* sect of Islām, i.e., the followers of the twelve *Imāms* last of whom is al-Mahdi al-Muntaẓar.

History also informs about several uprisings against the *Carmathians* in the region. ^{c}Ali ibn Mismār of ^{c}Abd al-Qais, together with Abu Zakariyya al-Baḥrāni, were among those who resisted the *Carmathians* and had to face death at the hands of Abu Sa^{c}īd al-Jannābi, the *Carmathian* chief.[124] It was only later when the *Carmathian* power began to dwindle, that the inhabitants were able to deport the Jannābi clan to the island of ?Awāl, then a place for political exiles.

Shaikh Yūsuf al-Baḥrāni in his *al-Kashkūl*[125] states that *Shīᶜism* was so strong in the region during the caliphate of ᶜAli, that Muᶜāwiyah could not dismiss the *wālis* appointed by ᶜAli. The *Shīᶜah* inhabitants of the region resisted the tyranny of ᶜAbd al-Malik ibn Marwān, the Umawi ruler, who was responsible for the massacre of many of their nobilities.

To weaken *Shīᶜism* in the area and to force its adherents into relinquishing their faith, ᶜAbd al-Malik mustered a great force which landed in the village of Dirāz, the stronghold of the *Shīᶜah* of ?Awāl. After bitter fighting his army blocked the main sweet water spring there, known locally as ?Umm as-Sujūr, with rocks and stones.

However, the *Carmathian* rule over the region lasted from 286–366 A.H. (app.). Their excesses, such as the massacre of pilgrims in the Holy Mosque, the removal of the Black Stone, and the covering of the House, militated against the movement and hastened their eventual decline.[126]

Finally, these lines from H.A.R. Gibb are quoted in support of the view that peninsular Arabia, not Persia, witnessed the birth of *Shīᶜism:*[127]

> "It should be said at once that the still far too prevalent view that Persia was the original home of *Shīᶜism* has no foundation at all, and it is noteworthy that converts from Zorastrianism adopted in general the *Sunni* rather than the *Shīᶜite* faith."

NOTES:

1. The year 1031 A.H. marks the political dissociation of the island of ?Awāl from al-Aḥsā? and al-Qaṭīf,
   dominions. See al-Muslim, *Sāḥil adh-Dhahab al-Aswad,* p. 148.
2. 1783 witnessed the Āl-Khalīfah take-over of the islands, hence historians are often inclined to consider this year the start of the recent history of Baḥrain.
3. *EI,* vol. 1, p. 941.
4. Abu Ḥākimah in *History of Eastern Arabia,* p. 104, informs us that "both Kuwait and Zubārah benefited from the conveyance of men and mail through the Persian Gulf and through the desert route from Mascaṭ to Aleppo."
5. Medieval Arab geographers refer to the sea between Baḥrain and the eastern coast of Arabia as "the green sea" most probably owing to the shallowness of the water which makes it look green.
6. *Ṣubḥ al Aᶜsha,* vol. 1, p. 411.
7. *Sabā?ik,* p. 8.
8. Arab geographers tend to write it with an initial *ḍamma* as well as *fatḥa,* i.e., *?Uwāl* or *?Awāl.*
9. *Ṣifat al-Jazīrah al-ᶜArabiyyah,* p. 130.
10. *Muᶜjam Mastaᶜjam,* vol. 1, p. 131. Note that unlike al-Bakri's account above, in certain Hebrew sources, the ancient capital of Yaman, I am told, is given as Azāl and not ?Awāl.
11. A. Sprenger's translation of *Murūj, Meadows of Gold and Mines of Gems,* p. 263.
12. Al-Balādhuri, *Futūḥ al-Buldān,* under al-Baḥrain.
13. *Murūj adh-Dhahab,* vol. 2, p. 135.
14. Al-Muslim in *Sāḥil adh-Dhahab al-Aswad,* notes that "al-ᶜAmāliqa were the original

diggers of the natural water springs that appear on the mainland of the old region and the island of ?Awāl."

15. *Tārīkh al-Rusul wal-Mulūk,* vol. 1, pp. 213–215.
16. As regards the *nisbah* i.e. attributive adjective to ^{c}Abd al Qais there are three versions, viz. (a) ^{c}Abdiyy (عَبْدِيّ) attributed to the first part of the compound form عَبْد القيس (b) Qaisiyy (قَيْسِيّ) attributed to the second part of the same (c) ^{c}Ab qasiyy (عَبْقَيْسِيّ) attributed to both parts See N*ihayāt al-Arab fi Ma ^{c}rifat Ansāb al-^{c}Arab* (Baghdad 1958) p. 311.
17. *Mu^{c}jam Masta^{c}jam,* vol. 1, pp. 52–7.
18. Famous, in Islamic times, for its spears, said to be made of imported Indian bamboo.
19. Famous for its dates, hence the Arab proverb, *ka jālib at-tamr ?ilā Hajar,* i.e., to take dates to Hajar, the land of dates!
20. *Ṣubḥ al-A ^{c}sha,* vol. 1, p. 337.
21. *Mu ^{c}jam Qabā?il al-^{c}Arab al-Qadīmah w-al-Jadīdah,* vol. 2, p. 727.
22. Ḥajji Muḥammad ^{c}Ali al-Tājir, in his *^{c}Uqūd al-Āl fi Tārīkh Jazā?ir ?Awāl* (unpubllished), p. 203, states, 'what is locally known as the tomb of Ṣa ^{c}ṣa ^{c}ah Ibn Sohan al-^{c}Abdi, is not the case. The inscription on the tomb, he adds, reads "Shamsiddīn ibn Ṣa^{c}ṣa^{c}ah ibn Shamsiddīn ibn Ṣa^{c}ṣa^{c}ah ibn Ṣōḥān al-^{c}Abdi, a grandson of Ṣa ^{c}ṣa ^{c}ah ibn Ṣōḥān.'"
23. Al-Hamdāni, *Ṣifat,* pp. 204–6.
24. *Mu^{c}jam Ma sta^{c}jam,* vol. 1, p. 56.
25. Sprenger, *Meadows,* p. 267.
26. *Annals,* vol. 7, pp. 30–31.
27. *Nihāyat al-Arab fi Funūn al-Adab,* vol. 2, pp. 299–300.
28. Note that when referring to an inhabitant of Baḥrain, medieval Arab sources invariably use the relative adjective Baḥrāni, as in Mas ^{c}ūdi's account above. In confirmation of the same see *Tāj al-^{c}Arūs,* vol. X Book 16 (Kuwait, 1972), pp. 122–24, where the relative adjective Baḥrāni appears regularly in the names: Zakariyya ibn ^{c}Aṭiyyah al-Baḥrāni, ^{c}Ali ibn Muqarrab ibn Manṣūr al-Baḥrāni, Dāwūd ibn Ghassān ibn ^{c}Īsa al-Baḥrāni, Muwaffaq ad-Dīn al-Baḥrāni.
29. At-Tanbīh *w-al-Ishrāf,* pp. 339–40.
30. *Ṣifat.* p. 136.
31. Ḥamdalla al Mustawfī of Qazwīn in his *Nuzhat al Qulūb* informs us that Hajar was founded by Ardashīr Bābakān. See Guy Le Strange's translation of the former book p 135. Also, al Bakri in his *Mu ^{c}jam* vol 2 p. 827 gives this account of Hajar: "A famous city of al Baḥrain said to be a borrowing from Persian Hakar ... also said to be named after a lady called Hajar bint Miknaf of the ^{c}Amālīq"
32. Jawād ^{c}Ali, *Tārīkh al-^{c}Arab Qabl al-Islām,* vol. IV p. 211.
33. Al-Bakri, *Mu ^{c}jam,* vol. II p. 741.
34. *A ^{c}yān al-Shī ^{c}ah,* vol. 1, p. 517.
35. Ibid.
36. Muḥarraq literally meaning 'the place of burning ', possibly had a fire-temple of the Magians or perhaps later a crematory for the Hindus. Although Yāqūt in *Mu ^{c}jam,* vol. VII, p. 393, mentions al-Muḥarriq being an idol of Bakr ibn Wā?il and most of Rabī ^{c}ah in pre-Islamic times, and that in every quarter of Rabī ^{c}ah lands there existed a place of worship dedicated to his two sons, Balkh ibn al-Muḥarriq and Ghufaylah ^{c}Umar ibn al-Muḥarriq, yet the pre-Islamic idol should not be confused with the island of Muḥarraq which got the name relatively recently and no connection whatsoever between the two is suggested in any of the reliable Arab sources.

Also M.B. Sinān in *al-Baḥrain Durrat al-Khalīj al-ᶜArabi* (Baghdad, 1963) p. 31 mentions al-Muḥarraq being an idol of the ᶜijl (عِجْل) branch of ᶜAbd al-Qais in pre-Islamic times.

37. *Mu ᶜjam Mastaᶜjam,* vol. II, p. 567.
38. See al-Suyūṭi, *al-Muzhir,* vol. I, p. 222. Also, Ibn Manẓūr, *Lisān,* vol. II p. 301.
39. *Mu ᶜjam Ma staᶜjam,* vol. II, p. 567.
40. *Mu ᶜjam al-Buldān,* vol. 5, p. 120.
41. Supplement to *Mu ᶜjam al-Buldān,* vol. 9, p. 208, under *Arad.*
42. *ᶜUqūd,* p. 248.
43. The change of the glottal *?* to *ᶜ* in ?Arād realized *ᶜArād* is perhaps due to what Arab grammarians call *ᶜan ᶜanah,* a peculiarity ascribed to Tamīmi tribes. Other examples of this phonetic feature abound in the Baharnah dialect.
44. *Mu ᶜjam al-Buldān,* vol. 4, p. 9.
45. Ibid., vol. 7, p. 157.
46. *ᶜUqūd,* p. 186.
47. *Mu ᶜjam al-Buldān,* vol. 3, p. 357.
48. Ibid., vol. 7, p. 314.
49. *ᶜUqūd,* p. 260. Kāflān is also mentioned by Lorimer (map Gazetteer)
50. *Mu ᶜjam al-Buldān,* vol. 3, p. 117.
51. *Kitāb al-Buldān* (Leiden, 1885) p. 30.
52. *Mu ᶜjam al-Buldān,* vol. 5, p. 187.
53. Ibid., vol. 7, p. 208.
54. Ibid., vol. 2, p. 383.
55. *EI*, pp. 941–942.
56. H Wahba, *Jazīrat al-ᶜArab fi al-Qarn al-ᶜIshrīn,* p. 80.
57. Ibid., p. 85.
58. S.A.R. al-Quṭb, *Ansāb al-ᶜArab,* p. 222.
59. Ibid., p 159.
60. *Nihāyat al-Arab,* p. 276.
61. F. al-Zayyāni, *Mujtama ᶜ al-Baḥrain,* p. 125.
62. S.A. R. al-Quṭb, op. cit., p. 162.
63. Wahba, op. cit., p. 113, adds bani Yās to the above.
64. Lorimer, *Gazetteer,* under Baḥrain, p. 883.
65. Wahba, op. cit., p. 109.
66. Ibid., pp. 109–111.
67. See Maps II and III (Appendices).
68. *ᶜUqūd,* p. 234. Perhaps it is worth mentioning here that ᶜĀli is an old village of ?Awāl island, where a group of the largest sepulchral tumuli, said to be over 80 feet high, are found.
69. In an interview with Mulla ᶜAṭiyya, a religious *Shī ᶜi* figure of the same village, I was told that the Jamārah as they are locally known are descendants of Jamarāt, an extinct Arab tribe whose homelands were in the Yemen.
70. *Mu ᶜjam Qabā?il al-ᶜArab,* vol. 1, p. 203.
71. Al-Mubarrad, *al-Kāmil,* vol. 2, p. 596.
72. *Mu ᶜjam al-Buldān,* vol. V p. 34.
73. *Ṣifat,* p. 136.
74. Ibn Manẓūr, *Lisān,* vol. IV, p. 345.
75. *I.O.R.,* R/15/1/192. Note that Shaikh Aḥmad ibn Muḥammad Āl-Mājid al-Bilādi, a member of Āl-Mājid family, was the leader of the Baḥārnah village of Bilād al Qadīm around 1783

76. I am told that the Āl Bu Kawwārah are Huwalah Arabs.

77 *Gazetteer*, p 208

78 He fails to mention Āl Madan of Jid Ḥafṣ, Āl-Rajab of Manāmah, and Āl-Nashrah of Sanābis, who were all involved in religious or political leadership of the Baḥārnah since late eighteenth century.

79. In Arabic Manāmah means 'the place of sleeping'. E. Mackay, in his report on *'Baḥrain and Hemamieh'*, accounting for the same, writes "Perhaps so called owing to its proximity to the largest field of Tumuli. It is a common term for a grave or tomb."

80. J.G. Lorimer, *Gazetteer of the Persian Gulf* (1915), p. 212, gives the total area of the island as 208 square miles. 18 square miles, he adds, are covered by date plantations.

81. In vol. XXIV of *Bombay Selections*, p. 104, the width of the main island is stated "from nine to six miles".

82. The island of Sitrah embraces the following villages: al-Qarya, Mhazza, Sfāla, Markubān, Wādyān, al-Khārjiyya, Ma^{c}āmir, al-^{c}Ikur, al-Fārsiyya, al-Ḥālāt.

83. S.M. Zwemer in *Arabia, the Cradle of Islam* (1900) mentions Muḥarraq "the place of burning" so named, he quotes local Arabs, because the Hindu traders used it for cremating their dead. E. Mackay is of the same opinion, see *"Baḥrain and Hemamieh"*, p.1.A.Rayḥāni in *Around the Coasts of Arabia*, p. 266, remarks in a footnote, "Muḥarraq is where the ancient Persians- the Magians-who occupied the island, burned their dead." Rayḥāni is perhaps mistaken, Hindus not Magians burn their dead.

84. *JRGS*, Appendix (1), vol. LXXI (1928), p. 463. Also in Gibb's translation of *Ibn Baṭṭūṭa's Travels*, we are given this note: "There is a story that a camel once fell into a spring at al-Ḥasa and was never seen again until it came up in the sea near Baḥrayn." *Travels in Asia and Africa* (1325–1354), p. 353.

85. Op. cit., p. 99.

86. F.O. Handbook, *The Persian Gulf* (London, 1920), p. 38. The significance of Baḥrain as a mart, from the earliest times, is attested by this verse from Yāqūt's *Mu^{c}jam*, vol. 1, p. 365, in which Tamīm ibn ʔUbayy ibn Muqbil says:

عَمِدَالحُداةُ بِهالِعارِضِ قَريَةٍ فَكَأَنَّهاسُفُنٌ بِسَيفِ أُوالِ

87. Col. D. Wilson, *JRGS*, vol. III (1833), p. 283. Further account of the same is given in *JRSA* (15 Mar. 1901), it runs: "At the season of fisheries, some 4,500 boats of every size and rig may be seen all busily employed. They carry from five to fourteen men each, and the total number of hands engaged is said to be 30,000 . . . the assorted pearls are dispatched to the Indian market, whence a great many go back again to Arabia and Persia . . . the Gulf banks give no indication of a failing supply."

88. C. Belgrave, *Personal Column*, pp. 79–83.

89. These figures are obtained from recent official publications.

90. S.N. Kramer, *"Dilmun: the Land of the Living," BASOR, No. 96*, Dec. 1944, pp. 18–28. See also De Lacy Oleary: Arabia before Muḥammad (London-1927) pp. 47–50.

91. G. Bibby, *Looking for Dilmun*, pp. 45–98.

92. For a full account see G. Rawlinson, *History of Phoenicia* (1889), p. 53. Also P. Ḥitti, *Lebanon in History*, pp. 67–73.

93. See Memorandum by L. Lockhart, *"The History of the Baḥrain Islands"*, *I.O.R.* 15/2/484 (E. 113/113/91), 2.3. 1945.

94. Al-Balādhuri, *Futūḥ al-Buldān*; or P. Ḥitti's translation, *The Origins of the Islamic State*, ch. XVII.

95. *Tārīkh aṭ-Ṭabari,* vol. III, pp. 301–313.
96. See Shaikh Yūsuf al-Baḥrāni's *Anīs al-Khāṭir wa Jalīs al–musāfir,* also known as *al-Kashkūl* (Bombay, 1291 A.H.).
97. A. Rayḥāni, *Around the Coasts of Arabia,* pp. 286–7.
98. Ḥitti observes "the rebellion of the Zanj (Ethiopian) slaves was mounted by negroes imported from East Africa and employed in the saltpetre mines on the lower Euphrates. The leader (Ṣāḥib al-Zanj) was one ^{c}Ali ibn-Muḥammad . . . probably of Arab origin." *History of the Arabs,* p. 467.
99. Aṭ-Ṭabari, *Tārīkh,* vol. 10, pp. 23–7.
100. Suhail Zakkār, *Tārīkh Akhbār al-Qarāmiṭah,* p. 95.
101. *Tārīkh al-Mustabṣir,* ed. Oscar Löfgren (Leiden 1951), pp. 300–1.
102. *Historical Memorandum on Baḥrain* (1934), *I.O.R.* (L/P+S/18) B. 436.
103. C. Belgrave, *"The Portuguese in the Baḥrain Islands", JRCAS,* vol. XXII, 1935.
104. *Gazetteer,* p. 79.
105. C. Belgrave, *Personal Column,* p. 202, gives this account of Huwala Arabs: "Holis are descended from Arabs who migrated from the Arab coast to Persia many centuries ago and later returned to the Arab side of the Gulf. They are *Sunnis* of the *Shāfi ^{c}i* sect whereas the Āl-Khalīfah family and the tribal Arabs belong to the *Māliki* sect."
106. *The History of Baḥrain Islands,* F.O. Research Dept, *I.O.R.* 15/2/484.
107. *Travels Through Arabia,* vol. II, p. 152 (R. Heron's English translation).
108. The exact year of the ^{c}Utbi occupation is disputed. Lorimer, *Gazetteer,* p. 839, on the same, writes: "The recent history of Baḥrain may be said to date from 1783, in which year, the Persians, then in possession, were expelled from the islands." J.B. Kelly, accounting for the same in *"The Persian Claim to Baḥrain", International Affairs,* vol. XXXIII, no. 1, Jan. 1957, observes, "Late in 1782 the Āl-Khalīfah had raided Baḥrain, plundered Manāmah, its principal town, and retired with a great loot."
109. Abu Hākimah, quoting al-Qinā ^{c}i in *Ṣafaḥāt min Tārīkh al-Kuwait,* mentions Qays island, ^{c}Abadān, etc., among places they settled briefly prior to moving to Kuwait. *History of Eastern Arabia,* pp. 50–1.
110. In his preface to *at-Tuḥfah an-Nabhāniyyah,* he says, "After the fall of Baṣrah around 1333 A.H. to the British, he was arrested to be freed in 1334 A.H. on Shaikh ^{c}Īsa's intervention, on his behalf, with the British authorities." He adds, "the original title of my book was *al-Nubdhah al-Laṭīfah fi l-Ḥukkām min Āl-Khalīfah."* In answer to a British demand for an English translation of the book, the ex-chief of Baḥrain Police, Mr. Ḥasan Siddīq produced a translation of the same.
111. Lorimer, *Gazetteer,* vol. I, p. 1002.
112. H. Wahba, *Jazīrat al- ^{c}Arab fil-Qarn al- ^{c}Ishrīn,* pp. 117–8. For a fuller account of the Baḥārnah conditions around 1782–3, see Y. al-Falaki's *Qaḍiyyat al-Baḥrain,* pp. 11–5.
113. Confidential report from C.K. Daly to A.P. Trevor-Political Resident-entitted: *Some Examples of Oppression of Baḥārnah Subjects by the Ruling Family in Baḥrain, I.O.R.* 15/1/327/No. 1/c 3.1.1922.

114. Confidential letter from S. G. Knox to His Highness Shaikh Sir ^{c}Abdul ^{c}Azīz ben ^{c}Abdul Raḥmān al-Faiṣal As-Sa^{c}ūd-Sulṭān of Najd and Dependencies. *F.O.* 371–No. 174, 15.6. 1923.
115. Ibid.
116. In a letter to the Foreign Secretary to the Government of India, T.C. Fowle, Political Resident, wrote in March 1935:" There has never been any attempt at a census of the Baḥrain population, but it is believed to be some 120,000 or more. Of this the Ālkhalīfah number perhaps two hundred . . . According to a rough estimate Arab *Sunnis* constitute 20% of the total population and foreigners 20%, the Baḥārnah 60%. Whatever amount of guesswork there may be in this computation it is agreed that the Baḥārnah number well over half of the total inhabitants." *F.O.* 371. No. C/43–18.3. 1935.
117. Letter from H. Weightman. P.A. to T.C. Fowls Political Resident. *I.O.R.* 15/2/176. No. C/666 1. b/5 27.10. 1938.
118. C. Belgrave, in his annual report writes, "An important event in the history of Baḥrain was the settlement of the long standing quarrel between Baḥrain and Qaṭar which for the last 14 years has caused bitter feelings between the ruling houses of Baḥrain and Qaṭar as well as between the people of these two neighbouring States. The situation of Zubārah on the Qaṭar coast opposite Baḥrain, the ancestral home of the Khalīfah family from the time when they migrated from Kuwait until they conquered Baḥrain, has now reverted to the status quo which existed before the quarrel." *Government of Baḥrain–Annual Report Rabī ^{c} al-Awwal 1369 A.H. (Jan. 1950).*
119. E.A. Nakhleh, *Baḥrain* (1976).
120. A. Zayyāni, *Baḥrain 1783–1973* (Beirut, 1973), pp. 176–177.
121. *A ^{c}yān ash-Shī ^{c}a h,* vol. 1, p. 14.
122. Ibid.
123. Ibid.
124. Al-Mas ^{c}ūdi, *at-Tanbīh w-al-Ishrāf,* pp. 339–340.
125. Otherwise known as *Anīs al-Khāṭir wa Jalīs al-Musāfir* (Bombay, 1291 A.H.).
126. H.F. Amedroz and D.S. Margoliouth's translation of Ibn Maskawaih's *The Experiences of the Nations,* vol. 1, p. 226.
127. *Islām,* p. 83.

Part II
The phonology of the Baḥārnah dialect

In this part of the present study we intend to investigate the phonological features of the Baḥārnah dialect, abbreviated as B. The investigation will involve both divisions, i.e., rural and urban B. It should be noted however that among the latter division there are members who have established themselves in Manāmah, the capital, and those who are still dwelling in their village of origin.

Before we present any systematic analysis of the phonology of B, here is a summary of the characteristic phonological features of B.

The *Hamza*

The occurrence of a lax, initial and medial *hamza,* but not of a final *hamza,* is a feature of B. The conditions affecting such an occurrence are discussed under the appropriate section.

velar *ḷ* : an allophonic variant of otherwise alveolar *l* is found in certain emphatic environments in B. However, a velar *ḷ* such as occurs in the vicinity of certain gutturals in the ᶜAnazi dialect, abbreviated as A, is not noted for B.

t > *ṭ*: As in many dialects certain speakers tend to realize non-emphatic *t* as *ṭ* in the neighbourhood of the guttural ᶜ in cardinal numbers from thirteen to nineteen.

s > *ṣ*: In the neighbourhood of the guttural *x* and the emphatic *ṭ* , non-emphatic *s* of certain Arabic forms is realized *ṣ*, as in *ʔaṣmax* (deaf).

Partial preservation of Arabic inter-dental fricatives

Arabic *ṯ, ḏ,* and *ẓ* are only partially preserved in B. Their occurrence is restricted to certain classical and koine forms such as names of Arabic months, Koranic (Qurʔanic) citations, etc. However, *ṯ, ḏ,* and *ẓ* have a higher frequency of occurrence in educated speech.

ṯ > *f*: Arabic *ṯ* has the free variant *f* in B.

Palatalization of *j*: In rural forms of B *j* , with some speakers, may be realized *y* in the vicinity of front and back, short and long vowels.

j > *g*: In certain areas of rural B, *j* is realized *g* as in: *gafiir* (basket).

Partial preservation of *q*: Arabic *q* remains stable in certain classical and koine forms circulating in B.

Realization of *q* as *k*: In rural forms of B *q*, with some speakers, is realized as *k*.

-*š* as a feminine marker: In B, -*š* corresponding to Arabic 2 f.s. suffix -*k*, has the grammatical function of a feminine marker.

Affricate *č*: Affrication of *k* to *č* occurs regularly in B, but not of *g* to *j*.

Omission of the sound -*h* in urban B

-*h* of Arabic 3 m.s. pronominal suffix, is retained only in rural B, e.g., *ᶜindeh* (he has) realized *ᶜinde* in urban B.

Word-final *imāla*

A peculiarity of this dialect is strong word-final *imāla*, viz. the realization of Arabic feminine suffixes -*a* and -*aa* as -*e*.

Word-final stressed -*é*

A phonetic feature found in B is the occurrence of stressed -*é* in sentence-final positions used to indicate questions, as in: *barazt-i?* (are you ready?).

The Consonants

The consonant system of the Baḥārnah dialect appears below.

	Plosive		Fricative		Affricate		Liquid	Nasal
Bilabial		*b*						*m*
Labio-dental			*f*	*w*				
Dental			*ṯ*	*ḏ*				
			s	*z*				
Denti-alveolar	*t*	*d*						
Alveolar			*š*		*č*	*j*	*r*	*n*
							l	
Emphatics	*ṭ*	*ḍ*	*ṣ*					
Palatal				*y*				
Velar	*k*	*g*	*x*	*ġ*				
Uvular	*q*							
Pharyngeal			*ḥ*	*ᶜ*				
Glottal	*?*		*h*					

What follows is a description of the above consonant sound-units.

The Plosives: the *hamza* or the glottal stop

A lax *hamza*, where a measure of glottal constriction accompanies the initial vowel sounds, appears when *hamza* occurs out of liaison. Thus compare the following pronominal forms:

1	m.s.	*?ane*	1	f.s.	*?ani*
2	m.s.	*?inte*	2	f.s.	*?intiin*

The above also applies to elative forms when realized out of liaison:

?a^{c}raf	(better informed)	*?aḥsan*	(better)
?aṣdag	(more truthful)	*?ašja^{c}*	(more courageous)

Medial glottal stop, as these examples show, is often audible where it is preceded by the short vowels *a* or *i:*

?ista?jar	(he hired), inf. 16
i?aṯṯir	(it affects), inf. 4

and in the passive form: *barra?ooh* (he was acquitted). The medial glottal stop of the following koine forms is normally retained:

ra?iis	(boss, head)	*(i) m?addab*	(well-behaved)
?a?imme	(imāms), inf. 1	*la?iim*	(ungrateful)
^{c}abd il-?amiir	(^{c}Abdul-Amīr-a proper name), inf. 16		
has-su?aal	(this question), inf. 1		
fi l-?idaa^{c}a	(on Baḥrain Radio), inf. 16		

Final glottal stop can normally be heard in educated speech only. It should be noted, however, that the occurrence of the glottal stop in B ought to be examined in view of its degree of audibility rather than its total non-existence. In these examples from B, Arabic *hamza* is systematically realized ^{c}, a feature known as *^{c}an^{c}anah:*

verb	*da^{c}am* < *da?am*	(he collided)				
adverbials	*^{c}ajal* < *?ajal*	(so, then)	*^{c}afar*	<	*?aṯar*	(as if, perhaps)
nominals	*^{c}aḍaafiir* < *?aẓaafir*	(nails)	*^{c}uum*	<	*?uum*	(sardines)

Elision of the glottal stop[1]

The main occasions when the glottal stop is elided may be summarized as follows: Initial glottal stop is normally elided in connected speech:

ifaṣṣil issiim	(he knits the wire), inf. 2

It is also elided in liaison with particles such as *b-*, *ma*, and *w-* and the definite article:

b-atsabbaḥ	(I shall bathe)	*ma-ariid*	(I don't want)
w-axad	(and he took)	*l-aḥmar*	(the red).

As a result of the elision of medial glottal stop, a compensatory lengthening of the vowel takes place:

faal	(fortune-telling)	*raas*	(head)

The *hamza* of lit. Ar. nominal patterns with the element *-aa?i* is regularly realized *-y:*

masaayil	(issues, affairs)	*naxaayil*	(date gardens)
daayib	(worn out)	*naayib*	(deputy)

The preconsonantal plosive *?* of the following Arabic forms is regularly realized *w*:

mawluuf	(familiar)	*tawkiid*	(assurance)

Cf. also: *?alaf* > *walaf* (got used to) *?akkad* > *wakkad* (he assured).

The plosive *b* [2]

b is normally realized as voiced bilabial plosive. In certain loan-words *b* arises from *p*. A feature found in A only is the occurrence of an emphatic *ḅ* in the contiguity of a following emphatic syllable. Thus:

A		B
ḅúgar	(cows)	*bágar*
ḅúṣal	(onion)	*báṣal*

The plosive *t*

t is normally realized as voiceless dentialveolar plosive.
The ultimate *t* of the following borrowing from Persian is often retained in liaision with an ensuing vowel:

hast irjaal	(there are men)	*hast aḥad?*	(anybody there?)

Out of liaison, the above *t* is often dropped:

has naas	(there are people)	*has waaḥid*	(there is someone)

The emphatic *ṭ*

Non-emphatic *t* is often realized emphatic in the vicinity of the guttural *c* in cardinal numbers from thirteen to nineteen:

ṯalaṭṭa ᶜ*aš*	(thirteen)	*sabaaṭa* ᶜ*aš*	(seventeen)

The plosive *d*

d in B is voiced denti-alveolar plosive. *d* usually replaces Arabic inter-dental *ḏ:*

deel < *ḏeel*		(tail)
ladiid < *laḏiiḏ*		(delicious)

With some speakers *d* is realized *ḍ* in emphatic environments:

ṣaḍur	(chest)	*ṣaḍag*	(he told the truth)

Devoicing of *d* to *t* [3]

In the rural speech of Dirāz village *d* is occasionally devoiced to *t* preceding the gutturals *x*, ᶜ, and *h:*

ʔaxathum < *ʔaxadhum* (he took them), inf. 26
maaᶜithe < *maaᶜidhe* (she doesn't have), inf. 26

The Emphatic *ḍ*

The voiced, emphatic *ḍ* usually replaces the Arabic inter-dental *ẓ*. Cf:

ḍaalim	(unjust)	*ġaliiḍ*	(thick)
naḍḍaara	(spectacles)		

In these examples emphatic *ḍ* replaces the Arabic interdental *d̲*:

maa aḍkur	(I don't remember)	*ḍakar*	(male)

The Plosive *k* [4]

The *k* of the 2 f.s. suffix is regularly realized *-š* in B;

ʔabuuš	(your father)	*šaᶜriš*	(your hair)

The above applies both to rural and urban forms of B.

Affrication of *k* to *č* [5]

(1) The affricate *č* of the ᶜAnazi-type dialects has the grammatical function of the 2 f.s. pronominal suffix, e.g. *ktaabič* (your book). Except for Sitrah forms, the *-k* of the 2 m.s. pronominal suffix remains stable in A and most of B. Cf:

	A		Rest of B	Sitrah B
2 m.s.	*fiik*	(with you)	*fiik*	*fiič*
	ktaabik	(your book)	*ktaabuk*	*ktaabeč*

(2) Both in A and B affricate *č* is found in the vicinity of short and long front vowels in non-emphatic environments. Cf:

A		B	A		B
čabid	(liver)	*čibd*	*čilme*	(word)	*čilme*
fačč	(he opened)	*fačč*	*smiče*	(fish)	*samače*
ničab	(he poured)	*načab*	*čidi*	(like this)	*čidi*
čaan	(if)	*čaan*	*čiis*	(bag)	*čiis*
baačir	(tomorrow)	*baačir*	*diič*	(cock)	*diič*
čeele	(scoop)	*čeele*	*čeef*	(how)	*čeef*

(3) Both in A and B affricate *č* is found in the neighbourhood of back vowel *uu*, but usually in forms derived from a root in which *č* occurs:

(i) fčuuč	(openings)	*(i) ᶜluuč*	(chewing gum)
čuuᶜ	(elbow)	*mančuus*	(sprats)

But contrast:

kuuma	(heap)	*kuub*	(cup)

k remains stable:
(1) in proper names, in penultimate as well as ultimate positions:

kamaal	(Kamal)	*(i)mbaarak*	(Mubārak)	*kariim*	(Karīm)

(2) in the nominal structure: C_1 C_2 aaC_3, where *k* is the initial consonant and the vowel is back αα.

(i) kbaar (big) *(i)knaar* (Indian kanard fruit) *(i)kṯaar* (many)

But contrast: *(i)člaab* (dogs).
(3) in these nominal forms that have the classical feminine termination *-ka:*

malaayka	(angels)	*baraka/brika*	(blessing)
šaraaka	(partnership)		

But note these pl. forms from B:

sammaače	(fisher folk)	*ḥayaayče*	(sail makers)

(1), (2), and (3) above apply to both A and B.
(4) in the ultimate syllabic structure -CaaC, when it is the closing consonant in these di-syllabic forms, both in A and B.

(?alla) hadaak	(may God guide your steps)	*de(e)laak*	(those)
ha(a)daak	(that)	*minnaak*	(there)

All the above forms, however, appear with an affricate *č* in Sitrah speech.
Affricate *-č* in the following ᶜAnazi demonstrative has the grammatical function of a feminine marker. Cf:

	A		B
fem	*ḏiič*	(that)	*diik*

(5) in the plural suffix *-kum* as in:

ᶜindikum, ᶜindkum (do you have?) *likum* (for you)

The above applies to A, to Manāmah B, and to a majority of the villages with the exclusion of Sitrah forms where the *k* is affricated, as in:

ᶜindčem (with you) *leečem* (for you)

(6) in loan-words both in A and B:

kaččе[6]	(learner's driving licence)	*balak*	(plug)
keemara	(camera)		

(7) in dialect forms corresponding to the Arabic verb type FaMuLa as in:

A		B
kubar	(he has grown)	*kabar/(i)kbur*
kufar	(he denied the existence of God)	*kafar*

(8) in the vicinity of back vowels *o* and *oo* in these items:

kora (ball) *koos* (south-easterly wind)

(9) in the neighbourhood of the emphatics *ṣ* and *ḏ̣* in these examples in A and B:

maṣkuuk	(closed)	*ṣakk*	(he closed)
ḏikart, ḏ̣akart	(I remembered)	*(i)ḏ̣kaara*	(males)

But note: *ṣičim* (pellet) *ṣčaač* < Arabic *ṣikaak* (obstacle, impediment)

(10) in certain Arabic forms that end in *-kuur* both in A and B;

maḏkuur	(it is mentioned)	*maḥkuur*	(stuffy)
maškuur	(thank you)	*maskuur*	(blocked)

The occurrence of *č* in Loan-Words

č of these borrowings is not an affricated form of Arabic consonant *k:*

hinč	(inch) inf. 6 (from English)
kačče	(a learner's driving licence)

In certain forms affrication of *k* occurs mainly in A. Cf;

A		B
ḏiič	(that)	*diik*
mačaan	(place)	*makaan*
mačtuub	(letter)	*maktuub*
čoočab	(female proper name)	*kawkab*
čalaam	(talk)	*kalaam*

Affrication of *k* in these forms from B occurs only in Sitrah speech. Cf:

Sitrah		Manāmah and the villages
čill	(every)	*kill*
leečem	(for you)	*leekum*
de(e) laač	(those)	*deelaak*

The plosive *q*

q is a voiceless, uvular plosive in B; it is preserved in certain classical forms:

d̲i l-qi ᶜde	(the eleventh month of the Muslim year)
qaḍa w-qadar	(fate and divine decree)
leelat il-qadr	(the night in which, according to Sura 97, the Qur?ān was revealed; celebrated on the night between 26th and 27th Ramaḍān)

q is also often preserved in these koine forms:

qarnaabiiṭ	(cauliflowers), inf. 6
burtuqaal	(oranges), inf. 1
?axlaaq	(moral behaviour), inf. 1

And also in this reference to a *Shīᶜi* religious occasion:

wafaat il-qaasim	(the day that marks the death of al-Qāsim, son of al-Ḥasan ibn ᶜAli ibn Abi Ṭālib)

And in these foreign names:

?iš-šarika l-afriqiyye	(The African Co.), inf. 1
qubruṣ	(Cyprus)

Initial *q* of the following forms remains stable in Dirāzi female speech:

qatal il-walad	(he killed the child), inf. 26
qafalat i ᶜyuune	(his eyes closed), inf. 26

The fronting of *q*

Voiceless *q* is realized voiced velar *g* in all positions. Cf:

init.	*geeṭaan*	(ornamental cord, attached to female trouser)		
	guble	(facing the *Ka ᶜba* during prayer)		
med.	*ragiig*	(thin)	*mugbara*	(graveyard)
fin.	*buxnug*	(head-veil for young girls)	*zarnuug*	(a narrow street)

Initial *g* followed by *ú* in stressed open syllables is found in A only. Cf:

	A		B
Cú-CaC			
	gúmar	(moon)	*gámar*
	gúfaṣ	(cage)	*gáfaṣ*

Realization of *q* as *k*

In rural forms of B, *q* is, with some speakers, realised as *k*. This phonetic process seems to be unconditioned and to occurr in all positions. Cf:

init.	*ka ᶜadt*	(I sat), inf. 5	*kuum*	(get up), inf. 4
	kafiif	(baskets) inf. 22		
med.	*bakil*	(clover), inf. 22	*(i) tkaffuḍ*	(it closes down) inf. 4
	?istakall	(it dwindled), inf. 4		
fin.	*l-axlaak*	(moral behaviour), inf. 6	*(i) nšikk*	(we cut), inf. 24
	ḥakk	(for), inf. 12		

In urban forms of B this realization is almost non-existent, except for the following two examples:

(a) Classical Ar. *q* in the adverbial particle *laqad* (already) is invariably realized *k*. Thus:

naade(e)te, lakid raaḥ (I called upon him but he had already left)

(b) The Cl. Ar. form *waqt* is regularly realized *wakt* (time), but note the plural form, *?awgaat* (times).

Final *g* of these loan-words is regularly rendered *k* . Cf:

balak	[*pləg*]	(plug) from English, inf. 11
tak	[*təg*]	(tug) from English, inf. 11

The occurrence of *q* as *ġ* in A[7]

A phonetic feature of A is the tendency of some speakers to realize *q* as *ġ* in contiguity with both front and back vowels. Cf:[8]

A		B
?istiġlaal	(independence)	*?istiqlaal*
?alġa	(he delivered (a talk))	*?alqa*
ġaraar	(decision)	*qaraar*
ġanaabil	(bombs)	*qanaabil*
ġora	(villages)	*qura*
raġum	(number)	*raqum*
barġ	(lightning)	*barq/barg*

Realization of final *g* as *ġ* does not occur in these forms from A:

šarg	(east)	*suug*	(market)

Arabic consonant *ġ* of these forms remains stable in B, whereas in A it is oftern realized as *q* in contiguity with front vowels, cf:

A		B
?aqaani	(songs)	*?aġaani*
qeer	(other than)	*ġeer*
qaamij	(dark)	*ġaamug*
?alqaw	(they cancelled)	*?alġaw/oo*
qarse	(bottle)	*ġarše*

The Affrication of *g* to *j* in B

It has been noted that *k* and *g* are affricated to *č* and *j* in a majority of Arab peninsular and related dialects.[9]

However, in ᶜUmāni, Qaṭīfi, Ḥasāwi and Baḥrāni Arabic regular affrication of *k* to *č* , but not of *g* to *j*, is noted. Cf. these examples from A and B:

A		B
jalᶜa	(fort)	*galᶜa*
jiime	(price)	*giime*
rijiij	(thin)	*ragiig*

Some scattered cases of $g > j$ can be found among speakers from Rās Rummān or Shahrakkān areas of B.
Examples of $g > j$ in B are:
(a) The proper name *qaasim* (Qāsim) is often realized *jaasim.*
(b) Occasionally, the ^{c}Anazi form *jatt* (lucerne) is heard in rural forms of B, as against the commoner form *gatt.*

The occurrence of *g* in A
$g < q$ remains stable in the vicinity of short and long vowels *a, aa* in these forms:

gabul	(before)	*gaam*	(he stood)
galam	(pen)	*gaal*	(he said)
ga^{c}ad	(he sat)	*gaad*	(he led)

g also remains stable before and after *uu* in the pattern CCuuC, as in:

yguum	(he stands)	*(i) tguum*	(you stand)
yguul	(he says)	*(i)nguud*	(we lead)
ysuug	(he drives)	*yruug*	(he likes)

g also remains stable when it occurs as an ultimate geminated sound in a closed syllable of the structure CaCC:

ṭagg	(he beat)	*dagg*	(he knocked)
ḥagg	(right)	*šagg*	(he tore)

The occurrence of $g < q$ as *j* in A
(a) *g* is realized *j* in the neighbourhood of short and long vowels *a* and *i* in all positions. Cf:

jal^{c}a	(fort)	*waajif*	(standing)	*ġaamij*	(dark)
jisme	(portion, share)	*šarji*	(eastern)	*baayij*	(thief)
jiriib	(near)	*yijiis*	(he measures)	*ṣidiij*	(friend)
jibiile	(tribe)	*rijiij*	(thin)	*^{c}atiij*	(old)

(b) In non-emphatic environments, initial *g* of the penultimate open syllable Caa- is rendered *j* in these nominal forms:

jaasim	(Jasim)
jaable	(tomorrow night)

In emphatic environments, initial *g* of nominal forms remains stable:

giṭ^{c}a	(piece)	*gaṣir*	(palace)	*guuṭi*	(tin box)
giḍḍ	(hole)	*gaaṣir*	(incomplete)	*giṭne*	(cotton)
geeḍ	(prime of summer heat)			*gaṣṣaab*	(butcher)
gooṭra	(bulk, wholesale)				

(c) *g* of certain FaML and FiML noun types is realized *j* when it is the closing consonant of a form in which the penultimate sound is also a consonant:

ḥalj	(throat)	^{c}*irj*	(vein)

j > *g* in B

Some speakers viz. from Shahrakkān, ^{c}Āli and Karrāna areas of B tend to realize non-final *j* as *g* in the vicinity of short front vowels:

rural B		urban B
gafiir	(basket), inf. 7	*jafiir*
gadiide	(new), inf. 12	*jadiide*
lignuub	(the south), inf. 8	*l-ijnuub*

Realization of *j* as *y*

The realization of *j* as *y* is found in a majority of South and E. Arabian dialects today. In Baḥrain, this phonetic feature is found in A, and to a lesser degree only in rural forms of B. Among the Manāmah community of B, the above feature is occasionally heard in Rās Rummāni speech only, to the exclusion of the rest of Manāmah speakers of B.

In A, the occurrence of *j* as *y* is categorical in the sense that it can occur in the vicinity of front and back vowels in all positions. Cf:

maynuun	(crazy)	*yilde*	(a piece of leather)
(i) nyuum	(stars)	^{c}*ayam*	(Persians)

In rural B, the occurrence of *j* as *y* is also categorical; it is found in contiguity with front as well as back vowels. Cf:

init.	*yaarim* < *fašt il-jaarim*	(shoal, reef), inf. 24
	yariid < *jariid*	(date fronds), inf. 3
med.	*ḥayar* < *ḥajar*	(stones), inf. 23
	i^{c}*aalyuun* < *i*^{c}*aaljuun*	(to cure, to treat), inf. 26
fin.	*miḥmal il-ḥayy* < *ḥajj*	(pilgrims' ship), inf. 4

In these illustrations, *j* is normally realized *y* in A, whereas in B it remains stable in Manāmah speech, excluding Rās Rummāni forms of B where *j* is rendered *y*. CF:[10]

A		Manāmah B
yiime	(bait)	*jiime*
maa tyuuz	(stop it!)	*maatjuuz*
yoo^{c}*aan*	(hungry)	*joo*^{c}*aan*
yufra	(hole)	*jufra*

In these two illustrations from rural B, *j* is palatalized only when out of liaison with *il-*; whereas in the second example it remains stable in liaison with *li-*. Cf:

j > *y*	*haade l-yazzaaf*	(this bulk-buyer of fish also retailer), inf. 2
j > *g*	*mihnati fi ijzaafe*	(my job is bulk-buying of fish), inf. 23

The velarized *ḷ*

A velar *ḷ*, an allophonic variant of otherwise alveolar *l*, is found in the contiguity of the emphatics *ṣ, ḍ,* and *ṭ* in B. The illustrations below show both types of *l* in different phonemic environments:

non-emphatic: environment	*tall*	(he pulled)	*salle*	(basket)	*yiddalla*^{c}	(enjoys fondling)
emphatic : environment	*ṭaḷḷ*	(he gazed)	*ṣaḷḷe*	(he prayed)	*yiḍḍaḷḷam*	(he complains)

Further examples of the same are:

raṭiḷ	(a pound (weight)	*ṣiḷm*	(nut)	*ḍiḷ*^{c}	(rib)
ṭiḷbe	(a wish)	*ṣiḷh*	(friendship)	*ḍiḷm*	(injustice)

In A, in addition to *ṣ, ḍ, ṭ,* the *l* is also velarized in the neighbourhood of emphatic *ḅ*, a feature not found in B. Cf:

A		B
gaḅuḷ	(before)	*gabil*
xaḅaḷ	(stupid)	*(i)mxabbaḷ*

A regular feature of A is the appearance of a velar *ḷ* and backing of front vowels in the contiguity of *x*, *ġ*, and *g* < *q*, a feature normally not found in B. Cf:

A		B
xαḷααḷ	(unripe, green dates)	*xalaal*
buxuḷ	(meanness)	*(i) bxil*
šuġuḷ	(work)	*(i) šġil*
gαḷαm	(pen)	*galam*
gαḷααḷi	(Galāli; place name)	*galaali*

An unconditioned feature is the occasional assimilation of *l* in these forms from B. Cf:

git	for	*gilt*	(I said)
wad	for	*wald*	(son of)
?a-ḥiin	for	*?al-ḥiin*	(now)

The Liquid *r*

r in B occurs as an alveolar liquid consonant in all positions. In rural B, a partially realized *r̥* is found in the vicinity of long stressed vowels:

taġyiir̥	(change), inf. 20
la l-fóor̥	(to the bull), inf. 22

Initial *r* followed by a voiced consonant, a peculiarity found in the nominal structure C–CuC–te(h) in A, does not occur in B. Cf:

A		B
r-ġub-te	(his wish)	*raġ-bate*
r-gub-te	(his neck)	*ragabate*

The Fricatives: the guttural *ġ*

ġ in B is a voiced velar fricative. A feature common to both A and B is the assimilation of voiced *ġ* as a result of progressive assimilation, in the root *bġy*. In B this is:

1	c.s.	*?abbi*	for	*?abġi*	(I want)
2	m.s.	*tubbi*	for	*tubġi*	(you want)

The guttural *x*

x in B is a voiceless velar fricative. In the following two forms from B, classical Arabic *x* is realized *ġ* [11]

laa tġabbi ^{c}*aliyyi* < *laa txabbi* (don't screen things from me), inf. 26
diġs < *duxas* (dolphin), inf. 24

The guttural *h*

h of Arabic 3 m.s. pronominal suffix, normally dropped in urban B, is retained in rural B. Cf:

urban		rural
^{c}*inde*	(he has)	^{c}*indeh*
?axad le	(he took)	*?axad leh*
šifte	(I saw him)	*šifteh*

h of the demonstrative *ihni* (here) and *ihnaak* (there) is regularly dropped in liaison with the particle *min* (from):

minni	for	*minihni*	(from here)
minnaak	for	*minihnaak*	(from there)

The fricative *w*

w in B is a labio-dental fricative. Other than its normal occurrence, *w*, corresponding to Arabic conjunction *waw*, is found in liaisons only. Cf:

has-sane w-kil sane (may (this grace) continue every year)

In sentence initial positions, and occasionally elsewhere to a varying extent the above *w* is realized *u*, as in:

u daak (and that)

The fricatives *f* and *ṯ*

Arabic inter-dental *ṯ* has the free variant *f* in B:[12]

fuum (garlic) *falaaf* (three), inf. 19

In the following classical and koine forms, ṯ is preserved:

ṯyaab	(gowns), inf. 2	*i?aṯṯir*	(it affects), inf. 4
ḥadiiṯ	(the Prophet's sayings)		

In the following forms from B, ṯ of the source word is invariably realized *f*:[13]

falam	<	*ṯalam*	(he broke into two)
fariid	<	*ṯariid*	(a traditional dish of sopped bread and broth)
nafye	<	*naṯye*	(female)

The fricative ḏ

Arabic inter-dental fricative ḏ is only partially preserved in B. It is found in classical and koine forms circulating in B:

ḏi l-qi^{c}*de*	(the eleventh month of the Muslim calendar)
ḏi l-ḥijje	(the last month of the Muslim calendar)
kaḏa waaḥid	(quite a few persons)

Elsewhere it is replaced by *d*.

The fricative *s*

In the following examples from B, non-emphatic Arabic *s* is realized emphatic *ṣ* in the vicinity of the guttural *x* and emphatic *ṭ*:

ṣixxaam	(soot, smut)	*ṣxuune*	(temperature)
yiṣxi	(he is willing to give)	*ṣaxle*	(lamb)
?aṣmax	(deaf)		
bṣaaṭ	(cotton or nylon rug)	*ṣaaṭuur*	(adze)
ṣaṭa	(he looted, confiscated)	*yiṣṭa*^{c}	(it shines)

Note that in emphatic environments, such as in the examples above, the vowel *a* is normally realized as α.

The fricative *z*

z in B is voiced dental fricative. It undergoes no changes. However, in the following examples from B, Arabic ḏ is regularly realized *z*:

za^{c}*ag*	<	*ḏa*^{c}*aq*	(he screamed)
zfur	<	*ḏafar*	(stench)
raziil	<	*raḏiil*	(mean)

In the following items Arabic *ṣ* is dissimilated to *z*:

zaġiir	for	*ṣaġiir*	(little), inf. 5.
l-izġayyir	for	*liṣġayyir*	(the younger), inf. 5.

The nasal *n*

In the following forms from B, Arabic *n* is dissimilated to *m* in the vicinity of the voiced bilabial plosive *b*:[14]

minbar	>	*mumbar*	(rostrum)
janb	>	*jamb*	(side)

In rural B *n* is often partially realized in the vicinity of stressed long vowels as in:

?inčáan̥	(if)	*famíin̥*	(precious, costly)

In liaisons, voiced *n* of certain particles is sometimes dropped:

le kaan	<	*leen kaan*	(if)
mi s-suug	<	*min issuug*	(from the market)

Assimilation of consonants

A phonetic feature common to B is the total assimilation of a voiceless consonant by an ensuing voiced one. Cf. these illustrations from B:

vd. *j* replaces vl. *t* before *j*

mijjahziin	<	*mitjahziin*	(they are ready)
mijjam^{c}*iin*	<	*mitjam*^{c}*iin*	(they have assembled)

vd. *d* replaces vl. *t* before *d*

middaa^{c}*miin*	<	*mitdaa*^{c}*miin*	(involved in accidents)
middaaxliin	<	*mitdaaxliin*	(they are entangled)

vd. *z* replaces vl. *t* before *z*

mizzaa^{c}*liin*	<	*mitzaa*^{c}*liin*	(they are not on speaking terms)
mizzawjiin	<	*mitzawjiin*	(they are married)

vd. *ḍ* replaces vl. *t* before *ḍ*

miḍḍaarbiin	<	*mitḍaarbiin*	(involved in a quarrel)
miḍḍaamniin	<	*mitḍaamniin*	(united or accomplices in an act)

Contractions

Contractions abound in rural varieties of B. No precise rules can be formulated for their occurrence. They seem to be extremely common and are indeed habitually used by many speakers but their occurrence is not governed by emphasis or any other obvious conditioning.[15]

The ultimate open syllable *-la* of the particle ^{c}*ala* (on) is often contracted to ^{c}*a-* in rural forms of B. Cf:

urban B		rural B	
^{c}*ala raaḥati*	(at my leisure)	^{c}*a raaḥati,*	inf. 5
^{c}*ala waṣa*	(on order)	^{c}*a waṣa,*	inf. 4
^{c}*ala n-naḍar*	(depends on my eye-sight)	^{c}*a n-naḍar,*	inf. 4

-ar of the ultimate closed syllable in the Arabic cardinal *ᶜašar* (ten) is deleted in B; in pause, it is normally realized *-ᶜaš* in numbers from eleven to nineteen. Cf:

falaṭṭaᶜaš (thirteen) *?arbaaṭaᶜaš* (fourteen)

The above also applies to the same forms in A.
The interrogative particle *čeef* (how come?!) is often contracted to *če* both in urban and rural B:

če maa tidri (how come you don't know?!)

The prefix *i-* of these adverbial particles is often contracted in rural forms of B in and out of liaison. Cf:

?ileen > *leen* (till, until), inf. 8
iji > *ji* (for about)

The initial element is similarly elided in B in the roots *?b* and *?x*. Thus:

bu-ṣeebiᶜ (Abu Ṣēbiᶜ village)
bu-ᶜašiira (Abu ᶜAshīra date garden)
bu-faame (Abu Fāme oyster bed)

and:

xuuk (for *?axuuk:* your brother)
buuk (for *?abuuk:* your father)

The Vowel System

A fourfold set of discriminations, in terms of frontness versus backness and closeness versus openness, distinguishes short vowels in B. These are:

a	open-front as in:	*ᶜala*	(on)
i	close-front as in:	*ᶜindi*	(I have)
α	open-back[16] as in:	*ṣαdαg*	(he told the truth)
u	close-back as in:	*?umkum*	(your mother)

In addition to the above main distinctions, two further short vowels are found, mainly as a result of the shortening of long vowels. These are:

e mid-front, which as a short variant of long *ee* is found in:

hadeleen for *hadeeleen* (these)
delaak for *deelaak* (those)

Final *e* also arises as a result of *imāla* of Arabic *a* as in:

?ane (I) same (sky)

A sentence final, sitressed *-é* is employed to indicate interrogation: *katabt-é?* (have you written?) *katabtin-é ?* (have you written ? fem.)

e also occurs as a conditioned variant of *i* and *u*. Thus compare the following pron. suffixes from Sitrah, where *e* corresponds to lit. Ar. *u:*

leečem	(for you)	*beeteč*	(your house)

o mid-back, is a short variant of long *oo* in:

(*xams*)	*nobaat* for	*noobaat*	((five) times)	
zojaate	for	*zoojaateh*	(his wives)	

In terms of degress of length, six long vowels can be distinguished in B, viz:

aa	open-front as in:	*mbaašar*	(regular care),	*mašaamur*	(long veils)
ee	mid-front as in:	*ᶜeen*	(fresh-water spring),	*mitḥeeriṣ*	(mean with)
ii	close-front as in:	*?intiin*	(you (f.s.)),	*il-jaziira*	(Nabīh Ṣāliḥ Island)
αα	open-back as in:	*sabααṭαᶜaš*	(seventeen),	*xααḍ*	(he waded)
oo	mid-back as in:	*mbooyuḍ*	(whitish),	*ṣooban*	(to soap)
uu	close-back as in:	*?intuun*	(you),	*ṭuus*	(pearl sieves)

It should be noted that the distinction between front *a* and back *α* relates chiefly to difference of consonantal environment.
Below are further illustrations of the occurrence of short and long vowels in B.

The front vowel *a*

In B forms below, *a* of the open stressed syllable is rendered *u* in the corresponding ᶜAnazi forms:

B		A
báṣal	(onion)	*búṣal*
gámar	(moon)	*gúmar*

In these nominal forms, viz. FaMaaMiiL, Arabic unstressed front *a* is retained in B only. Cf:

B		A
bagaagiil	(sellers of local vegetables)	*bgaagiil*
sačaačiin	(knives)	*sčaačiin*

The anaptyctic *a*

Anaptyctic *a* is found in these faMal < faMl forms:

laḥam	(meat)	*ṭaᶜam*	(taste)	*šaḥam*	(fat)

This anaptyctic *a* is elided when suffixes, e.g. *-e* or *-a* are added to the basic forms. Cf:

laḥme	(meat)	*ṭaᶜma*	(its taste)	*šaḥme*	(fat)

An anaptyctic vowel occurs after geminates in A to avoid the occurrence of triconsonantal clusters. In B a geminate does not occur in similar circumstances. Thus:

A		B
haṭṭaha	(he put it)	*ḥaṭha*
faččaha	(he opened it)	*fače*

Front *a* > back *α*

In B, in emphatic environments other than Koranic citations, front *a* is realized as back *α*. Cf. these minimal pairs:

samm	(poison)	*ṣαmm*	(in bulk(money))
tamm	(he remained)	*ṭαmm*	(it submerged, flooded over)
damm	(blood)	*ḍαmm*	(he employed, added)
salle	(basket)	*ṣαḷḷe*	(he prayed)
tall	(he pulled)	*ṭαḷḷ*	(he gazed or peeped)
dall	(he directed)	*ḍαḷḷ*	(he remained or stayed back)

In the vicinity of the gutturals *x* and *ġ*, *l* (in A only) tends to become velarized and concomitantly short front *a* is replaced by back *α*. Cf:

A		B
xαḷαα̣ḷ	(green, unripe dates)	*xalaal*
xαα̣ḷ	(uncle from mother's side)	*xaal*
nαġα̣ḷ	(bastard)	*naġal*
mbaġġαḷ	(hybrid)	*mbaġġal*

Word-final *imāla*

A phonetic feature found in B is the *imāla* of Arabic unstressed short vowel *-a* or *-a* < *-aa* to *e*. *Imāla* of *-a* to *-e* normally does not occur in post-emphatic positions viz. *ṣ*, *ḍ* and *ṭ* in B. Cf:

ᶜaṣa	(stick)
xabiiṣa	(tradional sweet made of flour, butter and sugar)
ġaliiḍa	(thick, mushy)
ᶜariiḍa	(wide)
ḥooṭa	(enclosure)
baṭṭa	(duck)

An exception to the above is found in certain Dirāzi forms where *-a* is affected by *imāla* in post- *ṭ* position:

murbaṭe	(harness), inf. 3
barbuṭe	(I shall tie it), inf. 3

Imāla does not take place in post- *ᶜayn* position in urban B. Cf:

galᶜa (fort) *bid ᶜa* (innovation) *rub ᶜa* (local weight = 4 pounds) *?arba ᶜa* (four) *sab ᶜa* (seven) *tis ᶜa* (nine)

Imāla in post-^{c}*ayn* position is found in certain Dirāzi forms not involving the feminine marker:

tbii^{c}*e*	(you sell it)	*yiṭla*^{c}*e*	(he will take it out)

Imāla after *f* in feminine forms occurs in Sitrah speech only. Cf:

Manāmah		Sitrah	
ġurfa	(room)	*ġurfe,*	inf. 22

Imāla after *b* similarly occurs mainly in nominal forms of the structure FaMLa or FiMLa:

wajbe	(meal)	*nihbe*	(looting)
ḥabbe	(a pinch of)	*šabbe*	(alum)

Imāla of *-a* in this position does not occur in nominal forms of the structure FaMaLa:

ragaba	(neck)	*ḥaṭaba*	(a piece of wood)

But exceptionally, ^{c}*atabe* (stepping path (of a house))
Imāla of *-a* after *m* occurs in the following:

(1) certain adjectival patterns:

mḍalme	(dark)	*mġayme*	(cloudy)

(2) certain FaMLa nominal forms:

faḥme	(coal)	*zaḥme*	(coniestion)
nijme	(star)	*ni*^{c}*me*	(grace, bounty)

(3) certain FaMaLa nominal forms:

janame	(a local brand of fish)	*ġaname*	(goat)

(4) certain FaMaaLa nominal forms:

salaame	(safety)	*ḥamaame*	(pigeon)

(5) certain FaMiiLa (p.n.) nominal forms:

nasiime	(Nasīma)	*na*^{c}*iime*	(Na^{c}īma)

Imāla of *-a* in post-*m* position does not occur in:

(1) certain FaMLa forms of nouns:

laṭma	(slap)	*raḥma*	(compassion)
nooma	(sleep)	*gooma*	(getting-up)

(2) these passive participials:

maxtuuma	(sealed)	*maḍluuma*	(prejudiced against)

Imāla of *-a,* corresponding to the lit. Ar. fem. ending *-aa,* occurs in the following nouns:

same	(sky)	*me*	(water)

Imāla of *-a,* corresponding to lit. Ar. *alif maqṣūra -aa* occurs in these verbal forms:

bane	(he built)	*samme*	(he named)
yitšable	(he climbs)	*yitsalle*	(he amuses himself)
yitḥačče	(he speaks)	*yitmašše*	(he walks)

Imala of *-a*, corresponding to lit. Ar. *alif maqṣūra -aa*, does not occur in these verbal forms:

rabba	(to bring up)	*ġabba*	(to hide)

The front vowel *i*

i is found in all positions, e.g.

?ani	(I (fem.))	*?intiin*	(you (fem.))

And in the imperfect preformatives:

3 m.s. *yi ᶜruf* 2 m.s. *ti ᶜruf* 1 c.pl. *ni ᶜruf*

And in the nominal participial prefix *mit-*:

mitsaamiḥ	(tolerant)	*mitkeesil*	(lazy)

In the adverbial particles below, the final *-i* of urban B has the allophonic variant *-e* in the corresponding rural forms. Cf:

urban B		rural B	
minni	(here)	*minne*	inf. 26
čidi	(like, as)	*čide*	inf. 22

In these forms from B, stressed *-á-* of the penultimate open syllable is realized *i* in the corresponding ᶜAnazi forms:

B		A
?inkatab	(it was written)	*?inkitab*
?infataḥ	(it got open)	*?infitaḥ*

In B, *i* appears with 2 f.s. suffix *-š* when the ultimate syllable of the unaffixed form is -CVVC, as for example:

?aduuniš	(your ear)	*ᶜyuuniš*	(your eye)

This *i* is normally dropped when the ultimate syllable of the unaffixed form is -CVC:

muᶜḍaḍš	(your bangle)	*jabhatš*	(your forehead)

Note that the equivalent suffix in A is *-ič*. Thus:

yabhatič		*glumič*	(your pen)

The *u* Variant of *i*

In this dialect, *i* of the Arabic ultimate syllable -CiC is often realized *u* when the consonantal environment is emphatic or emphatized. In the neighbourhood of *r*, for example, in verbal forms corresponding to Arabic imperfect verb type yaFMiL, cf. the following:

yiṣbur (he is patient) *yiᶜruf* (he knows)
yiḥfur (he digs) *yiġruf* (he scoops)

Arabic *i* of the above verb type remains stable when the aforementioned syllable has *r* for its opening consonant and a non-emphatic for its closing sound, such as:

yidris (he studies) *yiḥris* (he guards) *yitris* (he fills)
yubrid (it gets cold) *yixrid* (he changes money) *yišrid* (he escapes)
yubriz (he will be ready) *yifriz* (he sorts out)

The *i* of the -CiC syllable of the Arabic verb type *nuFaMMiL* is often realized *u*, mainly in the neighbourhood of emphatics and gutturals, as:

nxaṭṭur (We overtake) *nḥaḍḍur* (We make ready)
ngaṣṣus (We cut off) *nsaᶜᶜur* (We price)
nbaxxur (We perfume with incense) *nṣaḥḥuḥ* (We correct, mark)
nṣabbuġ (We paint)

The *u* variant of *i* is also found in the vicinity of the consonants *r* and *f*, as:

ndawwur (We search) *nxabbur* (We inform) *nṣaffuf* (We arrange).

But note that Arabic *i* remains stable in these nuFaMMiL verb types in the neighbourhood of *t, d, r, m:*

nfattit (We crumble) *njaddid* (We renew, renovate)
nbarrid (We cool) *nḥammil* (We transport, carry)

i is also realized *u* in these nominals, corresponding to Arabic plural maFaaMiL, where *r* is the opening or closing consonant in the ultimate syllable -CiC:

maxaaruf (baskets for ripe dates) *maᶜaaruf* (education)
maḥaabur (ink pots) *mašaamur* (long veils for ladies)

And in these nominals corresponding to Arabic active participle FaaMiL, where *r* is the opening or closing consonant such as:

šaarub (drunk) *ᶜaaruf* (knowing)
faaṭur (not fasting) *ḥaaḍur* (present)

But not in:

naahib (looter) *laabis* (dressed) *naazil* (descending)
gaatil (killer) *ᶜaagil* (wise) *ḥaamil* (pregnant)

Arabic *i* is realized *u* in the vicinity of the emphatic consonants *ṣ, ḍ, ṭ,* as in these forms:

yixṣum	(he deducts);	*yigṣub*	(he slaughters);
ixalluṣ	(he finishes);	*laaṣug*	(glued);
yinfuḍ	(it electrocutes);	*yiḥḍur*	(he is present);
ḥaamuḍ[17]	(sour);	*(i) mġammuḍ*	(with the eyes shut)
yilṭum	(he smacks the face)	*yirbuṭ*	(he ties)
yixṭur	(it occurs (to the mind)	*yifṭur*	(he breaks a fast)

The prosthetic vowel *i*

The prosthetic vowel *i* is mainly found in certain nominal and verbal forms: nominals iFMaaL < Arabic FiMaaL or FuMaaL as in:

iḥjaab	(amulet)	*iġbaar*	(dust)

and in verbal nouns corresponding to Arabic muFaaMaLa, as:

imkaafaḥ	(hard work)	*imbaašar*	(regular care)

and in quadriliteral forms of the verbal nouns:

itṣirwil	(trousering)	*itmiššuṭ*	(combing)

and in verbal forms corresponding to Arabic verb type taFaMMaL:

itmassaḥ	(he performed the ablution)	*itsabbaḥ*	(he bathed)

and in the imperatives: 2 f.s. *ikli* (eat) 2 c.pl. *iklu* and the adverbials: *ihni* (here) *ihnaak* (there)

In the following interrogative sentences, prosthetic *i* functions as a sort of connective. Cf:

leeš itṣarrux?	(why are you screaming?)
f-ween itḥawše?	(where is it obtainable from?)
weeš itsawwi?	(what are you doing?)

Finally, some ^{c}Anazi speakers also tend to realize certain nominal and verbal forms with the prosthetic *i*, as in:

ismiče	(fish)	*iḥṭuba*	(a piece of wood)
iktibat	(she wrote)	*iftiḥat*	(she opened)

Note that although throughout this work the occurrence of the prosthetic *i* as shown in A and B above, is not always mainfested in the transcriptions, it is to be understood that such a feature does exist.

The anaptyctic vowel *i*

Generally, anaptyctic *i* appears in the neighbourhood of *l, n, r* both in A and B.

In B, anaptyctic *i* appears in the structure FaMiL for lit. Ar. FaML, as:

baṭin	(stomach)	*^{c}adil*	(right; correct)
nadir	(vow)	*ḥabil*	(rope)

When FaML has *m* as its second radical, anaptyctic *i* is not employed as in these forms from B:

raml (sand) *tamr* (dried dates) *xamr* (wine)

In A, the above forms appear with anaptyctic *u:*

ramul *tamur* *xamur*

Certain lit. Ar. nominal forms of the structure FuML appear with the anaptyctic *i* both in A and B. Cf:

A	B
ḥizin (grief, sorrow)	*(i) ḥzin*
kiḥil (antimony, kohl)	*(i) kḥil*

In defined forms, initially closed syllables of the structure CiC- take anaptyctic *i*:

l-ibdayyi ^{c} (al-Budayya ^{c}) *l-ijfeer* (al-Jufayr)

Elision of the anaptyctic *i*

Anaptyctic *i* is elided when:

(a) a suffix such as *-e* is added to the form FaML:

baṭin	(belly)	*baṭne/h*	(his belly)
?akil	(food)	*?akle/h*	(his food)

(b) the suffix *-in* of tanwin is added:

baṭnin ^{c}*ood* (big belly) *?aklin zeen* (good food)

(c) the plural suffix *-iin* is added to the same:

^{c}*adil*	^{c}*adliin*	(correct)
sahil	*sahliin*	(easy or inferior)

The back vowel *u*

u is found in these forms from B:
beet umma (his mother's house)

Also in the penultimate closed syllable CuC-, as:

xuḍra (vegetables) *ḥumra* (lip-stick)

And in the 2 c.pl. imperative suffix:

ruuḥu (go) *iklu* (eat)

And in the plural suffixes *-kum* and *-hum*, as:

?axbaarkum	(your news)
?axbaarhum	(their news)

The occurrence of the long vowels: long *ii*

Long *ii* [18] occurs oftenest in the suffix *-iin:*

?intiin	(2 f.s., you)	*?al-ḥiin*	(now)
l-awwaliyyiin	(the previous ones)	*riḥtiin*	(you went?)

Long *ii* of these forms is normally shortened in liaison with the attributive suffixes *-iyye* or *i*, as in:

gaṭiif	*gaṭifiyye*	(of Qaṭīf (fem.))
jaziira	*jaziri*	(an inhabitant of Nabīh Ṣāliḥ island)

Long *ee*

ee is found as a reflex of Arabic diphthong *-ay* as in:

deen	(debt)	*been*	(between)

It is also found in certain participials:

mitkeesil	(lazy)	*mitbeexil*	(mean)

and also in certain diminutive forms which are local place names:

l-iġreefe	(Ghurayfa)	*(i) n ᶜeem*	(Na ᶜīm)
l-ijfeer	(Jufayr)	*l-iglee ᶜa*	(Qulay ᶜa)

Long *ee* such as found in the following forms from A, are realized differently in B. Cf:

A		B
gaameet	(I woke up)	*gomt*
naameet	(I slept)	*nimt*

But note these forms which are common to both A and B:

waafeet	(I met)	*naadeet*	(I called)

Long *ee* of the above forms is normally shortened to *e* in liaison with 3 m.s. pron. suff. *-e*, as in:

waafete	(I met him)	*naadete*	(I called him)

Long *aa*

Long *aa* is found in open as well as closed syllables as in:

ḥaamuḍ	(sour)	*baaṣug*	(tasteless)
banaat	(girls)	*?awlaad*	(boys)

It is also found in certain names pertaining to traditional professions:

l-iḥyaače	(sail making)	*l-ijzaafe*	(bulk-buying of fish)
?in-nasaaje	(weaving)	*l-iṭwaaše*	(pearl dealing)

And in these realtive adjectives:

naxaalwa	(attendants of date gardens)
ᶜakaarwa	(date planters)
ṣawaabᶜa	(people of Abu Ṣēbiᶜ)
jamaara	(people of bani Jamrah)

And in these verbal nouns derived from defective verbs:

tawdaat	(delivering)	*tarbaat*	(bringing up)
ramaay	(throwing)	*ᶜaṭaay*	(giving)

It is also found in these locally coined forms corresponding to Arabic noun type muFaaMaLa:

mᶜaabal	(regular attention)	*mgaabal*	(continuous attendance)
mbaašar	(regular care)	*mᶜaadal*	(arrangement, levelling)

The long *aa* of the following forms from A is absent from the same forms in B. Cf:

A		B
kalaaha	(he ate it)	*?akalhe*
xaḏaaha	(he took it)	*?axadhe*

Back Vowel αα

αα is a fully back vowel found mainly in contiguity with *ṣ*, *ṭ*, and *ḍ*. Cf:

ṣααr	(it is done)	*saar*	(the village of Sār)
ṭααb	(it is cured)	*taab*	(he expiated)
ḍααrr	(harmful)	*daar*	(room)

Long αα is also found in the vicinity of *ṭ* in these numerals:

?arbααṭαᶜaš	(fourteen)	*sabααṭαᶜaš*	(seventeen)

Long *oo*

óó is a mid-back rounded vowel corresponding mainly to the Arabic diphthong *aw*, as in:

xoox	(peaches)	*foog*	(up)
looz	(Terminalia-Indian fruit)	*ṣoob*	(towards)

óó is also found in these nominal forms:

middoorma	(lip-pigmented)	*mijjoorma*	(having a guilty conscience)
mbooyuḍ	(whitish)	*msoowid*	(blackish)

And in the diminutive suffix:

ḥamzóo	(Ḥamza)	*nijmóo*	(Nijma)

oo is also found in theme III(a) of the derived forms of triliteral verbs:

xoozar	(he stared fixedly)	*foošar*	(he showed off)

Long *oo* of these forms is normally shortened in liaison with the dual suff. *-een:*

loon	*loneen*	(two colours)
zooje	*zojateen*	(two wives)

Long *oo* of 3 c.pl. perf. forms functioning as passives is often shortened in liaison with the fem. suff. *-ha,* as:

raawooh	(he was shown)	*raawoha*	(she was shown)
jaabooh	(it was brought)	*jaaboha*	(she was brought)

Long *uu*

uu is a back rounded vowel found in 2 c.pl. pron. suff. *-uun* as in:

?intuun	(you)	*gada^{c}tuun?*	(have you eaten?)

It is also found in local forms of proper names:

ḥammuud	(Muhammad)	*?ammuun*	(Amīna)

It is also found in the imperatives:

guum	(get up)	*guul*	(say)
ruuḥ	(go)	*suug*	(drive)

Diphthongs

-ey < Arabic *-ay* is preserved in rural forms of B whereas in the comparable urban forms it is realized *ee.* Cf.

rural B		urban B	
ṣaḥeyne	inf. 4	*ṣaḥeene*	(he woke up)
xeyr	inf. 11	*xeer*	(grace, bounty)
rweyd	inf. 3	*rweed*	(raddishes)
xeybe	inf. 6	*xeebe*	(hopeless)
ġeyr	inf. 7	*ġeer*	(other than)
leyhum	inf. 20	*leehum*	(for, to them)
^{c}eyb	inf. 8	*^{c}eeb*	(unsound; blameworthy)

Final *-aw* corresponding to the lit. Ar. pl. suff. *-uu* is common to all speakers of B:

ᶜammaraw	(they lived long; they were constructive)
raaḥaw	(they went)
jaw	(they came)

Clear vowels such as characterize these urban forms are often diphthongized in rural speech. Cf:

		Urban		rural	
i > *iy*	as in:	*yaᶜni*	(that is to say)	*yaᶜniy*	inf. 4
		iḥuṭṭ	(he puts)	*iyḥuṭṭ*	inf. 4
		bijuun	(they will come)	*biyjuun*	inf. 22
ii > *ay*	as in:	*miinaa*	(port)	*mayne*	inf. 1
ee > *ey*	as in:	*beezaat*	(money)	*beyzaat*	
oo > *ow*	as in:	*hadoole*	(these)	*hadowle*	inf. 7

Consonant Clusters

Four types of initial consonant cluster are found in B. These are:

(a) a stop followed by a continuant as in:

b-waasṭat	(through)	*glaame*	(pens)

(b) a continuant followed by a stop as in:

ṣṭaar	(slap)	*mbaašar*	(attention, care)

(c) two continuants in succession as in:

mnazz	(cradle)	*mrašš*	(rose water sprinkler)

(d) two stops in succession as in:

ṭbuul	(drums)	*kbaar*	(big)

Note, however, that all the illustrations above can occur with the prosthetic *i* when realized out of liaison. Initial consonant clusters, such as are brought about by the presence of gutturals in A are not found in B. Cf:

A		B
ghawa	(coffee)	*gahwa*
ṣxale	(lamb)	*ṣaxle*

Nor in these forms either:

smiče	(fish)	*samače*
wriga	(a paper)	*waraga*

A final bi-consonantal cluster is found in these forms from Manāmah B where the closing consonant in the ultimate syllable is 2 f.s. suff. *-š*. Cf:

A		B
glumič	(your pen)	*galamš*
yabhatič	(your forehead)	*jabhatš*
wuldič	(your son)	*waladš*

In these forms from B, a tri-consonantal cluster is avoided by a momentary pause disconnecting the basic verb from the attached suffix:

šift-he	(I saw her)	*jibt-hum*	(I brought them)

Gemination or Duplication of a Consonant

Initial gemination is rare in B. Initially geminated consonants are often found in liaison with other items, such as:

ha n-nooba	(this time)	*ha š-šahar*	(this month)
ha s-safra	(this journey)	*ha d-dagiiga*	(this moment)

When the item *?um(m)* (mother) is compounded with another item, *m* is geminated as in:

?umm	*iššijeera*	(Um Shujayra (place name))
?umm	*iš ᶜuum*	(Um Shᶜūm (a natural spring in Baḥrain))

The final radical of the base-form of geminate verbs is long only in pre-vocalic positions, as:

verb +	2 m.s.	suff. *-a:*	*ḥišše*	(weed it out)	*ṣuffa*	(arrange it)
verb +	2 f.s.	suff. *-i:*	*xummi*	(sweep)	*limmi*	(collect)

Out of liaison the final radical of the base-form is realized as a single consonant.
In these forms gemination results from total assimilation of a sound:

assim. of	*?*	as in:	*?il-?awwal*	*?il-lawwal*	(in olden times)
assim. of	*l*	as in:	*ha l-rajjaal*	*ha r-rajjaal*	(this man)

Gemination also takes place when *e* < *a* of an elative form is in liaison with the interjective particle *maa*, as in:

min ?aḥle m-maa yumkin!	(the most beautiful)
min ?aġle m-maa yumkin!	(the most expensive)

n of the passive prefix *?in-* is regularly geminated in these forms where it is followed by front *a:*

?innaxad	(was taken)	*?innakal*	(was eaten)
?innase	(was forgotten)		

The Syllabic Structure of Certain Nominal and Verbal Forms

The table below sets out the syllabic components of certain basic nominal forms that are realized differently in A and in B. Cf:[19]

		A		B	
CCuCa	as in:	*rguba*	(neck)	CaCaCa	*ragaba*
CCiCe	as in:	*smiče*	(fish)	CaCaCe	*samače*
CCaCe	as in:	*nxale*	(date-palmtree)	CaCCe	*naxle*

CCaCa	as in:	*ghawa*	(coffee)	CaCCa	*gahwa*
CaCaC	as in:	*xaḍar*	(green)	?aCCaC	*?axḍar*
CaCuC	as in:	*ramul*	(sand)	CaCC	*raml*

Note the occurrence of a series of short syllables in this form from B:
Ca-Ca-Ca-Ce *ragabate* (his neck)
Cf. ᶜAnazi form of the same:
C-CuC-Ce *r-gub-te*

Below are the syllabic components of certain verbal forms which are realized differently in A and in B:

		A			B
CaCa	as in:	*kala*	(he ate)	CaCaC	*?akal*
CaCeeC	as in:	*kaleet*	(I ate)	CaCaCC	*?akalt*
CiCaC	as in:	*širab*	(he drank)	CaCaC	*šarab*
CuCa	as in:	*buga*	(he stayed)	CaCa	*baga*
CCuCaC	as in:	*wgufat*	(she stood)	CaCaCaC	*wagafat*
CaaCeeC	as in:	*naameet*	(I slept)	CiCC	*nimt*
CiCCiCaC	as in:	*?istilam*	(he received)	CiCCaCaC	*?istalam*

Stress in B

Stress in this dialect, as in other dialects of Arabic, is determined by the syllabic components of a given form. In disyllabic forms, stress falls on:
the initial syllable in the structure:

CV–CV	as in:	*šára*	(he bought)
CV–CVC[20]	as in:	*ráṭil*	(one pound (weight))
CVV–CVC	as in:	*máazaḥ*	(he joked)
CVC–CVC	as in:	*fállaᶜ*	(he threw stones)

the final syllable in the structure:

CV–CVCC	as in:	*labást*	(I dressed)
CV–CVVC	as in:	*nasíib*	(relative)
CVC–CVVC	as in:	*masdúud*	(blocked)

In trisyllabic forms stress falls on:
the initial syllable in the structure:

CV–CV–CV	as in:	*ḥáṭaba*	(wood)
CV–CV–CVC	as in:	*šárabat*	(she drank)

the pre-final syllable in the structure:

CV–CVV–CV	as in:	*jamáara*	(people of Bani Jamrah)

the final syllable in the structure:

CV–CVV–CVVC	as in:	*samaamíič*	(fisher folk)
CV–CV–CVVC	as in:	*gasamóoh*	(it was divided)

In quadrisyllabic forms stress falls on the second syllable as in:

CVC–CV–CV–CVC	*?indáᶜamat*	(it was hit)
	?ixtárabat	(it broke down)

NOTES:

1. Glottal stop is not transcribed before prosthetic vowels or the 3 m.s. imperfect suffix *i(y-)*.
2. *m* of this Arabic form from B is regularly realized *b:*
   ṭamaš > *ṭabaš* (nonsense, rubbish)
   m > *b* is a peculiarity ascribed to Māzin of Tamīm. Anīs, *Fi l-Lahajāt al-ᶜArabiyya,* p. 118.
3. Al-Lughawi in *al-Ibdāl*, vol. I, p. 107, observes that some Arab speakers tend to replace *d* by *t* in the form:
   kanᶜad > *kanᶜat* (mackerel)
4. See Map V, Appendices.
5. See Map VI, Appendices.
6. Note that medial *-čč-* of the Hindustani *word* kačča (unripe) is not an affricated form of *k*.
7. See Map VII, Appendices.
8. *q* of this borrowing from Latin is regularly rendered *x* in A and B:
   gawlanj > *xoolanj* (colic). See *al-Muzhir*, part I, p. 277.
9. T.M. Johnstone, '*The Affrication of KĀF and GĀF in the Arabic Dialects of the Arabian Peninsula*", *JSS*, vol. VIII, pp. 210–26 (1963).
10. In Manāmah B, *j* > *y* is found in one isolated example: *dyaaje* < *dajaajah* (hen). Cf. the ᶜAnazi form of the above: *dyaaye.*
11. Driver, *GCASP*, p. 9, mentions the occurrence of Arabic *x* as *ġ* in this example from Syrian Arabic: *xafiir* > *ġafiir* (guard, sentry). The replacement of *x* by *ġ*, however, is, we are told, an old Arabic feature. Cf. these forms from *al-Ibdāl*, vol. I, p. 335: *xabana* and *ġabana* (to cheat, defraud); also: *xamra* and *ġamra* as in *daxala fi xamrat innaas* (he plunged into the crowds). On the interchangeability of *x* and *ġ* in certain forms of Arabic, Ibn Manẓūr gives the examples: *xunna* and *ġunna* (slight nasalization of sounds)
12. See Map VIII, Appendices.
13. *ṯ* of the following Arabic form is regularly realized *s:*
    dayyuus < *dayyuuṯ* (procurer, vicious)
14. Ultimate *n* of this Arabic form is often replaced by *l:*
    fanaajiin > *fanaajiil* (small coffee cups)
15. See note 11 in Rabin's *Ancient West Arabian*, p. 122.
16. Occurring in transcriptions only of contrastive examples.
17. Reinhardt gives the form *ḥaamuḍ* with Arabic *i* > *u* for Banī Kharūṣ dialect of ᶜUmān, *Ein arabischer Dialekt*, p. 9. Also, H. Blanc mentions the same form for Muslim Iraqi, *CDB*, p. 38.
18. In certain rare cases Arabic FaMiiL is rendered FaMuuL as in: *ᶜanuud* (obstinate).
19. In A, as in a majority of north Arabian Beduin dialects, Arabic *a* in stressed open syllables is regularly realized *u* or *i* in these FaMaL forms:
    bágar *búgar* (cows)
    sámač *símač* (fish)
20. Also in the ᶜAnazi form *búṣal* (onion).

Part III

The morphology of the Baḥārnah dialect

In its basic structure, the morphological system of this dialect does not vary greatly from other dialects in the area. However, some archaic features indicative of older strata of language in the area are present in the Baharnah speech-forms. Forms like 2 f.s. *?intiin* (you), 2 c.pl. *?intuun;* verbal nouns of form II of the derived themes of the triliteral verb such as taFMaaL as in *taswaat* (making), taFMuuL as in *tasluum* (handing over), etc., have survived in B. The form of the relative adjective that takes the termination *-wa* and collectives that end in *-a* are in circulation in B.

Furthermore, since *a* can occur in open syllable in B, the FaMaL forms of verbs have remained stable. The ᶜAnazi pattern FiMaL corresponding to the lit. Ar. verb type FaMaL, therefore, does not occur in B.

Other morphophonemic changes such as the assimilation of certain verbal types to verbs with third radical *y*, a feature found in A, do not seem to occur in B. Cf:

A		B
kaleet	(I ate)	*?akalt*
naameet	(I slept)	*nimt*

Similarly, in liaison with the pronominal suffixes weak verbs that have *hamza* as their initial radical remain stable in B. Cf:

A		B
xaḏaaha	(he took it)	*?axadhe*
kalaaha	(he ate it)	*?akalhe*

The suffixes 2 f.s. *-iin* and 2 c.pl. *-uun* such as occur in the perfect verb are peculiar to B only. In A, *-ay* and *-aw* are employed for the same functions: Cf:

		A	B
2	f.s.	*kaleetay*	*?akaltiin*
2	c.pl.	*kaleetaw*	*?akaltuun*

In A the imperative forms 2 f.s. and 2 c.pl. of certain strong verbs are realized without the prefix *?i-*. Cf:

		A	B
2	f.s.	*sim ᶜay*	*?isma ᶜi*
2	c.pl.	*sim ᶜaw*	*?isma ᶜu*

Note above that the second person plural is of common gender both in A and B.
In A, the imperfect preformative of strong verbs of the FaMaL type is *ya-* for the third person masculine singular and the third person common plural; and *ta-* is used for the rest of the forms except first person. Whereas in B, the same is regularly realized *yi-*and *ti-*. Cf:

		A	B
3.	m.s.	*yaktib*	*yiktib*
3	f.s.	*taktib*	*tiktib*

In B, *y-* of the lit. Ar. 3 m.s. imperfect preformative is normally realized *i-* in the following verb forms:

hollow verbs, as:	*iṣuum*	(he fasts)
doubly weak verbs, as:	*iji*	(he comes)
geminate verbs, as:	*ijirr*	(he drags or pulls)

But Arabic *y-* of the above examples remains stable in liaison with the negative particles such as:

maa *yji* (he does not come) *laa yruuḥ* (he shouldn't go)

Furthermore, lit. Ar. 3 m.s. preformative *y-* remains stable in these verb forms from B;

weak final *y-*, as	:	*yirḍa*	(he agrees)	*yiṣḥa*	(he wakes up)
weak initial hamza, as	:	*yaakil*	(he eats)	*yaaxid*	(he takes)
strong verbs, as	:	*yišrab*	(he drinks)	*yiktib*	(he writes)

In B, the imperfect preformative of the themes V and VI is invariably *yit-* for the masculine and *tit-* for the feminine as in:

	masc.		fem.
V	*yitsabbaḥ*	(he bathes)	*titsabbaḥ*
VI	*yitšaawar*	(he confers or takes advice)	*titšaawar*

Both in A and B, instead of the derived themes of certain weak and geminate verbs, speakers use theme I:

weak final	*y*	:	*šara*	*?ištara*	(he bought)
			šaka	*?ištaka*	(he complained)
geminate verbs		:	*gall*	*?istagall*	(it dwindled)
			mall	*?istamall*	(he got bored)

In B, the passive of verbs is normally expressed by a verb of theme VII, such as:

masc.	*?inġasal*	(it was washed)	fem.	*?inġasalat*
	?inkasar	(it was broken)	fem.	*?inkasarat*

In addition, the passive is expressed by the use of a 3 c.pl. verb functioning as an impersonal, with or without the relative *?illi* (which, who), e.g.

^{c}*aṭooh* (he was given) *?illi šarooha* (that which was bought) . The common form of the imperative in B is FaMMiL on the analogy of theme II of the derived forms. Cf:

fahhim (explain) or *ḥawwil* (come down)

The Strong Verb

The simple verb: the perfect

The lit. Ar. perfect type FaMaLa has remained stable in B, e.g.,

zara^{c} (he planted) *ṣabar* (he was patient)

The lit. Ar. perfect type FaMiLa is also realized FaMaL in B, e.g.,

sama^{c} (he heard) *šarab* (he drank) *ḥalam* (he dreamed)

The above form, viz. FaMaL < FaMiLa, has the free variant iFMiL/iFMuL in B. Thus:

ismi^{c} *išrub* *iḥlim*

The ^{c}Anazi form FuMaL < Arabic type FaMaLa as in *wugaf* (he stood) and *ṭubax* (he cooked) does not occur in B, since it is a variant of FiMaL. In A FiMaL corresponds to lit. Ar. FaMaLa and FaMiLa.

The paradigm below illustrates the conjugations of the simple theme both in A (FiMaL) and B (FaMaL):

	A		B
3 m.s.	*kitab*	(he wrote)	*katab*
3 f.s.	*ktibat*		*katabat*
2 m.s.	*kitabt*		*katabt*
2 f.s.	*kitabtay*		*katabtiin*
1 c.s.	*kitabt*		*katabt*
3 c.pl.	*ktibaw*		*katabaw*
2 c.pl.	*kitabtaw*		*katabtuun*
1 c.pl.	*kitabne*		*katabne*

Note the elision in A of the lit. Ar. unstressed short vowel *i* of 3 f.s. and 3 c.pl.; and the presence of *-n* in the Baḥārnah 2 f.s. and 2 c.pl. forms.

The imperfect

Verbs which in the perfect have the base form 3. m.s. FaMaL in B, have imperfects of the pattern yiFMiL, yiFMaL, yiFMuL.[1] The conjugations of these three patterns, are adduced below:

3 m.s.	*yiġsil*	(he washes)	*yiḥlam*	(he dreams)	*yiḥfur*	(he digs)
3 f.s.	*tiġsil*		*tiḥlam*		*tiḥfur*	
2 m.s.	*tiġsil*		*tiḥlam*		*tiḥfur*	
2 f.s.	*tiġsiliin*		*tiḥlamiin*		*tiḥfuriin*	
1 c.s.	*?aġsil*		*?aḥlam*		*?aḥfur*	
3 c.pl.	*yiġsiluun*		*yiḥlamuun*		*yiḥfuruun*	
2 c.pl.	*tiġsiluun*		*tiḥlamuun*		*tiḥfuruun*	
1 c.pl.	*niġsil*		*niḥlam*		*niḥfur*	

Note that the regular occurrence of the unstressed short vowel *i* in the preformatives above prevents initial biconsonantal clusters arising in B.

However, it is difficult to demonstrate the phonemic conditions for the occurrence of these varying imperfect forms.

The table below sets out the imperfect conjugations of the verb types equivalent to the lit. Ar. perfect types FaMiLa and FaMaLa as realized in A and B. Cf:

	A	B
3 m.s.	*yi^{c}arf, yaktib*	*yi^{c}ruf, yiktib*
3 f.s.	*ti^{c}arf, taktib*	*ti^{c}ruf, tiktib*
2 m.s.	*ti^{c}arf, taktib*	*ti^{c}ruf, tiktib*
2 f.s.	*ti^{c}arfiin, taktibiin*	*ti^{c}rufiin, tiktibiin*
1 c.s.	*αα^{c}rif, ααktib*	*?a^{c}ruf, ?aktib*
3 c.pl.	*yi^{c}arfuun, yaktibuun*	*yi^{c}rufuun, yiktibuun*
2 c.pl.	*ti^{c}arfuun, taktibuun*	*ti^{c}rufuun, tiktibuun*
1 c.pl.	*ni^{c}arf, naktib*	*ni^{c}ruf, niktib*

Accordingly, the imperfect preformatives of the two strong verbs above, both in A and B, are:

	A	B		
3 m.s.	*yi-*	*yi-*	for Arabic strong verbs of the type	FaMiLa
	ya-	*yi-*	,, ,, ,, ,, ,, ,, ,,	FaMaLa
3 f.s.	*ti-*	*ti-*	,, ,, ,, ,, ,, ,, ,,	FaMiLa
	ta-	*ti-*	,, ,, ,, ,, ,, ,, ,,	FaMaLa
2 m/f.s.	*ti-*	*ti-*	,, ,, ,, ,, ,, ,, ,,	FaMiLa
	ta-	*ti-*	,, ,, ,, ,, ,, ,, ,,	FaMaLa
3 c.pl.	*yi-*	*yi-*	,, ,, ,, ,, ,, ,, ,,	FaMiLa
	ya-	*yi-*	,, ,, ,, ,, ,, ,, ,,	FaMaLa
2 c.pl.	*ti-*	*ti-*	,, ,, ,, ,, ,, ,, ,,	FaMiLa
	ta-	*ti-*	,, ,, ,, ,, ,, ,, ,,	FaMaLa
1 c.pl.	*ni-*	*ni-*	,, ,, ,, ,, ,, ,, ,,	FaMiLa
	na-	*ni-*	,, ,, ,, ,, ,, ,, ,,	FaMaLa

Note, however, with some speakers from A, *a* of the imperfect preformatives of certain strong verbs may be realized as *i*, thus:

yaktib and *yiktib* *yaḥlam* and *yiḥlam*

The imperative

Certain morphophonemic changes have affected Arabic imperative forms in B, viz. Arabic *ḍamma* is invariably realized *kasra*, as in *xuḏ* > *xid* (take). Also, the second person plural uses one form for both genders. Monosyllabic imperatives use the short vowel *i*:

2.m.s.	*kil*	(eat)	*xid*	(take)

Imperatives of certain weak verbs which are disyllabic in structure appear with the prefix *?i-* or *?u-*, as in:

2.m.s.	*?ib*^{c}*id*	or	*?ibti*^{c}*id*	(go away)
	?ugaf	(stand up)		

Certain trisyllabic forms are also realized with the prefix *?i-:*

2 m.s.	*?irtiḥil*	(go away)	*?istilim*	(take, receive)

Imperatives of hollow verbs appear with long (stressed) *áa* or *úu:*

2 m.s.	*naam*	(go to sleep)
	ruuḥ	(go away)

Lit. Ar. imperatives of form IV are normally realized on the analogy of theme II of the derived forms of the triliteral verbs i.e., FaMMal as in:

2 m.s.	*rassil*	(send)	*xabbur*	(tell)
	sarri^c	(make haste)	*daxxil*	(let in)

The above also applies to these weak verbs:

2 m.s.	*yabbis*	(make dry)	*?ayyis*	(despair)

Some common forms of the perfect, imperfect, and imperative

The perfect, imperfect, and imperative of certain strong verbs both in A and B appear below.

FaMaL/yiFMaL type:

B				A		
ga^c*ad,*	*yig*^{c}*id,*	*?ig*^{c}*id*	(to sit)	*ga*^{c}*ad,*	*yag*^{c}*ad,*	*?ig*^{c}*ad*
sama^c*,*	*yisma*^{c}*,*	*?isma*^{c}	(to hear, listen)	*sima*^{c}*,*	*yasma*^{c}*,*	*?isma*^{c}
šarab,	*yišrab,*	*?išrab*	(to drink)	*širab,*	*yašrab,*	*?išrab*
ṭabax,	*yiṭbax.*	*?iṭbax*	(to cook)	*ṭubax,*	*yaṭbax,*	*?iṭbax*

Derived themes

Specimens of the derived themes of perfect/imperfect in B are:

II	*jawwad,*	*ijawwid*	(to hold), v.n.	*tajwiid*
	baddal,	*ibaddil*	(to change), v.n.	*tabdiil*
	^{c}*allam,*	*i*^{c}*allim*	(to teach), v.n.	*ta*^{c}*luum*
	sabbaḥ,	*isabbiḥ*	(to bathe), v.n.	*tasbuuḥ*

III	*saamaḥ,*	*isaamiḥ*	(to forgive, condone), v.n.	*msaamaḥa*
	^{c}aašar,	*i^{c}aašir*	(to have social intercourse), v.n.	*m^{c}aašar*
	saa^{c}ad,	*isaa^{c}id*	(to help), v.n.	*msaa^{c}ade*
	saafar,	*isaafur*	(to travel), v.n	*safar*
V	*itkallam,*	*yitkallam*	(to talk or discuss), v.n.	*itkillim*
	itlabbas,	*yitlabbas*	(to dress), v.n.	*itlibbis*
	itfannan,	*yitfannan*	(to excel), v.n.	*itfinnin*
	itḥassan,	*yitḥassan*	(to have a hair-cut), v.n.	*itḥissin*
VI	*itṣaadag,*	*yitṣaadag*	(to befriend), v.n.	*mṣaadag*
	itsaalam,	*yitsaalam*	(to greet), v.n.	*msaalam*
	itmaazaḥ,	*yitmaazaḥ*	(to joke), v.n.	*immaazaḥ, mazaaḥ*

Note above, themes V and VI have the characteristic prefix *it-* in the perfect. The ^{c}Anazi forms of the same are realized without the prosthetic *i*, as in:

	theme V		*ti^{c}allam*	
	theme VI		*tiṣaadag*	
VII	*?inšaḥan,*	*yinšiḥin*	(to be filled). v.n.	*šaḥaan*
	?inġasal,	*yinġisil*	(to wash), v.n.	*ġasaal*
VIII	*?istalam,*	*yistilim*	(to receive), v.n.	*tasluum*
	?istama^{c},	*yistimi^{c}*	(to listen), v.n.	*tasmuu^{c}/itsimmi^{c}*

The Weak Verb

The *hamzated* verb: verbs with initial *hamza*

In B, only 3 m.s. perfect *?axad* and *?akal* have the shorter free variants *xad* and *kal*. The perfect form *kala* <*?akal* is a regular feature of A, not B. In B, the perfect, imperfect forms of the above and the verbal nouns derived from them are:

?axad,	*yaaxid,*	v.n.	*?axaad*
?akal,	*yaakil,*	v.n.	*?akaal*

The conjugations of the perfect verb *?akal* (he ate) both in A and B, are given below:

	Perf. B	Perf. A	imp. B	imp. A
3 m.f.	*?akal, kal*	*?ikal, kala*		
3 f.s.	*?akalat*	*kalat*		
2 m.s.	*?akalt*	*kaleet*	*kil*	*?ikil/kil*
2 f.s.	*?akaltiin*	*kaleetay*	*?ikli*	*?iklay*
1 c.s.	*?akalt*	*kaleet*		
3 c.pl.	*?akalaw*	*kalaw*		
2 c.pl.	*?akaltuun*	*kaleetaw*	*?iklu*	*?iklaw*
1 c.pl.	*?akalne*	*kaleene*		

The paradigm below sets out the conjugations of the perfect and the imperfect of *?axad* (he took) both in A and B. Note again that the unprefixed forms are a regular feature of A, not B:

	perf. B	perf. A	imperf. B	imperf. A
3 m.s.	*?axad/xad*	*xad̲*	*yaaxid*	*yaaxid̲*
3 f.s.	*?axadat*	*xad̲at*	*taaxid*	*taaxid̲*
2 m.s.	*?axadt*	*xad̲eet*	*taaxid*	*taaxid̲*
2 f.s.	*?axadtiin*	*xad̲eetay*	*taaxdiin*	*taaxd̲iin*
1 c.s.	*?axadne*	*xad̲eet*	*aaxid*	*aaxid̲*
3 c.pl.	*?axadaw*	*xad̲aw*	*yaaxduun*	*yaaxd̲uun*
2 c.pl.	*?axadtuun*	*xad̲eetaw*	*taaxduun*	*taaxd̲uun*
1 c.pl.	*?axadne*	*xad̲eene*	*naaxid*	*naaxid̲*

Verb medial *hamza*

Verbs with medial *hamza* are rare, and only *sa?al* (he asked) and *ra?as* (he presided over) occur frequently. The realization of the *hamza* in these forms is common to all speakers regardless of their educational status. In A the short, stressed *á* of B is realized *i*, as in *si?al* and *ri?as*. The paradigm below gives the conjugations of the verb *sa?al* in B:

	perf.	imperf.	imp.
3 m.s.	*sa?al*	*yis?al*	
3 f.s.	*sa?alt*	*tis?al*	
2 m.s.	*sa?alt*	*tis?al*	*?is?al*
2 f.s.	*sa?altiin*	*tis?aliin*	*?is?ali*
1 c.s.	*sa?alt*	*?as?al*	
3 m.pl.	*sa?alaw*	*yis?aluun*	
2 c.pl.	*sa?altuun*	*tis?aluun*	*?is?alu*
1 c.pl.	*sa?alne*	*nis?al*	

Verb final *hamza*

Lit. Ar. forms with a final *hamza* regularly lose the *hamza* both in A and B. Long *aa* of lit. Ar. forms is *imalized* to *-e*, as in *je* <*jaa?*.[2] In some cases the final *hamza* of Arabic forms is elided and the medial radical is geminated as in this example from B:

badde < *bada?* (he has started)

but note *gara* (he has read)

Some common verbs of this type are:

badde,	*ibaddi*	(to start) v.n.	*(i) tbiddi*
gara,	*yigra*	(to read), v.n.	*(i) graaye*
je,	*iji*	(to come, arrive), v.n.	*jiyye*

The conjugation of the verb *badde* (he has started) is given below:

	perf.	imperf.	imp.
3 m.s.	*badde*	*ibaddi*	
3 f.s.	*baddat*	*itbaddi*	
2 m.s.	*baddeet*	*itbaddi*	*badd*
2 f.s.	*baddeetiin*	*itbaddiin*	*baddi*
1 c.s.	*baddeet*	*?abaddi*	
3 c.pl.	*baddaw*	*ibadduun*	
2 c.pl.	*baddeetuun*	*itbadduun*	*baddu*
1 c.pl.	*baddeene*	*inbaddi*	

Note that the preformative *i-* of the imperfect form 3 m.s. and 3 c.pl. is realized *y-* remains in liaison with the negative particles *laa* or *maa,* as in: *laa ybaddi* (he does not start) or *maa ybadduun* (they do not start)

Verb initial *w*

The most common example of these is the verb *waṣal* (he came, arrived) which has the free variant *waṣṣal* in B. 3 m.s. perfect of the same verb has the characteristic penultimate open syllable Cu- in A, but Ca- in B. Also, 3 m.s. imperfect has the penultimate syllable Coo- in A, but Cuu- in B. Cf:

	A	B
3 m.s. perf.	*wuṣal/wugaf*	*waṣal/wagaf*
3 m.s. imperf.	*yooṣal/yoozan*	*yuuṣal/yuuzan*

The conjugation of the verb *wagaf* (he stood) in B, appears below:

	perf.	imperf.	imp.
3 m.s.	*wagaf*	*yuugaf/yuwgaf* (rural)	
3 f.s.	*wagafat*	*tuugaf*	
2 m.s.	*wagaft*	*tuugaf*	*?ugaf*
2 f.s.	*wagaftiin*	*tuugafiin*	*?ugafi*
1 c.s.	*wagaft*	*?awgaf*	
3 c.pl.	*wagafaw*	*yuugafuun*	
2 c.pl.	*wagaftuun*	*tuugafuun*	*?ugafu*
1 c.pl.	*wagafne*	*nuugaf*	

Derived themes

Some common examples of the derived themes of verbs initial *w* in B are:

II	*warraf, iwarruf*	(to bequeath), v.n.	*tawriif*
III	*waaṣal, iwaaṣil*	(to continue), v.n.	*imwaaṣal*
V	*(i)twaffag, yitwaffag*	(to be successful) v.n.	*tawfiig*
VI	*(i)twaada* ^{c}, *yitwaada* ^{c}	(to bid farewell), v.n.	*imwaada* ^{c}
VIII	*?ittasa* ^{c}, *yittisi* ^{c}	(to get larger), v.n.	*tawsii* ^{c}

Verb initial *y*

The paradigm below gives the inflection of the verb *?ayyas* (to despair):

	perf.	imperf.	imp.
3 m.s.	*?ayyas*	*i?ayyis*	
3 f.s.	*?ayyasat*	*it?ayyis*	
2 m.s.	*?ayyasat*	*it?ayyis*	*?ayyis*
2 f.s.	*?ayyastiin*	*it?aysiin*	*?aysi*
1 c.s.	*?ayyast*	*?a?ayyis*	
3 c.pl.	*?ayyasaw*[3]	*i?aysuun*	
2 c.pl.	*?ayyastuun*	*it?aysuun*	*?aysu*
1 c.pl.	*?ayyasne*	*in?ayyis*	

Derived themes:

Some examples of the derived themes of verbs with initial *y* are:

II	*yabbas, iyabbis*	(to dry), v.n.	*ityibbis/taybiis*
V	*tyabbas, yityabbas*	(to become dry)	

Hollow verbs

These are noted chiefly for two features. Firstly *y*- of the imperfect preformative of hollow verbs is normally realized *i*-. Secondly, the 3 m.s. imperfect *ibaat* (to stay overnight) has the free variant *ibiit* in B. Some common forms of hollow verbs in B are:

gaal, iguul	(to inform), v.n.	*gool, gawalaan*
šaal, išiil	(to carry), v.n.	*šayalaan*
gaam, iguum	(to rise up), v.n.	*gooma*
ṭaaḥ, iṭiiḥ	(to fall down), v.n.	*ṭeeḥa*

The paradigm below sets out the conjugation of the hollow verb *ṣaam* (he fasted):

	perf.	imperf.	imp.
3 m.s.	*ṣaam*	*iṣuum*	
3 f.s.	*ṣaamat*	*itṣuum*	
2 m.s.	*ṣumt*	*itṣuum*	*ṣuum*
2 f.s.	*ṣumtiin*	*itṣuumiin*	*ṣuumi*
1 c.s.	*ṣumt*	*ʔaṣuum*	
3 c.pl.	*ṣaamaw*	*iṣuumuun*	
2 c.pl.	*ṣumtuun*	*itṣuumuun*	*ṣuumu*
1 c.pl.	*ṣumne*	*inṣuum*	

Derived themes

The following verbs are illustrative of the derived themes of hollow verbs:

II	FaMMaL	*jawwad, ijawwid*	(to hold), v.n.	*tajwiid*
		xawwaf, ixawwuf	(to dread), v.n.	*taxwiif*
III	FaaMaLa	*ġaawar, iġaawur*	(to ignore), v.n.	*imġaawar*
V	taFaMMaLa	*itḥayyar, yitḥayyar*	(to be baffled), v.n.	*itḥiyyur*

Defective verbs

Defective verbs in this dialect have the characteristic vowel *i* in the imperfect preformative, normally realized *a* in A. Cf:

	B	A
3 m.s.	*yirmi, yimši*	*yarmi, yamši*

Some common form of these, together with their verbal nouns, appear below.

FaMaL, yiFMaL:

^{c}aṭa, yi^{c}ṭi	(to give), v.n.	*^{c}aṭaay*
rama, yirmi	(to throw), v.n.	*ramaay*
maše, yimši	(to walk), v.n.	*mamše/maši*
baġa, yubġi	(to want), v.n.	*baġiyye*
sawwa, isawwi	(to make), v.n.	*taswaat*
wadde, iwaddi	(to take to), v.n.	*tawdaat*
samme, isammi	(to name), v.n.	*tasmaat*
xalle, ixalli	(to leave), v.n.	*taxlaat*

Below is the conjugation of the verb *maše* (he walked) both in A and B. Cf:

	perf. B	perf. A	imperf. B	imperf. A	imp. B	imp. A
3 m.s.	*maše*	*miše*	*yimši*	*yamši*		
3 f.s.	*mašat*	*mišat*	*timši*	*tamši*		
2 m.s.	*mašeet*	*mišeet*	*timši*	*tamši*	*miš*	*?imiš*
2 f.s.	*mašeetiin*	*mišeetay*	*timšiin*	*tamšeen*	*?imši*	*?imšay*
1 c.s.	*mašeet*	*mišeet*	*?amši*	*?amši*		
3 c.pl.	*mašaw*	*mišaw*	*yimšuun*	*yamšuun*		
2 c.pl.	*mašeetuun*	*mišeetaw*	*timšuun*	*tamšuun*	*?imšu*	*?imšaw*
1 c.pl.	*mašeene*	*mišeene*	*nimši*	*namši*		

Note above: (a) the occurrence of the anaptyctic *i* in 2 m.s. imp. in A only.
(b) the occurrence, in A, of *i* in the penultimate open syllable of all the perfect forms, and that in B, *a* is regularly used in the same position, e.g., *maše, miše*

Perfect forms of the defective verb *ṣaḥa* (he recovered) have free variants in B. Cf:

	perf.
3 m.s.	*ṣaḥa, iṣḥi*
3 f.s.	*ṣaḥat, ṣiḥyat*
3 m.s.	*ṣaḥeet, iṣḥiit*
2 f.s.	*ṣaḥeetiin, iṣḥiitiin*
1 c.s.	*ṣaḥeet, iṣḥiit*
3 c.pl.	*ṣaḥaw, ṣiḥyaw*
2 c.pl.	*ṣaḥeetuun, iṣḥiituun*
1 c.pl.	*ṣaḥeene, iṣḥiine*

In rural forms of B, Manāmah *ee* is often replaced by the diphthong *ey*, as in:

ṣaḥeetuun > *ṣaḥeytuun*
ṣaḥeene > *ṣaḥeyne*

The conjugation of the verb *baġa* (he wanted, asked for) is given below:

	perf.	imperf.
3 m.s.	*baġa*	*yubġi/yubbi*[4] yabgi etc.
3 f.s.	*baġat*	*tubġi/tubbi*

2 m.s.	*bağeet*	*tubġi/tubbi*
2 f.s.	*bağeetiin*	*tubġeen/tubbeen*
1 c.s.	*bağeet*	*?abġi/?abbi*
3 c.pl.	*bağaw*	*yubġoon/yubboon*
2 c.pl.	*bağeetuun*	*tubġoon/tubboon*
1 c.pl.	*bağeene*	*nubġi/nubbi*

Cf. the ^{c}Anazi imperfect forms of the above:[5]

	imperfect	
3 m.s.	*yabbi*	yabi etc.
3 f.s.	*tabbi*	tabi
2 m.s.	*tabbi*	tabiin
2 f.s.	*tabbiin*	
1 c.s.	*?abi*	
3 c.pl.	*yabboon*	yabuun
2 c.pl.	*tabboon*	
1 c.pl.	*nabbi*	

Note, above, the use of back vowel *u* with the imperfect preformatives *y, t,* and *n* in B, as against *a* for the same forms in A. Also, note the use of the plural suffix *-óon* both in A and B.

The future particle *b(i)-* is to be derived from this root. With 1 c.s. forms it is realized *b-* or *?aba-*. Thus:

baṣiid	or	*?abaaṣiid*	(I am going to catch)
baruuḥ	or	*?abaaruuḥ*	(I shall go)

Doubly weak verbs

The most common form of these is the verb *je* (he came) rendered *ye* in A. Although palatalization of *j* to *y* is found in rural B, yet *j* of the above form remains stable in B. *y* of the imperfect preformative is invariably rendered *i* both in A and B. Total assimilation of the voiceless *t* to *j* occurs, e.g., the 3 f.s. *itji* > *ijji*. Cf:

	perf. B	perf. A	imperf. B	imperf. A
3 m.s.	*je*	*ye*	*iji*	*iyi*
3 f.s.	*jat*	*yaat*	*ijji*	*ityi*
2 m.s.	*jiit*	*yeet*	*ijji*	*ityi*
2 f.s.	*jiitiin*	*yeetay*	*ijjiin*	*ityiin*
1 c.s.	*jiit*	*yeet*	*?aji*	*?ayi*
3 c.pl.	*jaw*	*yaw*	*ijuun*	*iyuun*
2 c.pl.	*jiituun*	*yeetaw*	*ijjuun*	*ityuun*
1 c.pl.	*jiine*	*yeene*	*inji*	*inyi*

Geminate Verbs

Here again *y* of the imperfect preformative is regularly rendered *i* in A and B. In some forms total assimilation of the *t* of the imperfect to *d* takes place in A as well as B. Cf. 3 f.s. *itdill* > *iddill*. Assimilation of *t* does not seem to occur in the vicinity of *ṣ, r,* or *m*, etc. Cf:

itṣikk (to close), *itrišš* (to sprinkle), *itmidd* (to stretch)

Conjugation of the geminate form *dall* (to direct, guide) is given below:

	perf. B	perf. A	imperf. B	imperf. A
3 m.s.	*dall*	*dall*	*idill*	*idill*
3 f.s.	*dallat*	*dallat*	*iddill*	*iddill*
2 m.s.	*dalleet*	*dalleet*	*idill*	*idill*
2 f.s.	*dalleetiin*	*dalleetay*	*iddilliin*	*iddilliin*
1 c.s.	*dalleene*	*dalleene*	*indill*	*indill*
3 c.pl.	*dallaw*	*dallaw*	*idilluun*	*idilluun*
2 c.pl.	*dalleetuun*	*dalleetaw*	*iddilluun*	*iddilluun*
1 c.pl.	*dalleene*	*dalleene*	*indill*	*indill*

The Passive Verb

The passive, in this dialect, is either expressed by theme VII as, for example, *?inkasar* (it was broken), or by not expressing the agent in the sentence, for example, *?id-dikkaan it?ajjar* (the shop was let), or by a 3 c.pl. functioning as an impersonal verb. Accordingly, the prefix *?in-* is a regular feature of the passive perfect forms in this dialect; *yin-*, *tin-*, and *?an-* are regular features of the passive imperfect. The paradigm below, sets out the realization of perfect/imperfect passives in this dialect.

perfect:	3 m.s.	*?inḍarab*	(he was beaten)
	3 f.s.	*?inḍarabat*	
	2 m.s.	*?inḍarabt*	
	2 f.s.	*?inḍarabtiin*	
	1 c.s.	*?inḍarabat, etc.*	
imperfect:	3 m.s.	*yinḍurub*	(he is, beaten)
	2 f.s.	*tinḍurub*	
	2 m.s.	*tinḍurub*	
	2 f.s.	*tinḍurbiin*	
	1 c.s.	*?anḍurub, etc.*	

Hamzated forms of the passive verb

Hamzated verbs of the type FaMaL tend to take the prefixes *?in-* and *yinn-* for perfect and imperfect respectively. Cf:

perfect:	*?innaxad*	(it was taken)	*?innakal*	(it was eaten)
imperfect:	*yinnaxad*	(it is taken)	*yinnakal*	(it is eaten)

Initially hamzated verbs of the type FaMMaL, tend to use form V to express the passive, and thus:

perfect:	*it?ajjar*	(it was let)
	it?axxar	(he was late)
imperfect:	*yit?ajjar*	(it is let)
	yit?axxar	(he is late)

Note that the addition of the prefix *b-* to the imperfect forms of the passive changes the meaning from present to future, thus:

b-yit?ajjar	(it will be let)	*b-yinḍurub*	(he will be beaten)
b-yit?axxar	(he will be late)	*b-tinḍurub*	(she will be beaten)

Hollow verbs as passive forms

Hollow verbs take the prefixes *?in-* and *yin-* < VII for the perfect and imperfect respectively. Cf:

perfect:	*?injaab*	(it was brought)	*?inšaal*	(it was taken)
imperfect:	*yinjaab*	(it is brought)	*yinšaal*	(it is taken)

Defective verbs as passive forms

These also take the same prefixes as above:

perfect:	*?inšara*	(it was bought)	*?inrama*	(it was thrown)
imperfect:	*yinšara*	(it is bought)	*yinrama*	(it is thrown)

Geminate verbs as passive forms

These also take the same prefixes:

perfect:	*?inḥaṭṭ*	(it was put)	*?indagg*	(it was ground)
imperfect:	*yinḥaṭṭ*	(it is put)	*yindagg*	(it is ground)

Quadriliteral Verb

Both forms of the lit. Ar. quadriliteral verbs are found in this dialect. Those that are formed by the doubling of a biliteral root show a higher frequency of occurrence in speech. A salient feature of the imperfect of these verbs is the regular empolyment of the prefix *i* < *y*.

The paradigmatic behviour of two such verbs are adduced below:

perfect:	3 m.s.	*ṣarwal*	(to trouser)	*galgal*	(to shake)
	3 f.s.	*ṣarwalat*		*galgalat*	
	2 m.s.	*ṣarwalt*		*galgalt*	
	2 f.s.	*ṣarwaltiin*		*galgaltiin*	
imperfect:	3 m.s.	*iṣarwil*		*igalgil*	
	3 f.s.	*(i) tṣarwil*		*(i) tgalgil*	
	2 m.s.	*(I)tṣarwil*		*(i) tgalgil*	
	2 f.s.	*(i)tṣarwiliin*		*(i) tgalgiliin*	

Derived Themes

As the summary above shows, the basic themes of the triliteral verb are all found in this dialect. Theme III (a),[6] as in *soolaf* (he chatted) or *xoozar* (he stared fixedly, looked askance), is a common feature of B. Theme IV is normally replaced by theme II, thus *rassal* (he sent) and *xabbar* (he told). Voiceless *t* of certain forms of theme V undergoes total assimilation when followed by a voiced consonant, as in *iḍḍarrar* (he incurred damage) or *ijjamma* ᶜ (it accrued). Also, theme VI (a)[7] like *(i)tsoolaf* (he chatted) or *(i)tjooram* (he felt guilty) are common in B. Another common form arising from theme VI, hereafter called VI (b), is *(i)tFeeMaL* as in *(i)tmeeraḍ* (he malingered) or *(i)tkeesal* (he became lazy). Forms of theme IX chiefly express colours such as: *?iḥmarr* (it got red), *?ixḍarr* (it got green). Others of the same theme are also present, e.g., *?iḥtarr* (it got hot), *?iftarr* (he turned).

Certain Arabic forms of theme X normally lose their medial *hamza* and as a result of this loss, a compensatory lengthening of the vowel *a* takes place: Cf:

	?istaanas	(he was bemused)	*yistaanis*
but note:	*?ista?dan*	(he asked permission)	*yista?din*

Finally, the imperfect preformatives of most of the derived themes are *y-* or *i-* < *y*.

Here are the basic forms of the derived themes in this dialect:

	perf.		imperf.	imp.
II	*ᶜammar*	(he ploughed the soil)	*iᶜammur*	*ᶜammur*
III	*saafar*	(he travelled)	*isaafur*	*saafur*
III(a)	*foošar*	(he boasted)	*ifoošur*	*foošur*
IV	*xabbar*	(he told)	*ixabbur*	*xabbur*
V	*(i)tḥassan*	(he had his hair cut)	*yitḥassan*	*itḥassan*
VI	*(i)tšaawar*	(he consulted)	*yitšaawar*	*itšaawar*
VI(a)	*(i)tjooram*	(he felt guilty)	*yitjooram*	—
VI(b)	*(i)tfeeḍal*	(he poked his nose)	*yitfeeḍal*	*itfeeḍal*
VII	*?inšaḥan*	(it was filled)	*yinšiḥin*	—
VIII	*?istamaᶜ*	(he listened)	*yistimiᶜ*	*?istimiᶜ*
IX	*?iḥtarr*	(it got hot)	*yiḥtarr*	*?iḥtarr*
X	*?ista?jar*	(he rented)	*yista?jur*	*?ista?jur*

Note that the perfect forms V, VI, VI(a), VI(b) normally take the prefix *it-*.

Finally, locally coined forms, on the analogy of theme II, are frequently met with. Cf:

FaMMaL: *hawwas* (he put pressure) *fannaš* (he resigned, from English "finish")
bannad (he closed (a shop), from Persian)

Active and Passive Participles

FaaMiL and maFMuuL, corresponding to classical Arabic active and passive participles of the triliteral verb, are common in B. Defective verbs which do not exhibit a munFaMiL form in B, are realized as:

?illi nᶜaṭa	(which was given)
?illi nšara	(which was bought)

Arabic forms of the type maFMuuL as in *ma?kuul*, lose their *hamza* and as a result a compensatory lengthening of short *a* to long *aa* takes place, e.g., *maakuul* (is eaten), *maaxuud* (is taken).

Some common forms of FaaMiL/maFMuuL participles in B are:

act. part.		pass. part.	
baayiᶜ	(seller)	*mabyuuᶜ*	(sold)
ġaasil	(washer)	*maġsuul*	(washed)

ḥaamil	(carrier)	*maḥmuul*	(carried)
maaxid	(taker)	*maaxuud*	(taken)

Some examples of FaaMiL/munFaMiL forms of the participles are:

čaasi	(provider)	*minčasi*	(recipient of provision)
kaasib	(winner)	*minkisib*	(loser)
ḥaarig	(burner)	*miḥtirig*	(burnt)

Active participles as verbs

A characteristic feature found in B is the regular employment of the terminations *-inne* and *-tinne*, masculine and feminine respectively (sc. *tanwīn* + pron. suff.) with the active participle form FaaMiL in these verbal constructions:

masc.	*?abuuyi*	*šaarinne*	(my father bought it)
fem.	*?amiina*	*msawwitinne*	(?Amīna made it)

Cf. the A rendering of the above examples:

masc.	*?ubuuy*	*šaarye*
fem.	*?amiine*	*msawwite*

Some common forms of the active participles

Examples of common forms of active particples based on the derived themes of triliteral verbs are given below:

V[8]	mitFaMMiL	<	mutaFaMMiL
	mitbarriz		(prepared; ready)
	mitlabbis		(dressed)
	mitFooMiL	<	mutaFaMMiL
	middooliğ		(wearing socks)
	mitxoobil		(dismayed, alarmed)

Note the total assimilation of the voiceless *(t)* in the first example above.

VI	mitFeeMiL	<	mutaFaaMiL
	mitbeexil		(stingy)
	mitḥeeriṣ		(mean)

Examples of quadriliteral forms are given below:

I	(i)mFaMLuL	<	muFaMLiL
	mbarṭum		(cross, grim-faced)
	mṭa:ıgur		(unwilling to communicate)
II	mitFaMLiL	<	mutaFaMLiL
	mitṣarwil		(trousered)
	mitmalfi^{c}*a*		(veiled (fem.))
	mitFaMMiL	<	mutaFaMMiL
	mit^{c}*ammim*		(turbaned)
	mit^{c}*allim*		(educated)

The Nominal Patterns

A large number of Arabic nominal types, including some archaic forms have survived in B. The simplest and commonest forms of these are biconsonantal nouns such as are characterized by ultimate long (doubled) consonants, e.g., *xadd* (cheek). Others have undergone morphophonemic changes, such as the following plural forms, normally treated as sound plurals in Arabic, are realized as broken plurals in B:

baggaal,	pl.	*bagaagiil*	for lit. Ar.	*baqqaaluun*	(grocers)
ḥammaal,	pl.	*ḥamaamiil*	for lit. Ar.	*ḥammaaluun*	(porters)

Other forms of Arabic nouns appear with the anaptyctic *(a), (i),* or *(u)* as in:

faḥam	(coal)	*bagil*	(clover)	*gabur*	(grave)

Certain archaic forms of nouns and adjectives are preserved in B. Forms such as the adjective *xayyir* (calm and obedient), the irregular plural substantive pattern FiMLaan, as in *niswaan* (women); the pl. pattern FaMaaLa, as in *sakaara* (drunken); and the pl. pattern FaMaaLiL, as in *manaayir* (minarets) or *ḥaraayir* (silk).

Nouns of the type FaMMaaL, mostly pertaining to traditional crafts and trades, figure largely in B:

sammaač	(fisherman)	*ᶜakkaar*	(date planter)
ḥaḍḍaar	(owner of weirs)	*saffaaf*	(mat plaiter)

Some scattered old forms, such as *mamšaa* (disposal or sale), *ḥisbaan* (reckoning, calculation), *šarye* (a buy), *binye* (physical constitution), *ᶜubri* (passenger), *siif* (harbour), *sluum* (setting of the sun), are commonly met with in daily speech.

However, the ᶜAnazi (medial guttural) pattern FMaLa < FaMLa, eg., *ghawa* < *gahwa* (coffee) resulting in an initial biconsonantal cluster, does not occur in B. This also applies to FiMaL < FaMaL e.g., *liban* (sour milk) and *jimal* (camel) are realized *laban* and *jamal* in B. Similarly forms FiMiiL and FiMiiLa as in *ḥiliib* (milk) and *ḥijiije* (fact) are invariably realized *ḥaliib* and *ḥagiiga* in B. *Also* the ᶜAnazi pattern FMuLa < FaMaLa as in *rguba* (neck) realized *ragaba* in B is another example of the non-elision of the *a* of the first syllable of CaCaCa(C) forms in the pre- ᶜAnazi speech of eastern Arabia.

Certain Arabic adjectives of the type ?aFMaL (m.s.) may have the pattern FaMaL in A, where the initial radical is a guttural. Thus:

B		A
?aḥmar	(red)	*ḥamar*
?axḍar	(green)	*xaḍar*
	(red)	

Certain classical adjectives are also in circulation in B, e.g.,

FaMiiL/e as in *baṭiin/e* (a glutton)
FaMuuL as in *maluul* (easily bored) or *ᶜanuud* (obstinate) *ṣaduug* (truthful) *ṣabuur* (patient)
FaaMuuL as in *šaaġuul* (hard working)
FaMLaani FaMLaaniy as in *foogaani* (top one)
taḥtaani (bottom one)

MFaMMaL	< muFaMMaL	as in	*mšajjar*	(patterned)
			mdawwar	(circular)
mFooMi/uL	< muFawMaL	as in	*mṭoowil*	(longish)
			mḥoomur	(reddish)

Specimens of derivative adjectives in B are:

noun		adjective	
beelajaan	(egg-plant)	*beelajaani*	(violet)
ward	(rose)	*wardi*	(rose)
gahwa	(coffee)	*gahwači*	(dark-brown)

Some examples of pl. patterns of relative adjectives found in B are:

	sing.	pl.	
FaMaaLa as in	*jamri*	*jamaara*	(Bani Jamrah villagers)
	gaṭiifi	*gaṭaafa*	(Qaṭīfis)
FuMLa as in	*buhri*	*buhra*	(Indian Ismailis)
FaMaaw(i)La(h)	*draazi*	*daraawze*	(Dirāzi villagers)
FawaaM(i)La(h) as in	*ṣeeb^{c}i*	*ṣawaab^{c}a*	(Abu Ṣēbi^c villagers)
FaMaaL(i) wa(h) as in	*satraawi*	*sataarwa*	(Sitrah Islanders)
	hindi	*hanaadwa*	(Indians)
FaMaaLiL as in	*ḥalaayli*	*ḥalaayil*	(Baḥārnah villagers)
FaMaaLiyye as in	*ḥasaawi*	*ḥasaawiyye*	(Ḥasāwis)

The Formation of Nouns and Adjectives by Suffixes: The Singular

With few exceptions, the suffix *-e* or *-a* marks a noun or adjective as feminine singular, as in:

fem. noun	*mara*	(woman)	*bnayye*	(girl, daughter)
fem. adj.	*^{c}oode*	(big, elderly)	*ṣaġiira*	(young, small)

The Dual

Dual nouns are marked by the suffix *-een* and *-teen*, e.g.,

masc.	*waladeen*	(two boys or sons)	*bitteen*	(two girls, daughters)

Feminine nouns which have the termination *-a* or *-e* are characterized by the infix *-t* before the dual suffix *-een* as in:

fem. noun	*rṭaba*	*rṭabateen*	(two ripe dates)
	waraga	*waragateen*	(two papers)

The Sound Plural

The sound plural is made by the suffixation of *-iin*, *-aat* and *-iyye*. *-iin* is suffixed to masculine nouns and adjectives as in:

mwaḍḍafiin (civil servants) or *zeeniin* (good, excellent)

-aat is suffixed to feminine singular nouns that have the feminine ending *-a* or *-e* as in:

bnayye	(girl)	*banaat*	(girls)
marra	(once)	*marraat*	(several times)

-iyye occurs with nouns pertaining to trades or origins as in:

ḥasaawi *hasaawiyye* (Hasawis) or *ḥammaaliyye* (porters)

The Diminutive

Arabic forms of the diminutive, viz. FMeeL < FuMayL, FMeeLa < FuMayLa, and FMayyiL < FuMayyiL are also found in this dialect. A locally coined form of the diminutive ending in stressed *-óo* as in FaMaaLóo is a peculiarity common to Baḥrāni and ᶜUmāni speech. The following examples illustrate the diminutive forms in B:

(1) proper names:	(i) FMeeL			(i) FMeeLa	
	ḥmeed	(Ḥumayd)		*fdeeḍa*	(Fudayda)
(2) place names:	*jfeer*	(Jufayr)		*n ᶜeem*	(Nu ᶜaym)
	daar ičleeb	(Dār Kulayb)		*ġreefe*	(Ghurayfa)
(3) (i) FMayyiL:	*ḥbayyib*	(Ḥabīb)		*ᶜzayyiz*	(ᶜAziz)

The above are often used to denote maternal love, when said by a mother to her son.

(4) Certain classical forms have also survived in B. Cf:
šwayye (a little) *nteefe* (a small bit)
qiitat yoom (one day's meal), inf. 2.

(5) The local form of FaMaaLoo,[9] diminutive of proper names, is very common:
ḥasaanoo (Ḥasan) *faṭaamoo* (Fāṭma)

Collectives

In this dialect, one type of collective noun is characterized by a scatter of four related forms each appropriate to its own grammatical context, thus:

singulative		dual	collective	plural
waraga	(one paper)	*waragateen*	*warag*	*?awraag*
ṭamaaṭaye	(one tomato)	*ṭamaaṭayateen*	*ṭamaaṭa*	*ṭamaaṭa*

Certain plurals are characterized by the association of the plural form with one of the following specific words:

raas (head (of onion))	*raaseen*	*ruus baṣal*
čeele (one scoop)	*čeelateen*	*čammin čeele ᶜeeš*

Collective nouns are also formed by the addition of the fem. suff. *a* to the relative adjective of the type FaMMaaL. Cf: f:

xammaam	*xammaama*	(sweepers)
ḥammaar	*ḥammaara*	(donkey drivers)

Certain collective nouns denoting local crafts or trades have two realizations in B, viz.

ġaaṣa	*ġawaawiiṣ*	(divers)
baḥḥaara	*baḥaaḥiir*	(seamen)
xayaayṭa	*xayaayiiṭ*	(tailors)
sammaače	*samaamiič*	(fisher folk)

The Verbal Nouns: Derived Themes

Verbal nouns show a high rate of frequency in daily speech in B. The simplest form of these is FaMiL as in *gatil* (killing). Certain FaMiL forms have the free variant FaMaaL as in *ḥamil/ḥamaal* (carriage), *ġasil/ġasaal* (washing)

Verbal nouns such as derived from hollow verbs are mainly of the form: *gooma* (getting up) or *nooma* (sleeping).

Another common form is FaMaLaan,[10] also derived from hollow verbs. Cf:

fawaḥaan	(boiling)	*jayabaan*	(bringing)
gawalaan	(telling)	*šarayaan*	(buying)

Verbal nouns derived from defective verbs are also copious; these exhibit the form FaMaaL. Cf:

ramaay	(throwing)	*ᶜaṭaay*	(giving)
sagaay	(watering)	*ḥabaay*	(crawling)

Archaic forms such as taFMuuL and TaFMaaL (derived from defective verbs, viz. final *-y*), are found in B. Below is a list of the most recurring forms of the verbal nouns derived from triliteral verbs in this dialect:

II taFMuuL[11]

tasluum	(handing over)	*taᶜluum*	(training, teaching)
tasbuuḥ	(bathing)	*tasmuuᶜ*	(listening)

but note: *tasbiiḥ* (glorification of God on a bead), *taᶜdiil* (tidying) both of which also belong to form II of the derived themes of the triliteral verbs.

II (from verbs final *w, y*)
taFMaaL

	tawdaat	(delivering)	*taṣfaat*	(refining, purification)
	tarbaat	(bringing up)	*taxlaat*	(leaving, keeping)
III	(i) mFaaMal < muFaaMaLa			
	mkaafaḥ	(hard work)	*mjaabah*	(constant attention)
	mṣaafaf	(arrangement)	*mbaašar*	(regular care)
IV	taFMiiL, replacing ?iFMaaL)			
	takmiil	(completing)	*tabdiil*	(changing)
	taḥḍiir	(preparing)	*tabliiġ*	(notification)
V	(i) tFiMMiL < taFaMMuL			
	itᶜiddil	(tidying)		
	itmiddin	(keeping up with civilization)		
	itfinnin	(excelling)		
	itbirriz	(preparation)		

t of the above forms undergoes total assimilation in the vicinity of *ḍ* or *d*. Cf:

iḍḍillim	(complaining)
*iddilli*ᶜ	(fondling)

VI (i) tFeeMiL < taFaaMuL

itbeexil	(stinginess)
itḥeeriṣ	(meanness)

The commonest patterns of verbal nouns, derived from quadriliteral verbs are:

II (i) tFiMLiL or (i)tFuMLuL < taFaMLuL

itṣirwil	(trousering)
itburṭum	(state of being cross)
iṭṭungur	(unwillingness to communicate)
Itfurṣux	(disengaging)

Common Forms of Nouns and Verbal Nouns in B

Below is a representative list of some of the most frequently recurring forms of nouns and verbal nouns in this dialect:

1.	FaML as in:	*ṭal*ᶜ	(spadix or spathe of the palm tree)			
		warč	(thigh)			
	FaMaL < FaML as in:	*faḥam*	(coal)		*baḥar*	(sea)
	FaMiL < FaML as in:	*bagil*	(clover)		*baṭin*	(stomach)
	FaMuL < FaML as in:	*gabur*	(grave)		*ṣadur*	(chest)

Two rare forms, probably arising from FaML, are *ṣidḥ* (roof) and *fugur* (poverty). Certain forms of the above have different realizations, with or without anaptyctic *u*.

Cf: *tamr* *tamur* (dates)

The anaptyctic *i*, such as in FaMiL forms is frequently met with, particularly in the vicinity of plosives like *g* and *ṭ*.

2.	FiML:	ᶜ*idg*	(bunch)	*jid*ᶜ	(stem)
	(i) FMuL< FiML:	*bsur*	(ripening dates)	*ḥbur*	(ink)
3.	FuML:	*xums*	(1/5th)	*ruxṣ*	(cheapness)
	FiML <FuML:	*ḍilm*	(injustice)	*filf*	(1/3rd)
	(i) FMiL <FuML:	*šġil*	(work)	*ḥzin*	(sorrow, grief)
4.	FaMLa:	*wajbe*	(meal)	*fahwa*	(unfulfilled wish)
		šahwa	(wish)	*gahwa*	(coffee)
5.	FaMLa:	*ga*ᶜ*de*	(sitting)	*daxle*	(entering)
		nazle	(descending)	*jalse*	(getting together)
6.	FiMLa:	*filga*	(half or slice)	*ni*ᶜ*me*	(blessing)
7.	FiMLi:	*ši*ᶜ*ri*	(certain, local fish)		
		jinni	(evil spirit)		
8.	FuMLa:	*ṣuxma*	(waist-coat)	*ḥurma*	(lady)
	FiMLa <FuMLa	*ḥijra*	(room)	*ġitra*	(head-cloth)
9.	FaMaL:	*gadam*	(a holy spot)	*xabar*	(news, information)

10.	FaMaLa:	*tanaka*	(tin)	*xalaga*	(a piece of cloth)
11.	FaMaaL:	*naxaal*	(sieving)	*zalaal*	(skimming)
		nagaay	(combing—of rice)		
		^{c}ajaan	(dough kneading)	*galaay*	(frying)
		ḥalaab	(milking)		
12.	(i) FMaaL<FiMaaL:	*šraa^{c}*	(sail)	*ḥbaal*	(rope)
13.	(i) FMaaL<FuMaaL:	*n^{c}aas*	(drowziness)	*zraar*	(button)
14.	(i) FMuuL< FuMuuL:	*^{c}yuun*	(eye)	*ġyuum*	(clouds)
15.	FaaMLa <FaaMiLa:	*xaaṣra*	(waist)	*faatḥa*	(mourning ritual)
		baarḥa	(last night)	*naaṣfa*	(15th of Ramaḍān)
16.	FaaMiL:	*^{c}aamil*	(worker)	*jaahil*	(child)
17.	FaMaaLa:	*nadaafa*	(cleanliness)	*baraaḥa*	(open enclosure)
		xaraaba	(ruins)	*gawaaya*	(boldness, impudence)
18.	(i) FMaaLe <FiMaaLa:	*glaafe*	(boat building)		
		ṣfaara	(copper-smithing)		
		ḥdaade	(black smithing)		
		ṭwaaše	(pearl dealing)		
	but note:	*nasaaje*	(weaving)		
19.	FaMiiL:	*ṣariix*	(screaming)	*ḍariiḥ*	(shrine)
		fariid < *ṯariid*	(meat and bread broth)		
20.	FaMiiLa:	*hariise*	(grain porridge)	*xabiiṣa*	(sweet made of flour, butter and sugar)
21.	FaMuuL:	*gaduu^{c}*	(food offered as entertainment)		
		sabuu^{c}	(one week)		
22.	(i) FMuuLa < FuMuuLa:	*xšuune*	(coarseness)		
		ḥmuuḍa	(sourness)		
	but note the preservation of the short unstressed *u* in the koine form: *xuṭuuba* (engagement)				
23.	FaMMaaL:	*^{c}akkaar*	(date planter)		
		bazzaaz	(cloth dealer)		
		baḥḥaar	(seaman)		
		jazzaaf	(bulk-buyer of fish, also retailer)		
24.	FiMMaaLa:	*šiddaaxa*	(mouse-trap)		
		millaale	(a pendant; a wooden frame for keeping fruit or vegetables)		
		sillaaye	(thorn; fish bone)		
25.	FiMMiiL:	*sikkiir*	(alcoholic)	*^{c}irbiid*	(libertine)
26.	FaaMuuL:	*ḥaaguul*	(eel)	*xaafuur*	(a protected seedling)
		jaaruur	(shelf, drawer)		
27.	MiFMaL:	*milfa^{c}*	(head veil),	*mišmar*	(head and shoulder veil)
		misnad	(wall pillow, used for reclining)		
		miḥmal	(ship)		
28.	miFMaaL:	*mišxaal*	(sieve)	*misbaaḥ*	(beads)
29.	taFMaaL:	*taswaat*	(making)		
		tawdaat	(delivering)		

taṣfaat (refining)
taxlaat (vacating, placing)

30. taFMiiL: *tagḍiib* (pruning)
tanbiit (the cutting of the branches from a date palm)
taḥdiir (clustering and lowering of branches)
tamšiiṭ (combing)
talgiim (feeding by bits)

31. taFMuuL: *ta^{c}luum* (teaching; training)
tasluum (handing over)
tajmuu^{c} (collecting; saving)
tamsuuḥ (rubbing, massaging)

32. FaMaLaan: *mayalaan* (slanting, sloping)
šayalaan (handling) *jayabaan* (bringing)
šarayaan (buying)

33. maFMuuL: *mačbuus* (local dish made with meat in the bottom of the pan, covered with rice on top)
mašmuum (myrtle)
mamruus (local sweets made with flour, butter and sugar)

34. (i) tFiMMiL < taFaMMuL: *it^{c}iddil* (tidying)
itbirriz (preparing, making ready)
itsinnid (placing on the floor or against the wall)

35. (i) tFeeMiL < taFaaMuL: *itbeexil* (stinginess)
itḥeeriṣ (meanness)

36. (i) tFiMLiL or (i) tFuMLuL < taFaMLuL:
itṣirwil (trousering)
itburṭum (state of being cross, grim faced)

37. FaMLiyya: *^{c}aṣriyye* (evening) *ṣubḥiyye* (morning)
ga^{c}diyye (sitting, sedentary)

38. FuuMaaL: *duulaab* (date garden) *juuraab* (socks)

39. (i)mFaaMaL < muFaaMaLa: *imkaafaḥ* (hard work, toil)
im^{c}aabal (diligence)
imraakaḍ (regular attendance)
imbaašar (care, attention)
im^{c}aadal (aligning, arranging)

The Broken Plural

A large number of classical forms of the broken plural are preserved in this dialect. Some have undergone certain changes which are set out below. Since *i* and *u* are regularly elided in open syllable FiMaaL loses the short unstressed vowel *i* as in FMaaL: and FuMuuL loses *u* as in FMuuL. The elision of the vowels *i* and *u* in open syllable is also a feature of the ^{c}Anazi forms of the same. In lit. Ar. FaMMaaL forms of nouns, when used for persons, normally take the sound plural terminations. In B, such nouns are treated as broken plurals, e.g.,

gallaaf galaaliif (boat builders)
baggaal bagaagiil (donkey drivers who sell local vegetables)
gaṣṣaab gaṣaaṣiib (butchers)

Among the triliteral forms, the following occur most frequently in speech:

(1)FMaaL, (i) FMuuL, FiMLaan, FuMLaan
Among the quadriliteral forms, the following occur frequently:
maFaaMiL, maFaaMiiL, FaMaaLiiL, FaMaayiL
Certain words have more than one broken plural in B, e.g.,

?araaḍi	*?araaḍiin*	(lands)
ṣufr	*ṣufraan*	(the yellow ones)
zill	*zawaali*	(rugs)
ni^{c}l	*ni^{c}le*	(sandals)

Except for final *imāla* of *a* to *e*, the lit. Ar. type ?aFMiLa remains stable. Cf:

?amṯile (proverbs, examples) *?ajwibe* (answers, responses)

Some ?aFMiLa forms also have free variants with the termination *-aat*. Cf:

?abniye *binaayaat* (buildings)

Lit Ar. forms that end in long *aa* are realized with a short *-e* < *-a*. Cf:

?aFMiLe, as in:	*?atqiye*	(pious people)
	?aš̌qiye	(mischievous persons)

Certain lit. Ar. forms of the type ?aFMiLa(a), exhibit shorter forms peculiar to this dialect. Cf:

ġinye	*?aġniyaa?*	(the rich)
ridye	*?ardiya*	(cloaks)

The following items are specimens of rare forms of the broken plural found in this dialect:

FaMLe:	*mawte*	(the deceased)
FuML:	*ġurb*	(strangers)
FiMLe:	*ḥible*	(ropes)
FaMiiL:	*ḥariim*	(ladies)
(i) FMiiL:	*(i) nxiil*	(date plantations)
FaMaaLL:	*maxaadd*	(pillows)

Common patterns of the broken plural in B

The table below sets out some of the commoner patterns of the broken plural in this dialect:

1. ?aFMaaL occurs as follows:
   (a) ?aFMaaL < FiML, as: *?as^{c}aar* (prices)
   (b) ?aFMaaL < FaML, as: *?awqaat* (times)
   (c) ?aFMaal < FuML, as: *?axmaas, ?asdaas;* as in *yiḍrub ?axmaas fi ?asdaas* (he is counting his 1/5ths and 1/6ths)
   (d) ?aFMaaL < FaMaL, as: *?aš̌jaar* (trees)

Note that *?a ^{c}maam* and *(i) ^{c}muum* (paternal uncle) are equally common in B. Also note that certain forms of the lit. Ar. broken plural ?aFMaaL are replaced by FiMLaan where hollow roots are involved. Thus:

looḥ	>	*liiḥaan*	(planks of wood) in place of	*?alwaaḥ*
baab	>	*biibaan*	(doors) in place of	*?abwaab*

But note: *?ačyaas* (bags).

2. ?aFMiL < ?aFMuL, as:	*?alsin*	(tongues)	*aŝhi/ur*	(months)
3. ?aFMiLa/e, as:	*?adwiye*	(medicine)	*?ad ^{c}iye*	(prayers)
	?anbiye	(prophets)	*?adkiye*	(intelligent)

Note that the B form *waadye* (regions and not valleys) in this dialect, replaces the classical from *?awdiya,* in rural forms of B. Cf:

fi hal-waadye (in these regions) inf. 6 Karrānah

Also note the occurrence in B of the old form *samaayid* (rubbish) for *?asmide.*

4. FaMaaLiL, as:	*?awaadim* (people)		*?ajaanib*	(aliens)
	^{c}amaayir (buildings)		*manaayir*	(minarets)

Note that *?amaakin* (places) is invariably realized *makaanaat* in B.

5. FaMaaLiiL, as:	*?abaariig*	(pitchers)		
	?ajaawiid	(virtuous people)		
6. (i) FMaL <FuMaL:	*ijfar*	(holes)	*iḥfar*	(pits, holes)

7. (i) FMaaL< FiMaaL:

(a) arising from a sing. FaML, as:	*člaab*	(dogs)
(b) arising from a sing. FaMaL, as:	*jbaal*	(mountains)
(c) arising from a sing. FaMLa, as:	*dlaal*	(coffee pots)

Also note that the Baharnah form *rjaal* (men) is realized *ryaayiil* in A.

8. (i) FMuuL < FuMuuL:	*ḍluu^{c}*	(ribs)	*gluub*	(hearts
	ġyuum	(clouds)	*njuum*	(stars)
9. FiMiL < FuMuL:	*kitib*	(books)	*midin*	(cities)
10. FaMaLa < FuMaLaa?:	*ŝaraka*	(partners)	*nazale*	(occupants, tenants)
FuMaLe < FuMaLaa?:	*wukale*	(agents)	*zu^{c}ame*	(leaders)

11. FiMLaan is related to certain singular patterns. Thus:

	Sing.	Pl.	
FaMaaL	*ġazaal*	*ġizlaan*	(deer)
FiMaaL	*jdaar*	*jidraan*	(walls)
FaMiiL	*ṣadiig*	*ṣidgaan*	(friends)

Or with hollow roots, as:

siibaan	(brooks)
xiilaan	(uncles from mother's side)
jiiraan	(neighbours)
niiraan	(fires)

Note that the form *niswaan*[12] (women), a common lexical feature of B, has the singular form *mara* or *ḥurma* (woman, lady) in this dialect.

12. FuMLaan is related to certain singular patterns. Thus:

	FaMuuL	*xaruuf*		*xurfaan*	(sheep)
	FaMaL	*balad*		*buldaan*	(countries)
	?aFMaL	*?aḥmar*		*ḥumraan*	(red)
	FaMiiL	*jafiir*		*jufraan*	(straw baskets)
13.	FiMMaaL:	*ḥijjaaj*	(pilgrims)	*tijjaar*	(merchants)
14.	FuMMaaL:	*ḥuwwaal*	(shifters)	*zuwwaar*	(visitors)
15.	FaMaaLi:	*šakaawi*	(complaints)	*gaḥaafi*	(local caps)
		ḥačaawi	(gossips)	*malaali*	(Mullas)

Specimens of the commoner forms of broken plurals derived from quadriliteral stems are given below:

1.	FaMaaLi/uL:	*baxaanug*	(head veils for young girls)	*maḥaabur*	(ink pots)
		mašaamur	(long veils for women)	*ġaḍaayur*	(bowls)
2.	FaMaaLila:	*baḥaarne*	(Baḥārnah)	*ṣaraawle*	(trousers)
3.	FaMaaLwa < FaMaaLiwa:	*^{c}akaarwa*	(date planters)		
		naxaawla	(attendants of date gardens)		
		dalaalwa	(brokers)	*ṭaraarwa*	(beggars)
4.	FaMaaLiiL:	*dawaaliib*	(date gardens)	*nawaaṭiir*	(sentries)
		sanaaniir	(cats)	*basaatiin*	(gardens)
5.	FaMaayiL:	*masaayil*	(affairs, issues)	*fasaayil*	(transplants)
6.	taFaaMiiL:	*taḥaariim*	(religious mournings)		
		taxaariif	(myths, tales)		
7.	maFaaMiL:	*mawaatim*	(Shī^{c}i places of assembly)		
		madaawis	(weaver's treadles)		
		maḥaamil	(ships)	*masaanid*	(wall-pillows)
8.	maFaaMiiL:	*masaabiiḥ*	(beads)	*mawaa^{c}iin*	(kitchenware)

Tanwīn (Nunation): an Archaic Feature Preserved in B

Nunation, a phonetic feature of classical Arabic, has survived in B. Two common forms occurring in this dialect are *-an* < *-an* and *-in* < *-an, -in, -un.*

The former is found, mainly, in koine forms, and the latter is peculiar to dialect forms. Nunation does not affect cardinals in this dialect. Examples of the commoner forms of these are given below:

-an is frequently met with in these koine forms:

ġaṣban ^{c}anni	(I couldn't help it)	*ṭab^{c}an*	(of course)
taqriiban	(approximately)	*maṯalan*	(for example)

-in corresponding to lit. Ar. *-un, -an, -in* is found in:

beetin ma^{c}muur	(may this house be blessed)
ḥajjatin maqbuule[13]	(I hope you have had a perfect pilgrimage)
ziyaaratin mabruuka	(I hope you had a blessed visit)

Also in:

waladin zeen	(a good lad)
ḥurmatin ?ajwadiyye	(a virtuous lady)
samačatin ṭariyye	(a freshly caught fish)

It should be noted that dialect *-in* is caseless, and that the adjectives collocating with nouns do not have the termination *-in,* even when they are non-pausal.

The Construct State

Masculine and feminine plural nouns that end in *-iin* and *-aat* remain unchanged in the construct state, e.g.,

masc. pl.	*mufattišiin il-baladiyye*	(municipality inspectors)
fem. pl.	*mudarrisaat il-ma^{c}aaruf*	(school mistresses of the Ministry of Education)

Dual nouns have no affixed forms and are replaced by a plural + the dual cardinal, as in:

?awlaade l-iṯneen fi l-midrase	(his two sons are at school)
banaate ṯ-ṯinteen fi l-beet	(his two daughters are at home)

but not:

waladeen ir-rajjaal

or *bitteen ir-rajjaal*

Feminine singular nouns and collectives that end in *-a* take *-t* in the construct, e.g.,

fem. sing.	*sayyaarat iš-šarika*	(the company car)
collective	*xammaamat il-baladiyye*	(the municipality sweepers)

In rural forms of B, the particle *taba^{c}* is often used to indicate a possessive relationship. Cf:

taba^{c} il-ḥukuuma	(of the Government)
taba^{c} iš-šarika	(of the company)

The particle *hagg* (for) is also used similarly:

m.s.	*ḥagg aḥmad*	(for Ahmad)
f.s.	*ḥagg amiine*	(for Amina)
m.pl.	*ḥagg il-jahaal*	(for the children)
f.pl.	*ḥagg il-banaat*	(for the girls)

The particles *raa^{c}i* and *r^{c}aat* (owner of) are also used similarly. Cf.

raa^{c}i t-tiksi	(owner of the taxi)
(i) r^{c}aat ittiksiyye	(owners of taxis)

The Comparison of Adjectives

The pattern of the elative in this dialect is ?aFMaL, usually with *min* (than). Thus:

hal-xalag ?aškal min daak	(this garment is better than that)
?il-^{c}ood ?arzan min iṣ-ṣaġiir	(the elder is more composed than the younger)
l-idraaz ?ašraḥ min is-sanaabis	(Dirāz is pleasanter than Sanābis)

The elative of adjectives is found with all numbers and genders. Cf:

?il-walad ?akbar min l-ibnayye	(the boy is older than the girl)
?il-banaat ?agwa min l-awlaad	(the girls are stronger than the boys)

The superlative is normally expressed by placing the elative form of the adjective in a construct relation with the noun or pronominal suffix, as:

?abrak	(most auspicious day)
?a^{c}galhum	(the wisest among them)

The form *min* ?aFMaL *maa,* a common feature of the superlative usage in this dialect, is found in:

min abda^{c} maa yumkin	(one of the best)
min arxaṣ maa yumkin	(the cheapest available)

The Numerals

The cardinals one to ten

Below, are the cardinals from one to ten:

	with masc. *nouns*	*with* fem. *nouns*
1	*waaḥid*	*waḥde*
2	*?iṯneene*	*ṯinteen*
3	*ṯalaaṯe*	*ṯalaaṯ*
4	*?arba^{c}a*	*?arba^{c}*
5	*xamse*	*xams/xamis*
6	*sitte*	*sitt*
7	*sab^{c}a*	*sab^{c}/sabi^{c}*
8	*ṯamaanye*	*ṯamaan*
9	*tis^{c}a*	*tisi^{c}*
10	*^{c}ašara*	*^{c}ašir*

It should be noted that it is the urban forms of B which exhibit the structure FaML as in *sab^{c}* (seven) whereas in rural forms of the same, they are realized with the anaptyctic *i*. Cf:

sabi^{c}	*xamis*

ṯ can be replaced by *f* in all the forms above, as in *falaafe* (three).
waaḥid and *waḥde* always denote an indefinite number, e.g.,
looḥin waaḥid (one plank of wood) or *beeḍa waḥde* (one egg).
The masculine counterpart of the above, i.e., *ḥaadi* has wider currency in daily speech. Cf:

?il-yoom ḥaadi min rabii^{c} l-awwal (today is the first of Rabī^{c} al-Awwal—3rd month of the Muslim year)

Or as in these common phrases:

ḥaadi	*š-šahar*	(first day of the month)
tawaali	*š-šahar*	(last days of the month)

The numerals from three to nine

Masculine nouns, from 3 to 9, take the fem. form of the numerals; and feminine nouns are associated with the masc. form of the numerals as in:

	numeral + fem. pl.		numeral + masc. pl.
3 papers	*ṯalaaṯ waragaat*	3 boys	*ṯalaatat awlaad*
4 women	*?arba^c niswaan*	4 men	*?arba^{c}at irjaal*
5 cars	*xams sayyaaraat*	5 Dinars	*xamsat danaaniir*
6 tables	*sitt ṭaawilaat*	6 shirts	*sittat qumṣaan*
7 pommegranates	*sab^c rummaanaat*	7 thousand	*sab^{c}at aalaaf*
8 times	*ṯamaan marraat*	8 gardeners	*ṯamaanyat zaraarii^c*
9 pieces	*tisi^c ḥabbaat*	9 pens	*tis^{c}at aglaam*

Note that all the *ṯ* sounds above can be replaced by *f* by the majority of speakers.

Collective nouns, whose grammatical gender is fem. viz. those that end in the fem. suffix *-a/e* as, e.g., *sammaače* (fisher folk) and whose singular form is masculine, are associated with fem. numerals. Cf.

sab^{c}at ḥammaara	(seven donkey drivers)
falaafat xammaama	(three sweepers)
?arba^{c}at hanaadwa	(four Indians)

The cardinals eleven to nineteen

In pause, cardinals from eleven to nineteen normally take the following forms:

11	*?iḥda^{c}aš*
12	*?iṯna^{c}aš*
13	*ṯalatta^{c}aš*
14	*?arbaata^{c}aš*
15	*xamsta^{c}aš*
16	*sitta^{c}aš*
17	*sabaata^{c}aš*
18	*ṯamanta^{c}aš*
29	*tsaata^{c}aš*

Note that there is a strong tendency to realize non-emphatic *t* of *ṯalatta^{c}as* as emphatic *ṭ*, this also affects the quality of the front vowel *a* changing it to a fully back vowel, as, e.g. *ṯalɑṭṭɑ^{c}aš*.

The above applies to numbers from thirteen to nineteen.

Whereas in pause Arabic *^{c}ašar* is contracted to *^{c}aš*, in collocation with nouns, the longer form, with the loss of Arabic unstressed short *a*, is retained:

?iḥda^{c}šar nafar	(eleven persons)
xamsta^{c}šar waaḥid	(fifteen persons)

The numerals twenty to ninety

The above are normally realized with the morpheme *-iin*, in or out of liaison:

20	*^{c}išriin*	20	*ṯalaaṯiin*
40	*?arbi^{c}iin*	50	*xamsiin*
80	*ṯamaaniin*	90	*tis^{c}iin*

In rural B, in the case of eighty, palatal *y* is inserted before *-iin* such as:

ṯamaanyiin (eighty)

Note that the above numerals can appear in definite constructions, such as:

bil-^{c}išriin wiṯ-ṯalaaṯiin (by twenties and thirties)

Numbers above a hundred

١٠٠	*imye*
200	*imyateen*
300	*ṯalaaṯimye*
400	*?arba^{c}imye*
1,000	*?alf*
2,000	*?alfeen*
3,000	*ṯalaaṯat aalaaf*
9,000	*tis^{c}at aalaaf*

The above can appear in definite contexts such as:

waṣalaw l-imyateen (they rose to two hundred)

The ordinals one to ten

The ordinal *ḥaadi* (first) is more common than the koine form *?awwal* in daily speech in B. *?awwal* (first) and *?uula* (i.e., fem. counterpart of the former) show the influence of the schools particularly in the expression: *ṭala^{c} l-awwal* (he was first in his class)) or *ṭala^{c}at il-?uula* (she was first (in her class)).

The table below sets out the ordinals from one to ten:

	masc.	fem.
1st	*ḥaadi/?awwal*	*?uula*
2nd	*ṯaani*	*ṯaanye*
3rd	*ṯaaliṯ*	*ṯaalṯe*
4th	*raabu^{c}*	*raab^{c}a*
5th	*xaamis*	*xaamse*
6th	*saatt*	*saatte*
7th	*saabi^{c}*	*saab^{c}a*
8th	*ṯaamin*	*ṯaamne*
9th	*ṯaasi^{c}*	*taas^{c}a*
10th	*^{c}aašur*	*^{c}aašra*

The Personal Pronouns

Rural and urban speakers of B employ more or less similar forms of the personal pronouns. Forms such as 2 f.s. *?intiin/e* (you) and 2 c.pl. *?intuun/e* (you) are found in both. In B, first person masculine singular and first person feminine singular have two distinct forms; whereas in A one form is common to both. Plural forms of the personal pronouns are of common gender both in A and B, though each employs its own distinctive form.

Singular forms of the personal pronouns, both in A and B, are set out below:

	B	A		B	A
1 m.s.	*?ane*	*ααne*	1 f.s.	*?ani*	*?ααne*
2 m.s.	*?inte*	*?inte*	2 f.s.	*?intiin/?intiine*	*?intay*
3 m.s.	*hu (u)*	*?uhwa*	3 f.s.	*hi (i)*	*?ihya*

Note the use of the fully back vowel *αα* in the ᶜAnazi forms above; and the effect of the guttural *h* on the syllable structure of the 3 m/f.s. ᶜAnazi forms above. The pl. forms corresponding to the above are:

	B	A
1 c.pl.	*?iḥne*	*ḥinne/?iḥne*
2 c.pl.	*?intuun/?intuune*	*?intaw*
3 c.pl.	*hum*	*?uhma*

Note that the form 3 c.pl. *-hem* is invariably found in liaison with other items.

The pronominal suffixes[14]

Urban B, i.e, the Manāmah dialect of B, and the villages employ the same forms of the pronominal suffixes except for 3. c.pl. which has the free variant *-hem* in rural speech, used interchangeably with *-hum*. Sitrah islanders have slightly different forms characterized by the affrication of Manāmah *-k* to *-č* in all numbers and genders. The 2 f.s. has two realizations in Sitrah speech viz. *-(e)š* and *-eč*, depending upon the speaker's village of origin. *-(e)š* is found in Khārjiyyah, whereas *-ec* is used in Markuban.

Below, are the pronominal suffixes found both in A and B. Cf:

	rural and urban B	A	Sitrah Islanders
1 c.s.	*-i*	*-i*	*-i*
2 m.s.	*-(u) k*	*-(i) k*	*-eč*
2 f.s.	*-(i) š*	*-ič*	*-(e)š/-eč*
3 m.s.	*-eh*	*-eh*	*-eh*
3 f.s.	*-he*	*-he*	*-he*
1 c.pl.	*-ne*	*-ne*	*-ne*
2 c.pl.	*-kum, -čem*	*-kum*	*-čem*
3 c.pl.	*-hum, -hem*	*-hum*	*-hem*

Note that *h* of 3 m.s. suffix *-eh* is with majority of Manāmah speakers realized *-e;* it is retained, however, in rural B, as in:

Manāmah *raase* (his head) realized *raaseh* in rural B. Also, note that 2 c.pl. *-čem* is mainly found in Sitrah speech and occasionally in Shahrakkān village and the adjoining areas.

Cf. these examples from rural and Sitrah B:

ḥillaanhem	(their personal belongings) inf. 6 Damistān
?aḥaačihem	(I talk to them) inf. 6 Damistān
šiġilhem	(their job) inf. 7 Shahrakkān
zamaanhem	(their time) inf. 7 Shahrakkān
inbiiᶜhem	(we sell them) inf. 4 Bani Jamrah
tiᶜṭiič	(she gives you) inf. 22 Sitrah
beetčem	(your house) inf. 22 Sitrah

The particle *iyya*+pronominal suffixes

A classical Arabic feature, viz. *w + ?iyya*+pron. suff., where the *w* is the *wāw al-ma*^{c}*iyyah*, is preserved in B. It occurs with all persons and numbers. Thus:

3 m.s.	*wiyyaah*	(with him)	3 c.pl.	*wiyyaahum*	(with them)
3 f.s.	*wiyyaaha*	(with her)	2 c.pl.	*wiyyaakum*	(with you)
2 m.s.	*wiyyaak*	(with you)	1 c.pl.	*wiyyaanne*	(with us)
2 f.s.	*wiyyaaš*	(with you)			
1 c.s.	*wiyyaayi*	(with me)			

The reflexive pronouns *nafs* and *ruuḥ*

nafs and *ruuḥ* are interchangeably used to mean "self" in B. Often they are used in association with the personal pronouns, such as:

3 m.s.	*hu b-nafse maa yidri*	(he does not know himself)
3 f.s.	*hi b-nafishe maa tidri*	(she does not know herself)
2 m.s.	*?inte b-nafsuk maa tidri*	(you do not know yourself)
2 f.s.	*?intiine b-nafsiš maa tidriin*	(you do not know yourself)
1 m.s.	*?ane b-nafsi maa-dri*	(I do not know myself)
1 f.s.	*?ani b-nafsi maa-dri*	(I do not know myself)
3 c.pl.	*hum ib-nafishum maa yidruun*	(they don't know themselves)
2 c.pl.	*?intuune b-nafiskum maa tidruun*	(you don't know yourselves)
1 c.pl.	*?iḥne b-nafisne maa nidri*	(we don't know ourselves)

maal and *maalat* as possessive pronouns

The possessive pronoun *maal/maalat* (belongs to, owned by) is often found in liaison with the pronominal suffixes, such as:

	when the item concerned is masc.		or feminine
3 m.s.	*maale (h)*	(his)	*maalate(h)*
3 f.s.	*maalhe*	(hers)	*maalathe*
2 m.s.	*maaluk*		*maalatk*
2 f.s.	*maališ*		*maalatš*
1 c.s.	*maali*		*maalati*
3 c.pl.	*maalhum*		*maalathum*
2 c.pl.	*maalkum*		*maalatkum*
1 c.pl.	*maalne*		*maalatne*

A similar usage prevails for the possessive pronoun *ḥagg* (for, belongs to) which is also found in association with the pronominal suffixes such as:

3 m.s.	*ḥaggah*		3 f.s.	*ḥaggha*
2 m.s.	*ḥagguk*		2 f.s.	*ḥaggiš*
1 c.s.	*ḥaggi,*	etc.		

In addition to the above, *maal* can appear with nouns to mean "belonging to" or "owned by" as in:

ktaab maal aḥmad (Aḥmad's book)

A Baḥārnah villager

A Baḥārnah gardener displaying his tools

Ḥajji ᶜAli ᶜAbdalla Nijim at his ground-loom in Bani Jamrah

A fisherman in the process of finishing a wire trap

Fishermen from the village of Dirāz

Traditional houses of Baḥrain

Other traditional houses (of Baḥrain)

Demonstrative pronouns

Below appear the demonstratives such as employed in rural and urban B:

	nearness		remoteness	
m.s.	*hay/haade/de*	(this)	*ha(a) daak/daak/haak/haaka*	(that)
f.s.	*haadi/di*		*ha(a) diik/diik/heek/heeka/heeki*	

Note that *haak/haaka/heek/heeka* are met with in Dirāzi women's speech only. The suffix *-a/i* is added when the demonstrative is used to refer to prersons, as in:

	remoteness		
	objects	persons	
m.s.	*haak*	*haaka*	(that)
f.s.	*heek*	*heeka/heeki*	(that)

The ^{c}Anazi forms of the demonstratives are:

m.s.	*haay/haaḏi/ḏi*	(this)	*haḏaak/ḏaak*	(that)
f.s.	*haaḏi/ḏi*		*haḏiič/ḏiič*	

d and *ḏ* are used interchangeably in the ^{c}Anazi forms above. Short and long forms are equally common both in A and B. The long *aa* of the open syllable *haa-* is often shortened to *ha-* both in A and B.

The plural forms of the demonstratives are, both in A and B, of common gender. Cf:

those indicative of near objects:

	A		B	
c.pl.	*haḏeele/ḏeele*	(these)	*hadeleen/deleen*	(these)
	haḏoole/haḏool	(these)	*hadoole*	(these)

those indicative of remote objects:

c.pl.	*haḏelaak/ḏelaak*	(those)	*hadelaak/delaak*	(those)
			hadoolaak	(those)

Note that the *oo* of *hadoole* and *hadoolaak* is often diphthongized to *aw* in rural forms of B. as: *hadawle* and *hadawlaak*

The demonstrative *haade* (this) is often contracted to *ha-*, as in:

har-rajjaal	(this man)
hal-mara	(this woman)

Often, the prefix *ha-* of the demonstrative *haččidi* is dropped, as in:

čidi (like this) *čidaak* (like that)

The demonstrative of place

The following forms of the above demonstratives recur in B:

ihni(i)/ihna	(here)	ihnaak/ihnaaka (there)
minni/minne < *min ihni*	(from here)	
minnaak < *min ihnaak*	(from there)	

The forms: *ihna,ihnaaka,* and *minne* are found in rural B only.

The demonstratives in liaison with pronominal suffixes

Demonstratives in liaison with pron. suff. are common both in A and B. Both in A and B different forms of these are employed. Cf:

near persons or objects:

	B		A
3 m.s.	*haadahu*	(this is him, it)	*kaahwa*
3 f.s.	*haadahi*		*kaahya*
2 m.s.	*hadante*		*kaante*
2 f.s.	*hadantiin*		*kaantay*
1 m.s.	*hadaane*		*kaane*
1 f.s.	*hadaani*		*kaane*
3 c.pl.	*haadahum*		*kaahma*
2 c.pl.	*hadantuun*		*kaantaw*
1 c.pl.	*hadaḥne*		*kaaḥne*

for far persons or objects:

3 m.s.	*hadakku, hakku*	(that is him, it)	*kaahwa*
3 f.s.	*hadakki, hakki*		*kaahya*
3 c.pl.	*hadakkum, hakkum*		*kaahma*

Note above that the ^{c}Anazi forms for near and far persons or objects are the same.

The relative pronoun *?illi*

The relative *?illi* (which, who) is of common gender in B:

masc.	*šahr illi ngaḍa*	(the month that elapsed)
	sabuu ^{c} illi raaḥ	(the week that elapsed)
fem.	*?il- ?arḍ illi btaa ^{c}at*	(the land which was sold)
	?is-sayyaara lli nda ^{c}amat	(the car which had an accident)

Particles

Prepositions

Both types of prepositions i.e., separable and inseparable units are found in B.

Separable units: the most recurring forms of these are: *b-, ?ila, ^{c}ala, ^{c}an, fi, min, janb, ^{c}ugub, ba ^{c}ad, ^{c}alašaan, ḥagg*

These are used as follows:

?ila (for), as:	*haade ?ila ?aḥmad*	(this is for Aḥmad)
la < *?ila*, as:	*haade la-xtuk*	(this is for your sister)
^{c}*ala* (on), as:	*ṣallu* ^{c}*ala n-nabi*	(say your prayers; cool down)

^{c}*an* (of, about), as: *yirwoon* ^{c}*an ?amiir il-muumniin*
(it is said of Imam ^{c}Ali (Commander of the Faithful))
fi (in), as: *axuuyi fi l-midrase* (my brother is at school)
min (from) as in this proverbial expression:
min foog hallahalla, min taḥat yi^{c}*lam alla*
(lib. God knows what is beneath this neat appearance, viz., appearances are deceitful)
(*n*) of *min* is more often assimilated in liaison with (*l*). Cf:
mil-leel laṣ-ṣubḥ (from night to morning)
^{c}*ugub* (after, later), as: *haade* ^{c}*ugub daak* (this comes after that)
ba^{c}*ad* (also), as: *?iḥne ba*^{c}*ad* . . . (we also . . .)
^{c}*alašaan* (for the sake of), as ^{c}*alašaan* ^{c}*een tikram ?alf* ^{c}*een* (for the sake of one person (loved-admired) I will please a thousand)

^{c}*ind* (with), as:	*l-iktaab* ^{c}*indi*	(the book is with me)
	l-iktaab ^{c}*indiš*	(the book is with you)
miṯil (as, like), as	*haade miṯil daak*	(this is like that)

Examples of prepositions with affixed pronominal suffixes are:

	b + pron. suff.		*l* + pron. suff.
3 m.s.	*beh*	(with him/it)	*leh*
3 f.s.	*ibhe*		*leehe*
2 m.s.	*buk*		*luk*
2 f.s.	*biš*		*liš*
1 c.s.	*bi*		*li*
3 c.pl.	*ibhum*		*leehum*
2 c.pl.	*ibkum*		*leekum*
1 c.pl.	*ibne*		*leenne*

Note the use of prosthetic *i*, particularly in the plural forms above.

Adverbial particles

Adverbial particles figure largely in daily speech. Some common forms of these are:

those indicating present time :

kill-yoom	(every day);	*kill-saa*^{c}*a*	(every hour);
kill-wakt	(any time).	*?al-ḥiin*	(now)

These can appear in initial or final position in a construction. Cf:

?al-ḥiin maa niḥtaaj	(we don't need them now)
imgaffuḍ al-ḥiin	(he is closed now)

(indicating emphasis)	init.	*kill-yoom yaaxid diinaar* (every day he takes a dinar)
	fin.	*yaaxid diinaar kill-yoom*

Note that Sitrah form of the above is invariably *čill-yoom.*

those indicating past time:

gabl iš̌wayy	(a moment ago);	*?il-baarḥa*	(last night);
?ams	(yesterday);	*?awwal-ams*	(day before yesterday);
baarḥat l-uule	(last night);	*?il-la ^{c}aam*[15]	(last year).

these indicate future:

han-nooba	(next time)	*door is-sane*	(after this year)
raas iš-šahar	(opening days of the month)		
tawaali ša ^{c}baan	(the end of Sha ^{c}bān)		

The adverbial particle *taww* (just, now) in these examples is regularly followed by participials:

tawwa	*gaa ^{c}id*	(he has just woken up)
tawne	*mwaṣliin*	(we have just arrived)

In the following example, *taww* is used interjectively:

tawhum biruuḥuun! (just now they are setting off ! i.e., they are late)

Often, the adverbial particle *taww* (just, now) is followed by the imperfect, as in:

tawwa yaakil	(he is just eating)
tawne nit ^{c}ašše	(we are just having supper)

The adverbial particle ^{c}*ajal* (so):

^{c}*ajal* is, in these negated constructions, employed to confirm a previous statement:

^{c}*ajal maa bijji?*	(So you are not coming then ?)
^{c}*ajal maa saafart?*	(So you have not travelled then?)

The adverbial particle ^{c}*aad* (make sure) is used in the following imperative constructions to confirm or emphasize a statement. It may begin or end a statement, as in:

^{c}*aad, dawwur ši z-zeen, laa yġiššuunuk* (make sure you choose the good ones, don't let them cheat you)

or in: *laa tinse ^{c}aad* (make sure you don't forget)

^{c}*aad* with the imperative may be used to mean "please". Cf:

^{c}*aad* ^{c}*iṭni šwayy*	(please, give me some)
saa ^{c}idni fi š-šeel ^{c}aad	(help me in lifting please)

Adverbs of place, such as appearing below, are very frequent, Cf:

minni	(here)	*ihni*	(here)	*minnaak*	(there)
ihnaak	(there)	*ṣoob*	(towards)	*mgaabil*	(opposite)

Note that often the Manamah form *ihni* is realized *ihne* in rural forms of B.

Conjunctions

(a) Conditional conjunctions
Below are some of the commoner forms of conditional conjunctions:

?in,	*?in gadart marreet ^{c}aleek*	(if I am able, I shall look in)
?inčaan,	*?inčaan wudduk, ḥayyaak*	(if you like, come along)
?illa ?ida,	*?illa ?ida maṭarat, ma-ḥne raayḥiin*	(only if it rains, we shall not go)
?amma,	*?amma l-yoom yaa baačir*	(either today or tomorrow)
?aw,	*?aw is-sabt, ?aw il-laḥad*[16]	(either Saturday or Sunday)
lo(o),	*lo ?adri maa riḥt*	(had I known I wouldn't have gone)
ḥatte,	*ḥatte yinbit, laazim tisgiih kill-yoom*	(in order that it grows, you should water it daily)
leekaan,	*leekaan il-^{c}ood maa gadar, čeef iṣ-ṣaġiir?*	(if the elder couldn't do it, how could the younger?)

(b) Conjunctions as connectives

laakin (but), as in:	*waṣṣeete laakin nase*	(I reminded him but he forgot)
?u (and), as in:	*ṭabaxne ^{c}eeš ?u samač*	(we cooked rice and fish)

Conjunctions as adverbs

ba^{c}deen	(later):	*xalle la ba^{c}deen*	(leave it to some other time)
taali	(afterwards):	*bašuufuk taali*	(I shall see you later)

Interjections
Some common examples of such usage are:

bass	as in:	*bass iḥne maa dareene*	(only but we did not know!)
šuuf. . . weeš	(look, what!) as in:	*šuufi weeš jaayib!*	(look what he has brought!)

maa baġa (wouldn't), interjective *maa* is often used with the perfect verb *baġa* in exclamatory contexts. The paradigm below illustrates its occurrence:

3 m.s.	*maa baġa y-ji!*	(wouldn't he have wanted to come!)
3 f.s.	*maa baġat itji!*	
2 m.s.	*maa baġeet itji!*	
2 f.s.	*maa baġeetiin itjiin!*	
3 c.pl.	*maa baġaw ijuun!*	
2 c.pl.	*maa baġeetuun itjuun!*	

Note that the *t* in the above examples, is often totally assimilated by the *g*. Thus *itji* *ijji*. The interjective particle *čeef čaan!?* (how come!?) is regularly followed by the perfect in interjective usage. Cf:

čeef čaan bayyan!	(how come he came!?)
čeef čaan maar ᶜaleenne!	(how come you paid us a visit!?)

Interrogative particles

Some of the common interrogative particles in B are:

čeef (how), as: *čeef bitruuḥ?* (how will you to (there) ?)
čamm (how much/many). Cf. also *čammin waaḥid?* (how many?, masc, and *čammin waḥde?* (fem.)
weeš lit. Ar. *wa-?ayyu šay?* (what), as:
weeš fiik? (what is wrong with you?);
weešhu? (what is it?)
leeš *li-?ayyi šay?* (why), as:
leeš maa jiit? didn't you come?)
min (who), as: *min gaal luk?* (who told you?)
or, *minhu?* (who (is it)?)
la < *?il a* (to, for), as *la-ween?* (where to?)
mate (when), as: *mate s-safar?* (when will you travel?)
(i)b-čam (for how much?), as: *(i) bčam ?axadte?* (for how much did you buy it?)
?ayy (which), as *?ayy waaḥid?* *?ayy waḥde* (which one?: masc. and fem respectively);
?ayyhu, ?ayyhi (which one?: masc. and fem. respectively).
ḥagg weeš (what for?), as: *ḥagg weeš maa jiit? ḥagg weeš maa jiitiin?* (why didn't you come? masc. and fem. respectively.
maa (haven't, don't (you)), as:
maa riḥt il-midrase? (haveen't you been to school?)
maa tubġi? (don't you want?)

Two common particles found in A, to the exclusion of B, are *šuule* (why?) and *wara* (why?). In B, alternative particles are found as in:

A: *šuule/wara maa yiit?* (why didn't you come?)
B: *leeš/ḥagg weeš maa jiit?*

NOTES:

1. The regular employment of *kasra* for classical Arabic *fatḥa* in the imperfect preformatives in B above, is, we are told (*Lisān*, vol. 20, p. 283) a linguistic peculiarity of the tribes: Qais, Tamīm, Asad, and Rabīᶜa; only the Hijāzis and some members of al-Hawāzin, the Azd of Sarāt and Hudhayl, retain the classical *fatḥa* in the above forms. This phonetic feature is called *taltalat Bahrā?* after the Bahrā? tribe of Quḍāᶜah, says Anīs in *Fi al-Lahajāt al-ᶜArabiyyah*, p. 139.
2. The ᶜAnazi forms of the above are invariably *ye* and *yiit*.
3. The ᶜAnazi form of the above is *?ayyisaw*.
4. The above forms are equally common.

5. Perfect forms such as are used in B are not found in A, though occasionally they may appear in ^{c}Anazi speech as borrowings from B. However, in A alternative usages are found, as:

gaal yabbi	(he said he wanted)
čaan ?abi	(I wanted)
kinne nabbi	(we wanted)

6. See *EADS*, p. 45.
7. Ibid.
8. See *WGAL*, Part II, p. 143.
9. Al-Muslim, M.S. in his *Sāḥil adh-Dhahab al-Aswad*, p. 147, expresses the view that the suffix *-oo* is a reflex of anti-Portuguese feelings. The Portuguese ruled over the islands from 1521 to 1602, i.e., just over 80 years. Jayakar in *ODA*, Part I, pp. 654–5, notes the occurrence of the above *-oo* in ^{c}Umāni Arabic.
10. In *WGAL* the above type is given under form XXI. See part II, p. 111.
11. Reinhardt mentions it for the Bani Kharūṣ dialect (op. cit., p. 4); Landberg notes it in Ḥaḍrami (*Études*, vol. I, p. 393); Rhodokanakis, for Ẓafāri (op. cit., vol. II, p. 153); Rossi for Ṣan^{c}āni Arabic (*Appunti*, p. 249); (*L'Arabo Parlato*, p. 30); and finally Johnstone for Dōsiri dialect of Kuwait (Article, *BSOAS* vol. XXIV, Part II, 1961) and the majority of east Arabian dialects (*EADS*, p. 45).
12. Also found in Ṣan^{c}ā speech, Rossi, *L'Arabo Parlato*, p. 14.
13. Such greeting terms as this and the following one are conferred upon a *ḥaajj* (pilgrim) or a *zaayir* (i.e., somebody who has just visited the shrines of *Shī^{c}i* Imāms) immediately after his safe return.
14. See Map IX, Appendices.
15. Viz. *^{c}aam* with a reduplicated *l* deriving from the article.
16. Lit. Ar. *al-?aḥad.*

Part IV
Some syntactic features

Generally speaking, this part of the study is concerned with (a) the peculiarities that set the syntax of B as against other dialects, and (b) what local variations, viz. inter-dialectal features, there are and how they function.

More specifically, this section examines the grammatical functions performed by perfect and imperfect verbs in B, and the positional permutations that these can asssume in relation to other items in a given structure. Also, among the items considered in this section are: the regular appearance of the particle *lakid* < *laqad* (already, etc); *baruuḥ, raayiḥ,* in verbal constructions; and the use of the imperfect verb *iji* as an adverbial particle to mean "for, about"; interrogative particles; relative pronouns; compounds such as interrogative particle + pron. suff., viz., *weešhu?, weešhi?;* local peculiarities such as *ḥagg weeš?, min weeš?* in B, and *šuule?, wara?* in A; the classical Arabic interrogative particle *?ayy;* and the employment in sentence final positions of a rising *-é?* to indicate questions, a feature peculiar to Umāni and Baḥrāni Arabic and not reported elsewhere.

Also treated are: concord in relation to the concept of definiteness and indifiniteness; gender and number concord; the employment of intensifiers such as *waajid* and *killiš* in adjectival structures; negated forms of the pronouns, viz *ma(a)hu* and *ma(a) hi,* and their shorter counterparts *mu(u)* and *mi(i);* the preservation in B of an old Arabic feature, namely *iyya* + pron. suff.; the conditional sentences; and the verbal permutations in the protasis and apodosis of conditional sentences.

The Verb

The perfect

The perfect, in this dialect, is used mainly to indicate an act accomplished in the past. It can occur in sentence-initial, and post-nominal positions. Thus[1]

a)	*?ištaġalt fi š-šarika xams isniin*	(I worked with the Company (i.e., BAPCO) for five years)
b)	*killhum raaḥaw sawa*	(They all left together)

In negated constructions, the perfect invariably follows the negative particle, as in:

ba ᶜde maa je	(he hasn't arrived yet)
maa sa?al ᶜannuk	(he hasn't asked about you)
maa šifte	(I haven't seen him)

In optative constructions, the perfect may appear either with or without a particle. In the examples below, where the particles yaa *reet* and loo are used, the perfect is in a post-particle position. Cf:

yaa reetik kint ḥaaḍir	(I wish you were present)
lo (o) zeen jiit	(I wish you had come)

Again, in optative constructions, in which the perfect is employed without a particle, it is often found in sentence initial position, such as:

	ṣaaḥabatk issalaame	(may safety be yours (i.e., may you be preserved))
or	*ḥafaḍk aḷḷa*	(God save you)

The emphatic particle *lakid*[2] (already, etc.), arising from lit. Ar. *laqad*, systematically precedes the perfect form of verbs, such as:

maa ṭala ᶜt waraah, lakid raaḥ (when I went after him, he had already gone)

Often, *lakid* in the above sentence, can be separated from the perfect by an adverbial phrase viz., *min zamaan* (a long time ago):

maa waṣal, lakid min zamaan akalne w-itgahweene
(when he came, we had long ago eaten and drunk our coffee)

Note the employment of *maa* meaning "when" in the constructions above.

Finally, when giving instructions, as in the following construction where the speaker is explaining how to grow lucerne, the perfect may appear where the imperative is expected:

it ᶜaddil il-maḥal, ?ileen ᶜaddalte ?u naḍḍafte ḥaṭṭeet samaad, ?u sageete door . . . dooreen . . . (you prepare the place (i.e., the land), then when you have prepared it and cleaned it, you add manure and you water it once or twice. . .)

This is virtually a conditional construction.

The imperfect

The imperfect in B, as in other dialects of Arabic, is employed for various grammatical functions. Chief among these is to denote a habitual action, as in this description from a gardener describing his customary activities:

in ᶜaabil il-?arḍ ?u nisgi z-zarᶜ, ?u njizz gatt . . .
(we till the soil, water the plant, and cut lucerne)

It is also used to make a statement of fact, as:

yig ᶜid min ġubše	(he wakes up at daybreak (i.e., very early)
?issaa ᶜa sitt iruuḥ l-išġil	(he goes to work at six o'clock)

In conjunction with an adverbial particle the imperfect in the following construction denotes continuity or progression of action:

?al-ḥiin yištiġil, maa b-yigdar išuufuk
(he is working now so he won't be able to attend to you)

In conjunction with *b(-)* the imperfect in the following constructions is employed to indicate a future action:

baruuḥ is-suug baštari samač (I am going to the market to buy fish)
and *baačir bisaafruun il-ḥijjaaj* (the pilgrims will travel tomorrow)

The imperfect may also appear in optative structures, in which case it regularly follows the subject of the sentence as in these common expressions:

?aḷḷa yiḥfaḍk min iš-šarr wiḍ-ḍarr
(May God guard you against evil and harm)

or in *?aḷḷa iṭawwil ^{c}umruk* (May god give you longer life).The imperfect can occur in sentence-final position when a purpose is to be expressed, such as:

šiil l-iskaar, ^{c}alašaan il-maay imurr
(remove the stopper, in order that water can pass)
?ilbas ṣuuf, ḥatte laa tubrad
(get dressed in wool, lest you should feel cold)

A perfect preceding a following imperfect, indicating intentions, is found in these common constructions:

raaḥ yixruf l-irṭab	(he has gone to pick dates)
gaam iṣalli	(he has got up to pray)
ga ^{c}ad yiḥsib	(he has settled down to count)

Note that the items *raaḥ, gaam, ga ^{c}ad,* as used in the above sentences are very common in daily speech.

The use of the imperfect verb *iji* (for about, since) as an adverbial particle
iji in the following examples functions as an adverbial particle:

iji šahar al-ḥiin maa šifnaah	(we have not seen him for about a month now)
iji sabuu ^{c} min saafar	(it has been a week now, since he left)

The imperative
Besides the normal uses of the imperative, it can occur in reported speech in a sequence of perfect verbs, in which case it does not function as an imperative in the normal sense,[3] e.g.

ba ^{c}id maa ?akalaw, raaḥaw ^{c}adaari, nazalaw yitsabbaḥoon, xid ruuḥuk inte ba ^{c}ad u nuṭṭ min foog, fi saa ^{c}ateh t ^{c}awwar u waddooh il-ḥakiim
(after they had eaten they went to ^{c}Adāri pool, (just as) they started swimming, you take yourself (i.e., what does he do but take himself) and jump from a height, immediately he injured himself and was taken to hospital)

The active participle

A feature commonly met with in B is the occurrence of two successive participials the former invariably having the nunation *in*, e.g.

gaayimin gaa ^{c}*id*	(standing up and sitting down—said of a boy who cannot settle in one place)
maakilin šaarub	(eating and drinking—said of an unproductive person)
daaxilin ṭaali ^{c}	(coming in and going out—said of a mischievous boy)

The employment of participials to indicate past or future time

As in all Arabic dialects the active participle most frequently indicates a past action the effect of which lasts up to the time of speaking. Often, however, the participles of verbs of motion such as *raayiḥ* and *jaay* are employed to indicate an immediate future. In this usage *jaay* and *raayiḥ* maintain their concordial relationship with the preceding subject, e.g.,

2 m.s.	*?inte jaay wiyyaanne, w-ulla la?* (are you coming with us or not?)
2 c.pl.	*?intuun jaayyiin loo la?* (are you coming or not?)
3 f.s.	*hi (i) raayḥa s-suug* (she is going to the market)
3 c.pl.	*hum raayḥiin is-suug* (they are going to the market)

In two-word collocates, the negated forms of the pronouns are often followed by participials. Thus:

mahu ḥaaḍir	(he is not present)
mahi raayḥa	(she is not coming)

In the following constructions the participial always follows the particle *?illi:*

?illi ḥaadur w-illi ġaayib	(he who is present and he who is absent)
?illi raagid w-illi ṣaaḥi	(he who is sleeping and he who is waking)

The passive verb

As mentioned earlier, the passive voice in B is expressed mainly by the use of the VIIth form of the triliteral verb, by a 3 pl. verb or by not expressing the agent, e.g.

active perf.	*zara* ^{c}	(he planted)
passive perf.	*?iṭ-ṭamaaṭa nzara* ^{c}	(tomatoes were planted)
active imperf.	*yizra* ^{c}	(he plants)
passive imperf.	*?il-jazar b-yinzara* ^{c}	(carrots will be planted)

In a passive context, the subject normally follows the verb:

?inkasar iṣ-ṣaḥan	(the plate is broken)

But to denote emphasis, the above order can be reversed:

ʔiṣ-ṣaḥan inkasar

When the agent is not expressed, the passive construction takes the following sequential order:

l-inxiil maatat (the date palms have died out)
or *maatat l-inxiil*

In the first example above, the initial item carries the emphasis.

Subject-verb concord

Subject-verb concord, in regard to gender and number, is closely maintained in this dialect. Cf:

m.s.	*naam il-walad*	(the boy has slept)
f.s.	*naamat il-bitt*	(the girl has slept)
m.pl.	*naamaw l-awlaad*	(the boys have slept)
f.pl.	*naamaw il-banaat*	(the girls have slept)

To emphasize the subject of the sentence, the above order may be reversed thus:

l-awlaad ragadaw (the boys slept)
or *ʔin-niswaan itgaddamaw* (the women left first)

Interrogation

Interrogative particles and pronouns usually appear in initial positions in sentences. The interrogative sentence has, in the main, the same sequential order as a statement. The syntactic bahaviour of certain interrogative particles and pronouns are examined below. For example:

čeef[4] *bitšiile?* (how are you going to handle it?)
čam[5] *waaḥid?* (how many?)

weeš (what?) is normally found in initial positions in a sentence. This order is reversed when *weeš* is not the carrier of the emphasis. Cf:

weeš haade? (what is this?)
haade weeš? (this now, what is it?)

Often *weeš* appears in liaison with the pronominal suffixes *-hu* and *-hi* in interrogative contexts. Cf:

3 m.s.	*weešhu lli nkasar?*	(what was broken?)
3 f.s.	*weešhi has-saalfe?*	(what kind of a tale is it?)

weeš can also appear in liaison with the prepositions *ḥagg* (for) and *b-* (with), as in:

ḥagg weeš maa katabt? (why didn't you writer?)
b-weeš šilte? (what did you remove it with?)

or in liaison with a preposition *min,* as in:

min weeš maa je?	(why didn't he come?)
min weeš maa jiitiin?	(why didn't you come? (fem.))

The ^{c}Anazi counterpart of *weeš* is *?eeš*, which is sometimes contracted to *š-*, as in:

š-gaal lik? (what did he tell you?)

However, *?eeš* or *š-*, syntactically, are analogous to *weeš* in B. The interrogative particle *šinhu?* (what?) is another example of a contracted interrogative compounds found both in A and B. It is contracted from lit. Ar. *?ayyu šay?in huwa* (what is it?) and syntactically behaves like *weešhu*. Cf:

šinhu lli naagṣinne min is-suug (what do we need from the market?)

Like *weeš*, it is also found in liaison with the 3 f.s. *-hi,* as:

šinhi l-muškile? (what is the problem?)

The interrogative particle *min* (who?) is also found in liaison with pronominals, as, e.g., in:

3 m.s.	*minhu lli ^{c}arras*	(who got married? : masc. sing.)
3 f.s.	*minhi lli ^{c}arrasat*	(who got married? : fem. sing.)
3 c.pl.	*minhum illi maa stalamaw*	(who are the ones who have not received anything yet?)

The interrogative pronoun *?ayy* (which) is also often found in liaison with pronominals. Thus:

3 m.s.	*-hu:* as in	*?ayyhu l-^{c}ood fiihum?*	(who is the elder among them?)
3 f.s.	*-hi:* as in	*?ayyhi l-^{c}oode fiihum?*	(who is the elder among them?)
3 c.pl.	*-hum*:as in	*?ayyhum illi bitbii^{c}hum?*	(which are the ones you intend to sell?)

When realized in isolation, *?ayy* is often collocated with indefinite pronouns, such as:

m.s.	*?ayy waaḥid ?*	(which one?)
f.s.	*?ayy waḥde?*	

but note that *čam* (how many?) is invariably found out of liaison:
masc. *čam waaḥid?* (how many?) fem. *čam waḥde?*
mu(u) čidi? (isn't it?), *mu(u) ^{c}adil?* (right or note?), *^{c}adil-la?* (isn't that right?), expressions corresponding in grammatical function to English question-tags such as isn't it?, etc., are often found in ultimate positions in sentences. Cf:

baačir falaafiin fi š-šahar, mu(u) čidi?
(tomorrow is the 30th of the month, isn't it?)
^{c}aṭaani xamsat danaaniir giddaamuk, mu(u) ^{c}adil?
(he gave me five dinars, in front of you, isn't it right?)

ṣaar luk al-ḥiin ᶜašrat ayyaam min jiit, ᶜadil-la?
(ten days have elapsed since you came, isn't that right?)

Other examples of interrogation, where the rising tone rather than the explicit use of particles conveys the question, are given below:

verb + obj.	*riḥt is-suug?*	(have you been to the market?)
obj. + verb + subj.	*l-iktaab, gareete?*	(the book, have you read it?)

In the last example, the object of the sentence is transposed to initial sentence position to indicate emphasis. Such a shift is also found in this example:

?axuuk, leeš maa tḥaayeet wiyyaah? (your brother, why didn't you greet him?)

A peculiarity found in B, not in A, is the employment of the suffixed vocal termination *-é?* denoting interrogation, such as:

?akalt-é? (have you eaten?) *katabt-é?* (have you written?)

Two interrogative particles found in A, to the exclusion of B, are *wara* and *šuule.* These, and there counterparts in B, are used as follows:

A	B
wara maa tguul lene? (why don't you inform us?)	*ḥagg weeš maa tguul leen-ne?*
šuule maa tmur ᶜleen-ne? (why don't you visit us?)	*leeš maa tmurr ᶜleen-ne?*

(Note: *wara maa* is a compound of Arabic adverbial *waraa?* and the interrogative particle *maa;* and *šuule = iš-leh.* In interrogative contexts both items are found in association with *maa.*)

Negation of verbs

The particle *ma(a)* (not) is used to negate a statement of fact, as in:

	perf.		imperf.	
sing.	*maa gara*	(he has not read)	*maa yiktib*	(he doesn't write)
pl.	*maa garaw*	(they have not read)	*maa yiktibuun*	(they don't write)

The particle *laa* also appears with verbs. One of its functions is to negate the imperative verb, as in: m.s. *laa tiṣrax* (don't scream) f.s. *laa tistaᶜjiliin* (don't make haste) *wala* (not) is also employed to negate all forms of verbs, such as:

perf.	*gaal biji, wala je*	(he said he was coming, but he didn't come)
imperf.	*ṣaar le mudde, wala ybayyin*	(it's been long time and he has not shown up)

In certain constructions, *maa* and *wala* are interchangeable. Cf:

maa je (he didn't come) *maa bayyan* (he has not shown up)

Double negation

laa . . . wala (neither . . . nor) is found mainly in the following constructions:

(a) with adverbials, as: *laa hni wala hnaak* (neither here nor there)
(b) with aux. + imperf. as: *laa yubġi yaakil, wala yišrab* (he does not want to eat or drink)
(c) with imperf., as: *laa yigra, wala yiktib* (he neither reads nor writes)
(d) with perf., as: *laa ?akal, wala šarab* (he has not eaten or drunk)

maa . . . u maa . . . (neither. . . nor), found with the connective *u*, is interchangeable with *laa . . . wala*. Cf:

maa ybii ^{c} *u maa yištari* (he neither sells nor buys)
laa ybii ^{c} *wala yištari* (he neither sells nor buys)

The Noun

The indefinite noun

As in other Arabic dialects indefiniteness can be expressed simply by the absence of the definite article *al-:* e.g. *daar* (a room). However, indefiniteness may also be expressed by *waaḥid* (someone) and *waḥde* placed before the relative adjective as in:

waaḥid jamri (someone from Bani Jamrah)
waḥde manaamiyye (some lady from Manāmah town)

Often, *min* (from) may be inserted after *waaḥid* or *waḥde*, such as:

waaḥid min l-idraaz (someone from Dirāz village)
waḥde min l-iġrubaat (some lady from the remote villages)

min (from, of) is inserted between two nouns where the first is indefinite in the singular and the other definite in the plural, as in:

sane min l-isniin (a certain year)
safra min is-safaraat (a certain journey)

The concept of the indefiniteness of a number of persons is also conveyed through the use of the item *naas* (a crowd), as in:

naas waajid ḥaḍaraw iz-zaffe
(a big crowd attended the wedding procession)

Cf. similarly, the use of *xalg* (people) as in:

xalgin ^{c}*aḍiim* (a great number of people)

Note the *tanwīn -in* above (which is of course caseless),[6] and also the concordial relationship between the common plural *xalg* and the singular adjective ^{c}*aḍiim.* Such usage is not uncommon in B.

Definite and indefinite concord

As in Arabic, concord operates in respect of gender, number and definition in B. Thus, nouns can be defined in many ways:

(a) by the addition of the article *?il-* < *al-*, e.g., *?in-naxle* (the date palm)
(b) by the addition of a pron. suff., e.g., *xawaathe* (her sisters)
(c) by belonging to the category of proper nouns, such as: *?ahil sitra* (people of Sitrah)
(d) by close association with a following noun which is itself defined:

fariig il-ḥaṭab	(the alley of al-Ḥaṭab)
suug il-xamiis	(the al-Khamīs market)
beet abu naxle	(the house with the palm tree)

(e) by association with the vocative particle, such as: *yaa ḥajji* (Oh! Ḥajji)

Nouns defined in the manner (a) to (d) above, must be accompanied in the noun-adjective phrase by adjectives which are also defined by the prefixation of the article *?il-* e.g.,

?il-qaaḍi l-jadiid	(the new judge)
?is-sihle l-foogiyye	(the upper Sihlah)

Nouns defined in the manner of (e) are accompanied by definite adjectives with which *yaa* is associated, e.g.

yaa ?aḥmad ya l-haddaar (oh talkative Aḥmad)

?illi is also employed to define an adjectival phrase whose antecedent is a defined noun, such as:

?il-beet illi thaddam (the house which came to ruins)

Gender and number concord

The typical sequence is N + A, viz. the adjective regularly following the noun. The following concordial combinations are found in B:

m.s. noun + m.s. adj:	*naxal ᶜood*	(big date palm garden)
	beetin kabiir	(a big house)
	walad faahim u haab riiḥ	(an educated and smart boy)
f.s. noun + f.s. adj:	*naxle ᶜoode*	(a long date plam)
	ḥijratin kabiira	(a big room)
	bitt faahme ?u haabbat riiḥ	(an educated and smart girl)

Note that gender distinction in the above examples is associated with the presence or absence of the fem. suffix *-a* or *-e*.

Exceptions to the above are found in these examples where feminine adjectives are associated with masculine nouns in figurative usages:

m.s. noun + f.s. adj.:	*hal-walad aafe*	(this boy is a glutton)
	hal-walad naṭfa	(this boy is mischievous)
f.s. noun + f.s. adj.:	*hal-bitt aafe*	(this girl is a glutton)
	hal-bitt naṭfa	(this girl is mischievous)

Compound adjectives such as consisting of two nouns are also common in B. Gender concord is regularly maintained between such compounds and the nouns they collocate with:

?amiine šeexat il-banaat	(Amīna is the best of all the girls)
?aḥmad šeex l-awlaad	(Aḥmad is the best of all the boys)

Relative adjectives, which take the suffix *-i* in the masculine singular and *-iyye* in the feminine singular show gender distinction in the singular only:

m.s.	*rajjaal ingiliizi*	(an Englishman)
f.s.	*mara ngil iizi yye*	(an Englishwoman)

The plural is of common gender:

m.pl.	*rjaal ingiliiz*	(Englishmen)
f.pl.	*niswaan ingiliiz*	(Englishwomen)

Adjectives of colour

Adjectives of colour show gender distinction in the singular only:

m.s.	*?il-mišmar il-wardi*	(the rose-coloured, head-and-shoulder veil)
f.s.	*?il-giṭ ᶜa l-xamriyye*	(the wine-coloured piece (of cloth))

The adjectives of colour, which in the plural take the suffix *-aan,* are of common gender:

m.pl.	*?il-qumṣaan iṣ-ṣufraan*	(the yellow shirts)
f.pl.	*l-ifyaab il-biiḍaan*	(the white gowns)

Often, adjectives of colour are preceded by intensifiers such as *killiš* and *waajid,* both meaning "very":

m.s.	*hal-iḥbur killiš mḥoomur*	(this ink is intensely red)
f.s.	*has-sayyaara waajid msoowde*	(this car is very black)

Certain nouns, which are used to describe material, show no gender or number distinction, but agree for definiteness, such as:

m.s.	*mišṭ plaastiik*	(a plastic comb), or *?il-mišṭ l-iplaastiik* (the plastic comb)
	xaatam dahab	(a golden ring)
f.s.	*tirkiyye dahab*	(a golden ear-ring)
	ṭaawle plaastiik	(a plastic table)
m.pl.	*mšuuṭ plaastiik*	(plastic combs)
f.pl.	*taraaki dahab*	(golden ear-rings)

In the following examples, relative adjectives retain their immediate post-nominal position:

ᶜeeš pišaawari, ?abu ḥabbe ṭawiile
(Pishawari rice of long grain)
ḥaliib hoolandi, ?abu warde
(Dutch milk—Carnation brand)

When a descriptive of material co-occurs with a relative adjective, the former immediately follows the noun and immediately precedes the relative adjective, as in:

f.s.	*faaniile ṣuuf ingiliiziyye* (an English woollen cardigan)	
m.pl.	*ġtar giṭin sweesri* (Swiss cotton head-cloths)	

Negation of the nominal sentence

The negative particle *maa-fi* (there is/are not) which does not inflect for gender or number, is used to negate nominal sentences:

m.s.	*maa-fi galam fi š-šanṭa*	(there is no pen in the bag)
f.s.	*maa-fi ṯamara naaḍje*	(there is no ripe fruit)
m.pl.	*maa-fi najaajiir hal-ayyaam*	(there are no carpenters these days)
f.pl.	*maa-fi sayyaaraat fi d-diira*	(there are no cars in the village)

The following particles show gender distinction:

masc.	*mu(u) jawaad, ?axuuh*	(not Jawad, his brother)
fem.	*mi(i) l-ᶜoode, xithe*	(not the elder, her sister)

In the following proverbial expressions *mu(u)* is followed by the item *kill* (every):

mu(u) kill ḥamle b-walad	(not every pregnancy will yield a male)[7]
mu(u) kill imdaḥrab jooz	(not every round object is a nut)

laa . . . wala (neither . . . nor), besides appearing in verbal constructions, is also employed to negate nominal constructions:

laa haade wala daak	(neither this nor that)
laak l-kabiir wala ṣ-ṣaġiir	(neither the elder nor the younger)

Finally, the particle *maaku* (there is/are no), a salient feature of Iraqi and Kuwaiti Arabic, is also common in B. It is not inflected for gender or number:

maaku ?aḥad fi ṭ-ṭariig	(there is no one in the street)
maaku xuḍra fi s-suug	(there are no vegetables in the market)
maaku sayyaaraat lil-ijra	(there are no cars for hire)

Negated forms of the personal pronouns

Negated forms of the personal pronouns have a high rate of frequency in daily speech. They are found with nominals as well as verbals. Below are those found in B:

3 m.s.	*ma(a)hu*
3 f.s.	*ma(a) hi*
2 m.s.	*mante*
2 f.s.	*mantiin*
1 m.s.	*maane*
1 f.s.	*maani*
3 c.pl.	*maahum*
2 c.pl.	*mantuun*
1 c.pl.	*maḥne*

Note that the Baḥārnah forms *ma(a) hu* < Arabic *maa huwa,* and similarly *ma(a) hi* < Arabic *maa hiya,* have the shorter forms *mu(u)* (masc.) and *mi(i)* (fem.).

In A, also, two variants are present, viz. *mhub* < lit. Ar. *maa huwa b-* and *mhib* < *maa hiya b-*. However, the shorter form *mub,* which is of common gender in A, has higher frequency in daily speech than the inflected variants.

In B, in statements, negated forms of the pronouns are normally found in collocation with adjectives, in which case the latter follow the former, e.g.

ma(a)hu	or	*mu(u) zeen*	(he, it is not good)
ma(a)hi	or	*mi(i) xayra*	(she is not gentle)

Negated forms of the pronouns are also common in verbal sentences where they are regularly followed by participles. Cf. these interrogative constructions:

mante jaay?	(aren't you coming?) (masc.)
mantiin jaayye?	(aren't you coming?) (fem.)
mantuun raayḥiin ?	(aren't you going?) (c.pl.)

Sentence Structure

Below are specimens of nominal and verbal sentences selected for the structural variations which they exhibit:

The nominal sentence

haadi gallat tamr	(this is a sack of dates)
beetne taḥt il-maatam	(our house is near the Matam, i.e., *Shī ^{c}i* place of assembly)
?axuuyi muu hni	(my brother is not here)
?il-^{c}ood wiṣ-ṣaġiir fneenhum msaafriin	(the elder and the younger are both abroad)
haadaak waajid ib ^{c}iid	(that is very far away)
killhum b-xeer	(they are all good)
?intuune mistaansiin	(you seem to be happy)

The verbal sentence

The simplest forms of verbs, in this dialect, are found with or without a specified subject, such as:

je	(he came)	*raaḥat*	(she went)

The verbal sentence may have the sequential order subject + verb or verb + subject, e.g.

subj. + verb:	*faaṭma raja ^{c}at*	(Fāṭma came back)
	?inte ruuḥ is-suug	(you, go to the market)
verb + subj.:	*iġli l-^{c}eeš*	(The price of rice has risen)
	ṭaffaw il-ḥariiga	(the fire was extinguished)

Initial imperative in liaison with a pronominal suffix is another common feature of the verbal sentence in this dialect:

sawhum ᶜala raaḥatk	(make them at your leisure)
xidhum ᶜala baġiyyatk	(buy them according to your liking)
wadne l-manaame	(take us to Manāmah)

The effect of emphasis on positional variations

Transpositions of one kind or another are very common in this dialect. Often, where the sentence order verb + noun is normally expected, the reverse order, i.e., noun + verb is found instead; this kind of positional shift is normally made to emphasize an item, as:

ᶜala lla twakkalne	(on God we rely)
ʔil-ḥabb ʔawwal nibdira	(the seeds are first sown)
fi d-dawaaliib ʔaštiġil	(on date gardens I work)

The above also applies to these proverbial expressions which are copious in speech:

yoom ṣaxxanne l-maay, farr id-diič
(after we had boiled the water, the cock has escaped)
or in: *ʔil-kilme lli tistaḥi m-minhe, badhe*
(that word which you are shy of mentioning, enunciate it first)

The sequential order: adj. + noun

The normal sequence in a nominal sentence, where the predicate is an adjective or a noun with an adjectival function, is sometimes reversed to indicate emphasis as in:

iḥleewiin hal-igṭaᶜ	(these pieces (fabric) are pretty)
saaḥir hal-walad	(this boy is a magician, i.e., smart)

The adjective *xo(o)š* (good, excellent)

The adjective *xo(o)š*, a borrowing from Persian, is common to both A and B. It is of common gender and number and placed before the noun it qualifies, as in:

sing.	*xo(o)š šayy*	(what a good thing!)	*xo(o)š walad!*	(good boy!)
	xo(o)š bitt!	(good girl!)		
pl.	*xo(o)š awlaad!*	(good boys!)		
	xo(o)š ṭaawilaat!	(good tables!)		

The particle weeš

weeš,[8] (what a . . .! or how!) besides functioning as an interrogative particle in B, has the function of expressing surprise and wonder; it is often found in pre-nominal positions.[9]

Cf. these examples from B, where *weeš* functions as *maa:*

weeš ḥalaawte!	(how pretty!)
weeš ḥalaawathum!	(how pretty they are!)
weeš hal-ḥajaayij	(what (fake) pretexts!)

The particle kill/e

kill (every, each, all) which collocates with nouns only is often found in pr-nominal positions:

kill ?arba^{c} saa^{c}aat, ?ibla^{c} ḥabbe
(every four hours, take one tablet)
Often *kill* carries the emphasis in a statement. Cf:

	kill yoom yištiġil	(he works everyday)
or	*kill leele yigra ?u yiktib*	(he reads and writes every night)

The adverbial particle *kille* (regularly, always) is regularly found in pre-participial positions in these sentences. Cf:

3 m.s.	*kille ta^{c}baan*	((you are) always tired)
3 f.s.	*kille ta^{c}baane*	((you are) always tired)
c. pl.	*kille raagdiin*	((you are) always sleeping)

Demonstratives

Near objects
The demonstratives which indicate near objects in this dialect are *haade* (this) and *haadi* (this) for masculine and feminine singular respectively; and the common plural form is *ha(a)deleen* (these). Cf:[10]

m.s.	*haade beetne*	(this is our house)
f.s.	*haadi sayyaaratne*	(this is our car)
c.pl.	*hadeleen iwlaad axuuy*	(these are my nephews)
	hadeleen banaat ixti	(these are my nieces)

Note that *haadi* may also appear with masculine and feminine plurals, as in:

m.pl. *haadi š-šawaari^{c} illi šaggathe l-ḥukuuma*
(these are the roads constructed by the government)
f.pl. *haadi sayyaaraat iš-šarika*
(these are Company (BAPCO) cars)
Demonstratives, as shown above, precede the noun when occurring predicatively in statements; this also applies to questions, except when a shift of emphasis takes place and then the above order is reversed. Cf:

demon. + noun:	*haade l-beet la-min?*	(whose house is this?)
noun + demon.:	*?il-beet haade leekum?*	(is this your house?)

Remote objects
ha(a) daak (that) and *ha(a) diik* (that) are used for the masculine and feminine singular respectively. These inflect for gender and number as in:[11]

m.s.	*ha(a)daak il-baab iš-šargi*	(that is the eastern gate)
f.s.	*ha(a) diik id-dariiše l-ġarbiyye*	(that is the western window)

The plural forms of the above, viz. *hade(e) laak* (those (masc.)) and *diik* (fem.) are used as follows:

m.pl.	*hadelaak byuut il-ḥukuuma*	(those houses are owned by the government)
f.pl.	*diik is-sayyaaraat la š-šarika*	(those cars belong to the Company)

Finally, in Dirāzi female speech distinction is made between two sets of demonstratives, viz.

	far objects		far persons
m.s.	*haak*	(that)	*haaka*
f.s.	*heek*	(that)	*heeka/heeki*

The above forms are less common than their Manāmah counterparts viz. *daak* and *diik* used for both persons and objects. In contexts, however, the Dirāzi forms appear thus:

m.s. objects	*haak il-yoom*	(that day) for	*daak il-yoom*
m.s. persons	*za ᶜag haaka*	(that man yelled) for	*za ᶜag daak*
f.s. objects	*heek al-ḥiin*	(at that time) for	*diik al-ḥiin*
f.s. persons	*raaḥ ila heeka*	(he went to that woman) for	*raaḥ ila diik.*

Demonstratives in liaison with pronominal suffixes

Compounds consisting of the base-demonstrative in liaison with pronominal suffixes *haada* (this) in B and its counterpart *kaa* in A are regularly found.[12] These forms, viz. 1 m.s. *hadaane* (here I am) or its corresponding ᶜAnazi counterpart, *kaane*, are used similarly. In sentences they are regularly followed by verbs or adverbs, such as:

with verbs	B		A
1 p.m.s.	*hadaane jaay*	(here, I am coming)	*kaane yaay*
1 p.f.s.	*hadaani jaayye*		*kaane yaayye*

Note above that the A-forms are the same for both genders.

with adverbs:	B		A
3 c.pl.	*hadakkum ihnaak*	(there they are)	*kaahma hnaak*
3 c.pl.	*haadahum ihni(i)*	(here they are)	*kaahma hni(i)*

Unlike B, where two distinct sets of these are used for near and far persons or objects, in A only one set is used for both. Cf:

	B		A
3p.m.s. (near)	*haadahu*	(here he, it is)	*kaahwa*
3 p.m.s. (far)	*hadakku*	(there he, it is)	*kaahwa*

The particle *-iyya*

An old Arabic feature which has survived both in A and B is the item *-iyya* + pronom. suff. In B, *-iyya* + pron. suff. is often found in sentence-initial positions when used in cautionary exclamations, e.g.

2 m.s.	*?iyyaak itruuḥ b-ruuḥuk*	(don't go by yourself)
2 f.s.	*?iyyaaš itsawwiin šaṭaane*	(don't make mischief)

-iyya in liaison with *w-*, i.e., *waw al-ma ᶜiyye,* is found regularly in post-verbal positions, as in:

1 c.s.	*ta ᶜaal wiyyaayi*	(come with me)
2 c.pl.	*?intiḍur, baji wiyyaak*	(wait, I am coming with you)
3 m.s.	*bitsaafur wiyyaah?*	(are you travelling with him?)

Conditional sentences

The conditional particles are *?ida(a), lo(o), (?in)čaan, (?i) leen, ?in, ?illi.* These are all equally frequent in daily speech. *?ida(a)* in the *protasis,* is used with:

(a) the imperfect tense, as:
?ida(a) bitruuḥ is-suug baji wiyyaak
(if you are going to the market I'll come with you)
?ida(a) b-taakluun, bininčib il-ᶜaše
(if you feel like eating, we will serve the supper)
(b) the perfect tense, as:
?ida(a) ji ᶜt, kill
(if you feel hungry, (go ahead) eat)
?ida(a) t ᶜibt, naam
(if you are tired, go to sleep)
(c) participials and adjectives, as:
?ida(a) mant ta ᶜbaan, guum saa ᶜidne
(if you are not tired, come give us a hand)
?ida ntiin mašġuule, maani maarra
(if you are busy, I shan't call)
(d) nominals as in:
?ida(a) yoom il-jim ᶜa, maa bagdar aji
(if on Friday, I won't be able to come (make it))
or as in: *?ida(a) kill waaḥid nuṣṣ, bijazzi*
(if everybody (takes) half, it will suffice)
(e) in proverbial expressions the condition is implied without the explicit use of a conditional particle as in:
?iḍrub il-čalb, yit?addab il-?asad
(chastise the dog, and the lion will behave)

A more explicit form of the aobve is: *?ida ḍarabt il-čalb, it?addab il-?asad.*
lo(o) in the protasis appears with:
(a) the imperfect tense as in:
lo(o) ?axuuk yidri, čaan axadk wiyyaah[13]
(if your brother knew, he would have taken you with him)
or as in: *lo(o) yištiġluun kill yoom, čaan kamal il-beet*
(if they work (daily) regularly, the house will have been completed)
(b) the perfect tense as in:
lo(o) šara l-la ᶜaam, čaan dafa ᶜ agall
(if he had bought last year, he would have paid less)
lo(o) daras čaan najaḥ

(if he had studied, he would have passed)

(c) active participles as in:

lo(o) laabis čaan axadnaak wiyyaanne

(if you were dressed, we would have taken you with us)

lo(o) mgafḍiin yoomeen, čaan waajid it ᶜaṭṭalne

(if they had remained closed for two days, we would have had a lot of delay)

(d) nominal constructions such as:

lo(o) huu hni(i), čaan saa ᶜadne

(if he were here, he would help us)

or in this proverbial expression,

lo(o) fiih xeer, maa ramaah iṭ-ṭeer

(if it were worthy, the bird wouldn't have discarded it)

(?in) čaan in the protasis appears with:

(a) the imperfect as in:

(?in) čaan ti ᶜruf, di raawne

(if you know, then show us)

(b) the perfect as in:

(?in) čaan xallaṣ min idruuse, xalle yiṭla ᶜ

(if he has finished (revising) his lessons, let him go)

(c) the future as in:

(?in) čaan bitruuḥ, baji wiyyaak

(if you are going, I'll come with you)

(d) nominal constructions as in:

(?in) čaan is-sayyaara ṣaaḥye, bawaddiikum

(if the car is in order, I shall take you)

?ileen (if, when, in case) has the free variant *leen*, both being equally common in speech. *(?i) leen* can appear with:

(a) the perfect in the protasis + the imperfect (with a future particle) in the apodosis:

leen ᶜarrast, bitgiib awlaad

(when you get married, you will have children)

(b) the perfect (in the protasis) + the imperative (in the apodosis):

leen baġeet, xid

(if you felt like having (some), do (take some)

leen iḥtijt, guul liyyi

(when you need (some), let me know)

Note that the perfect forms above have a future meaning.

(c) the negative imperf. (in the protasis) + neg. imperf. (in the apodosis)

leen maa biṭṭaawu ᶜ, maa bitḥaṣṣil

(if you don't obey, you won't get)

The conditional particle *?in* (if, whether) is found in the protasis, mainly with the perfect. Cf: perfect:

?in gadarne, marreene ᶜaleekum

(if we are able, we shall drop by)

?in šiftuk ḥaafi, baštaki ᶜaleek ᶜind abuuk

(if I find you barefooted, I shall complain you to your father)

or as in: *?in ittaṣal aḥad fi ġyaabne, xid numrate*

(if anybody calls in our absence, take down his number)

Again, note in the apodosis above, the verb is in the imperative. The relative pronoun *?illi* (who, which) is commonly used as a conditional particle. It is found in the protasis with imperfects as well as adverbials. Cf:

imperf. (protasis):
?illi yidris, yinjaḥ
(he who studies, passes (the examination))
adverbials (protasis):
?illi fi l-igdur, iṭal ᶜa l-millaas
(the scoop can reveal what the pan conceals)

And less frequently with nominals in the protasis as in this proverbial expression:
?illi beete min kazaaz, maa yfalli ᶜ iḥjaara
(those who live in glass houses should not throw stones)

yaa, besides functioning as a vocative particle, is used to mean "either. . . or" in conditional contexts. It is found with:
(a) nominals in the protasis and apodosis:
naad liyyi yaa ?abuuk, yaa ?axuuk
(call me either your father or your brother)
(b) imperfects: *yaa tji wiyyaanne, yaa tig ᶜid fi l-beet*
(either you come with us, or else sit at home)
(c) adverbials: *yaa hni, yaa hnaak, makaan ġeer la*
(either here or there; nowhere else)

Note that *yaa,* as used in conditional contexts, is not found with the perfect.

Relative clauses

If the subject or object is defined, relative clauses are introduced by the relative *?illi* (which, who), as: subject definite: *?il- ᶜummaal illi yištiġluun fi š-šarika, ḥaṣṣalaw zyaade*
(The workers who work with the company have received a rise (in wages))
object definite: *?ir-risaale lli katabthe, waddeethe l-bariid*
(the letter which I wrote, I have posted)

Relative clauses where the subject or object is not defined are put bogether without *?illi,* as:
subj. indef.: *haadi mis?ale tiḥtaaj ila naḍar*
(this is an issue (which) requires thinking)
obj. indefl.: *šift sayyaara ṭuulhe yumkin ṯalaaṯiin fuut*
(I saw a car (which) is about thirty feet long)

When the antecedent is object definite, the pronominal suffix attached to the main verb of the relative clause is in gender and number concord with its antecedent. Cf:

l-idlaaġ illi štareete ?ams, labaste
(I wore the socks which I had bought yesterday)
?il-balad illi jawha baarid, laa ṯṭubha
(The country with a cold climate, avoid going to it)
Note the inversions in constructions such as the following:
hum illi waṣalaw gabilne

(it's they who arrived first)
gillat il-maṭar hi lli txalli z-zar ^{c} *imuut*
(it is lack of rain which makes the plant shrivel)

A common feature is the occurrence of *min* in association with *?illi,* in which case *min illi* is used to mean "by or of what" as in:

t ^{c}*ajjabt min illi šifte*
(I was amazed by what I saw)
^{c}*iṭni min illi* ^{c}*induk*
(give me of what you have)

Temporal clauses

Below are some of the common particles used to introduce temporal clauses. *?ileen* < *?ilaa?an* (until, *when)* has the short form *leen.* It is found with the:

(a) imperf. as in:
?iṣbur ileen axalliṣ
(wait until I have finished)
haaris ileen axuuk yiḥḍur
(wait until your brother arrives)

(b) perf. as in:
xalle yiġli, w-leen faaḥ šiile
(let it simmer, when it boils remove it)
?ane basaa ^{c}*idk ileen inte t* ^{c}*ibt*
(I shall help you when you feel tired)

Often *?ileen* appears with *maa* to introduce a clause in the perfect, as in:
nasooh ^{c}*ala n-naar ileen maa ḥtarag*
(it was left on the fire until it burnt)
xallooh fi š-šams ileen maa yabas
(they exposed it to the sun until it got dry)

Like *?ileen, yoom* (when) is also used to introduce a clause in the perfect:
yoom xallaṣ, raaḥ
(when he had finished, he left)
yoom ikbur, gaam iṣalli
(when he grew up, he started praying)

The particle *lamma* (when) is found more often with the perfect than with the imperfect verbs in temporal clauses. Cf:

perf.: *lamma waṣalaw ihnaak, maa šaafaw aḥad*
(when they arrived there, they found no one)
lamma xallaṣat il-midrase, raja ^{c} *il-beet*
(when the school had finished, he came home)

lamma as used above, is interchangeable with yoom (when). Cf:
yoom waṣalaw ihnaak, maa šaafaw aḥad

With a majority of speakers, *?ileen* + perf. replaces lamma + imperf. in these clauses:
less common: *lamma txalliṣ it-ṯanawi, ruuḥ il-jaam* ^{c}*a*

(when you finish secondary schooling, go to the university)

more common: *?ileen xallaṣt iṯ-ṯanawi, ruuḥ il-jaam ^{c}a*

(when you have finished secondary schooling, go to the unversity)

less common: *lamma tinjaḥ baštari luk saa ^{c}a*

(when you pass (the exams.) I shall buy you a watch)

more common: *?ileen najaḥt, baštari luk saa ^{c}a*

(when you have passed (the exams.) I shall buy you a watch)

NOTES:

1. Occasionally, an elderly interlocutor may begin his speech with an adverbial phrase indicative of a past event, the exact date of which is unknown to him, as in:
   sanat illi je ṭ-ṭaa ^{c}uun. . . (the year plague hit the country (appr. 1247 A.H.))
   or *sanat iṭ-ṭab ^{c}a . . .* (the year of the mass foundering of local boats (appr. 1288 A.H.))
2. Arabian dialects almost all have (*č, ts*) in this particle and not *q*.
3. Such usage is also noted for the Shammar- ^{c}Abde speech of north Arabia. See Cantineau, *Études*, III, p. 188.
4. *čeef* has the free variant *čeefe.*
5. *čam* has the nunated form *čammin,* which denotes scarcity, as in *bass čammin waaḥid* (only few ones) and is equally common.
6. *Tanwīn,* in this dialect, is examined under Morphology, Part III.
7. Baḥraini husbands, like most Arabs, prefer a male child from an expectant wife.
8. Also examined, in the previous pages, under Interrogation.
9. For classical Arabic *maa,* see *WGAL,* part II, p. 98.
10. Note that *haade* and *haadi* have shorter free variants, which are equally common. These are *de* for the former and *di* for the latter; their syntactic behaviour is analogous to their longer counterparts. Note also that *ha(a) deleen* has the shorter free variant *deleen* which syntactically behaves like its longer counterpart and is equally common.
11. *ha(a) daak* and *ha(a) diik* also have the shorter free variants *daak* and *diik* for the former and the latter, and the shorter forms behave similarly to their longer counterparts.
12. The above forms also appear in the appropriate section under Morphology.
13. *čaan,* the shorter form of *?inčaan,* is used interchangeably with the latter. Both forms are equally common.

Part V
Lexical features

Lexical features constitute an important part of a dialect survey. The present study of Baḥārnah lexis was directed at speakers with different registers of language. The aims laid down for this part of the investigation were, primarily, two-fold:

(a) to acquire sufficient data representing both urban and rural forms of B;
(b) to obtain a large number of specialized lexis, in particular items pertaining to cottage industries.

The prevailing date-culture and the concomitant traditional activities, some of which are solely dependent upon the former, are long-established traditional pursuits of the Baḥārnah rural community.[1] However, one should note here that owing to a strong tide of sweeping modernization some such industries have already diminished and others which are extant are rapidly dwindling away. Shortly after the craft disappears, its specialized vocabulary is subsequently forgotten.

The present study of the Baḥārnah lexis has revealed the following:

(1) Items circulating in daily speech are to a great degree common to both rural and urban forms.
(2) A large number of classical items have survived in B.
(3) Pan-Arabic koine forms show a high rate of frequency in current urban speech
(4) A large number of proverbial expressions are in circulation, especially in the speech of the elderly.
(5) Foreign words, old and recent, occur frequently in the entire dialect area.
(6) Specialized lexis is found in all the areas within Bahrain where similar traditional activities are found.
(7) Finally, a large number of Arabicized forms are in current use.

Lexical data is studied under three sections, the first deals with specimens of two-word collocates, localisms, proverbial expressions, classical and koine forms in current speech. Section two (B) looks into old and recent borrowings; and section three (C) examines specialized lexis pertaining to certain traditional activities.

Section A

Specimens of two-word collocates, i.e., noun + adjective

ḥawin ^{c}ood	a big enclosure (of a house)
maayin faatir	lukewarm water
jins barraani	foreign fabric

naas ?ajaawiid	virtuous or good people
?iṯ-ṯoob l-imšajjara	the patterned gown
tamrin zeen	good dates
wzaar jamri	a Bani Jamrah loin-cloth, i.e, one made in Bani Jamrah village
rde ṣeeb ^{c}i	an Abu Ṣēbi ^{c} cloak, i.e., one made in Abu Ṣēbi ^{c} village

Specimens of common verbal forms

Below is a specimen list of some common verbal forms chosen from the texts of interviews with local people:

nṣaffiih u nimši	we dispose of it (sell it) and then leave
nitmaṣlaḥ	we make a profit
maa yinfug	it can't be sold
načaf	he changed his mind
faraš	he has opened his shop
gaffaḍ	he has closed his shop
tyassar	he has set out
twaffa	he has passed away
?akruf ruuḥi	I toil laboriously
ixayyim ^{c}ind il-jiiraan	He lingers at the neighbours

Specimens of localisms

The following items, most of which are of Arabic origin, have undergone certain morphophonemic changes or acquired a new range of meaning in this dialect:

mahaayin	trades and crafts
igḥaafaat	sea-beds
waadye	local regions or areas (not valleys)
mkaafaḥ	toil, struggle
m ^{c}aabal	diligence, constant attention
mraakaḍ	regular attendance
jadaḥaat	drilled holes
?abuuk il-^{c}ood	your grandfather
?ummuk il-^{c}oode	your grandmother
yoom u tark	every alternate day
baaluul	a small hamur (fish of the grouper family)
naknuuk	a small hāmūr (Sitrah)
baġle[2]	a clay jar for cooling water
ḥalaayil	native Baḥārnah Arabs
nasiib	a relative; when used by the *ḥalāyil*, i.e., Baḥārnah villagers, the term indicates a sense of belonging to the same stock
iġrubaat	remote areas
diira	village
jawwadne l-mihne	(from a weaver) we stuck to our (inherited) trade
?iz-ziraa ^{c}a ḍa ^{c}iife	gardening is in decline
weeš in-naḍar	what course of action should we adopt?
?astaad	head mason; skilful worker
xašab	boats, local ships (lit. wood)

?aafe	glutton
maḥmuul u yitraffas	lit. a kicking (grumbling) dependant; lib. beggars can't be choosers.
ḥamiihe ḥaraamihe	lit. the protector is a crook; lib. if the enforcer of the law is criminal, what sort of justice can you expect?
ḍaa^c fi ṭ-ṭoose	he got lost in the crowds
hi b-šiime w hi b-giime	first beg for his favour and also pay for his labour (said of an ungrateful worker)
jaahil	a child, a lad
^{c}eeš	rice
xubz	bread

Some common proverbial expressions

(1) *maa tirtifi^c illa s-samaade, wala yi^{c}tali ?illa d-dixxaan*
(rubbish and smoke both rise up!)

(2) *?illi y^{c}azzi w-illi maa y^{c}azzi yaakil ^{c}eeš l-iḥseen*
(lit. he who beats his chest (during Muḥarram) and he who doesn't receive (Imām) Ḥussein's rice! Cf. one man sows and another reaps!; one beats the bush and another catches the birds!)

(3) *čafan bi-blaaš, ?ariid amuut!*
(for a free shroud, I am willing to die!)

(4) *kiṯr id-dagg ifičč l-ilḥaam*
lit. constant striking undoes the welding; lib. constant dripping wears away the stone, or little strokes fell great oaks

(5) *waraak yaa baṣal tiġle, gaal ane fiz-zaad aḥle*
(should you raise your price ye onion? yes, he said, 'cause, with me, food tastes nicer!)

(6) *l-ifluus itjiib il-^{c}aruus*
(lit. money can buy you a bride; lib. a golden key opens every door)

(7) *maa ntageet min l-injuum ?illa sheel!*
(out of all the stars you chose but Canopus!)[3]

(8) *^{c}atiig iṣ-ṣuuf wala jadiid l-ibriisam*
(better old wool than new silk!)

(9) *yaa maaši fi ?arḍ iz-zalag, laa ti?man iṭ-ṭeeḥ*
(he who treads a slippery path, is doomed to fall)

(10) *Ya lli waaṣil been il-baṣale w-gišrathe, maa yintaabuk illa dmuu^c*
(he who breaks in between the onion and its skin, gets naught but tears)

(11) *ḥsaab umm il-beeḍ!* (lit. the calculation of the lady who sells eggs!; lib. don't count your chickens before they are hatched! or, catch your bear before you sell its skin!)

(12) *?iṣbur ^{c}ala majnuunuk laa yjiik ?ajann im-minne*
(better the devil you know than the devil you don't know!)

(13) *šiil il-xara ^{c}ala r-raas, wala l-ḥaaje ?ila n-naas*
(lib. better a scavenger, than a solicitor of favours)

(14) *^{c}adaari tisgi l-ib^{c}iid, ?u tinse l-gariib*
(lib. ^{c}Adāri (a natural pool) pours water in remote areas, forgetting the adjoining ones, i.e., charity begins at home!)

(15) *midd irjuuluk ^{c}ala gadd ilḥaafuk*
(stretch your legs according to your coverlet or cut your coat according to your cloth.)

(16) *laa tsawwi l-ḥabbe dabbe*
(don't make a mountain out of a molehill)

Classical Arabic Items in B

Below are specimens of classical Arabic items in current use in B, regardless of the educational status of the speaker:

raḍii ^{c}*a*	(sister)
ḍane	(offspring, son)
nasaal	(lady's hair washing)
naxaal	(sieving or sifting)
zalaal	(skimming)
maḥaaḥ	(egg yolk)
fuṣṣ	(stone such as used on rings)
xeezaraane	(cane, stick)
buxnug	(head-veil for young girls)
maa ?aṭiig	(I can't stand. . .)
ġubše < *ġabaš*	(daybreak)
^{c}*afse*	(disarray, confusion)
zabra(h)	(a scream of anger)
laṭma(h)	(a slap on the face)
hooše	(conflict, brawl, fray)
ḥooba < *ḥawbah*	(poverty, ill-fortune)
ḥaniin	(longing, screaming)
waniin	(wailing)
ḥaafi	(barefoot)
zataat	(quick)
ṣaxxa	(quiet)
binč < *bunuk*	(prime of)
baṭiin	(glutton)
ḥazze	(time of)
ġabbat il-muġrub	(at night)
sluum iš-šams	(at sunset)
tawaali š-šahar	(the closing days of the month)
raas is-sane	(opening days of the new year)
wajbe	(meal)
mawaa ^{c}*iin*	(kitchen utensils)
saniin	(sharp)
faatir	(tepid)
mnazz	(cradle)
mxamma	(broom)
?adnaat ši	(a minimum of)
haab riiḥ[4]	(smart, dexterous)
sihle[5]	(plain, lowland)
mitbarje	(said of a lady who appears in public uncloaked or unveiled)
falag < *falaġ*	(to split)
za ^{c}*ag* < *ḏa* ^{c}*aq*	(to scream or yell)
faṭas	(to strangle, to drown)
gašaṭ	(to chip)
nadab	(to send for)
^{c}*adan*	(to become familiar with)
kawwad	(to heap or pile)
?il-karr	(circular rope with a soft back, used for climbing date palm trees)
dibs	(date honey (syrup))
dalu	(leather-bucket)
tanbiit	(the process of cutting the branches off the date palm)
taḥdiir	(the clustering and lowering of the bunches of a date palm so that they can grow unobstructed)
gallaaf	(boat builder)

Pan Arabic koine forms in current speech

The dialectal forms appearing to the left hand side of this list are often replaced by the koine forms shown on the right:

ġurb	foreigners, strangers	*?ajaanib*
baazaar	market	*suug*
šaagardi	labourer, worker	^{c}*aamil*
glaaṣ	glass	*kaas*
ličče	stingy, mean	*baxiil*
?aalu	potatoes	*baṭaaṭa*
^{c}*eeš*	rice	*ruzz*
dlaaġ	sock	*juuraab*
motar il-ḥariiga	fire brigade	*sayyaarat il-?iṭfaa?*
tawdaat	delivering	*naql*
karwa	fees, fares, wages	*?ijra*

šiġil/mihne	job, work	*waẓiife*
luumi	lime	*laymuun*
daxtar	doctor	*ṭabiib*
binsil	pencil	*galam raṣaaṣ*
kamče	spoon	*mil ^{c}aqa*
kašme	spectacles	*naẓẓaara*
duuni	ordinary, usual	*^{c}aadi*
yikruf ruuḥa	he toils	*yijhid nafse*
sille	thorns; fish bones	*šook*
timbe	ball	*kora*
xaṭṭ/maktuub	letter	*risaale*
bugše	envelope	*ẓarf*
ḥakiim (in ^{c}eem)	(Ni ^{c}eem) hospital	*mustašfa*

Comparative lexis: specimens of regional variations

The following lexical items are normally exclusive to the dialect under which they appear. Cf:

B		A
ḍarab	he hit	*ṭagg*
ġarše	bottle	*buṭil*
sannuur/sannuura	cat	*gaṭu/gaṭwa*
rid wara	move back	*waxxir, tna ^{c} ^{c}az*
ixawwuf	causing alarm or dread	*ixarri ^{c}*
mxabbal	stupid	*xabal*
weeš itguul?	what is it?	*šin-gaayil*
weeš in-naḍar	what course of action should we take?	*šinsawwi* (also *š-in-naḍar*)
haadahu	here it is	*kaahwa*
ḥalaawate	how nice!	*ḥle(e) laate*
duulaab	date garden	*naxal*
ḥawi	enclosure, compound (house)	*ḥooš*
ijirr	to drag, tow	*idiff* (also *iyirr*)
rama	he threw	*gaṭṭ*
?akil	food, provisions	*ignaad* (also *?akil*)
bil-jumle	in bulk	*gooṭra*
gdur	cooking pan	*ṣifriyye* (also *jidir*)
ḥjaara	stones	*ḥaṣa*
jafur	well	*jiliib*
leeš (maa jiit?)	why didn't you come?	*wara (maa yiit?)*
faag buuze	he opened his mouth fig. he screamed abuse	*faačč ḥalje*
xalaga	a piece of cloth	*xirje*
maṣkuuk	closed, shut	*msakkar* (also *maṣkuuk)*

Specimens of inter-dialectal variations: rural and urban forms of B

The forms given below are exclusive to the division under which they appear:

Rural B		Urban B
nṣe(e) fiyye	sack	*juuniyye*
(ᶜajuuz) mzimne	elderly (lady)	*ᶜoode*
mamšaah	its disposal, sale (said of hand-woven cloaks)	*bee ᶜah*
?inxaraṭ	disappeared (said of a trade or craft)	*raaḥ, ?ixtafe*
(?id-diira) tgišš	(the village) is deserted (during pearling season)	*tixtali*
ᶜala marbaah	according to habit, customary	*ḥasab it-ta ᶜwiid*
?adoobiš	do all sorts of jobs	*?aštiġil fi kill ši*
ma ᶜṣuuma	grave yard	*mugbara*
tnabbur	you dig with the hands	*tiḥfur* (also *tnabbur)*
tdimm (ᶜaleeh ir-raml)	you cover it(with sand)	*tġaṭṭiih . . .*
diiwaaniyye	spacious sitting-room	*mijlas*
ṭamar	jumped over	*naṭṭ*
imzayyin	hairdresser	*imḥassin*
taliil	evil spirit	*jinni*
looga	ornamental box for keeping perfume bottles, etc.	*guuṭi*
ṣirj	light, lantern	*fanar, šim ᶜa*
ḥaṣiir imraaje	straw mat	*ḥaṣiir xuuṣ*
yitġattar ᶜaliyyi	difficult (for me) to distinguish	*yiṣ ᶜab it-tafriig beenhum*
tagḍiib	pruning	*gaṣaaṣ*
gaadu	the dried end part of a date palm bough, raceme	*karab*
maḥaariir	spices	*?abzira,bahaaraat*
mitbarje	said of an unveiled, uncloaked lady	*ḥaasra*

Section B

Notes on English loan-words

A tendency among educated speakers is to eschew loan-words, particularly those for which an Arabic equivalent exists. Nevertheless, loan-words from English, Persian and Urdu are in copious use in daily speech. A large number of these words is, however, of relatively recent acquisition. They are recent because the bulk of these words came into use, apparently, after the discovery of oil in 1932 and the subsequent establishment of the Baḥrain Petroleum Company (BAPCO).

The above company has always employed a substantial number of indigenous workers who came into linguistic contact with expatriate work-mates, mainly British and Indian serving in technical and clerical capacities. Furthermore, with the coming of oil, trade and travel greatly flourished. These further developments have emphasized the actuality of broad linguistic interaction between the indigenous and the expatriate population of the country.

Many villagers abandoned gardening in preference for the more lucrative jobs that the nascent oil industry had created. A new range of borrowings came into use. Items such as *?il-kumbani* (the Company, i.e., BAPCO), *forman* (foreman), *oof* (off-duty), *ṣaaḥub* (from Indian *saab,* sir), not only gained wide currency, but also brought into being a new range of vocabulary, hitherto unknown to local speech. Workers employed as assistant pipe-fitters soon acquired a specialized form of vocabulary, viz. *beebfitar* (pipe-fitter), *hoozaat* (fire hoses), *beebaat* (pipes), *sbaanaat* (spanners), *ringaat* (rings), etc.

BAPCO was not the only source for these new lexical acquisitions. Certain items, firmly ingrained in current speech, came through contact with other British-Indian firms operating in the area. The terms *fuṣṣ* (first) and *fuṣṣiglaas* (first class), *sikin* (second class), *deek* (deck passengers) are normally associated with the two classes of sea travel available on the British India Steam Navigation Company's ships which had a long-standing monopoly on the sea route from Bombay, through the Gulf ports, ending up in Baṣrah. Thus, a Gulf passenger can travel to Bombay or Baṣrah either *fuṣṣ, sikin* or *deek.*

Notes on Hindustani loan-words

Hindustani (Urdu) words were acquired through two channels:

(1) trade and travel

(2) contact with the quite sizable Indian community existing in Baḥrain.

Trade between the old region of al-Baḥrain and India is of long standing.[6] Trade with India introduced new lexical items which were completely alien to Arab culture. Trade items such as *čiit* (course Indian calico), *sabaataat* (sandals), *malmal* (Indian voile), *jawaati* (shoes), *rawaamiil* (handerkchiefs), *jawaani* ^{c}*eeš* (sacksful of rice (sing. *juuniyye* < *gooni*)), etc., were incorporated into local speech. The Indians living in Baḥrain were familiar with the clerical side of the Gulf trade; and insurance, clearance and commercial correspondence were among the activities normally conducted by the Indian clerks who often worked for local importers. It is in this sphere of economic activity that words like *sii aay ef* (C.I.F., i.e., Carriage, Insurance and Freight), *biime* (bailment), *draaft* (bankdraft) were acquired.

A large number of Baḥrainis paid, and still pay, regular visits to Bombay, once described as the "London of the East". Among these were pearl dealers, locally called *ṭawaawiish, ṭreešiyye* (regular commuters on business trips) and many others who sought medical treatment there, for the want of it back home. Also, a large number of Baḥārnah Arabs, disenchanted for various reasons with their situation back home, settled for long years in Bombay. All of these had to communicate in Hindustani and many acquired a good deal of it. The pearl dealers learnt new Indian words such as *daana* (a single, large, very expensive pearl), *jiiwan* (well-rounded, large, white, expensive pearl), *buuka* (the smallest and least expensive of pearls), etc.

The Baḥraini travellers witnessed new modes and ways of life in Bombay. *sbiitaal* (hospital), *ṭraam* (tram car), and *rees* (horse racing), all became part of their newly acquired vocabulary.

Notes on Persian loan-words and place names

The Baḥārnah Arabs pay annual visits to the shrines of their Imāms in Iraq and Persia. A large Persian community has long existed in Baḥrain. The dhow trade between the adjacent Persian and Arab coastal towns is of long-standing. For long periods, sometimes with interruptions, the local chiefs of the islands were tributaries to Persian monarchs. Persian place names, such as are still found in Baḥrain, are a vestige of the past. The Baḥārnah village of *deeh* (Dēh) which is perhaps derived from a Persian word meaning "village", *samaahiij*[7] (Samāhīj) from Persian *se* (three), *maahi* (fish), and *damistaan* (Damistān) arising from Persian *dabistaan* (school) attest to the extent of Persian lexical influence which the old region of al-Baḥrain and specifically the island of ?Awāl witnessed in pre-Islamic and post-Islamic times. Also, *baaġše* < *baaġče* (garden) a specific garden once created in Manāmah by a Persian sovereign of the islands, is another example. It is not surprising then to find certain Persian items in current use in the area; the ubiquitous adjective *xo(o)š* (good, fine) and the equally omnipresent *hast* (is, has), are in circulation in most Gulf dialects starting from Kuwait to Abu Dhabi.

Other items, such as *šahrabaani* (police station), *mišhad* <*mašhad* (shrine, sanctuary), *qand* (sugar cones), *samaawar* (samovar), etc. are items often heard in local traveller's accounts of Iran.

Further notes on Persian and Hindustani loan-words

Certain other items, viz. from Persian and Urdu are in use in current Baḥraini speech. Items like *p/binsil* (pencil) or *pa/urde* (curtain, screen) are common to contemporary Gulf Arabic.[8] Whether these items were acquired through Persian or Bombay Hindustani,[9] is often difficult to determine because words such as these are found in both of these languages. It is thought, however, that such items were acquired during the days of the British Raj in India when large numbers of Baḥrainis and other Gulf Arabs used to frequent the Indian port of Bombay.

The word *buuz*, from Persian *puuz* (mouth), should not be treated on equal footing with other borrowings such as *tindeel* (foreman, tally clerk) or *dirwaaze* (door, gateway), both from Persian. The difference is that *buuz* is much older and therefore has a wider currency in East Arabian speech than the latter two items. Shaikh Jalāl al-Ḥanafi, accounting for the occurrence of the same item in Baghdadi speech, dates its adoption to the fourth century A.H.[10] It is sometimes difficult to ascertain the chronology of an acquisition, particularly in view of inadequate historical data.

Arabicized forms in current circulation in the area

In their account of Arabicized forms, Arab grammarians list noun-forms which were incorporated into Arabic a long time ago. Some such forms, acquired largely from Persian, ceased to exist in the original language, yet their Arabicized forms are in circulation in the Gulf area as well as in *MDA*. Some common examples of these, such as recur in Baḥraini speech, are:[11]

ṣurwaal	(trouser)	*tannuur*	(coal oven)
?ibriisam	(silk) bay)	*jaṣṣ, yaṣṣ*	(gypsum)
?ibriig, briij	(pitcher)	*ṭašt*	(a metal wash-trough)
diibaaj	(brocade, soft pillow stuffing)	*ṭarz*	(form, shape)
		maaš	(Indian peas)
finjaal/n	(coffee-cup)		
juuraab	(sock)		
sirdaab	(cellar)		
dabbuus	(pin)		

Specimens of borrowings from English

The borrowings appearing in this list are of relatively recent incorporation, found both in A and B:

fannaš	he resigned (inf. 4)
fannašooh	he was dismissed
bančar/fančar	to have a puncture, or to be unable to continue an action
?anwaaṭ	notes (currency)
teem	time (inf. 11)
l-igliiz	the glaze (pottery) (inf. 12)

šalfaat	shelves (inf. 12)
beebaat	pipes (inf. 12)
bulisiyye	police
baabko	BAPCO (Baḥrain Petroleum Company)
l-sčinjaat	telephone exchanges (inf. 1)
tiksiyye	taxis (inf. 1)
kankari	concrete
albe	ALBA (Aluminium Baḥrain)
ḥaliib karnešan	"Carnation" milk (inf. 1)
aayil	oil
hoozaat	hoses (inf. 5)
lanjaat	launches (inf. 2)
ringaat	rings
salandaraat	cylinders (inf. 5)
čeenaaw	China (inf. 4)
dabal	double
?il-yoom oof	I am off-job today (inf. 5)
fuṣṣ iglaaṣ	first class
taraktaraat	tractors (inf. 6)
dreewliyye	drivers (inf. 6)
mawaatir	motor-cars (inf. 6)
čaakleeti	of chocolate colour
waayaraat	electric wires (inf. 6)
hinč	inch (inf. 6)
kumbani	company (inf. 7)
baasaat	passports (inf. 7)
l-ikreen	the crane (inf. 19)
it-taawaraat	the towers (inf. 19)
beebfitar	pipe-fitter (inf. 19)
preemar	primer (inf. 19)
beet griibaal	Messrs. Gray Paul and Co. (inf. 7)
jaalbuut	jolly-boat
minwar	man-of-war
fariig it-teel	a locality in Manāmah named after the Telegraphic Office built there in the early forties.

Specimens of borrowings from Hindustani (Urdu)

The items appearing below are common to both A and B:

baxšiiš	tip, gratuity (also found in Persian)
jookam	risky
beezaat	money (from paysa the smallest unit of Indian corrency)
abannid	I close (inf. 12) (Persian *bindan*)
dabbe	a small tin or box
saamaan	furniture (inf. 12) (also found in Persian)
namuune	kind, type (inf. 1.) (also found in Persian)
siide	straight (inf. 1)
man (waaḥid)	one maund (inf. 2) (a unit of weight in current use in India, Persia, also Portugal and western Asia (*O.E.D.*))
čeeku	Indian fruit (inf. 3)

gaari	cart (such as a fisherman's donkey cart) (inf. 3)
baanka	fan
juuri	pair (also found in Persian)
santara	Indian mandarin
huuri	a small boat (inf. 6)
tiizaab	acid (also found in Persian)
battaat	door hinges
ruumaal	handkerchief (also found in Persian)
kamče < *čamča*	spoon
čitti	note or written order (in Hindustani meaning letter or a doctor's prescription)
kašamaat	goggles, spectacles (also found in Persian *čašm* meaning "an eye" and *čašme* meaning "a fountain".

Specimens of borrowings from Persian

Below is a list of borrowings from Persian, most of which are of relatively recent incorporation and circulate in A and B:

zari	silver or gilded cord
roozane	niche
naġde	lamé
bištaxte (from piiše taxte[12]*)*	a small chest or coffer
doošag (from doosak)	mattress (also Turkish *dawšak*)
karaafi from čaar payye	folding bed
čarx	wheel
baadagiir[13]	wind-circulating tower
meewa	fruit
trinj <*toronj*	citron
naarjiil	cocoanut
dariiše <*dariiče*	window
leewaan< *?iiwaan*	hall or gallery
kišmiš	sultanas
xaašuuga <*qaašoq*	spoon, ladle
daane	one piece (also found in Hindustani)
irsi <*uruusi*	sash or verandah
bandar	anchorage
fašt	reef, shoal
falle	good, excellent, or wholes, bulks
ṭamaaše	a public scene
pahlawaan	hero, stunt
tindeel	tally clerk or head worker
siim (pl. *?asyaam*)	metal wire
neešaan	scar mark or target
kašte	picnic
bisyaar	plentiful, abundant
baxšiiš	present, gift, gratuity
rang, as in	colour, kind, brand
weeš ranga?	what sort is it?
uuti	iron for ironing clothes
fatiile	wick of a candle or a lantern

zanjafeh < *ganjiifeh*	playing cards
bugše < *buqča*	knapsack, envelope
buuk < *buqča*	wallet
dismaal < *dastmaal*	handkerchief
lagan < *lakan*	tub, basin
ʔaṭlas	satin
ġawaazi	money (from Persian *ġaazi*, a Persian coin)
ṣooġa	gift, present < Persian *sawġaat*
ġalyuun < *qalyuun*	hubble-bubble
mizraab < *miizaab*	spout
naxxaj < *nuxud*	chick-peas

Specimen of borrowings from Turkish

booš	empty, useless as in: *kill ta ^{c}abne raaḥ booš* (our efforts have been wasted)
jigaayir	cigarettes
ġuuzi	whole, roasted and stuffed lamb
fašag/fišag < *fišek*	cartridge[14]
baaše	Pasha, rich man
tambal	stupid, lazy (also found in Persian)
gumrug	custom house

Section C

Specimens of specialized lexis: items pertaining to *l-izraa^{c}a* (gardening)

Perhaps *l-izraa ^{c}a* (gardening) is one of the oldest professions pursued by the native islanders. It is as old as the existence of the numerous subterranean, natural springs found on the mainland and in the sea surrounding the islands. Below, is a specimen list of specialized lexis drawn up from the text of an interview with a Baḥrāni gardener:

tagḍiib	pruning
xaafuur	a protected seedling; transplant
binni l-ʔarḍ b-imḥašš	raking of the soil with a sickle so that the sun's rays permeate the soil
yiḥriš il-ʔarḍ	he stirs up the soil with a spade
ʔis-sawaagi	narrow channels which allow water to pass into planted areas
ʔil-ʔašraab	planted beds
ʔil-xaṭṭ	a furrow dug in preparation for the sowing of seeds
ijizz gatt	he cuts off lucerne
waḍaḥ waaḥid	one watering
yi ^{c}mur il-ʔarḍ	he ploughs or prepares the soil
ʔaḥiṭṭ il-^{c}uud is-sane haadi ʔu s-sane l-faanye yiḥmil	I plant the seedling this year, and it blossoms next year
nista ^{c}mil samaad, ʔu ^{c}uum	we use manure, and sardines
ʔil-ʔarḍ ṭab ^{c}aane	the land is soggy with water
il-ʔarḍ tiḥtaaj ila mbaašar	the soil requires systematic attendance

idiff^{c}aleehe r-raml	he covers it with sand
n^{c}aabil il-ʔarḍ	we till the soil

Items from the text of an interview with a date planter

^{c}akkaar	a native date-planter
naxlaawi	an attendant or owner of a date garden
nirkab bil-karr	we climb the date palm with the help of the *karr* (i.e, a circular rope with the middle part plaited to support the back of the climber while picking dates)
nixruf b-yaadiin-ne	we pick dates with both hands
w-unnabbit	we cut off the branches from the date palm to lighten it
w-unrawwis	we remove the prickles from the plant
w-unḥaddir	we cluster the bunches and lower them
w-inšallix jariid	we cut the dry fronds into pieces
w-insallix in-nabaat w-inyadne	we remove the leaves and plait them together
ṭal^{c}	spadix or spathe
jduu^{c}	trunks of date palm trees
ḍruuf	plaited baskets also known as *gaa^{c}uudiyye* used for sitting on bare floors
jraab	a plaited basket, deep enough to hold food remnants, such as bread, dates and date-stones, which form part of the cows' and donkeys' food
ḥṣur	mats
gafiif	straw-baskets
ziblaan	big straw-baskets

Specimens from the nautical vocabulary of a local *baḥḥaar (seaman)*

siif	harbour
ṣaṭwa	spots where there is abundant seaweed, used locally as fish-bait in traps
mislaat	net with a wooden handle used for scooping out trapped fish from a weir
garaagiir	fish-traps made of wire
ḥḍuur	weirs, fish-traps built from palm branches
saalye	fish-net
jazzaaf	bulk-buyer of fish also retailer from Arabic *juzaaf* (bulk-buying)
Pearl diving	
ġeeṣ	diver
snaan	anchor
baa^{c}	fathom
ġubba	deepest spot in the sea
maḥḥaar	pearl oysters
dayyiin	knitted basket for holding the oysters
seeb	seaman in charge of the rope tied to the diver
magaaliṭ	ropes used for lowering or pulling divers

gaḥamaat	rounds, turns (of diving)
tabbaat	dives
zaad	foodstuff consumed during the pearling season
rakba	the start of the pearling season
ṭaraḥ	dropped anchor
ixraab	rope attached to the anchor
baraax	hauling the anchor
sadur	prow, stem of a ship
tafur	poor, stern
nahhaam	boat chanter
jiib	small sail
ijyaab	the two big oars attached to the prow

Specimens from a weaver's specialized vocabulary[15]

rde	lady's cloak
wzaar	loin-cloth
fijje	one piece
ʔanaajir	red stripes such as made on the fringes of a lady's cloak
dfaaf	breast beams of a ground loom
liiṭa[16]	reed beater
igfuul	side beams of a ground loom
kariib	shuttle
madaawis	treadles
sadaat	the process of separating dust from cotton by beating the cotton with two sticks
sooj	the process of starching the newly spun thread
ḥirš	weft
ġazil	threads, warps, yarn

Specialized lexis: folk-medicine

The following items are obtained from the text of an interview with the owner of a traditional laboratory for the extraction of folk-medicine.[17] Some items are Arabic in origin, others have come from Persian, all of which were known to the Arabs since earlier times.

maay l-igruuf also known as *maay il-liggaaḥ:* liquid extracted from the outer crust of the male pollen of a date palm tree used for scenting tea and making soft drinks. Its medicinal properties are widely believed to cure minor heart troubles and to stop dizziness.

margaduuš < *mardaquuš:*[18] liquid extracted from marjoram and origanum. Recommended for abdominal pain and the activation of the bladder.

maay iz-zamuute: liquid extracted from origanum and thyme, recommended for stomach upset and acidity.

maay il-kawzabuun (from Persian) known to the Arabs as

ward ilsaan iṯ-ṯoor: from Persian "ox-tongue rose". It is a rose-coloured herb imported from Iran. It is believed that its medicinal properties help regulate the functioning of the heart. It is also recommended as anti-cough syrup. Ibn Manẓūr observes, "it was called so for its analogy to ox-tongue".[19]

maay iš-šaatirra: liquid extracted from a medicinal herb imported from Iran. Recommended for the alleviation of blood pressure, allergy, and *al-sawdaaʔ*, i.e., the liver ailment caused by excessive intake of dates.[20]

maay il-hindibaan: this liquid is extracted from wild chicory or endive. *hindib* is defined as "a pungent herb",[21] and is recommended for abdominal ailments
maay il-ḥilwa: liquid extracted from aniseed, recommended for the regulation of heart malfunctioning. Also given to children as, a sort of vitamin.
maay il-ḥiij < *maa? ?al-ḥaaj:* a wild thorny medicinal herb with deep-seated roots.[22] This herb is found in the plains of Baḥrain. It is recommended as a cure for jaundice and also believed to be effective for the release of blocked urine.

Finally, these items are among common folk-medicine in use today:

ḥadaj	colocynths, recommended for colds and rheumatic pains
bleelaj	myrobalana bellerica, prescribed for stomach upsets (imported from India)
ḥilbe	fenugreek plant (trigonella), recommended for chest or breathing difficulties; also good for regulating the function of the liver and bladder
^{c}išrig	circoea, a species of cassia, used mainly as a laxative.

NOTES

1. For the geographical distribution of the traditional industries of Bahrain, see Map X—Appendices.
2. The above form should not be confused with *baġala* (largest of the indigenous seagoing vessels). See H.R.P. Dixon, *The Arab of the Desert,* p. 473.
3. *Lexicon,* vol. II, p. 1554, defines *sheel* as: (reference is made to *Tahdhīb* of al-Azhari and *The Ṣiḥāḥ*) "A certain star (well known, namely, Canopus) not seen in Khurasān, but seen in al-^{c}Irāq; as Ibn Kunāsah says, seen in al-Ḥijāz and in all the land of the Arabs, but not seen in the land of Armenia."
4. From classical Arabic: *ka-habbati r-riiḥ* (like a gust of wind)
5. As in the local place-name: *?is-sihle l-foogiyye* (the upper Sihlah) or *?is-sihle l-ḥadriyye* (the lower Sihlah).
6. Medieval Arab sources render accounts of the flourishing trade between the island of ?Awāl and India. However, talking of eloquence among Arab tribes, Abu Naṣr al-Fārābi, in his *al-Alfāẓ wal-Ḥurūf* observes that Quraish were the most eloquent therefore a source of reference on good Arabic . . . that Bakr ibn Wā?il were excluded from such a prestige because they had as neighbours the Copts and the Persians, and so were ^{c}Abd al-Qais (of Baḥrain) and Azd (of ^{c}Umān) who mixed with the Indians and the Persians (see al-Suyūṭi, *al-Muzhir,* vol. I, pp. 211–212).
7. For a fuller treatment of this item, see part I of this study, p.22.
8. The item *purde* is also found in *MDA*. See *CDB*, p. 18.
9. The *Shorter Oxford Dictionary* defines Hindustani as "The Language of the Moslem conquerors of Hindustan, being Hindi with a large admixture of Arabic, Persian, etc.; also called Urdu. It is now a kind of lingua franca over all India."
10. *Mu ^{c}jam al-Alfāẓ al-Kuwaitiyya,* p. 52. Some such items are also adduced by Blanc as occurring in *MDA*.
11. For a fuller account of these, see al-Jawālīqi, *al-Mu ^{c}arrab min al-Kalām al-?A ^{c}jamiy* (Leipzig, 1867); also al-Tha ^{c}ālibi, *Fiqh al-Lugha;* and al-Suyūṭi, *al-Muzhir.*
12. From Persian *piiš* (under, beneath) and *taxt* (bed), normally this item is kept under the bed in olden times.
13. From Persian *baad* (air, wind) and *giir* (catcher), i.e., wind-catcher.
14. Also found in Persian, viz. *fišang.*

15. These items are extracted from the texts of interviews with informants from Bani Jamrah village. For the woven garments of the Arab world in the first two centuries of the Hijri calendar see article by Ṣāliḥ al-^{c}Ali, *"al-Ansijah fi l-Qarnayn al-Awwal wath-Thāni"*, *al-Abḥāth* (Quarterly Journal of the American University of Beirut), No. 4, vol. XIV, 1961, pp. 550–600. On the woven garments of al-Baḥrain and ^{c}Umān, see pp. 574–8 of the same article.
16. From the Arabic verbal form *yuliiṭ* (to join, to stick together), *Lisān al-^{c}Arab*, vol. VII, p. 395.
17. This laboratory is situated in ^{c}Ayn Dār village within the periphery of the greater village of Jid Ḥafṣ.
18. *Lisān*, vol. 6, p. 346.
19. Ibid., vol. 13, p. 227
20. Ibid., vol. 3, p. 227.
21. Ibid., vol. I, p. 788.
22. Ibid., vol. II, p. 246.

Part VI
Comparative analysis

In this final part of the study we shall examine the characteristic features of dialects A and B as described in the preceding parts, noting also the presence or absence of any particular features in one or the other of these two dialect groups. In addition, we shall indicate the comparable forms found in the adjoining dialect areas and in particular in ^{c}Umāni and Yamāni, as these two, in certain respects, show closer correspondence with Baḥrāni speech-forms than the other dialects of the area. It would seem indeed that Qaṭīfi and Ḥasāwi are also close to Baḥrāni Arabic but no detailed study of these two has yet been undertaken.

Phonology

The plosives

We will begin our analysis with the phonology of the Baḥārnah dialect, starting with the plosives and selecting here only those features of the dialect relevant for our present purpose. In our study of the phonology of B we have found that the occurrence of a medial and final *hamza* is relatively rare, and that initial *hamza* though somewhat lax, is found in items where it is also found in lit. Arabic, such as:

?ane (I) and *?ani* (fem.) etc.

A feature found in B is the realization of the *hamza* of certain items as pharyngal ^{c}. This feature, known as ^{c}*an* ^{c}*anah* ascribed to the Tamīmi tribes of eastern Arabia, has survived in these forms from B: *?uum* > ^{c}*uum* (sardines), *da?am* > *da* ^{c}*am* (he collided), etc.[1]

On the interchangeability in lit. Ar., of *hamza* and ^{c}, al-Lughawi (died 351 A.H.) adduces quite a number of items which can appear with a *hamza* as well as ^{c}. Some such items are:

kaṯa?a l-labanu[2] or *kaṯa* ^{c}*a* . . .
(the milk has thickened and the oily matter floated upon its surface)
mawtun zu?aaf[3] or *zu*^{c}*aaf* . . .
(quick death)
la?aṭahu b-sahmin[4] or *la* ^{c}*aṭahu* . . .
(he hit him with an arrow)

Ibn Jinni also observes the presence of ^{c}*an* ^{c}*anah* in certain Tamīmi forms.[5]

Reinhardt[6] notes the occurrence of the same feature in these forms from the Bani

Kharūṣ dialect of ᶜUmān:

?aṣl > *ᶜaṣl* (origin) and *?arnab* > *ᶜarnab* (rabbit)

Rhodokanakis[7] observes the occurrence in certain Ẓafāri forms of pharyngal ᶜ as glottal *?*.

Another transformation of penultimate *hamza* in B is its realization as *w*, in the following examples:

twaxxar for *ta?axxar* (he was late)
twaalafaw for *ta?aalafuu* (they got on well)

The above feature is also reported for Yamāni Arabic.[8]

The sound *p*, a borrowing from Persian as well as English, is often heard in these forms:

parde/purde (curtain, screen (from Persian))
pančar (puncture (from English))
pahlawaan (hero (from Persian))

The occurrence of the sound *p* is also reported for *MDA*,[9] and for some other contemporary east Arabian dialects.

Non-emphatic initial *b* of the stressed open syllable *Cá-* of *bágar*, etc. in B, has a different realization in A, where *b* is realized emphatic in combination with back vowel *u*. Cf.

	B			A
Cá-CaC	*bá-gar*	(cows)	Cú-CaC	*ḅú-gar*
	bá-ṣal	(onion)		*ḅú-ṣal*

Emphatic *ḅ* such as occurring in the phonemic environment in A above, is also noted in north Arabian speech. Cantineau[10] mentions the occurrence of non-emphatic *b* as an emphatic one in the neighbourhood of a *mufakhkham* consonant or the back vowels *o*, *u* and *α* in most north Arabian dialects. The presence of the same feature is also noted in *MDA*.[11] However, emphatic *ḅ* such as noted in A-forms above, is not found in Baḥarnah Arabic, nor in ᶜUmāni or Yamāni dialects.

A peculiarity of B, also reported for ᶜUmāni Arabic,[12] is the tendency to realize non-emphatic *t* as *ṭ* in the vicinity of fully back vowels in cardinals from thirteen to nineteen, such as:

?arbααṭα ᶜaš (fourteen) or *sabααṭ αᶜaš* (seventeen)

Devoicing of *d* to *t* in the vicinity of the gutturals *x* and *h* such as in these items from B: *tihin* for *dihin* (animal fat) or *?axathum* for *?axadhum* (he took them), is also noted in these demonstratives from Daṯīnah Arabic:[13]

taak for *daak* (that) and *haataak* for *haadaak*

Total assimilation of the voiceless *t* in the neighbourhood of voiced consonants *j*, *z*, *d*, *ṣ*, *ḍ* a feature common to B:

t > *j* *mijjannis* (naturalized)
t > *z* *mizzawwij* (married)

t > *d*	*yiddalla*^{c}	(he enjoys fondling)
t > *s*	*miṣṣaadig*	(befriending)
t > *d*	*miḍḍaarub*	(quarrelled)

Total assimilation of *t* mainly in the vicinity of emphatic consonants is also mentioned for ^{c}Umāni,[14] Ẓafāri,[15] and the Ḥarb dialect of Arabia.[16].

Affrication of *k*

The affricate *č* < *k* is found both in A and B, and it is also reported for a majority of East Arabian dialects. Cantineau,[17] notes it among the sheep nomads of the northern deserts of Arabia; Johnstone[18] mentions it for the Dōsiri and ^{c}Anazi dialects of eastern Arabia. Blanc[19] mentions it for Iraqi Arabic and notes: "evidence from present distribution as well as from older sources points to non-affrication in old sedentary populations versus conditioned affrication in populations descended from, or influenced by, north Arabian nomads."

Affrication of *k*, however, does not seem, except for the affricate *-č* of Arabic 2 f.s. *-k*, to be a regular feature in the majority of the Yamāni dialects. Cf. these forms from Daṯīnah Arabic with their counterforms from B:[20]

Daṯīnah		B
kalb[a]	dog	*čalb*
kam[b]	how much/many?	*čam*
kawa[c]	he cauterized	*čawa*
kuu^{c}[d]	elbow	*čuu*^{c}

Diem's[21] account of the affricate *č* in Yamāni Arabic confirms the view that affrication is not a regular feature of most Yamāni dialects. Except for the affricate *č* of the second person feminine singular found in the dialects of the northern uplands, viz. Khamir, Sinnatain, Raideh, ^{c}Amrān, affrication is markedly less frequent in Yamāni than in Baḥrāni Arabic.

Both in A and B affrication occurs in the following forms mainly in the neighbourhood of front, short and long vowels in non-emphatic environments:

A		B
simač	fish	*samač*
ḥeeč	toil, labour	*ḥeeč*
čibiir	elder, bigger	*čabiir*
ničaf	he changed his mind	*način*
itaḥačče	he speaks	*yitḥačče*

Affricate *č* in the vicinity of back vowels, less common than the above, is nonetheless found in these forms from A and B

A		B
^{c}*luuč*	chewing-gum	^{c}*luuč*
čuu^{c}	elbow	*čuu*^{c}
fčuuč	openings, funnels	*(i)fčuuč*

In the following demonstrative from A, affricate *č* has the grammatical function of a feminine marker. Cf:

A		B
diič/hadiič	(that (fem.))	*diik/ha(a)diik*

Affricate č such as noted in the ᶜAnazi form above, is also reported in the same form for *MDA*;[22] and in some north Arabian Beduin dialects;[23] and also in East Arabian dialects of the ᶜAnazi type.[24]

However, as in B, the *-k* of the above demonstrative remains stable in the following dialects: south Arabian,[25] central Arabian,[26] Yamāni[27] and ᶜUmāni[28] Arabic.

The *k* of the 2 m. plural suffix *-kum* is affricated in Sitrah. Cf:

A	Manāmah (B)	Sitrah (B)
lukum	*leekum*	*leečem*
ᶜindikum	*ᶜindkum*	*ᶜindčem*

The *k* of the 2 m.s. pronominal suffix is affricated to *-c* in Sitrah forms of B only. Thus:

ktaabeč	(your book(masc.))	*galameč*	(your pen (masc.))
ᶜaleeč	(on you)	*wiyyaač*	(with you)
?abġaač	(I need you)	*bawaddiič*	(I'll take you)

In A, the affrication of the 2 f.s. *k* to *č* serves a grammatical function. Thus:

ktaabič	(your book (fem.))	*glumič*	(your pen (fem.))

The affrication of *k* in these forms is noted in A only:

A		B
mičaan	place	*makaan*
mačtuub	letter	*maktuub*
čoočab	Kawkab, proper name; offshore spring	*kawkab*
čalaam	speech	*kalaam*

Finally, the affrication of *k* in these forms occurs in Sitrah speech only:

čill yoom	(every day)	*čillene*	(all of us)
niḍhač	(we were joking)	*?ačal*	(he ate)
		niftačč minčem	(we get rid of you)

2 f.s. *-k* > *-š*

A feature peculiar to B is the realization of *-k* of 2 f.s. as *-š*. Thus, *ragabatš* (your neck), and *ṯoobiš* (your gown). Thus feature known to Arab grammarians as *kashkashah*, and is ascribed to the Ribīᶜah tribes of the area. Sībawayhi, commenting on the same, gives these examples:[29]

	ra?aytu ġulaamiš	(I saw your servant)
and	*daxaltu daariš*	(I entered your house)

Ibn Jinni, accounting for the same, mentions these examples:[30]

ᶜalayš	(on, to you)	*minš*	(towards you)

Jayakar,[31] mentions the occurrence of the same in ᶜUmāni Arabic; Reinhardt[32] notes it for Banī Kharūṣ; Rhodokanakis[33] reports it for Ẓafāri Arabic; and Cantineau[34] mentions it in these forms from Banī Ṣakhar speech:

hawaajbeš	(your eyebrows)	*?abuuš*	(your father)

Rossi[35] also observes the occurrence of 2 f.s. *š* and *iš* in Ṣan ᶜā Arabic, as in: *baytiš* (your house) and *ḥaggiš* (for you); and Rhodokanakis[36] reports the same for Ẓafāri Arabic. Diem[37] commenting on this feature, notes that in the northern uplands of Yaman both *-č* and *-ič*, *-š* and *-iš* are found in the town dialects of Khamir, Sinnatain, Raideh, and ᶜAmrān; whereas in the southern uplands only *-š* is found in the dialects of Ẓafār, ad-Dāmighah and Bainūn; in the south-western areas, only *-š* is found in the dialects of al-Maḥall and Qafr.

The occurrence of the 2.f.s *-š* is also reported for Ḥasāwi Arabic.[38]

Devoicing of *q* to *k* in rural B

The realization of *q* as *k* in the contiguity of front and back vowels, is found in rural forms of B, particularly Sitrah forms. Cf.

urban B		rural B[39]
guum	get up	*kuum*
bagil	clover	*bakil*
ḥagg	for	*ḥakk*

On the interchangeability of *q* and *k* in Arabic, al-Lughawi[40] provides these examples:

naqiib or *nakiib*	(headman, leader)
?aqhab or *?akhab*	(dust colour)
?a ᶜraabiyyun quḥḥ or . . . *kuḥḥ*	(pure Arab)

Also on the occurrence of *q* as *k*, Landberg[41] gives these examples from Ḥaḍrami speech:

kaam for *qaam* (he stood up); *tkuum* for *tquum* (you stand up)

Rossi[42] also reports the presence of the above feature in Ṣan ᶜā speech. He observes that whenever *q* is followed by a voiceless consonant it is pronounced *k*, and when it is followed by a vowel it is pronounced *g* as in these illustrations from Ṣan ᶜā Arabic:

yikfiḍ	for	*yiqfiḍ*	(it shrinks)	*wakt*	(time)
bukšeh	for	*buqšeh*	(envelope)	*?awgaat*	(times)

q > *k* is also noted in these items from Baghdādi Arabic:[43]

waket	(time)	*ketal*	(he killed)	*kufax*	(he slapped)

q > *ġ* in A

A feature noted among the ᶜAnazi speakers of Baḥrain is the realization of non-final *q* as *ġ* in the neighbourhood of front and back vowels as in this example: *raġum* (number). This feature is not found in Qaṭīfi, Ḥasāwi, ᶜUmāni or Baḥrāni speech forms of eastern Arabia. It is, however, mentioned for the Jabal Reimah district of the Yaman.[44] It is also reported for the Yamāni Arabic of the western mountain chains and the Ḥugariyeh region to the south of it, as these examples from al-Hadiyeh dialect of the south-western mountain chains show:[45]

xulaġat	(she was born)	*maa tuġuul*	(what do you say?)
ʔaġdir	(I can)	*ġahweh*	(coffee)

Cantineau[46] also mentions the presence of the above feature in north Arabian Beduin dialects. Johnstone[47] reports the same for Kuwaiti and the ᶜAnazi dialects of Baḥrain.

ġ > *q* in A

Another feature noted for the ᶜAnazi forms of Bahrain is the realization, by some speakers, of non-final Arabic *ġ* as *q*. *q* < *ġ* is also reported for Mawāli speech of north Arabia, as these examples show:[48]

qarbal < *ġarbal* (to trouble)
qanamhum < *ġanamhum* (their sheep)

The affrication of *q* in A

q realized *j* is a phonetic feature peculiar mainly to nomadic Arabic. It is found in northern speech in Arabia[49] and also in their East Arabian branches, viz. Kuwaiti, the ᶜAnazi of Baḥrain, Qaṭari and in the dialect of Abu Ẕabi and the adjoining areas. *q* > *j*, however, is not a regular feature of Baḥrāni, Ḥasāwi, Qaṭīfi, ᶜUmāni or Yamāni, all of which are sedentary dialects.

Johnstone[50] notes the affrication of *q* in the contiguity of front vowels in the ᶜAnazi speech of eastern Arabia; Blanc[51] accounting for the reflexes of *q* in *MDA*, confirms the presence of *g*<*q* and *k* <*q*, and to a lesser extent *j* < *q*. In certain forms, Blanc notes, old Arabic *q* exhibits two distinct realizations in Baghdādi Arabic, viz. *šarji* /*šargi* (eastern); *jeddaam*/*geddaam* (before); *ṣadiij*/*ṣadiig* (friend). Blanc concludes that some of his Muslim informants who have more forms with *j* than with *g* show the influence of the rural dialects of Iraq, where *j* reflexes are commoner.

Although *q* shows a higher rate of frequency in ᶜUmāni than Baḥrāni Arabic, its affricate form *j* < *q* is almost absent in both. A reading of Landberg, Rossi and Diem does not lead to the conclusion that the affricate *j* < *q* is a regular feature of Yamāni Arabic.

However, affrication of *q* to *j* in ᶜAnazi forms of Baḥrain is found in the neighbourhood of short and long front vowels, such as:

jisme	(division, portion)	*waajif*	(standing)
ġaamij	(dark)	*rifiij*	(friend)

Palatalization of *j*

j realized as *y*, a regular feature of the ^{c}Anazi dialects of Baḥrain and somewhat less so in rural forms of B is found in all positions, as in these examples from rural B:

yariid for *jariid* (fronds) *ḥayar* for *ḥajar* (stone)
ʔil-ḥayy for *ʔil-ḥajj* (the pilgrimage)

Cantineau[52] and Socin[53] mention the presence of the above feature in northern and central dialects of Arabia. Johnstone[54] also reports the same for the majority of east Arabian dialects which have emanated from the former dialects. Landberg[55] observes the same feature in Ḥaḍrami speech and Rhodokanakis[56] in Ẓafāri Arabic. This appears to be a cross-dialectal feature.

A feature of rural B is the realization of non-final *j* as *g* mainly in the vicinity of front vowels, as in these examples:

jafiir > *gafiir* (basket) *l-ijnuub* > *l-ignuub* (the south)

The above feature is absent in the ^{c}Anazi forms of Eastern Arabia. Reinhardt,[57] however, reports it for the Bani Kharūṣ of ^{c}Umān, Thus:

yuugid (it is found) *wugh* (face)

j > *g* is also noted for Ẓafāri Arabic in forms such as:[58]

geles (he sat) *šigra* (a tree) *dgaag* (hens)

Cantineau[59] also notes the same for Shammari and ^{c}Anazi speech of north Arabia; Rossi[60] mentions it for Tihāmah and the Ta^{c}izz Arabic of the Yaman; and Diem[61] reports the occurrence of *j* as *g* and g^{y} for the Yamāni dialects of the western mountain chain and Ḥugariyeh, and for the south-western dialects viz. Qafr in these examples:

giik	(I came)	*giina*	(we came)
gamal	(camel)	*gabal*	(mountain)

Velar *ḷ*

Velar *ḷ* [ɫ] such as is found in the contiguity of the emphatics *ṣ, ḍ, ṭ* in: *ṣaḷbuux* (shingle), *(i) ḍḷuu* ^{c} (ribs), *tiḷbe* (a wish), is common both to A and B; but the occurrence of the velar *ḷ* in contiguity with the consonants *x, ġ, g* < *q*, is exclusive to A. Cf:

A		B
xaḷaaḷ	(green unripe dates)	*xalaal*
šuġuḷ	(work)	*šiġil*
gabuḷ	(before)	*gabil*

Velar *ḷ*, such as noted for ^{c}Anazi forms of Baḥrain above, is also reported in these forms from *MDA*:[62] *xaaḷ* (mother's brother); *xaḷḷ* (vinegar); *šuġuḷ* (work).

Velar *ḷ* such as occurs in the vicinity of *x, ṣ, ḍ, ṭ,* is also reported for Ḥaḍrami[63] and Daṯīna[64] Arabic, Ẓafāri[65] and for the majority of the north Arabian dialects.[66]

The fricatives

A feature noted in B, and to a lesser degree in A, is the tendency to realize non-emphatic *s* of certain forms as *ṣ* in the neighbourhood of the guttural *x* and the emphatic *ṭ* such as in these illustrations:

suxma	(vest)	*ʔaṣmax*	(deaf)
ṣaaṭuur	(adze)	*bṣaaṭ*	(rug)

On the interchangeability of *s* and *ṣ* in certain Arabic words, al-Lughawi[67] provides these examples:

maġas > *maġaṣ*	(stomach pain)
yanbis > *yanbiṣ*	(to utter, whisper)

Sībawayhi,[68] accounting for the above feature, notes its occurrence in the vicinity of *x* and *ṭ* in these Arabic forms:

salax > *ṣalax*	(he has slain)
*saaṭi*ᶜ > *ṣaaṭi*ᶜ	(glittering, shining)

Reinhardt[69] also on the same feature, provides these examples from the Wādi Bani Kharūṣ:

s > *ṣ* as in: *waṣax* (dirt); *ṣixxaam* (soot or smut)

Rhodokanakis[70] also notes this feature in this example from Ẓafāri Arabic:

ṣulṭaan for *sulṭaan* (sovereign, ruler)

Rossi[71] mentions the occurrence of *s* as *ṣ* in the neighbourhood of emphatic *ṭ* in Ṣan ᶜā speech, and Landberg[72] notes it for Ḥaḍrami Arabic.

The occurrence of *ṯ* as *f* in B

Arabic inter-dental *ṯ* has the free variant *f* in B, e.g.,

fuum	(garlic)	for	*ṯuum*	*nafye*	(female)	for	*naṯye*
falaafe	(three)	for	*ṯalaaṯa*				

Arab grammarians, accounting for the same feature, adduce large lists of words wherein *ṯ* and *f* are interchangeable. Specimens of these are:[73]

init.	*ṯarwa/farwa*[74] (wealth)		*ṯaalaj/faalaj*[75]	(paralysis)
med.	*ḥuṯaala/ḥufaala*[76]	(dregs, worst parts)		
	ʔinṯajar/ʔinfajar[77]	(burst, gushed out)		
fin.	*jadaṯ/jadaf*[78]	(grave)		
	taḥannaṯ/taḥannaf[79]	(he relinquished the worship of idols)		

Landberg[80] notes the occurrence of *ṯ* as *f* in Ḥaḍrami Arabic; Rhodokanakis[81] mentions it for Ẓafāri Arabic in these examples:

ṯehem/fehem	(he understood)	*ṯoog/foog*	(up, upstairs)
ṯimhe/famhe	(her mouth)		

Rossi notes it in these forms from Yamāni Arabic:

Ṣan ᶜā speech:[82]	*miṯl/mifl*	(like, as)
Ta ᶜizz speech:[83]	*ḥadiiṯ/ḥadiif*	(talk)
al-Ḥudaidah: [84]	*ṯumm/fumm*	(mouth)

Smeaton[85] confirms the occurrence of *ṯ* as *f* in Ḥasāwi speech.

The partial preservation of *d* both in A and B has been mentioned. However, the occurrence of *ḏ* in the following demonstratives is found in A only. Cf:

A		B
haaḏi	(this)	*haade*
haḏeele	(these)	*hade (e) leen*

The occurrence of *ḏ* in demonstratives is also reported for Daṯīnah and Ḥaḍrami speech.[86]

The replacement of Arabic inter-dental *ẓ* by *ḍ* both in A and B, has a parallel in ᶜUmāni Arabic, as in:[87]

naḍar	(eye-sight)	*ḥafaḍ*	(he learnt)

The above feature is also mentioned for Ḥaḍrami,[88] north Arabian,[89] and for Ḥudaidah Arabic.[90]

The preservation of *-h* of Arabic 3 m.s. pronominal suffix *-hu* in rural forms of B is also reported for Ṣan ᶜā[91] and ᶜUmāni[92] Arabic, e.g.

ᶜindeh	(he has it)	*?ileh*	(for him)

The occurrence in B of sentence-final, stressed *-é,* used to indicate question, is also mentioned for ᶜUmāni Arabic,[93] e.g.

min ḍarabk? imḥammad-é? (who hit you? Muḥammad?)

The occurrence of *-n* in 2 f.s. and 2 c.pl. in B

The occurrence in B of an idiosyncratic feature, viz. *-n* in the pronouns 2 f.s. *?intiin* (you) and 2 c.pl. *?intuun* (you), is also attested in a number of dialects. Jayakar[94] mentions the presence in ᶜUmāni Arabic of 2 f.pl. *-n* , but not of 2 f.s. *-n.* Cantineau[95] reports the occurrence of *-n* in Sba ᶜa and the Rass forms: 2 f.pl. *?antan;* Rossi[96] notes only the preservation in Ṣan ᶜā Arabic of 2 f.pl *-n* but not of 2 f.s. *-n.* Blanc[97] reports the occurrence of *-n* in the imperfect 2 f.s. and 2nd and 3rd person plural as in these Muslim forms: *tketbiin* (you write) (f.s.), *tketbuun* (2nd. pl.), *yketbuun* (3rd pl.). But in his account of independent pronouns, *-n* does not appear in the 2 f.s. nor 2 c.pl. forms of the pronouns as these examples from *MDA* show:

	Muslim	Jewish	Christian
2 f.s.	*enti*	*enti*	*enti*
2 c.pl.	*entu*	*entem*	*entem*

As regards the ^{c}Anazi forms of Baḥrain, Johnstone[98] does not report the occurrence of 2 f.s. or 2 c.pl. *-n* in the independent personal pronouns, although he reports the presence of 2 f.pl. *-n* in certain other East Arabian forms. He also mentions the presence of 2 f.s. and 2 c.pl. *-n* in verb-forms from the ^{c}Anazi dialect of Baḥrain. Thus:

2 f.s.	*thiḏriin*	(you chatter)	2 c.pl.	*t^{c}arfuun*	(you know)

Diem[99] writing on the same feature in Yamāni dialects mentions it for the northern uplands in the 2 f.pl. form *?antinna,* and *?antin;* and in the southern uplands in 2 f.pl. *?antain;* and in the coastal plain, viz. Tihāmeh, in 2 m.pl. *?antun;* and al-Ḥudaideh 2 f.pl. *?antin;* and in the south-western dialects he mentions for Ta ^{c}izz the 2 f.pl. *?antin,* al-^{c}Udain 2 f.pl. *?antan,* and al-Maḥall 2 f.pl. *?antun.* As regards Ẓafāri Arabic,[100] this feature is absent as these examples show:

2 f.s.	*enti*	2 c.pl.	*entum*

It is also absent from the Ḥasāwi form of the same:[101]
2 f.s *inti* (you)

Imāla in B

Imāla, a salient phonetic feature of both A and B, is ascribed to the Tamīm and ^{c}Abd al-Qais tribes of Eastern Arabia.[102] Arab grammarians, including Sībawayhi, distinguish between two types of *imāla,* viz. internal and word-final both of which are regarded as a variety of palatalization.[103]

In the Baḥārnah dialect only word-final *imāla* is found. It is found in certain consonantal environments where Arabic unstressed short and long vowels *-a* and *-aa* are realized *-e.* Wright[104] accounting for the same feature defines it as the 'deflection' of the sound *a* and *aa* towards *e* and *ee,* respectively.

In B *imāla* affects the Arabic nominal and verbal suffix *-a(a).* Thus:

ni^{c}me	(grace, bounty)	*same*	(sky)
yitmašše	(he is walking)	*yithačče*	(he is talking)

Imāla in urban B and to a large degree in rural B is normally absent in words that have the emphatic consonants *ṣ, ḍ, ṭ* as their final radical, as:[105]

raṣaaṣa (bullet) *fawḍa* (noise, confusion) *ḥooṭa* (enclosure)

However, in the following forms from a Dirāzi speaker, *imala* occurs in post-*ṭ* position:

murbaṭe ((donkey's) harness) *barbuṭe* (I shall tie it)

In the following forms from rural and urban B, *imāla* occurs in the former only. Cf:

rural B		urban B
yiṭla^{c}e	(he takes it out)	*yiṭla^{c}a*
tbii^{c}e	(he sells it)	*tbii^{c}a*
ġurfe	(room)	*ġurfa*

Rhodokanakis[106] notes the occurrence of word-final *imāla* in these examples from Ẓafāri Arabic:

?ane	(I)	*ᶜaše*	(supper)

Rossi,[107] accounting for the same in Ṣan ᶜā Arabic states that the vowel, i.e., *-a* is less *imālized* in context and more in pause as in these illustrations from the same:

giime	(price)	*giimat*	(price of)

Further examples of *imāla* in Ṣan ᶜā Arabic, also shared by B are:[108]

ḥilbe	(trigonella)	*?il-mee*	(water)	*jee*	(he came)

Blanc, writing on the same feature in *MDA,* notes the presence of both internal and word-final *imāla.* He mentions the realization of word-final *-a* as *-e,* particularly in Syrian speech.[109]

Diem,[110] also notes the occurrence of *-a* as *-e* in the Yamāni dialects of the northern uplands, in pause only, viz.

je	(he came)	*katabne*	(we wrote)

But not in liaison: *jat* (she came)

In his introductory remarks, Alexander Borg[111] mentions *imāla* of *-aa* and *-a* for the dialects of Iraq, Aleppo, Ḥawrān, Negev Beduins, Upper Egypt and North Africa. *Imāla* of the feminine ending *-a,* he adds, is to be found in a number of dialects not having any other kind of umlaut, medial or final. These include the dialects of Damascus, Ḥamā and various Lebanese and Palestinian dialects.

Diphthongs

The lit. Ar. diphthongs *-ay-* and *-aw-* are realized *-ee-* and *-oo-* respectively both in A and urban B. *-ey-* (arising from lit. Ar. *-ay-)* is preserved in rural B, less so in the urban varieties of B, e.g.

ṣaḥeyne	(we woke up)	*xeyr*	(good, grace)

In B, the 3 pl. suffix *-uu* is invariably diphthongized to *-aw* as in: *?akalaw* (they ate). This is a feature which B shares with all the A dialects of E. Arabia. Certain vowels, such as found in urban B, are diphthongized in rural B Cf:

	urban B		rural B
i > *ay*	*biruuḥ*	(he will go)	*bayruuḥ*
i > *iy*	*ḥači*	(talk)	*ḥačiy*
oo > *ow*	*hadoole*	(these)	*hadowle*
ee > *ey*	*beezaat*	(money)	*beyzaat*

Reinhardt[112] notes the occurrence of *-aw* as *-oo* in Bani Kharūṣ forms of speech;

Rhodokanakis[113] mentions two types of diphthongization in Ẓafāri Arabic, viz. *ii > ey* after *h,* ^{c}*, ḥ, ṭ, x* as in: *ṣób* ^{c}*ey* (my finger) and *mwaá* ^{c}*eyn* (utensils) and *uu > éw* or *ów*, as in: *yisma* ^{c}*ewn* (they hear). Partial preservation in Ẓafāri Arabic of an older diphthong *ay* is also noted as in the example: *hi* and *hey* (she) both of which are found. Cantineau,[114] notes the occurrence in north Arabian speech of *aw* as *oo* and *ay* as *ee*. Rossi[115] mentions the preservation in Yamāni speech of the diphthongs *aw* and *ay*. Blanc[116] notes the preservation in *MDA* of Arabic diphthongs *ay* and *aw;* and Johnstone[117] observes the occurrence of Arabic *ay* and *aw* in addition to *-uy* and *-ei* in a majority of east Arabian dialects.

Morphology

Verbal forms

Arabic strong verb of the type FaMaL undergoes phonemic changes in A, not found in the same forms in B. The Arabic stressed short vowel *a* in the initial syllable of the perfect of the simple verb is retained in B, whereas in A, since *a* occurs in open syllable only in limited circumstances, it is realized as *i*.[118]

A		B
kitab	(he wrote)	*katab*
širab	(he drank)	*šarab*

Cantineau[119] notes the occurrence of FaMaL as FiMaL for most of the north Arabian dialects; Blanc[120] reports the same for certain areas of *MDA;* Johnstone[121] mentions the sound change involved for the ^{c}Anazi forms of Kuwait and Baḥrain as well as the majority of east Arabian and Najdi dialects. However, the sound change involved in A dialects are not mentioned for ^{c}Umāni or Yamāni Arabic. On the other hand, the Baḥārnah forms above correspond closely to ^{c}Umāni[122] and Ṣan ^{c}ā[123] Arabic.

Certain perfect forms of Arabic weak verbs, viz. *?akal* and *?axaḏ* lose the prefix *?a-* in A. Cf:

	A		B
1 & 2 m.s.	*kaleet*	(I ate)	*?akalt*
1 & 2 m.s.	*xaḏeet*	(I took)	*?axadt*
3 m.s.	*kalaaha*	(he ate it)	*?akalhe*
3 m.s.	*xaḏaaha*	(he took it)	*?axadhe*

Similar renderings such as are noted for A above are also reported for the Shammari dialects of north Arabia and those of the sheep nomads.[124] Johnstone also reports the same for the majority of the East Arabian dialects of the ^{c}Anazi type.[125] However, comparable forms of these, viz. 3 m.s. *xad* and *kal,* such as are present both in A and B, are also noted for ^{c}Umāni[126] and Daṯīnah[127] Arabic.

A feature of B is the replacement of the perfect theme ?aFMaL by the theme FaMMaL, as: viz.:

xabbar < *?axbar* (he told) *rassal* < *?arsal* (he sent)

The above feature is also noted for ^{c}Umāni,[128] Ṣan ^{c}āni,[129] Ḥaḏrami[130] and the dialect of Daṯīnah.[131]

A feature found in the ᶜAnazi forms of Baḥrain is the elision of the Arabic unstressed short vowel *a* in the initial syllable of a series of short vowels, such as occur in the perfect forms 3 f.s. and 3 c.pl. This feature does not occur in B. Cf.

	A		B
3 f.s.	*ktibat*	(she wrote)	*katabat*
3 c.pl.	*ktibaw*	(they wrote)	*katabaw*

Cantineau[132] notes this kind of elision in north Arabian dialects; Rossi[133] observes the same for Ṣan ᶜā Arabic; Blanc[134] mentions the occurrence in Muslim forms of *e* and *u* for Arabic unstressed vowel *a*, in:

3 f.s.	*ketbat, kuḅrat*	3 c.pl.	*ketbaw, kuḅraw*

Johnstone[135] notes the elision of the vowel *a* in the majority of East Arabian dialects in comparable patterns as in the these illustrations:

3 f.s.	*ktibat*	3 m.pl.	*ktibaw*	3 f.pl.	*ktiban*

The imperfect preformative *y-*

Both in A and B the Arabic imperfect preformative 3 m.s. *y-* of certain verbs is realized *i-* as in these examples from B:

y- >*i-*	hollow verbs	*iṣuum*	(he fasts)
		ibaat	(he stays overnight)
	weak verbs	*iji*	(he comes)
		iḥayyi	(he greets or salutes)
	geminate verbs	*imurr*	(he passes by)
		idill	(he directs)

Cantineau[136] reports the occurrence of the above feature in examples from Shammari speech, as:

iriid	(he wants)	*išuuf*	(he sees)

Rossi[137] also notes it for Yamāni Arabic, in:

Ḥudaidah forms:	*iruuḥ* (he goes)	*isiir*	(he walks)
Tihameh forms:	*išuuf* (he sees)	*iḥiid*	(he deviates, gives up)

In ᶜUmāni Arabic the 3 m.s. imperfect preformative *y-* remains stable as these examples show:[138]

yaridd	(he returns)	*yiji*	(he comes)
yamill	(he gets bored)		

The imperfect preformative of the FaMaL pattern both in A and B is:

	A		B	
3 m.s.	*ya-*	as in *yaktib*	*yi-*	as in *yiktib*
2 pl.	*ta-*	as in *taktib*	*ti-*	as in *tiktib*
1 pl.	*na-*	as in *naktib*	*ni-*	as in *niktib*

As the above examples show, the Baḥārnah forms of the imperfect preformatives employ, invariably, *i* and not *a*. The replacement of *a* by *i* is known to Arab grammarians as *taltalat Bahrā?*, already mentioned in Part III. The imperfect preformatives of strong verbs for ᶜUmāni Arabic are:[139]

3 m.s.	*yarkab*	2 m.s.	*tarkab*	1 pl. *narkab*
3 m.s.	*yijlis*	2 m.s.	*tijlis*	1 pl. *nijlis*
3 m.s.	*yu/iktib*	2 m.s.	*tu/iktu/ib*	1 pl. 1 pl. *nu/iktu/ib*

And in Ṣan ᶜā Arabic these are:[140]

3 m.s.	*ya-*	2 pl.	*ta-*	1 c.pl.	*na-*

But the imperfect preformatives of verbs of the type FaMiLa in Ṣan ᶜā Arabic are:

3 m.s.	*yi-*	2 pl.	*ti-*	1 c.pl.	*ni-* as in:
	yišrab		*tišrab*		*nišrab*

And for certain verbs of the type FaMaLa:

3 m.s.	*yuxrij*	2 pl.	*tuxrij*	1 c.pl.	*nuxrij*

In Ẓafāri Arabic[141] the preformatives are more frequently:

3 m.s. *yi-*, 2 pl. *ti-*, 1 c.pl. *ni-*,
and less frequently *ya-*, *ta-*, *na-*

In north Arabian dialects the preformatives *ya-*, *ta-* and *na-* are reported for the majority of them.[142]

As regards Iraqi Arabic, Blanc gives these examples for Muslim Baghdādi:[143]

3 m.s.	*yeftehem*	2 c.pl.	*teftehmuun*	1 c.pl.	*neftehem*

Johnstone,[144] accounting for the same in East Arabian speech, mentions the occurence of 3 m.s. *ya-*, 2 m./f. *ta-* and 1 c.pl. *na-* in the majority of East Arabian dialects including the ᶜAnazi forms of Baḥrain which tally closely with Cantineau's account for north Arabian.

The terminations *-inne* and *-tinne*

A feature shared by both ᶜUmāni[145] and Baḥrāni Arabic is the employment of *-inne/h* and *-tinne/h* in verbal forms. These terminations, viz. *energetic -n(n)* + pronominal suffix *-eh* are added to the form FaaMiL, as:

min šaarinne/h? (who bought it?)
fariide ṭaabxitinne/h (Farida cooked it)

The occurrence of *-inne,* such as noted above, is also mentioned for Ḥaḍrami speech.[146]

FaMaaMiiL for FaMMaaLuun

A salient feature in B and some other dialects of the area is the replacement of the sound plural pattern FaMMaaLuun by FaMaaMiiL, particularly in nouns that denote crafts or professions, as:

galaaliif	(boat builders)	*xabaabiiz*	(bakers)
gaṣaaṣiib	(butchers)	*bagaagiil*	(grocers)

The FaMaaMiiL pattern is also noted for ^{c}Umāni Arabic.[147]

In Ṣan ^{c}āni,[148] Ẓafāri[149] and north Arabian[150] speech, only the pattern FaMaaLiiL, but not FaMaaMiiL is reported.

B.H. Smeaton reports the occurrence of FaMaaMiiL in these examples from Ḥasāwi Arabic:[151]

samaamiik	(fishermen)	*najaajiir*	(carpenters)

?aFMaL > FaMaL in A

In ^{c}Anazi dialects the ?aFMaL pattern is realized FaMaL where the first radical is a guttural, as, for example, *ḥamar* for *?aḥmar* and *^{c}awar* for *?a ^{c}war.* This phenomenon, which is not characteristic of B, is also reported for some other dialects of the area.

Forms such as noted for A are also reported for Bani Kharūṣ[152] and north Arabian[153] speech, but not for Ṣan ^{c}ā Arabic[154] wherein the same forms are realized ?aFMaL as in B. Perhaps the presence in Bani Kharūṣ of FaMaL for ?aFMaL is indicative of an old Najdi influence.

Tanwīn

A classical Arabic feature that has survived in B is the (caseless) nunation *-in,* as in:

rṭabatin zeene	(good ripe date)
čammin waaḥid	(a few persons)

Tanwīn has also survived in some other dialects of the area. Rhodokanakis[155] mentions the occurrence of *-en and -in* in Ẓafāri Arabic; Cantineau[156] also notes the occurrence in pause of *- ăn, -en, -in* in north Arabian speech. Johnstone,[157] accounting for the same in east Arabian dialects, writes that: "indefinite nouns in non-final positions may have the ending *-an, -in, – ən* which, however, is not inflected for case." Al-Ḥāzmi,[158] in his study of the dialect of Ḥarb tribes, mentions the absence of *tanwīn* among the settled population, but notes its frequent occurrence in adverbs in the same dialect. In the dialects of Qaṣīm all nouns in collocation must have *-in,* thus distinguishing them from pausal forms.

- ^{c}aš and ^{c}ašar

Another feature found in B and some other dialects is the occurrence of both *- ^{c}ašar and - ^{c}aš* for Arabic cardinal *- ^{c}ašar* in the numerals from eleven to nineteen.

Reinhardt,[159] accounting for cardinals in ^{c}Umāni notes the presence of both long and short forms. Rhodokanakis[160] reports the occurrence in Ẓafāri Arabic of the longer form only, viz. *- ^{c}š(y) ar* and *- ^{c}šer;* Rossi,[161] writing on the same in Ṣan ^{c}ā Arabic, mentions the presence of both forms as in: *ḥad ^{c}ašir* and *ḥad ^{c}aš* (eleven). Blanc[162] notes the presence in *MDA* of the shorter form only; and Cantineau[163] on the same in north Arabian observes that before a following noun the short form - *ᶜaš* is employed as in: *t̲na ᶜaš sene* (twelve years), but the longer form may occur in isolation only. Johnstone,[164] accounting for the same feature in east Arabian dialects notes the presence only of the shorter form - *ᶜaš* in cardinals from eleven to nineteen. As regards the ᶜAnazi forms of Baḥrain, he mentions the occurrence of the longer form only, viz. - *ᶜášar.*

Personal Pronouns

A peculiarity in B, to the exclusion of A, is the distinction between 1 m.s. *ʔane* (I) and 1 f.s. *ʔani.*[165] Such a distinction is also reported for certain Yamāni dialects,[166] and for Aden Arabic.[167]

Diem[168] notes, specifically, the occurrence of *ʔana* (masc.) and *ʔani* (fem) in the dialects of the southern uplands of the Yaman, viz. Ẓafār, and in the coastal plains, such as Tihāmah and Ḥudaidah, and also in a number of dialects in the south-western areas.

However, the above distinction is not reported for ᶜUmāni,[169] Dat̲īnah,[170] Iraqi,[171] and Ṣan ᶜā[172] Arabic.

3 m.s. *hu(u)* and 3 f.s. *hi (i)*

The independent pronouns for the third person are realized differently both in A and B. Whereas in A, their realization tallies closely with north Arabian Bedouin dialects, in B they are paralleled by ᶜUmāni and Yamāni forms. Cf:

	A		B
3 m.s.	*uhwa*	(he)	*hu(u)*
3 f.s.	*ihya*	(she)	*hi(i)*

hu(u) and *hi(i),* such as found in B, are also reported for ᶜUmāni,[173] Dat̲īnah,[174] Ẓafāri,[175] Ṣan ᶜā Arabic[176] and for the majority of the Yamāni dialects of the northern uplands, the coastal plains, viz. Tihāmeh and Ḥudaidah, and the southwestern areas including Ta ᶜizz[177] and for Ḥasāwi.[178] In *MDA,* the Muslim and Christian forms of the same are: *huwwa* (m.) and *hiyya* (f.)[179]

Negated forms of the pronouns in B, such as *ma(a)hu* (he isn't) and *ma(a)hi* (she isn't) are also mentioned for the dialects of the northern uplands of the Yaman,[180] Ẓafāri[181] and Dat̲īnah[182] Arabic. Johnstone[183] notes the occurrence, in the ᶜAnazi dialects of Baḥrain, of *mub, mhub* and *muu;* and *m[h]uu* (masc.), *m[hii]* (fem.) in the ᶜAjmi dialect of Kuwait.

Demonstratives

Demonstrative pronouns have shorter free variants both in A and B. A characteristic feature in A is the occurrence of the shorter form *d̲iič* (that) (fem.), invariably realized, except for Sitrah form *ha(a)diič, diik* in B. Whereas in A, *d̲i* (this) is of common gender, in B its counterpart *de* (this) is employed for the masculine gender and *di* for the feminine.

In Ẓafāri Arabic, *d̲ee* is used for masculine gender only, whereas *d̲ii* is employed for both.[184]

The demonstratives *haak(a)* (that) (masc.) and *heek(a)* (that) (fem.) found in rural B are absent from the rest of B and A. Cf:

	rural B	A		urban B
f.s.	*heek, heeka, diik*	*d̠iič*	(that)	*diik*
m.s.	*haak, haaka, daak*	*d̠aak*	(that)	*daak*

haak, as reported for rural B, is also noted for Najdi[185] and Moroccan[186] Arabic; and *haaka* for Tunisian Arabic.[187]

The occurrence of a series of short syllables in B

A feature peculiar to B is the occurrence of front *a* in a series of short syllables. Cf. these forms from A and B:

	B		A
nouns:	*ḥaṭaba*	(a piece of wood)	*ḥtuba*
	samace	(a fish)	*smiče*
	waraga	(a paper)	*wriga*
verbs.	*ḍaraba (h)*	(he hit him)	*ḍruba*
	ṣafaga(h)	(he slapped him)	*ṣfuga*
	ḥamalateh	(she bore him)	*ḥmilteh*

Diem[188] notes the occurrence of a series of short open syllables in the southern uplands, particularly in the Ẓafāri dialect of Yaman in these examples:

ḥámalateh (she carried it) *kátabateh* (she wrote it)

Cantineau,[189] accounting for the same feature in north Arabian speech, notes that in a succession of short syllables with the vowel *a* the first is elided, as in these examples:

bgara < *bagara* or *ktabat* < *katabat*

The effect of gutturals on the syllable structure in A

The effect of the gutturals on the syllable structure where the non-final Arabic closed syllable CaC- is realized CCa-, is a feature typical of Najdi and ᶜAnazi forms of A, and is not found in pre-ᶜAnazi east Arabian speech. Cf:

A		B
ghawa	(coffee)	*gahwa*
ḥmise	(turtle)	*ḥamase*

Cantineau,[190] accounting for the same in north Arabian speech, notes that after gutturals *x, ġ, ḥ,* ᶜ, *h* an open *a* is employed as these examples show:

ṣxala (a lamb) *ghawa* (coffee)

Hess[191] also notes it for ᶜUtaibi speech and Johnstone[192] mentions it for a number of East Arabian dialects, including the ᶜAnazi dialects of Baḥrain.
However, this ᶜAnazi feature is not found in B, as these comparisons show:

		A		B
CGa– <	CaG–[193]	*ṣxale*	lamb	*ṣaxle*
Ga– <	?aG–	*ḥamar*	red	*?aḥmar*
GCu– <	Ga–Ca	*ᶜrubi*	Arab	*ᶜarabi*
CGi– <	CaG–	*šḥime*	fat	*šaḥme*

Lexis

Notes on comparative lexis

Generally speaking, quite a number of lexical items circulating in Baḥārnah Arabic are also found in ᶜUmāni and Yamāni speech. Such items, in the above dialects, are not only analogous in form to their Baḥārnah counter-forms but also share the same range of meaning. Similarly, certain lexical items, peculiar to ᶜAnazi Arabic of Baḥrain are also present in central and north Arabian speech.

However, when dealing with comparative lexis, it seems worth while to look into, in particular:

(a) Specimens of lexical similarities present in Baḥrāni and some other pre- ᶜAnazi dialects of the area, such as ᶜUmāni or Yamāni.

(b) Specimens of loan-words in circulation in the same dialects.

The following items from ᶜUmāni Arabic are also shared by B:[194]

ir-rajjaal il-ᶜood	the big man
haab riiḥ	dexterous, skilful
jaahil	infant
sluum iš-šams	sunset
baarḥat ams	last night
weeš	what?
hakkuuh	there he is
zaffe	wedding procession
zariibe	cow shed
ġeelame/ḥamase	turtle
jariid	date palm fronds
sanaaniir	cats
xariiṭ	meaningless chat
nawwax	he lingered
rajaajiil	men
ḥamaamiil	porters
najaajiir	carpenters
šaarinne	I bought it
jaaybinne	I brought it
wiyyaaš	with you
ḥaggiš	for you

Loan words are by no means restricted to a specific dialect in the area. The following loan words from Persion are in current circulation in ᶜUmāni as well as in Baḥrāni Arabic:[195]

daraayiš	windows
juuniyya/jawaani	sacks
ġawaazi	money
ṣooġa	present, gift
xaašuuga	spoon
mizraab	spout
karraani	clerk
ġalyuun	hubble-bubble

Below is a list of lexical items found both in Ḥaḍrami and Baḥrāni Arabic.

dalu [196]	leather bucket
karab[197]	lower parts or ends of date palm branches, raceme
jraab[198]	a bag or receptacle for left-over food
sufra[199]	straw mat used as a table cloth
t̠ariid [200]	crumbled bread in broth
minḥaaz [201]	mortar
jaahil [202]	lad
sluum iš-šams [203]	sunset
mšaahara [204]	salary
šabbat [205]	it caught fire, flared up
ġabba for *xabba* [206]	he concealed
lakid [207]	already
zabar [208]	he scolded
dallaal [209]	broker
bazzaaz [210]	cloth dealer
ḥumraan [211]	reds
biiḍaan [212]	whites
furḍa [213]	place where ships unload, jetty
samak [214]	fish
baqara [215]	cow
gamar[216]	moon

Some Persian loan-words common to both Ḥaḍrami and Baḥrāni Arabic are:

juuniyya/jawaani [217]	sacks
lagan [218]	tub, basin
bandar [219]	anchorage
karraani [220]	clerk, tally-clerk

The following lexical items are found both in Dat̠inah and Baḥrāni Arabic:

sannuur [221]	cat
ġabba for *xabba* [222]	he concealed
ṣaxx [223]	he became quiet
sajam [224]	local wooden bed
zabrah[225]	a scold
dalu [226]	leather bucket

barṭam [227]	he ceased from verbal communication as a sign of dissatisfaction
bazz [228]	cloth, fabric
šabb in-naar [229]	he let the fire
karab [230]	lower parts of the branches of a palm tree, raceme
ṯarad [231]	he crumbled bread into broth
jraab [232]	a bag for left-over food
karr [233]	circular rope for climbing a date palm
maa ᶜuun/mawaa ᶜiin [234]	cooking utensils
lakid [235]	already
jaahil [236]	lad
mšaahara [237]	salary
baqar [238]	cows
samak [239]	fish
furḍa [240]	place where ships unload, jetty

Certain loan-words, viz. from Persian, are also found both in Daṯīnah and Baḥrāni Arabic:

zabiil [241]	basket
karraani [242]	clerk, tally-clerk
juuniyya [243]	sack
laqan [244]	tub, basin
sawġaat [245]	presents
ġalyuun [246]	hubble-bubble
mizraab [247]	spout
buuz [248]	mouth

The following lexis from Ṣan ᶜāni Arabic are also present in B:

al-me(e)? [249]	the water
?ane(e)? [250]	I
mifl [251]	like, as
ḥilbe [252]	trigonella
ṣiiniyyah [253]	tray
daar/duur [254]	room, house
haadawla? [255]	these
haadawlaak [256]	those
diik [257]	that (fem.)
li (i) š [258]	to, for you
ḥaggiš [259]	for you
guumi (i) [260]	stand up
bagareh [261]	cow
ḥajareh [262]	stone
šijareh [263]	tree
saadeh [264]	descendants of the Prophet
?aniis [265]	amusing
dinye [266]	world
ṭaagah [267]	a roll of cloth

gahweh [268]	coffee
marateh[269]	his wife
ta ᶜmuul [270]	making
mgahwi [271]	coffee pourer

We will now evaluate the comparative closeness of links in the field of phonology between B and the other dialect-areas referred to above statistically. Not all the features listed are perhaps of the same importance but for what it is worth the number of parallels is as shown in the tabulation given below (where the asterisk indicates the presence of the given feature).

Distribution of comparative data

Phonological Features	A	B	ᶜUmāni	Yamāni	Ẓafāri	ᶜIrāqi	N.A.
Hamza > ᶜ		*	*				
Non-final *?* > *w*		*		*			
Presence of emphatic *ḅ*	*					*	*
Absence of emphatic *ḅ*		*	*	*	*		
t > *ṭ* in cardinals 13 to 19		*	*				
Affrication of *k* to *č* [272]	*	*	rare	rare	rare	*	*
2 f.s. *-k* > *-š* [273]		*	*	*	*		Bani Ṣakhar only
Devoicing of *q* to *k*		*		*			
Fronting of *q* to *g*	*	*	*	*	*	*	*
Presence of *ġ* < *q*	*			*			*
Absence of *ġ* < *q*		*	*		*	*	
Affrication of *q* to *j*[274]	*					*	*
Absence of *q* > *j*		*	*	*	*		
Palatalization of *j* to *y*	*	*	*	*	*	*	*
Velar *g* < *j*		*	*	*	*		*
ṯ > *f* [275]		*		*	*		
Employment of sentence final *-é*?		*	*				

Phonological Features	A	B	ʿUmāni	Yamāni	Ẓafāri	ʿIrāqi	N.A.
Occurrence of final *-n* in 2 f.s. *?intiin* & 2 m./f. pl. *?intuun*[276]		* *	*	*			Sbaʿa & ar-Rass
Occurrence of final-*n* in the imperfect forms 2 f.s. & 2 f. pl.	*	*				*	
Imāla of word-final-*a* > -*e*	*	*	*	*	*	*	*
Preservation of Arabic diphthongs-*ay* and -*aw*	*	*	*	*	*	*	*

From the list of phonological data given above it emerges that out of a total of nineteen features found in B, there are:

13 features which match with ʿUmāni Arabic
12 features which match with Yamāni Arabic
10 features which match with Ẓafāri Arabic
7 features which match with ʿIrāqi Arabic
7 features which match with N.A. Arabic

The tabulation on the following page sets out the morphological links between B and the dialects of the neighbouring areas referred to above:

Morphological features	A	B	ʿUmāni	Yamāni	Ẓafāri	ʿIrāqi	N.A.
FaMaL > *FiMaL*	*					*	*
FaMaL >*FaMaL*		*	*	*	*		
?akalt > *kaleet*	*					*	*
?akalt > *?akalt*		*	*	*	*		
3 m.s. imperf. preform. *y-* > *-i*	*	*		*			*
Occurrence of the pl. pattern FaMaaMiiL for FaMMaaLuun[277]	*	*	*				
Arabic nominal type ?aFMaL > FaMaL as in ḥamar – ʿawar	*		*				*
Presence of *tanwīn*	*	*	*	*	*	*	*
Contraction of Arabic - *ʿašar* to - *ʿaš* in numerals 11–19	*	*	*	*		*	*

Morphological Features	A	B	^{c}Umāni	Yamāni	Ẓafāri	^{c}Irāqi	N.A.
Occurrence of the longer form *^{c}ašar*	*	*	*	*	*		*
Independent personal pronouns realized 3 m.s. *hu(u)*, 3 f.s. *hi(i)*[278]		*	*	*	*		
Presence of the negated forms of the personal pronouns viz. *ma(a) hu/ma(a)hi*[279]	*	*	*	*	*	*	
Occurrence of a series of short syllables		*	*	*	*		
Effect of gutturals on syllable structure	*					*	*
Presence of *tanwīn -n(n)* in verbal forms	*	*	*	*			

From the morphological data provided in the tabulation above, it emerges that out of a total of eleven features found in B,

10 tie with ^{c}Umāni Arabic
10 tie with Yamāni Arabic
7 tie with Ẓafāri Arabic
3 tie with ^{c}Irāqi Arabic
4 tie with N.A. Arabic

The total number of phonological and morphological links with the dialects of the area are:

23 with ^{c}Umāni
22 with Yamāni
17 with Ẓafāri
10 with ^{c}Irāqi
11 with N.A.

Links are, accordingly, far closer with south Arabian than with ^{c}Irāqi or north Arabian speech.

No analogous statistical data from the field of lexis are given because samples in that field were chosen in a somewhat random way and not with a systematic coverage of certain selected aspects. However, the material presented above likewise bears witness to the existence of a strong linkage between B and ^{c}Umāni and Yamāni in particular.

SUMMARY AND CONCLUSION

From the foregoing analyses, it arises that certain inter-dialectal variations of phonological, morphological and lexical nature, affect rural and urban varieties of Baḥārnah Arabic. Unlike urban B, where the reappearance of Arabic inter-dentals is alregly due to expansion in education and the increasing influence of the media, partial preservation of the same in rural B is, to some extent, the result of religious teaching, particularly the type of teaching children undergo at the hands of traditional teachers.

Among the features noted for rural B is the realization of 3 m.s. pronominal suffix -*-h*, which is normally absent in urban B. Another feature is the unconditional fronting of *q* to *k*,[280] and the wider distribution, in Sitrah forms, of the affricate *č* < *k*, including the affrication also in Sitrah forms of *-k* of the 2 m.s. pronominal suffix and the partial realization in rural forms of ultimate *r* and *n*, when these are preceded by stressed long vowels.

Among the peculiarities reported for both divisions of Baḥārnah speech community is the realization of Arabic *ṯ* as *f*. This phonetic feature together with some others such as *j* > *g* or *j* > *y*, etc., are, we found, ascribable to certain tribes of old Arabia. Another characteristic feature of Baḥrāni Arabic is the word-final *imāla* of *-a* to *-e*.

We also noted that the phonetic features known as *ᶜan ᶜanah*,[281] *taltalah*,[282] and *kashkashah*[283] have left traces in current Baḥārnah speech. Also noted was the preservation, particularly in rural B, of the old diphthongs *-ay* and *-aw;* and the employment both in Baḥrāni and ᶜUmāni of a word-final interrogative *-é?*[284] not reported for most other dialects of the area.

As regards morphological features, other than the presence in rural B of the suffixes 2 c.pl. *-čem*, 3 c.pl. *-hem*, and the Dirāzi demonstratives *haak/a, heek/a,* the rest of the features are shared by all speakers of B. Salient among these features are that preformative *y-* of the 3 m.s. imperfect of certain weak verbs is realized *i-;* and that lit. Ar. verbs of the perfect type ?aFMaL are replaced by FaMMaL, as in: *xabbar* and *rassal.* (i)tFooMaL and (i) tFeeMaL are two forms of theme II of the quadriliteral verbs found in B, as in: *itṣooban* (he soaped himself) and *itḥeeraṣ* (he was mean with). An archaic feature that has survived in B and in ᶜUmāni Arabic is the verbal form FaaMil + energetic *-nn* as in *?ane šaarinne* (I bought it), *hu(u) baay ᶜinne (he* sold it). TaFMaaL and TaFMuuL, archaic forms of the verbal noun derived from theme II of the triliteral verbs have survived in B, as in: *taswaat* (making) and *tasbuuḥ* (bathing). Also the verbal noun muFaaMaLah, derived from theme III of the triliteral verbs, is regularlyrealized mFaaMaL, as *mbaašar* (regular attendance), *mkaafaḥ* (struggling, toiling). A peculiarity of B, also reported for ᶜUmāni Arabic, is the replacement of the plural form FaMMaaLuun by FaMaaMiiL as in: *samaamiic* (fisher folk) and *galaaliif* (boat builders). Other such peculiarities in B are *ḥayyiin* for *?aḥyaa?* (living), *maytiin* for *?amwaat* (dead), both are plural. The last example co-occurs with a less common form *mawte.* Also found in B and in ᶜUmāni are the forms *liiḥaan* for *?alwaaḥ* (planks of wood), *biibaan* for *?abwaab* (doors). Among other features that have survived in B are *tanwīn -in* and *-an;* and the archaic forms of the personal pronouns:

2 f.s.	*?intiine*
2 c.pl.	*?intuune*

compound pronouns, viz. *iyya+* pronominal suffixes, such as

wiyyaak (with you) and *wiyyaaha* (with her)

the demonstratives:

hadakku	(from lit. Ar.	*haaḏaaka huwa*	(that's him/it))
hadakki	(from lit. Ar.	*haaḏiika hiya*	(that's her/it))

And finally the particles:

čeef maa čaan	(somehow, one way or another)
lakid	(already)
ḥagg	(for)

Conclusions

The pre- ᶜAnazi dialects of Eastern Arabia which form the older stratum in present-day east Arabian speech are (a) Qaṭīfi, (b) Ḥasāwi, and (c) Baḥrāni.

To the above one may add ᶜUmāni, for what is now known as U.A.E. was, to medieval Arab sources, part of ᶜUmān proper. Hence, ᶜUmāni Arabic shows traces of eastern as well as southern Arabic.

Central and northern peninsular Arabic, particularly Najdi, have influenced ᶜAnazi, Muḥarraqi and Ḥiddi dialects of Baḥrain.

As regards Baḥrāni Arabic, our comparative data confirm a strong correspondence, in certain respects, with ᶜUmāni and to a slightly lesser extent, Yamāni Arabic. Therefore, Baḥrāni Arabic ought to be grouped with southern Arabic in some respects, but its main significance is that it clearly represents the ancient Eastern Arabian type before the spread of ᶜAnazi-type dialects. This is not, however, to deny the emergence, throughout the years, of features that are peculiar to the Baḥārnah dialect of Eastern Arabia.

The evidence of history confirms the evidence of linguistic findings in that Yamāni Arabic influenced both Baḥrāni and ᶜUmāni. The Azd tribes of ᶜUmān (Oman) had their original homelands in the Yaman, their settlement in ᶜUmān is said to date back to the burst of the Maʔrib dam. Similarly, the ᶜAbd al-Qais tribes of the ancient region of al-Baḥrain and the island of ʔUwāl, had their earlier settlements in Tihāmah (see Part I, Section A).

It is understandable therefore, that the pre- ᶜAnazi dialects of East Arabia show close parallels to the dialects of the settled population of east and south Arabia; whereas the ᶜAnazi forms of Baḥrain are closer to central and northern peninsular Arabic.

The presence in East Arabian speech of a large number of Arabicized forms, and loan-words, is indicative chiefly of two factors:

(a) old trade links with Persia and India
(b) Persian rule of the region in pre-Islamic times.

Persian lexical influence, more conspicuous in Baḥrāni Arabic, is said to date back to Persian control of the island. Some such loan-words, however, are as we have seen in the foregoing analysis, also present in ᶜUmāni, Ẓafāri and Yamāni Arabic.

Koine forms, such as are circulating currently in B, are to a large extent due to expansion in the school system and the spread of the media.

Finally, lack of adequate published data on Qaṭīfi and, except for Smeaton's little data on Ḥasāwi forms, unfortunately makes it impossible at present, to comment on these two dialect communities; although ethnic ties and shared history between these two and the Baḥārnah of Baḥrain are well established.

NOTES:

1. See above, p. 42.
2. *Al-Ibdāl,* vol. II, pp. 554–557.
3. Ibid.
4. Ibid.
5. *Al-I ᶜrāb,* vol. I, pp. 234–237.
6. *Ein arabischer Dialekt,* p. 22.
7. *Dialekt im Ḍofâr,* vol. II, p. 76, parag. 4(f)
8. Rossi, *"Appunti di dialettologia del Yemen",* *RSO,* XVII, 1938, p. 235.
9. Blanc, *CDB,* p. 18.
10. *Études sur quelques parlers de nomades arabes d'Orient,* III, p. 129.
11. Blanc, *CDB,* pp. 18, 40.
12. Reinhardt, op. cit., p. 10. But also in many non-Arabian dialects.
13. Landberg, *Études sur les Dialectes de l'Arabie Méridionale (Daṯīnah),* vol. II, p. 447.
14. Reinhardt, op. cit., p. 14.
15. Rhodokanakis, op. cit., vol. II, p. 81, parag. (a).
16. Al-Ḥāzmi, *A Critical and Comparative Study of the Spoken Dialect of Ḥarb Tribe in Sa ᶜūdi Arabia* (Ph.D. Thesis, Leeds University, 1975), p. 63.
17. *Études sur quelques parlers de nomades arabes d'Orient,* III, p. 141.
18. *EADS,* p. 4. Also, *"The Affrication of kāf and gāf in the Arabic Dialects of the Arabian Peninsula",* *JSS,* vol. VIII, 1963. In central Najd *ts,* not *č,* is the affricated variant of *k.*
19. *CDB,* p. 26.
20. Landberg, *Glossaire Daṯīnois,* vol. III (a) p. 2581, (b) p. 2584, (c) p. 2598, (d), p. 2598.
21. W. Diem, *Skizzen jemenitischer Dialekte,* pp. 14, 36.
22. W. Fischer, *Die demonstrativen Bildungen der neuarabischen Dialekte, pp.* 89, 92.
23. Ibid.
24. Johnstone, *EADS,* p. 67.
25. Fischer, op. cit., p. 65.
26. Ibid., pp. 90–92.
27. Ibid., pp. 89, 93.
28. Ibid., p. 90.
29. *Al-Kitāb,* vol. II, p. 295.
30. *Al-I ᶜrāb,* vol. I, p. 235.
31. *ODA,* part I, pp. 664–665.
32. *Ein arabischer Dialekt,* p. 22.
33. Op. cit., vol. II, p. 106, parag. (c).
34. *Études,* II, p. 141.
35. *L'Arabo Parlato,* p. 20, parag. 28.
36. *Dialekt im Ḍofâr,* vol. II, p. 78, parag. 6 (d).
37. Op. cit., pp. 33, 36, 41, 60, 84, 89.
38. Smeaton, *Lexical Expansion due to Technical Change,* p. 48.
39. This is also a feature of some of the rural dialects of the Jabal al-Akhḍar area of ᶜUmān according to Prof. Johnstone.
40. *Al-Ibdāl,* vol. II, pp. 353–359.
41. *Études . . . (Ḥaḍramoût),* vol. I, pp. 130–131.
42. *L'Arabo Parlato,* pp. 5–6, parag. 7(2). Also *Appunti,* p. 235.
43. Blanc, *CDB,* p. 27.

44. Rossi, *Appunti,* p. 235.
45. Diem, op. cit., pp. 9, 77.
46. *Études,* III, p. 140.
47. *EADS,* p. 20.
48. Cantineau, op. cit., p. 144
49. In central Najd the equvalent sound is *dz.*
50. *EADS,* pp. 2, 6, 31–32. Also *"The Affrication of kāf and gāf in the Arabic Dialects of the Arabian Peninsula", JSS,* vol. VIII, 1963. A similar affricate occurs in ᶜUmān only in dialects of the E. Ar. type, viz. on the Bāṭinah coast and the central desert area.
51. *CDB,* pp. 26–28.
52. *Études,* III, pp. 136–137.
53. *Dīwan aus Centralarabien* (1900).
54. *"The Sound Change j > y in the Arabic Dialects of Peninsular Arabia", BSOAS,* vol. XXVIII, part II, 1965.
55. *Études . . . (Ḥaḍramoût),* vol. I, pp. 32–34.
56. *Dialekt im Ḍofâr,* vol. II, pp. 78–79, 86.
57. Op. cit., pp. 3, 9. 13. So too in all Jabal al-Akhḍar dialects.
58. Rhodokanakis, op. cit., vol. II, pp. 78–79, parag. (f).
59. *Études,* III, p. 138.
60. *Appunti,* p. 236.
61. Op. cit., pp. 9, 71, 93–94.
62. Blanc, *CDB,* pp. 19–20.
63. Landberg, *Études . . . (Daṯīnah),* vol. II, p. 1189.
64. Ibid., vol. I, p. 51.
65. Rhodokanakis, op. cit., vol. II, pp. 82–84.
66. Cantineau, op. cit., p. 136.
67. *Al-Ibdāl,* vol. II, p. 178.
68. *Al-Kitāb,* vol. II, p. 428.
69. Op. cit., p. 10.
70. Op. cit., vol. II, p. 81, parag. (e).
71. *L'Arabo Parlato,* p. 7, parag. 9 (b).
72. *Études . . . (Ḥaḍramoût),* vol. I, p. 389.
73. See al-Lughawi, *al-Ibdāl,* vol. I, pp. 181–200.
74. Ibid. Also *Lisān,* vol. XIV, p. 110.
75. *Al-Ibdāl,* loc. cit.
76. Ibid., Also *Lisān,* vol. XI, p. 142.
77. *Al-Ibdāl,* loc. cit. Also *Lisān,* vol. IV, p. 101.
78. *Al-Ibdāl,* loc. cit. Also *Lisān,* vol. II, p. 128.
79. *Al-Ibdāl,* loc. cit. Also *Lisān,* vol. II, p. 138.
80. *Études . . .* (*Ḥaḍramoût*), vol. I, p. 510.
81. Op. cit., vol. II, p. 83, parag. (c).
82. *L'Arabo Parlato,* p. 8, parag. (11).
83. *Appunti,* p. 261.
84. Ibid., p. 264.
85. *Lexical Expansion due to Technical Change,* p. 23.
86. Landberg, *Études,* vol. II, p. 447.
87. *ODA,* Part I, p. 652.
88. Landberg, *Études,* vol. I, p. 118.
89. Cantineau, *Études,* III, p. 132.

90. Rossi, *Appunti,* p. 264.
91. Rossi, *L'Arabo Parlato,* p. 20, parag. (28).
92. Jayakar, *ODA,* Part I, pp, 664–666.
93. Ibid., p. 657. Also, Reinhardt, op. cit., p. 9.
94. *ODA,* Part I, p. 664.
95. *Études,* III, p. 173.
96. *L'Arabo Parlato,* p. 19, parag. (27).
97. *CDB,* pp. 6 (f), 59, 60, 63.
98. *EADS,* pp. 66, 94, 104.
99. Op. cit., pp. 26, 31–32, 41, 68, 71, 79, 84, 94, 104, 119.
100. Rhodokanakis, op. cit., vol. II, p. 106, parags. (c), (d).
101. Smeaton, *Lexical Expansion,* p. 48.
102. EI, vol. III (under *Imāla*)
103. Sībawayhi deals with the *imāla* of *alif* when there is a *kasra* in the syllable that immediately follows or precedes it, such as: ^{c}*ālim* (knowing), *kilāb* (dogs) or *bayyā*^{c} (seller). He mentions, also, the seven consonants that prevent the occurrence of *imāla,* viz. *ṭ, ḍ, ẓ, ṣ, ġ, x, q.*
104. *WGAL,* Part II, p. 10.
105. Also noted by Johnstone, *EADS,* p. 35.
106. Op. cit., vol. II, pp. 90–91.
107. *L'Arabo Parlato,* p. 3, parag. (4).
108. Ibid.
109. *CDB,* pp. 41–50.
110. Op. cit., p. 24.
111. *"The Imāla in Maltese", I.O.S.* (no. 6), 1976, pp. 191–193.
112. Op. cit., p. 8.
113. Op cit., vol. II, p. 92, parags. (p) (q) (t); also p. 99, parag. (j).
114. *Études,* III, pp. 151–152, 230.
115. *L'Arabo Parlato,* p. 4, note (4).
116. *CDB,* p. 6.
117. *EADS,* p. 25.
118. On the elision involved, see p. 159 below.
119. *Études,* III, p. 185.
120. *CDB,* p. 97.
121. *EADS,* p. 42.
122. Jayakar, ODA, Part I, pp. 652–656.
123. Rossi, *L'Arabo Parlato,* p. 26, parags. (42–43). Also *Appunti,* p. 247.
124. Cantineau, *Etudes,* III, pp. 193, 234.
125. *EADS,* p. 47.
126. Reinhardt, *Ein arabischer Dialekt,* p. 8.
127. Landberg, *Glossaire Daṯīnois,* vol. I, pp. 69, 82.
128. Jayakar, *ODA,* Part I, p. 656.
129. Rossi, *L'Arabo Parlato,* p. 30, parag. (50).
130. Landberg, *Études . . . (Ḥaḍramoût),* vol. I, p. 124.
131. Landberg, *Glossaire Daṯīnois,* vol. II, p. 717.
132. *Études,* III, p. 185.
133. *L'Arabo Parlato* p. 26, parags. (42), (43).
134. *CDB,* p. 98.
135. *EADS,* p. 42.
136. *Études,* III, p. 198.

137. *Appunti*, p. 242.
138. Jayakar, *ODA*, Part I, pp. 678–680.
139. Ibid., pp. 673–674.
140. Rossi, *L'Arabo Parlato*, pp. 26–27, parags. (44) (45).
141. Rhodokanakis, op. cit., vol. II, pp. 165–168.
142. *Études*, III, p. 186.
143. *CDB*, p. 114.
144. *EADS*. p. 43.
145. Jayakar, *ODA*, Part I, pp. 657, 681.
146. Landberg, *Études . . . (Ḥaḍramoût)*, vol. I, pp. 166–167 (fn.2).
147. Jayakar, *ODA*, Part I, pp. 659–661. Also Reinhardt, op. cit., p. 75.
148. Rossi, *L'Arabo Parlato*, p. 13.
149. Rhodokanakis, op. cit., vol. II, p. 162.
150. Cantineau, *Études*, III, p. 218.
151. *Lexical Expansion due to Technical Change*, p. 37.
152. Reinhardt, op. cit., p. 8.
153. Cantineau, op. cit., III, p. 169.
154. Rossi, op. cit., p. 16, parag. (22).
155. Op. cit., vol. II, p. 143.
156. *Études*, III, pp. 189, 203–204.
157. *EADS*, p. 63.
158. *A Study of the Spoken Dialect of Ḥarb Tribes*, p. 132.
159. Op. cit., p. 10.
160. Op. cit., vol. II, p. 141.
161. *L'Arabo Parlato*, p. 23.
162. *CDB*, pp. 91–92.
163. *Études*, III, p. 206.
164. *EADS*, pp. 64–65, 117.
165. Johnstone, *EADS*, p. 66. Cf. ᶜAnazi forms of the same.
166. *L'Arabo Parlato*, p. 20, parag. (27) (note 2)
167. Ghānem, *Aden Arabic*.
168. Op. cit., pp. 41, 68, 79, 84, 89, 104, 119.
169. Jayakar, *ODA*, Part I, p. 664.
170. Landberg, *Études . . . (Daṯīnah)*, vol. II, p. 1391.
171. Blanc, *CDB*, p. 59.
172. Rossi, *L'Arabo Parlato* p. 19.
173. Jayakar, *ODA*, Part I, p. 664.
174. Landberg, *Études . . . (Daṯīnah)*, vol. II, p. 1391.
175. Rhodokanakis, op. cit., vol. II, p. 106.
176. Rossi, *L'Arabo Parlato*, p. 19.
177. Diem, op. cit., pp. 26, 31–32, 41, 68, 71, 79, 84, 89, 94.
178. B.H. Smeaton, *Lexical Expansion*, p. 48.
179. Blanc, *CDB*, p. 60.
180. Diem, op. cit., p. 25, fn. 5, 6, 7.
181. Rhodokanakis, op. cit., vol. II, p. 106.
182. Landberg, *Glossaire Daṯīnois*, vol. III, p. 2672.
183. *EADS*, p. 157.
184. Rhodokanakis, op. cit., vol. II, pp. 107–108.
185. Fischer, *Die demonstrativen Bildungen der neuarabischen Dialekte*, p. 83.
186. Ibid., p. 87.

187. Ibid., p. 84.
188. Op. cit., p. 11.
189. *Études*, III, p. 223, parag. (c)
190. Ibid.
191. *Von den Beduinen des inneren Arabiens*, 1938.
192. *EADS*, pp. 6–7.
193. *G* is an abbreviation of Guttural.
194. The ᶜUmāni items cited above, including loan-words, appear in Jayakar's *ODA*, Parts I and II.
195. The above loan-words are also discussed in Part V of this book.
196. Landberg, *Études . . . (Ḥaḍramoût)*, vol. I, p. 575.
197. Ibid., p. 701.
198. Ibid., p. 541.
199. Ibid., p. 608.
200. Ibid., p. 538.
201. Ibid., p. 278.
202. Ibid., p. 544.
203. Ibid., p. 611.
204. Ibid., p. 394.
205. Ibid., p. 136.
206. Ibid., p. 668.
207. Ibid., p. 712.
208. Ibid., p. 596.
209. Ibid., p. 575.
210. Ibid., p. 530.
211. Ibid., p. 23.
212. Ibid.
213. Ibid., p. 673.
214. Ibid., p. 613.
215. Ibid., p. 532.
216. Ibid., p. 696.
217. Ibid., p. 545.
218. Ibid., p. 428.
219. Ibid., p. 535.
220. Ibid., p. 701.
221. Landberg, *Glossaire Daṯīnois*, vol. III, p. 1989.
222. Ibid., vol. III, p. 2356.
223. Ibid., vol. III, p. 2119.
224. Ibid., vol. III, p. 1903.
225. Ibid., vol. III, p. 1818.
226. Ibid., vol. I, p. 840.
227. Ibid., vol. I, p. 157.
228. Ibid., vol. I, p. 166.
229. Ibid., vol. III, p. 2013.
230. Ibid., vol. III, p. 2563.
231. Ibid., vol. I, p. 247.
232. Ibid., vol. I, p. 276.
233. Ibid., vol. III, p. 2562.
234. Ibid., vol. III, p. 2709.
235. Ibid., vol. III, p. 2643.

236. Ibid., vol. I, p. 303.
237. Ibid., vol. III, p. 2089.
238. Ibid., vol. I, p. 189.
239. Ibid., vol. III, p. 1980.
240. Ibid., vol. III, p. 2408.
241. Ibid., vol. III, p. 1819.
242. Ibid., vol. III, p. 2571.
243. Ibid., vol. I, p. 315.
244. Ibid., vol. III, p. 2642.
245. Ibid., vol. III, p. 2156.
246. Ibid., vol. III, p. 2378.
247. Ibid., vol. III, p. 1831.
248. Ibid., vol. I, p. 166.
249. *L'Arabo Parlato,* p. 9.
250. Ibid., p. 19.
251. Ibid., p. 8.
252. Ibid., p. 3.
253. Ibid., p. 7.
254. Ibid., p. 13.
255. Ibid., p. 21.
256. Ibid.
257. Ibid., p. 22.
258. Ibid., p. 41.
259. Ibid., p. 21.
260. Ibid., p. 33.
261. Ibid., p. 14.
262. Ibid.
263. Ibid.
264. Ibid., p. 13.
265. Ibid., p. 7.
266. Ibid., p. 11.
267. Ibid., p. 7.
268. Ibid., p. 6.
269. Ibid., p. 8.
270. Ibid., p. 30.
271. Ibid., p. 6.
272. In ^{c}Umāni, Yamāni and Ẓafāri, affrication does not seem to be a regular feature.
273. Also in Ḥasāwi.
274. Affrication of *q* to *j* is not a regular feature of B, although a small number of speakers both from urban and rural areas of B, tend to realize *q* as *j*.
275. Also found in Ḥasāwi Arabic. See above, p. 151.
276. 2 f.s. *-n* is absent from the Ḥasāwi form of the same.
277. Also found in Ḥasāwi.
278. Also found in Ḥasāwi.
279. Also found in Ḥasāwi.
280. See above, Part II, p. 47.
281. See above, Part II, p. 42.
282. See above, Part III, Note 1, p. 106.
283. See a bove, Part VI, p. 146.
284. See above, Part II, p. 55.

Appendices and texts

DISTRIBUTION BY NATIONALITIES

Nationality	Census 1941 (1360)	Census 1950 (1369)	
Baḥrain subjects	74,040	91,179	
Persians	7,547	6,934	
Indians Anglo-Indians Goanese	1,424	3,043	
Saudi Arabs	6,959 (Saudi Arabs to Europeans: Others)	2,526	8,494 (Saudi Arabs to Europeans: Others)
Omanis and Muscatis		2,466	
Qataris		438	
Kuwaitis		149	
Yemenis		105	
Iraqis		224	
Palestinians		28	
Syrians and Lebanese		52	
Egyptians		30	
Others		268	
Europeans:			
British		1,840	
Americans		290	
Others		78	
	89,970	109,650	
Baḥrain subjects	74,040	91,179	
Foreigners	15,930	18,471	

INCREASE BY NATIONALITIES

Nationality	Increase in 9 years
Baḥrain Subjects	17,139
Foreigners	2,541

DISTRIBUTION BY RELIGION

Religion	Census 1941 (1360)	% of population	Census 1950 (1369)	% of population
Muslims	88,298	98	105,401	96
Non-Muslims	1,672	2	4,249	4

DISTRIBUTION OF NON–MUSLIMS

Religion	Census 1941 (1360)	Census 1950 (1369)
Christians	not recorded	2,932
Jews		293
Hindus		975
Others		49
Total	1,672	4,249

DISTRIBUTION BY TOWNS AND VILLAGES

Towns or villages	Census 1941	% of population	Census 1950	% of population
Manāmah, Muḥarraq and Hedd	49,274	56	65,225	61½
Other Towns and Villages	39,164	44	40,579	38½
Total	88,438		105,804	

CENSUS OF DWELLING HOUSES

Towns or Villages	Census 1941 (1360)	Census 1950 (1369)
Manāmah	4,649	5,703
Muḥarraq	3,317	3,720
Hedd	719	619
Other Towns and Villages	5,697	6,232
Total	14,382	16,274

TOTAL POPULATION OF MAJOR CIVIL DIVISIONS

BY URBAN/RURAL RESIDENTS, SEX AND NATIONALITY, 1971

GEOGRAPHIC DIVISION AND URBAN/RURAL RESIDENCE	TOTAL POPULATION			BAḤRAINIS			NON-BAḤRAINIS		
	BOTH SEXES	MALE	FEMALE	BOTH SEXES	MALE	FEMALE	BOTH SEXES	MALE	FEMALE
Total	216,078	116,314	99,764	178,193	89,772	88,421	37,885	26,542	11,343
Urban	168,819	92,276	76,543	132,015	66,692	65,323	36,804	25,584	11,220
Rural	47,259	24,038	23,221	46,178	23,080	23,098	1,081	958	123
Manāma division	89,399	50,525	38,874	59,496	30,008	29,488	29,903	20,517	9,386
Manāma town	88,785	50,215	38,570	58,884	29,700	29,184	29,901	20,515	9,386
Rural	614	310	304	612	308	304	2	2	–
Muḥarraq Island	49,540	26,279	23,261	45,774	23,257	22,517	3,766	3,022	744
Muḥarraq town	37,732	20,240	17,492	34,112	17,318	16,794	3,620	2,922	698
Ḥidd town	5,269	2,737	2,532	5,172	2,672	2,500	97	65	32
Rural	6,539	3,302	3,237	6,490	3,267	3,223	49	35	14
Jiddhafs division	19,521	10,051	9,470	19,065	9,742	9,323	456	309	147
Jiddhafs town	11,152	5,844	5,308	10,743	5,574	5,169	409	270	139
Rural	8,369	4,207	4,162	8,322	4,168	4,154	47	39	8
Northern division (Rural)	10,614	5,347	5,267	10,454	5,205	5,249	160	142	18
Western division (Rural)	8,689	4,381	4,308	8,355	4,097	4,258	334	284	50
Central division	14,228	7,231	6,997	13,946	7,003	6,943	282	228	54
Isa town	7,501	3,831	3,670	7,285	3,666	3,619	216	165	51
(Rural)	6,727	3,400	3,327	6,661	3,337	3,324	66	63	3
Sitrah division	11,323	5,628	5,895	11,263	5,583	5,630	60	45	15
Sitrah town	6,665	3,287	3,378	6,624	3,259	3,365	41	28	13
Rural	4,658	2,341	2,317	4,639	2,324	2,315	19	17	2
Rafāᶜ division	12,633	6,741	5,892	9,766	4,803	4,963	2,867	1,938	929
Rafāᶜ town	10,731	5,593	5,138	9,171	4,486	4,685	1,560	1,107	453
ᶜAwāli town	984	529	455	24	17	7	960	512	448
Rural	918	619	299	571	300	271	347	319	28
Other Islands	131	131	–	74	74	–	57	57	–

SPECIMENS FROM BAḤĀRNAH TEXTS[1]

Informant 1

A *?il-?ism il-kariim ḥajji?*

B *sayyid aḥmad is-sayyid ḥaašim.*

A *mihnatk weešhi, ḥajji?*

B *?ane ?al-ḥiin ^{c}aamil fi l-keebal wayarles ?aštiġil ?ayyaam zamaan kunt aštiġil fi z-ziraa ^{c}a.*

A *mumkin ti ^{c}ṭiini fikra ^{c}an iz-ziraa ^{c}a?*

B *?iz-ziraa ^{c}a yaa waladi tibġa ya ^{c}ni mbaašar . . . ?ileen ḥaṣṣalat ileehe m-baašar ?iz-ziraa ^{c}a tinjaḥ.*

A *naas wajid yištiġluun fi z-ziraa ^{c}a hni fi l-idraaz?*

B *?al-ḥiin ?aġlabhum fi l-baḥar . . . ṣayyaadaat samač . . .*
?u ^{c}immaal fi l-a ^{c}maal.

A *hal iz-ziraa^{c}a ?al-ḥiin ?arbaḥ loo ?ayyaam zamaan?*

B *?awwal ?arbaḥ . . . ?awwal il - ^{c}aamil raxiiṣ . . . ya ^{c}ni mafal ^{c}induk bagiiše ?aw zraa ^{c}a tḥiṭ luk fiihe ^{c}aamil, fneen imaššuun l-išġil, ?u ynaḍmuun il-maḥal . . . ?al-ḥiin maḥḥad yištiġil . . . galiil ?ii . . . maa tḥaṣṣil.*

A *?ayyaam zamaan yoom kint fi z-ziraa ^{c}a weeš kint tizra ^{c}?*

B *mifil jazar, qarnaabiiṭ, mifil malfuuf, mifil luuba, baamye . . . ?akil wulla ġeer akil... ?ištaġalt ^{c}ind il-ḥukuuma ṯalatta ^{c}šar sane.*

A *zeen hadeleen l-adawaat qaṣdi mumkin ti ^{c}ṭiini fikra ^{c}anhum?*

B *hay l-adawaat . . . haade mgaṣṣ, mgaṣṣ maal šeel ya ^{c}ni, . . . maal tagḍiib . . . ?u haade maal binni l-?arḍ . . . ya ^{c}ni han-namuune čidi . . . maa nista ^{c}mil mḥašš ^{c}an laa ynagguf iš-šiif . . . ?u maal sayyaara biddif ^{c}aleehe ramil šwayy . . . haade lo bitigla ^{c} fiihe wruud walla zhuur . . . guul bass čidi w-itšiilhe . . . biṭṭiine maalhe . . . w-itxalliihe fi makaan ġeer.*

A *?in-naxle čeef tinzara ^{c}?*

B *?in-naxle tizra^c . . . leen miṯil ^{c}indik naxle bitizra ^{c}ha fi-l-beet . . . taaxid leek šwayy samaad gad zabiil waaḥid ?u šwayy ramil ?u txilṭa jamii ^{c}, w-itsawwi ḥufra fuut fi fuut, w-il-fasiile tjiibhe baarze w-itḥiṭṭ ^{c}aleehe šwayyat ramil min taḥt, ^{c}ugub tnazzil il-fasiile, w-iddiff ^{c}aleehe ramil w-itsawwi leehe ḥooḍ čidi w-itlifhe min foog ^{c}an iš-šams, ?u ti ^{c}ṭiihe maay yoom ?u tark . . . wida t-turba mafal nafs l-idraaz čidi mišxaal, laa ^{c}iṭha maay kill yoom ma-yxaalif.*

A *wil-gatt šloon?*

B *it ^{c}addil il-maḥal, ?ileen ^{c}addalt il-maḥal ?u naḍḍafte, ḥaṭṭeet samaad, sageete door, dooreen, nabbašt il-?arḍ . . . ?ileen tnabbašat il-?arḍ, ?il-badir ^{c}induk . . . ?il-ḥabb tibdirah ?u falatt ayyaam bass*

A *iguluun fi milḥ waajid fi l-?arḍ . . . čeef titxallaṣ minne?*

B *?arḍ il-baḥreen kilhe ṣbaax, bas haadi l-?arḍ yisguunhe yi^{c}tuunhe maay yoom, yoomeen, falaafe, ifičč minhe l-milḥ haade, ?u yimši z-zar ^{c} fiihe, ?u leen čaafaw il-?arḍ maṭalan xaayne ^{c}ala z-zar ^{c}, ya^{c}ni ḍa^{c}iif izzar ^{c} fiihe, nabbašaw il-?arḍ, ?u ḥattaw ^{c}aleehe samaad ṣinaa^{c}i,, sammaraw ^{c}aleehe tasmiir . . . ixilṭuune wiyya l-maay, yimši b-ruuḥa.*

TRANSLATON (Informant 1)

A Your noble name, *ḥajji?*

B Sayyid Aḥmad as-Sayyid Hāshim.

A What is your job, *ḥajji?*

B I am now a labourer at Cable and Wireless (Ltd.). In the past I used to work in gardening.

A Could you tell us something about gardening?

B Gardening, my son, requires regular attendance . . . when it receives regular attendance, it pays.

A Are there many people involved in gardening here in Dirāz?

B Nowadays most of them are at sea. . . fishermen . . . and (some) are labourers in different jobs.

A Is gardening more lucrative nowadays than it used to be in the past?

B In the past it was more lucrative. . . in the past the labourer was cheaper . . . if you had a garden or cultivated land . . . with one, two or three workers the job could be done. They will prepare the place (i.e., land, soil) for you . . . nowadays few take to it . . . very few. . . you won't find any.

A In the past when you were a gardener, what were you growing?

B Like carrots, cauliflower, cabbage, beans, okra, food or something else . . . lucerne . . . I worked with the government for thirteen years.

A Well these tools, could you tell us something about them?

B These tools . . . this is a pruner . . . it is used for removing . . . i.e., trimming . . . this one is used for levelling the soil . . . like this . . . we don't use a sickle in case it might uproot seedlings, or if you want to cover up the track of a car . . . This one is for transplanting flowers . . . you just do it like this and remove it with its soil . . . and put it in a different spot.

A How is a date-palm grown?

B The date palm is grown . . . for example when you have a date palm tree to plant at your house. . . you take some manure, a basketful of manure and a little sand, mix them together, dig a hole one foot by one foot . . . and you get the palm-shoot ready and put some sand underneath and then you put in the palm-shoot and cover it with sand and make a bed for it like this . . . and you cover the top part of it to protect it from the sun and water it every other day; if the soil is like what we have here in Dirāz . . . like a sieve, you will have to water it daily . . . it won't do it any harm.

A How about lucerne?

B You prepare the place and when you've prepared it and cleaned it, put on manure, and water it once or twice, then rake the soil. . . when you've raked the soil you have the seeds ready, the seeds are sown . . . it takes only three days.

A It is said that the amount of salt in the soil is high . . . how do you get rid of it?

B The land in Baḥrain is all marsh salt . . . this land is to be watered, to be given water for one, two or three days until the salt is removed, then the plant grows . . . if the soil is incapable of cultivation, i.e., it produces a weak plant, the land is raked and covered with chemical fertilizer . . . which is added to the water and penetrates the soil by itself.

Informant 2

A *?il-?ism il-kariim?*
B *?aḥmad ^{c}ali ?aḥmad l-akraf.*
A *weeš tištiġil?*
B *?aštiġil baḥḥaar.*
A *čeef tṣiiduun is-samač ihni fi l-idraaz?*
B *bil-garguur . . . ?aw il-ḥaḍra.*
A *čeef?*
B *?il-garguur nḥišš leh ḥašiiš min il-šisme, min is-saṭwa, ?u ba^{c}deen nxalli fih il-ḥašiiše, ?u ndišš ^{c}aad il-maaye. . . ?indišš ni ^{c}mur il-garaagiir, ?u yoom ṯaani indišš winjammi^c.*

. . . .

A *ween itwadduun is-samač? ya^{c}ni ween itbii^{c}unne?*
B *fii ^{c}idne ši ysammuune yazaaziif ḥagg is-samač. haade l-yazzaaf iruuḥ la-raa^{c}i l-miḥmal, ?il-baḥaaḥiir illi miṯlaati, ya^{c}ni maa ^{c}indeh miḥmal, ?adfa^c xums, ya^{c}ni kil xams rub^{c}aat ?adfa^c leh rub^{c}a waḥde . . . ya^{c}ni qabiil ta^{c}abe maal il-miḥmal . . . ?u haade l-yazzaaf biyaaxid is-samač min ^{c}ind raa^{c}i l-miḥmal ?u min ^{c}ind il-baḥaaḥiir . . . willi maa y-bii^{c}a^{c}ala l-yazzaaf biwaddiih is-suug . . . ya^{c}ni biyit^{c}ab ^{c}ala tawdaate s-suug li?anna suugne maa t-sa^{cc}i la bee^c is-samač ?akṯarhum baḥaaḥiir.*

A *kll miḥmal čam iṣiid?*
B *ya^{c}ni l-wazin . . . iṣiid leh min ṯna^{c}šar, ?arbaaṭa^{c}šar mann, haade ?idaa fii samač, ya^{c}ni.*
A *?il-mann čam rub^{c}a?*
B *?aftikur . . . čam? . . . ?arbaaṭa^{c}šar rub^{c}a, ?u ?aḥyaanan ma-yṣiiduun ši.*
A *?u waaldik weeš kaan yištiġil?*
B *kaan baḥḥaar . . . kaan isawwi garaagiir . . . ḥagg il-baḥaaḥiir.*
A *šloon isawwuun il-garaagiir?*
B *ijibuun ṭayyaat siim . . . ?u yig^{c}id ifaṣṣil is-siim ^{c}ala gadar illi yubġaah ya^{c}ni . . . maṯalan ?ay ḥajim yubġi . . . ?u ba^{c}deen yi^{c}mal mifl is-saffaaf leen isiff xuuṣ . . . ?il-ḥuṣraan . . . bigaṭṭi^c issiim ^{c}ala gad maa yibġi . . . ba^{c}deen isawwi leeh fčuuč.*

. . . .

A *?al-ḥiin il-baḥar, fi ha l-ḥaale weeš isammuune?*
B *fabor . . . fabor.*
A *w-leen il-maaye jat foog?*
B *sagi.*
A *šinhi l-axṯaar illi twaajihha fi l-baḥar?*
B *?al-ḥiin maa fii? ?axṯaar mifil ?awwal . . . ?awwal yaraayiir waajid, fii samač ḥaraam . . . ?alḥiin min ṭala^{c}at il-makaayin maal lanjaat maa yṣiir šii . . . lanna tsawwi rajje fi l-baḥar ?u samačat il-ḥaraam tibti^{c}id.*
A *leeš itsammiihe ḥaraam?*
B *xaṭiira.*

Translation (Informant 2)

A Your noble name?
B Aḥmad ᶜAli Aḥmad il-Akraf.
A What sort of a job do you do?
B I am a fisherman.
A How do you catch fish here in Dirāz?
B With wire traps or weirs.
A How?
B As regards a wire trap, we cut seaweed for it from the sea and put it inside the trap; then we enter into the sea and lay the traps, and the following day we go and collect(them).

. . . .

A Where do you take the fish? I mean, where do you sell it?
B We have what are called *yazāzīf* (i.e., bulk purchasers of fish). The *yazzāf*[1] approaches the owner of the boat. Fishermen like me, (somebody) who doesn't own a boat . . . pays a fith of the catch to him. That's to say I give him one *rubᶜah* (four pounds) against every five *rubᶜah* of fish, for using his boat. The *yazzāf* takes the fish from the owner of the boat and also from the fishermen . . . He who does not sell to the *yazzāf* takes it to the market. He will have to put himself to trouble . . . he will have to carry it on his head from here, from the sea to his house . . . then from his house to the market. In fact carrying it to the market is a tiring job . . . because our market can't take all our fish (since) most of the people are fishermen.
A How much fish does each boat catch?
B You mean in weight. . . each boat catches from twelve to fourteen maunds (a maund = 56 pounds), that is when the sea abounds with fish.
A How many *rub ᶜahs* are there in a maund?
B I think . . . how many? . . . fourteen *rub ᶜahs* . . . sometimes they don't catch any fish.
A What did your father do (for a living)?
B He was a fisherman . . . he used to make wire traps for fishermen.
A How do they make wire traps?
B They get pleats of wire mesh, and he cuts the wire according to the required length . . . for example, whatever size is required . . . then he works like a mat plaiter when he plaits straw mats . . . he cuts the wire according to what is required, then he makes funnels in it.

. . . .

A What do you call the sea at this state, now?
B Ebb tide . . . low tide.
A And when water is high?
B High tide.
A What kind of hazards do you face at sea?
B Nowadays, there are not the hazards there used to be in the past. In the past there were many sharks, and dangerous (lit. illicit) fish . . . now since the introduction of motor launches . . . nothing happens. . . because these produce a noise in the water which keeps the dangerous fish away.
A Why do you call it *ḥarām* (i.e., illicit)?
B It is dangerous.

1. The *jazzāf* or *yazzāf* buys fish in bulk from fishermen; he also retails it. Some *jazāzīf* own boats and therefore receive one fifth of the catch from the fishermen using their boats.

Informant 3

A *?il-?ism il-kariim?*
B *?ismi ᶜabdalla ᶜabd il- ᶜaziiz iḥseen madan.*
A *weeš tištiġil?*
B *fallaaḥ.*
A *mumkin tiᶜṭiinne fikra ᶜan iz-ziraaᶜa?*
B *maa nizraᶜ iḥne . . . bass inxiil . . . ?u nixruf rṭab.*
A *šloon tixrufuun l-irṭab?*
B *nirkab il-karr, w-un ᶜallig is-subbaag foog raasne, ?u nixruf b-yaadiinne . . . ?ii . . . w-unnabbit, w-unḥaddir, w-unrawwis.*
A *baᶜad šinhi l-ašyaa ?illi tizraᶜuunhe?*
B *nizraᶜ zeytuun, nizraᶜ rummaan, nizraᶜ čeyko, rweyd, ṭamaaṭa, ṭruuḥ, baṭṭiix, bagil, beelajaan, baamye.*
A *fween tbiiᶜuune?*
B *inḥiṭṭa fi s-sayyaara . . . inwaddiih il-manaame.*
A *mitzawwig hajji?*
B *?ii.*
A *čam zooje ᶜinduk?*
B *ᶜindi waḥde.*
A *čam walad?*
B *ᶜindi sabᶜa.*
A *?alla yxalliihum . . . weeš asmaa?ahum?*
B *raḍi, ᶜabd il-jabbaar, ᶜabd il-?amiir, ?u ḥabIIb, ?u ᶜIIse, ?u ᶜubbaas, ?u kawkab, ?u nuuriyye.*
A *tiᶜṭiinne sinhum . . . kil waaḥid cam sane?*
B *waaḥid wald ifnaᶜšar sane, waaḥid wald tisᶜe, l-ibnayye bitt tisᶜe, ?u waaḥid wald sitt, ?u waaḥid xams, ?u waaḥid wald falaaf, ?u waaḥid wald ᶜišriin yoom.*
A *?al-ḥiin bitruuḥ il-baḥar weeš bitsawwi?*
B *?abaaruuḥ l-iḥmaar ᶜindi, ?u baṭraḥ il-ḥadra, ?u baaṣiid samač, ?u baaji ?u baabiiᶜe ᶜala l-jazzaaf, baᶜdeen baṣalli, ?u bass xalaaṣ.*
A *inzeen . . . haade l-gaari yidxil lal-baḥar yaᶜni?*
B *?ii . . . lal-baḥar . . . ?u taali ?arbuṭa hnaak . . . w adxil il-gadiil yaᶜni l-ḥaḍra. ?u taali weeš tsawwi?*
A *?al-ḥiin, tikram, ?abarkab l-ḥmaar, ?u baruuḥ -il-ḥaḍra ?u baarbuṭe fi murbaṭe, ?u baᶜdeen basiir b-il-murḥale ᶜala ḍahri, ?u baruuḥ ibhe l-gadiil, baᶜdeen baṣiid is-samač, ?u baṭlaᶜ min il-gadiil ?u baruuḥ il-gaari ?u bafurr l-iḥmaar mijnib ?u baayi l-izraaᶜa ?u barbuṭe, ?u bajnib il-beet ?u bass.*
A *?u mate yinbaaᶜ haade s-samač?*
B *yinbaaᶜ ?arbaᶜ . . . ?awaddiih is-suug.*
A *šloon twaddiih issuug?*
B *?awzane bil-miizaan, ?u ?ašakle.*
A *tšakle šloon?*
B *?ašakle b-xuuṣ . . . maal in-naxal.*
A *čam wazin kil šakle?*
B *neṣ rubᶜa . . . raṭleen.*
A *ᶜala čam tbiiᶜa?*
B *?ane ?abiiᶜa ṯamantaᶜšar lal-ᶜišriin.*

Translation (Informant 3)

A Your noble name?
B My name is ᶜAbdalla ᶜAbd al-ᶜAzīz Ḥusayn Madan.
A What sort of work do you do?
B I am a farmer.
A Could you give us some idea about gardening?
B We don't grow . . . only date palm trees . . . and we pick ripening dates.
A How do you pick dates?
B We put on a *karr* (a circle of rope) and hang the basket on our head, and we pick the dates with our hands . . . yes . . . we cut off the leaves, we let down the bunches, and remove the prickles.
A What else do you grow?
B We grow guava, pomegranate, chiku (Indian fruit), radishes, tomatoes, cucumbers, melon, clover, egg plant, and okra.
A Where do you sell it?
B We transport it by car to Manāmah.
A Are you married, *ḥajji?*
B Yes.
A How many wives have you?
B One.
A How many children?
B I have seven.
A May God preserve them . . . what are their names?
B Raḍi, ᶜAbd al-Jabbār, ᶜAbd al-Amīr, Ḥabīb, ᶜĪsa, ᶜAbbās, Kawkab, Nūriyyah.
A Give us their age . . . how old is each of them?
B One is twelve years old, one is nine, the girl is nine years of age, one is six years old, and one five, and one three, and one is only twenty days old.
A You are heading towards the sea now . . . what are you going to do?
B I am going with the donkey and I'll stop at the weir, and I'll catch fish. Then I'll come back to sell it to the *jazzāf* (bulk purchaser), then I'll pray and that's it.
A Well, can this cart go into the sea?
B Yes . . . into the sea . . . then I'll tie it there and enter the *gadīl* (i.e., the weir).
A What will you do next?
B Now, may you be honoured, I shall get on the donkey . . . and go to the weir; I'll tie it with its rope, then I'll walk around with the sack on my back to the weir. Then I'll catch the fish, and leave the weir and walk to the cart. I'll turn the donkey south and make my way to the garden, and I'll tie it. Then I'll go south to the house and that's it.
A When will the fish be sold?
B It will be sold at four . . . I'll deliver it to the market.
A How are you going to take it to the market?
B I'll weigh it with a scale . . . then I'll make it into bundles.
A How are you going to make it into bundles?
B With date palm straws.
A How much does each bundle weigh?
B Half a *rubᶜah*, two pounds.
A How much do you sell it for?
B I sell it for eighteen to twenty (i.e., one *dīnār* and eight hundred *fils* or two *dīnārs*).

Informant 4

A *?il-?ism il-kariim?*

B *^{c}ali ^{c}abdalla nijim.*

A *min mate ḥajji nte fi ha š-šaġle haadi ?*

B *yumkin foog il-xamsiin sane . . . min yoom ?ane jaahil.*

A *weeš tiṣna ^{c}?*

B *haade ?asawwi rde . . . l-awwal yoom ?ane ṣaaḥi, ?asawwi rde yoomi, ?al-ḥiin yoom ane šwayy maane ṣaahi, ?asawwi . . . maa-sawwi l-irde, nuṣṣ irde bass . . . ?amma l-awwal asawwi rde kaamil . . . naas ba ^{c}ad yiṣna ^{c}uun wizra . . . ba ^{c}aḍhum ^{c}ala l-waṣa . . . yiṣna ^{c}uun aswad lal-mamlaka, ?uw ihni . . . ya ^{c}ni l-bahreen ba ^{c}ḍ iš-šay yilbasuune l-ḥariim . . . ha l- ^{c}aam . . . ?il-ḥukuuma ^{c}ataṭni ġazil . . . ?alla yṭawwil ^{c}umurhum jamii ^{c}, maa kaṣṣaraw.*

A *?išraḥ leenne šwayy ^{c}an l-ašyaa ?illi tsawwuunhe.*

B *haade l-ġazil . . . ijiibe mḥammad ḥabiib, ijiibeh min čeenaaw, ?u haade z-zari jaapa-ani, naaxde min is-suug . . . mḥammad ḥabiib huu l-imwarrid maalne.*

A *ġeer ir-ridye ba^{c}ad weeš itsawwi?*

B *?aṣna ^{c} ba ^{c}ad wizra . . . ?u min ?aṣil ṣana ^{c}ne bšuut . . . haay šaġlatne ba ^{c}ad, aaxrat aabaanne čidi, w-eḥne ^{c}aleehem mašeene.*

A *čam yaaxid l-irde . . . čam yoom?*

B *l-irde haabb ir-riiḥ isawwi waaḥid fi l-yoom. ?u hast naas isawwuun waaḥid u nuṣ, ^{c}idne nafareen bass isawwuun ^{c}ala rde w-nuṣ, haadaak ^{c}abd il- ^{c}aḍiim, ?u haadaak ḥajji ḥseen ba ^{c}ad al-ḥiin ^{c}ajjaz . . . maa ysawwi lla rde.*

A *l-irde čam ṭuule?*

B *sittat waaraat, ya ^{c}ni fna ^{c}šar idraa ^{c} . . . ?u ^{c}urḍa iji draa ^{c}een, ya ^{c}ni fuuteen u nuṣ . . . . . . killhum min fijjateen yaaxduune ?u yxuṭfuune hnaak . . . libse kille fi l-mamlaka, ?aġlabe kille lal-gatiif.*

A *ġeer il-mamlaka, maḥḥad iji yištari min ^{c}induk min ihni?*

B *ingareez u ġeer ingareez . . . haade maa yi ^{c}timid ^{c}aleehum, haade mamšaah kille fi l-is ^{c}uudiyye.*

. . . .

A *haade weeš itsammiih ḥajji?*

B *haade dfaaf, ?u haade sme ḥirš, ?u haadi liiṭa, ?u haadi l-madaawis.*

A *zeen, il-waalid il-kariim kaan fi nafs il-mihne?*

B *?abuuyi . . . ?ii . . . l-awwal yiṣna ^{c} bšuut, wi-šraa ^{c} . . . raaḥat aalat l-ibšuut, raaḥat aalat l-išraa ^{c}.*

A *?iš-šir ^{c} gaamaw ijibuun min barra?*

B *?iiy . . . mi l-mihne tkaffoḍ, aalathe raaḥat xalaaṣ, ?inxaraṭat.*

Translation (Informant 4)

A Your noble name?

B ^{c}Ali ^{c}Abdalla Nijim.

A Since when did you take up this job, hajji?

B Perhaps over fifty years . . . since I was a lad.

A What are you making?

B This . . . I am making a (lady's) cloak . . . in the past when I was in good health I used to weave a cloak a day. Now that I am not in good health I might or might not weave a cloak . . . half a cloak only . . . in the past I used to weave a whole cloak. Some also weave loin-cloths . . . Some (weavers) make them only on receiving orders . . . they make black ones for Saudi Arabia, also for here . . . in Baḥrain quite a few are worn by ladies. This year, the government gave me yarn . . . may God give all of them longer life, they've never failed us.

A Can you explain a little about what sort of things you make?

B This yarn is imported by Muḥammad Ḥabīb, he brings it (i.e, imports it) from China, and this golden thread is Japanese. We buy it from the market. Muḥammad Ḥabīb is our supplier.

A Other than cloaks what else do you make?

B I make loin-cloths. When I first started I wove men's cloaks . . . after all, this is our craft. Our ancestors were in the same line and we followed them.

A How many days does a cloak take?

B The dextrous weaver takes a day to make a cloak. There are others who weave one and a half (i.e. a day). We have only a couple of people here who can make one and a half . . . there's that ^{c}Abd al- ^{c}Aḍīm and that *Ḥajji* Ḥusain who is older now and can't make more than one.

A What is the length of a cloak?

B Six yards, i.e., twelve cubits . . . width-wise it is two cubits, i.e., two foot and a half . . . they are all (made in) two pieces. They take them and put them together there . . . . it is all worn in Saudi Arabia . . . most of it goes to Qaṭīf.

A Other than Saudi Arabia, does anybody buy from you from here?

B Englishmen and other than Englishmen, but one does not rely on them. Its main outlet is in Arabia.

A What do you call this, *hajji?*

B These are breast beams, and this is the weft, and this is the reed beater and these are the treadles.

A Well, your honoured father, was he in the same craft?

B My father. . . yes . . . In olden days he used to weave men's cloaks, and sails . . . the tools for making cloaks and sails have disappeared.

A Have they started importing sails from abroad?

B Yes . . . when a craft diminishes, its tools also disappear. They cease to exist.

A *?il-?ism il-kariim?*

B *^{c}ali bin ḥasan.*

A *?inte min ween?*

B *min banī jamra.*

A *mumkin ti ^{c}ṭiini fikra ^{c}an šiġluk?*

B *?ii . . . šiġli . . . ?ane kunt l-awwal fī hay l-iḥyaače ba ^{c}d . . . ?asawwi wuzra, ?u saa ^{c}aat iġtar . . . ṣaarat ḍa ^{c}iife l-mihne, ?u dabbart ba ^{c}ad duulaab il-ḥukuuma, w-uštaġalt ḥawaale ji sane, ?u taali raddeet ba ^{c}ad ?u fannašt ?u riḥt il-mamlaka.*

A *weeš ištaġalt fi l-mamlaka?*

B *mu ^{c}aawin najjaar . . . ?u taali jiit il-baḥreen w-utzawwajt, ?u ḍammeet fī š-šarika ḥawaale xamse w- ^{c}išriin sane.*

A *weeš itsawwi fi š-šarika?*

B *?aštiġil fi qism il-ḥariiq wis-salaame, inšaḥḥin ṭaffaayaat ?u nsawwi, ?ida mafal hooz mingaṣṣ, inḥiṭṭ ileeh ringaat, ?u nṣabboġ salandaraat.*

A *ba ^{c}ad maa txalliṣ min šiġluk fi š-šarika . . . ya^{c}ni l-^{c}aṣaari weeš itsawwi?*

B *walla ?ida xallaṣt iššigil, saa^{c}a ?ane najjaar . . . ^{c}indi beet ?aštiġil fiih, hadaane tawwi jaay ?al-ḥiin min il-beet mištiġil l-awwal ba ^{c}ad ?asawwi karaafi w kbaate.*

A *?al-ḥiin maḥḥad yubġi karfaayaat.*

B *laa ?a-ḥiin kille maal haade . . . hal-karaafī ween . . . ?al-ḥiin haddeet ba ^{c}ad l-injaara . . . ga ^{c}adt ?azaawil il-bunaaye . . . bannaay ya ^{c}ni . . . bass fi l-beet, beeti . . . w-uda mafal waaḥid yubġa daraj ?asawwi, ?aw injaara mafal ?antar leh, ?u wakt faraaġi saa saa ^{c}aat ?aruuḥ in-naadi.*

A *weeš itsawwuun fi n-naadi?*

B *walla, fii ?al ^{c}aab, tenis ?u kora ṭaayra, korat qadam.*

A *kam zooje ^{c}induk?*

B *waḥde.*

A *?u l-awlaad?*

B *sab ^{c}a.*

A *weeš asmaa?hum?*

B *waaḥid ^{c}abd il-ḥasan, ?u waaḥid ḥabiib, ?u naaji, haade z-zaġiir, ?u waḥde simhe zeynab, ?u faaṭma, ?u aasye, ?u ^{c}indi fowziyye ?ii . . . hay ?awlaadi. falaaf fil-midrase fi l-xamiis daak il-walad il-^{c}ood bohil, ?u hadd u raaḥ ?al-hiiṇ fil-baladiyye yištiġil.*

A *?inzeen ^{c}ajal tištiġil fi n-nijaara ?u fi l-bunyaan?*

B *l-bunaay ?u ba ^{c}ad marrant ruuḥi ^{c}ala l-masaaḥ . . . wallah beeti štaġalt fiih b-nafsi.*

A *b-nafsuk sawweete?*

B *b-nafsi ?ane ?u waladi.*

A *fi čam šahar sawweete?*

B *kul sane aaxid ir-ruxṣa w-ag ^{c}id la-hadaak, ?u ?aštiġil ^{c}a-raaḥati, ya ^{c}ni muu ?akruf ruuḥi, ?aštiġil saa ^{c}teen, ṯalaaṯ, ?u ?abannid.*

A *čam ṭaabuq sawweete?*

B *ṭaabuq waaḥid.*

A *saafart šii?*

B *marrateen.*

A *fween riḥt?*

B *riḥt il- ^{c}iraaq, ?u riḥt il-?iiraan, bass maa riḥt ġeer . . . ?u riḥt il-ḥajj ba^{c}ad.*

A *šloon kaan il-ḥajj ?ayyaamkum?*

B *walla raaḥa.*

A *riḥt b-ruuḥuk?*

B *riḥne taabi ^{c} muqaawil, ?ii.*

Translation (Informant 5)

A Your noble name?

B ^{c}Ali bin Ḥasan.

A Where do you come from?

B From Banī Jamrah (village).

A Could you give me some idea about your job?

B Yes . . . in the past I was also engaged in weaving . . . I used to weave loin-cloths and sometimes head-cloths . . . the craft began to dwindle, so I joined government garden where I worked for about a year . . . then again I resigned and went to Saudi Arabia.

A What sort of work did you do there?

B Assistant carpenter. And after that I came (back) to Baḥrain and got married, and joined the Company (i.e., Bahrain Petroleum Co.) for about twenty five years.

A What sort of work do you do in the Company?

B I work in the department of fire and safety . . . we fill fire extinguishers. And also we make . . . for example, if a fire hose is worn, we fix rings to it. We also paint cylinders.

A What do you do when you finish your (daily) work at the Company. . . I mean, in the evening?

B In fact, when I finish working, sometimes I become a carpenter. I have a house where I work. I have just come from the house where I have been working. In the past I used to make charpoys and cupboards.

A Nowadays nobody wants charpoys.

B No, nowadays everybody opts for . . . the charpoys not at all . . . I have left carpentry now. I've started working on building. I mean I'm a builder . . . but only in the house, my house . . . and if anybody wants a staircase (built) I do it. . . or carpentry (jobs) like a lintel, I do it for him. In my leisure time I go to the club.

A What do you do in the club?

B Well, there are games like tennis, volley ball, football.

A How many wives do you have?

B One.

A And children?

B Seven.

A What are their names?

B One is called ^{c}Abd al-Ḥasan and one Ḥabīb, and Nāji who is the youngest, and a girl by the name of Zaynab, and Fāṭma and Āsya, and I have Fawziyya too. Yes . . . these are my children. Three attend schools in the village of al-Khamīs. That elder boy is stupid. He left school, and at present he works with the Municipality.

A Well, so you work both in carpentry and in building?

B Building. And I also practised plastering . . . I did my house by myself.

A You built it yourself?

B Myself and my son.

A How many months did it take to do?

B Every year when I am on leave I devote my time to it. I work as I please, I mean I don't work to exhaustion . . . I work for two or three hours and then stop.

A How many floors did you do?

B One floor.

A Did you ever travel?

B Twice.

A Where did you go?

B I went to Iraq . . . and also Iran, but I've been nowhere else. Also I went on pilgrimage.

A How was pilgrimage in your days?

B It was comfortable indeed.

A Did you go by yourself?

B I went with a contractor . . . yes.

Informant 6

A *?il-?ism il-kariim, ḥajji?*

B *?aḥmad mḥammad ^{c}ali ḥseen.*

A *mumkin ti^{c}ṭiinne fikra, ḥajji, ^{c}an šiġluk?*

B *^{c}amali l-izraa^{c}a . . . tiḥruf il-?araaḍiin, wi-t^{c}addil . . . hal-ayyaam muusim iṭ-ṭamaaṭa, ?u muusim iṭruuḥ, xuḍra haade lli . . . nizra^{c} w-ileen zara^{c}ne n^{c}aabilhe m^{c}aabale.*

A *čeef tizra^{c}uun iṭ-ṭamaaṭa?*

B *?awwal in^{c}addil il-?araaḍi, wi-njiib traktaraat tiḥruf il-?araaḍiin, ?u taali niġris fiihe ṭ-ṭamaaṭa, wi-n^{c}aable bis-samaad il-keemaawi . . . ?ilaa stawa ḥada-ḥne staṯmarnaah . . . . ?u min ba^{c}de nizra^{c} iṭruuḥ.*

. . . .

C *ḥajji, ?ayyaam zamaan . . . ihni diiratkum ya^{c}ni gabil ṯalaaṯiin sane . . . loo hal-ayyaam?*

B *muddat a-ḥiin haay falafiin sane, ?arbi^{c}iin sane tġayyar waajid, l-awwal iḥne fi l-ġooṣ, ?id-diira tgišš, maa ttimm ?illa l-ḥariim bass b-ruuḥha... ?al-ḥiin il-ḥayaa ġeer, duun l-awwal.*

C *ya^{c}ni ?al-ḥiin ?aḥsan min l-awwal?*

B *?ii . . . ?aḥsan min l-awwal, ?aryaḥ . . . ?amma l-awwal laa ta^{c}baaniin fi l-ibḥuur, ?id-diira ngaarub biš-šahreen ?u nuṣ maa njiihe, kille fi l-ġooṣ . . . ?awwal betrool maa fiih, ?il-^{c}aamil b-^{c}asir rubbiyyaat ?u xams rubbiyyaat l-awwal . . . ?al-ḥiin b-sittiin rubbiyye . . . hay ^{c}indi šaġaaġiil yištiġluun ^{c}ala xamsiin rubbiyye ?u ma^{c}ruuf^{c}ala raasi, wala ?anwas ?aḥaačihem.*

C *min ahaali d-diira?*

B *min ahaali d-diira . . . maa-nwas ?aḥaačihem, ?atbaa^{c}ad b^{c}iid . . . fwaalathum^{c}išriin rubbiyye . . . l-awwal gaduu^{c}hum fardat tamr. ?al-ḥiin la . . . ?al-ḥiin b-xamsiin rubbiyye r-rooḥa wala-nwas ?aḥaačiih huu^{c}ammi, ?ane muu^{c}amme, huu^{c}ammi lli ?ane ?astaajur w-a^{c}ṭiih il-beezaat . . . huu^{c}aamil ma^{c}ruuf^{c}ala raasi . . . hii b-šiime, w-hii b-giime . . . ?in-nufuus tġayyarat, wal-xeer hast.*

Translation (Informant 6)

A Your noble name, *ḥajji?*
B Aḥmad Muḥammad ᶜAli Ḥusain.
A Can you give us some idea about your work?
B My work is gardening . . . the ploughing of the lands (i.e., soil), raking . . . and now is the season for tomatoes, and the season for cucumbers . . . vegetables that is what we grow . . . and when we have planted we look after them with great care.
A How do you grow tomatoes?
B First we prepare the lands then we bring tractors to plough the lands and afterwards we plant tomatoes, then we treat it with chemical ferilizers, when it has grown . . . then we have made it usable, and after that, we grow cucumbers.

. . . .

C How did this village use to be thirty years ago compared with today?
B Over a period of thirty or forty years great changes have occurred. In the past we were engaged in pearl diving, the village was vacated, except for women. Nowadays life is different, different from what it was in the past.
C So it is better now from what it used to be?
B Yes, it is better than olden times, it is more comfortable. In the past work at sea was tedious. For about two and a half months we were away from the village, all spent in pearl diving . . . there was no oil in the past, the worker used to take ten rupees or five rupees in those days . . . nowadays it is sixty rupees. I have some workers who work for fifty rupees and besides they are doing me a favour, and I dare not say a single word to any of them.
C Are they from the same village?
B Yes, people from the village. I don't dare even talk to them . . . I keep myself at a distance. Their snacks and soft drinks cost me twenty rupees. A few dates used to satisfy workers in the past. It is not the same now. Nowadays it is fifty rupees a go (i.e., daily) and I don't dare say anything to him. He is my boss, I am not his boss. Although I hire his services and pay him for it, he is my boss. He thinks he is doing me a favour . . . you beg for his favour and you also pay for it. Attitudes have changed . . . but people are better off.

Informant 12

A *?il-?ism il-kariim?*

B *^{c}abd ir-raḥiim ^{c}abd il-^{c}aziiz il-^{c}aali.*

A *ṣaar luk čam sane fi hal-mihne?*

B *?aštiġil fiihe min yoom sinni sab^{c} sniin ?ila l- ?aan fneene w-?arbi^{c}iin sane.*

A *weeš tiṣna^{c}uun?*

B *niṣna^{c} min kill šii . . . l-aškaal l-awwaliyye . . . killhe ni^{c}malhe ḥatte l-gadiide.*

A *miṯil?*

B *miṯil ?azhaar, ṭaffaayaat, manaara, dalle maal gahwa, gdaawa, ruus.*

A *hal fi ?aḥad yištiġil wiyyaak . . . isaa^{c}idk ya^{c}ni?*

B *ḥazzat ḥaaḍir bass ib-ruuḥi . . . ?u^{c}indi ^{c}aamil iji ṣ-ṣubḥ las-saa^{c}a ṯna^{c}aš iruuḥ.*

A *fahamt ?inna ?axuuk kaan yištiġil wiyyaak ?u tarak . . . leeš?*

B *lanna maa ṣarrafa l-^{c}amal . . . barra ma^{c}aaš ?aḥsan.*

A *?awlaaduk isaa^{c}duunuk?*

B *?i . . . laazim.*

A *š-isawwuun?*

B *iṣalḥuun iṭ-ṭiin . . . isawwuun ba^{c}ad ḥaṣṣaalaat . . . ?u ruus, ?u daak illi ?akbar ?astaad ṣaar.*

A *?ax ^{c}abd ir-raḥiim. . . ?il-maṣna^{c} haade maa yiḥtaaj ila tajdiid?*

B *qaṭ^{c}an . . . iḥne waajid zawwadne l-^{c}amal . . . ?u maa jawwadne l-^{c}amal illa ^{c}ala ḥsaab ya^{c}ni mwaa^{c}diinne, biyi^{c}ṭuunne . . . ?u byibnuun leenne maṣna^{c} . . . id-daayra . . . ha daḥne nitraggab . . . ?inšaaḷḷa^{c}an gariib yibnuun lene maṣna^{c}.*

A *?inzeen ?ax ^{c}abd ir-raḥiim . . . haay iz-zarga wil-xaḍra mumkin tišraḥ leenne ^{c}anhe?*

B *haadi ?alwaan maal gliiz . . . jaaybiine min il-?eeraan li-anna ?ane riḥt šahar ^{c}ala ḥsaab id-daayra . . . šahar waaḥid ?axadt fikra ^{c}an l-igliiz min ^{c}indhum ?u jibt wiyyaayi šwayy . . . wil-?aan mintiḍir asawwi furun ^{c}ala ḥsaab l-igliiz . . . li?anna furun maalne iṭubb minne waṣax ^{c}ala l-igliiz yitwaṣṣax . . . ?ileen sawweene furun jadiid b-ṭaabuug il-ḥaraari iṣiir ?aḥsan min illi ^{c}indine.*

A *?u l-igliiz haade mumkin yit^{c}amal ihnii?*

B *?i . . . bass ^{c}ala ḥsaab il-furun yistawi . . . ṯaaniyan il-furun maal l-igliiz laazim šalfaat . . . ?ileeh šalfaat . . . kul giṭ^{c}a tiḥtha b-ruuḥha.*

A *?iṭṭiin haade min ween itjiibe?*

B *injiibe min maḥal ^{c}ind ġarbi r-rafaa^{c} il-ġarbi . . . maḥal isammuune l-maaš. . . laazim inruuḥ leh bis-sayyaara . . . l-awwal kinne njiibe ^{c}ala ḥamiir . . . ?al-ḥiin fi sayyaaraat . . . inruuḥ leh inguṣṣa ^{c}ala baġiyyatne w-injiibeh.*

A *itguṣṣuune ?u hu jaaf ya^{c}ni?*

B *? i . . . iṭṭiin xašin . . . injiibeh w-inṣaffiih taṣfiyeh ikuun inṭalli^{c} minneh il-ḥašiiš . . . w-irraml ḥak nigdar ni^{c}male ?adawaat faxxaariyye. w-il-^{c}aamil yoomiyye walbe iṣaffi gufraan iṯneene . . . ṯalaaṯe . . . bas lanna taṣfaate waajid ṣu^{c}ub.*

Translation (Informant 12)

A Your noble name?

B ^{c}Abdul-Raḥīm ^{c}Abd al-^{c}Azīz, al-^{c}Āli.

A For how many years have you been doing this job now?

B I have been working at this craft since I was seven years of age . . . until now when I am forty two years old.

A What do you make?

B We make every kind . . . traditional forms . . . we make everything, even the new stuff.

A Like . . .?

B Like vases (lit. flowers), ash-trays, minarets, coffee pots, hubble-bubbles, (and their) tops.

A Is there anybody who shares work with you, you know, helps you?

B For the time being I am by myself. . . I have a labourer who comes in the morning, works until 12 (noon) and then goes.

A I am told your brother used to work with you and then he left . . . why?

B Because he didn't find this work lucrative . . . outside he gets a better salary.

A Do your sons help you?

B Yes . . . they have to.

A What do they do?

B They prepare the clay . . . they also make money-boxes . . . (and hubble-bubble) tops. The elder is master now.

A Brother, ^{c}Abd al-Rahim . . . this factory . . . does it not need refurbishing?

B Of course, we have expanded work here . . . I have adhered to this craft because they have promised us they'll give us . . . and they'll build us a factory, the Department. We are looking forward to it. If God wills, they are going to build us one soon.

A Well, brother ^{c}Abd al-Raḥīm . . . these blue and green (things) could you tell us about them?

B These are colours for glazing . . . we brought them from Iran . . . I went there for a month at the expense of the Department . . . one month . . . I formed some opinion about glazing there, and brought some with me . . . now I am looking forward to make a kiln for glazing . . . because our kiln drops dirt which affects the glazing . . . when we have built a new kiln . . . using thermal bricks it is going to be better than the one we have now.

A Can glazing be carried out here?

B Yes, but only when the kiln is made . . . also, the kiln for glazing requires racks. It has racks so that each piece can be placed separately.

A Where do you get this clay from?

B We get it from a place to the west of Western Rafā^{c} . . . a place called al-Māsh. We have to go there by car . . . in the past we used to bring it on donkeys, now in cars . . . we go there and cut it as we wish and carry it to here.

A You cut it while it is dry . . . you mean?

B Yes, the clay is hard . . . we bring it and refine it. We remove the grass and the sand so that it can be made into pottery items . . . the worker can, at his best, purify two to three baskets . . . only . . . because the process of refining it is very difficult.

A folktale from a Dirāzi female informant (26)

marra rayyaal ^{c}ala m-maa gilt ya^{c}ni ẖaakum, ?il-ḥaakum allah. taḥt beete ^{c}išše ?ila ya^{c}ni jaara faqiir ṣaaḥib ^{c}išše. ṣaaḥib il-^{c}išše^{c}indeh ḥadiiqa sġayra ^{c}ala gadara . . . miflaat immaa tguul haade l-beet hna w-il-ḥadiiqa hnaaka barra b ^{c}iid šwayy . . heek il-leele ḥarr waayid . . . ?illa hu yguul iṣ-ṣulṭaan: xalluunne nguum is-saa ^{c} nruuḥ ḥadiiqat il-faqiir, nitnazzah šwayy . . . ṭala ^{c}aw yitnazzahoon . . . ?ida fneen waagfiin, waaḥid f-iide girṭaase w-galam . . . ?illa hu yguul: yaa-xuuk iktib! gaal: weeš aktib? gaal: iktib inna mart iṣ-ṣulṭaan tiḥmal w-ityiib walad, ?u mart il-faqiir tiḥmal w-ityiib bitt, ?u yitzaawajoon . . . bitt il-faqiir yaaxithe wald il-ġani, inzeen ḍamm ^{c}ala ḍamiimate w-sakat . . . haada nte ya ṣ-ṣulṭaan . . . ye l-beet . . . ?alla qasam, hu marate ḥimlat u yaabat iṣbayy, wil-faqiir ḥimlat u yaabat bitt . . . ^{c}ala gool il-haatif yee . . . min yoom gaalaw heeki wuldat mart yiiraanne w-yaabat ibnayye . . . weeš sawwa . . . raaḥ ila ?abuuha . . . ?illa hu yguul ileeh: . . . jaabaw luk bitt. gaal: ?ii jaabaw liyyi bitt . . . gaal: bii ^{c}ne y-yaaha! gaal: čeef ?abii ^{c}uk iyyaaha! ?ane rḍiit ?umha yumkin maa tirḍa . . . gaal: laa guul leehe, ?aba ^{c}ṭiikum hal-kiṯir ifluus ?u ba ^{c}ṭi-ikum . . . ?u ba ^{c}ṭiikum . . . raaḥ ileehe gaal leehe: bitt iflaan . . . gaayil yubbaaha, yištari-ihe . . . inbii^{c}he yyaaha? ?intiin weeš naḍarš . . . gaalat: yuu! tawha lla majyuuba, ba ^{c}adhi ṣaġiira, ibii ^{c}uunhe-é? gaal: ?aguul liš i ^{c}ṭiih iyyaaha . . . iqitluunne . . . yaw ^{c}aṭoohum iyyaaha . . . ^{c}aṭoohum iyyaaha . . . weeš sawwa . . . ta ^{c}aal xithe b-xalaagiinhe ?u wadhe fi ġaaba, maalat, tikram, l-ičlaab, taḥat čide gabr . . . ?u šigg baṭin l-ibnayye ?u ruuḥ ^{c}an il-ġaaba . . . haak il-yoom ṭala ^{c}at umha wiyya ?abuuha biruuḥuun ḥadiiqathum bitisma ^{c} nasam fi l-ġaaba . . . ?illa hii tguul ileh: flaan? gaal: weeš? ?illa ḥiss nasam fi l-ġaaba . . . gaal: yumkin, tikram, čalbe waalde . . . ?u haadi wlaadhe . . . gaalat: laa . . . maa ?atgalgal ?awwal ta ^{c}aal wiyyaayi . . . wala daxalaw ?illa bithum marmiyye fi l-ġaaba . . . ?u nasamhe fiihe . . . ?u mašguug baṭinhe . . . ?axadooha . . . raaḥaw la-beethum ga ^{c}adaw i ^{c}aalyuun fiihe . . . buri l-jirḥ . . . ?illa hu yguul bitt iflaan . . . gaalat: yaalla . . . gaal: xalliinne niṭla ^{c} min hal-balad . . . maa leenne ḥaaje fiihe . . . yoom haade ?awwaliyyaathum . . . laa xiirat alla fi t-tawaali . . . xalliinne nsaafur . . . saafaraw ween biruuḥuun . . . raaḥaw il-baṣra.

Translation (Informant 26)

Once upon a time there lived a man, he was a ruler—there is no ruler but God! Near his house there was a hut which belonged to his poor neighbour. The owner of the hut had a small garden . . . according to his limited means, so then the house was here and the garden was there, outside . . . a little bit further away. It was very hot that night. The Sultan (i.e., the ruler) said, "Let us go to the poor man's garden for a short walk." They went out for a walk. Suddenly there were two persons standing, one with a piece of paper and a pen. One said, "Write, brother" The other answered, "What should I write?" He said, "Write down that the Sultan's wife will conceive and will give birth to a boy, and the wife of the poor man will conceive and will give birth to a girl, and they will get married. The poor man's daughter will get married to the rich man's son." The Sultan kept what he had heard to himself, and he went home. God decreed, and the Sultan's wife conceived and gave birth to a boy and the poor man's wife gave birth to a girl. It happened as the voices predicted. As soon as he knew of the poor man's wife giving birth to a girl . . . what he did was that he went to her father and said to him, "A girl was born to you." He replied, "Yes, a girl was born to me." He said (i.e., the Sultan), "Sell her to us." The man said, "Why should I sell her to you? If I agreed to do so, her mother wouldn't." He said, "No, you should persuade her. I shall give you this much money . . . and I shall give you . . . and give you." So the man went to his wife and said "Oh! daughter of so-and-so[1] he says (i.e., the Sultan) he wants to buy her. Shall we sell her to him? What is your opinion?" She exclaimed, "Yuu! She is a new-born babe! She is young; We couldn't sell her!" "I am telling you to give her to him," he said, "or they will kill us." They came (i.e., the Sultan's men) and she was given to them. She was given to them . . . what he did (I.e., the Sultan) was that he took her in her wrappers to the forest, may you be honoured, where dogs live . . . . . . near a grave . . . he disembowelled the girl and ran away from the forest. That day, the mother and the father of the girl were going to their garden. She (the mother) heard somebody breathing in the forest. So she said to him (i.e, her husband) "So-and-so!" He answered "What?" "Do you hear anybody breathing in the forest?" "Perhaps," he replied, "a bitch has given birth and these are her puppies." She replied, "No . . . I am not going to budge from here . . . unless you accompany me." When they entered they found their daughter lying in the forest . . . still breathing . . . with her stomach cut open. They took her home and nursed her wounds. The wound healed. He said, "Daughter of so-and-so" She (the wife) answered, "Yes." He said, "What is your opinion?" Regarding what?" she answered. "Let us leave this country," he said, "we don't need it any longer. If this is the beginning, the end is surely worse! Let us go abroad." They travelled . . . where did they go? They went to Basrah.

NOTE:

1. "Daughter of . . . " and "mother of . . ." are two terms of reference normally employed by husbands when calling the attention of their wives.

THE INFORMANTS AND THEIR VILLAGES[1]

Informant No. 1

Name	:	Sayyid Aḥmad as-Sayyid Hāshim
Age	:	over fifty
Educational status	:	illiterate
Occupation	:	ex-gardener
Village	:	Dirāz

Informant No. 2

Name	:	Aḥmad ᶜAli Aḥmad al-Akraf
Age	:	thirty one
Educational status	:	illiterate
Occupation	:	fisherman
Village	:	Dirāz

Informant No. 3

Name	:	Ḥajji ᶜAbdalla bin ᶜAbd al-ᶜAzīz bin Ḥusain Madan
Age	:	forty five
Educational status	:	illiterate
Occupation	:	gardener and fisherman
Village	:	Dirāz

Informant No. 4

Name	:	Ḥajji ᶜAli ᶜAbdalla Nijím
Age	:	over fifty five
Educational status	:	illiterate
Occupation	:	weaver
Village	:	Bani Jamrah

Informant No. 5

Name	:	ᶜAli bin Ḥasan bin Salmān
Age	:	forty two
Educational status	:	illiterate
Occupation	:	employee of the Baḥrain Petroleum Company (BAPCO)
Village	:	Bani Jamrah

Informant No. 6

Name	:	Aḥmad Muḥammad ᶜAli Ḥusain Falāḥ
Age	:	sixty
Educational status	:	illiterate
Occupation	:	gardener
Village	:	Damistān

Informant No. 7

Name	:	Ḥajji Aḥmad Ḥusain Abū Rwais
Age	:	seventy five
Educational status	:	illiterate
Occupation	:	retired fisherman and gardener
Village	:	Shahrakkān

Informant No. 8

Name	:	Yūsif Salmān Yūsif
Age	:	fifty
Educational status	:	illiterate
Occupation	:	in charge of a water pump in a garden
Village	:	Karrānah

Informant No. 9

Name	:	ᶜAbdalla bin Ḥasan
Age	:	fifty one
Educational status	:	illiterate
Occupation	:	labourer and part-time weaver
Village	:	Bani Jamrah

Informant No. 10

Name	:	Khamīs Muḥammad Swēlim
Age	:	seventy
Educational status	:	illiterate
Occupation	:	fisherman
Village	:	Budayyiᶜ

Informant No. 11

Name : Yūsif ^{c}Abdur-Raḥmān al-Kawwāri

Age : thirty four

Educational status : semi-literate

Occupation : member of a tug crew at Mīna? Salmān

Village : Budayyi ^{c}

Informant No. 12

Name : ^{c}Abd ar-Raḥīm ^{c}Abd al- ^{c}Azīz al- ^{c}Āli

Age : forty two

Educational status : illiterate

Occupation : potter

Village : ^{c}Āli

Informant No. 13

Name : ^{c}Abd al-Ḥusain

Age : twenty six

Educational status : illiterate

Occupation : ex-potter

Village : ^{c}Āli

Informant No. 14

Name : Mulla ^{c}Aṭiyyah

Age : sixty

Educational status : literate

Occupation : Shī ^{c}i religious preacher

Village : Bani Jamrah

Informant No. 15

Name : Husain bin ^{c}Ali

Age : sixty

Educational status : illiterate

Occupation : weaver

Village : Bani Jamrah

Informant No. 16

Name	:	Sa ^{c}īd Shaikh ^{c}Abdalla ^{c}Arab
Age	:	fifty five
Educational status	:	illiterate
Occupation	:	retired
Village	:	Bani Jamrah

Informant No. 17

Name	:	Sayyid Sa ^{c}īd al-As ^{c}ad
Age	:	thirty seven
Educational status	:	semi-literate
Occupation	:	Owner of a traditional laboratory for the extraction of folk-medicine
Village	:	^{c}Ain Dār (Jid Ḥafṣ)

Informant No. 18

Name	:	Raḍi Aḥmad Ḥammād
Age	:	thirty three
Educational status	:	literate
Occupation	:	BAPCO employee
Village	:	Jid Ḥafṣ

Informant No. 19

Name	:	Ḥajji Ṣāliḥ bin ^{c}Īsa bin Aḥmad
Age	:	forty five
Educational status	:	illiterate
Occupation	:	ex gardener, presently (BAPCO) painter
Village	:	Jid Ḥafṣ

Informant No. 20

Name	:	Ja ^{c}far ^{c}Abdalla
Age	:	forty
Educational Status	:	illiterate
Occupation	:	fisherman
Village	:	Sfālah (Sitrah Island)

Informant No. 21

Name	:	Ḥajji Ḥusain bin ^{c}Abdalla bin Jim ^{c}ah
Age	:	over seventy
Educational status	:	illiterate
Occupation	:	gardener
Village	:	Sitrah

Informant No. 22

Name	:	Manṣūr Raḍi ^{c}Abd ^{c}Ali
Age	:	sixteen
Educational status	:	literate
Occupation	:	student
Village	:	Markubān (Sitrah)

Informant No. 23

Name	:	Ḥajji Aḥmad bin ^{c}Ali bin Aḥmad
Age	:	seventy
Educational status	:	illiterate
Occupation	:	jazzāf (bulk-buyer of fish)
Village	:	Dirāz

Informant No. 24

Name	:	Ḥajji ^{c}Ali bin Ṣāliḥ
Age	:	fifty five
Educational status	:	illiterate
Occupation	:	gardener
Village	:	Dirāz

In addition to the above male informants, there were five female informants who were of more advanced age and four out of five were illiterate, the only exception being an informant from Manāmah.

Note:

1. Note that personal names given on this and the following pages conform to local pronunciation, regardless of how they are spelt in written Arabic.

Bibliography

Abboud, Peter F. (1970). *"Spoken Arabic."* In *Current Trends in Linguistics,* vol. VI, 439–66. The Hague.

Abū Ḥākimah, A.M. (1965). *History of Eastern Arabia* 1750–1800. Beirut.

Ali, Jawad. (1968–73). *Tārīkh al-ᶜArab Qabl al-Islām.* 10 volumes. Beirut.

Amedroz, H.F. and Margoliouth, D.S. (1920–1). *The Experiences of the Nations.* (Being a translation of Ibn Maskawaih's *Tajārib al-Umam.* Oxford.

Al-Ani, Salman Hassan. (1970). *Arabic Phonology.* The Hague.

————. and May, D.R. (1973). *"The Phonological Structure of the Syllable in Arabic,"* American Journal of Arabic Studies, I, 37–49, The Hague.

Anīs, Ibrāhīm. (1951). *"Taᶜaddud as-Ṣīyaġ fī al-Luġah al-ᶜArabiyyah,"* MMLA, XIII, 159–65. Cairo.

————. (1965). *Fī al-Lahajāt al-ᶜArabiyyah.* Cairo.

Al-Anṣāri, M.J. (1970). *Lamaḥāt min al-Khalīj al-ᶜArabī.* Baḥrain.

Al-Baḥrāni, Shaikh Yūsuf (1874–5). *Anīs al-Khāṭir wa-Jalīs al-Musāfir, known as al-Kashkūl.* Bombay.

Bakalla, Muḥammad Ḥasan. (1975). *Bibliography of Arabic Linguistics.* London.

————. (1981). *An Introduction to Arabic Language and Literature.* Taipei.

————. (1981). *Arabic Linguistics: An Introduction and Bibliography.* London.

Al-Bakri al-Andalusi. (1876–7). *Muᶜjam Mastaᶜjam.* Paris.

Al-Balādhuri. (1957–8). *Futūḥ al-Buldān.* Beirut.

Beeston, A.F.L. (1962). *"Arabic Sibilants," JSS,* VII, 222–7.

Belgrave, C. (1960). *Personal Column.* London.

Belgrave, J. (1973). *Welcome to Baḥrain.* Hong Kong.

Bibby, G. (1970). *Looking for Dilmun.* New York.

al-Bilādi al-Baḥrāni, Shaikh ᶜAli. (1377 A.H.). *Anwār al-Badrayn fī Tarājim ᶜUlamā? al-Qaṭīf wal-Aḥsā? wal-Baḥrain.* Najaf.

Blanc, Haim. (1964). *Communal Dialects in Baghdad.* Harvard.

————. (1970). *"Dual and Pseudo-Dual in the Arabic Dialects," Language,* XXXXVI.

Blau, Joshua. (1972). *"Middle and Old Arabic Material for the History of Stress in Arabic", BSOAS,* XXXV.

Bloch, A. (1970–1). *"Morphological Doublets in Arabic Dialects," JSS,* vol. XV, XVI (1970–1)

Borg, Alexander. (1976). *"The Imāla in Maltese", IOS,* no. 6.

Baḥrain Government Annual Reports. (Book I, 1949–1952); (Book II, 1952–1954); (Book III, 1957–1958); (Book IV, 1959–1961);

Bombay Selections, (1856). Vol. XXIV, Bombay.

Cantineau, Jean. (1936–7). *"Études sur quelques parlers de nomades arabes d'Orient"* in *Annales de l'Institut d'Études Orientales d'Alger*, II, 1–118; III, 119–237

Diem, W. (1973). *Skizzen Jemenitischer Dialekte.* Beirut.
Al-Dirāzi, H.M.A. (1896). *al-Fawādiḥ al-Ḥusayniyyah.* Bombay.
Driver, G.R. (1925). *A Grammar of the Colloquial Arabic of Syria and Palestine.* London.

Faroughy, A. (1951). *The Baḥrain Islands.* New York.
Fischer, W. (1959). *Die demonstrativen Bildungen der neuarabischen Dialekte.* The Hague.

Gairdner, W.H.T. (1925). *The Phonetics of Arabic.* London.
Garbell, I. (1958). *"Remarks on the Historical Phonology of an East Mediterranean Arabic Dialect," Word*, XIV.
Ghanem, H.A. (1958). *Aden Arabic for Beginners.* Aden.
Gibb, H.A.R. (1963). *Travels in Asia and Africa, being a translation of Ibn Baṭṭūṭa's Riḥalāt.* London.
Goitein, F. (1932). *"Jemenische Geschichten," ZS* VIII.
Greenberg, J.H. (1950). *"The Patterning of Root Morphemes in Semitic," Word*, VI.

al-Ḥamawi, Yāqūt. (1906). *Mu^cjam al-Buldān.* Edited by al-Khānji. Cairo. (8 vols. and 2 supplements)
al-Hamdāni. (1884–91). *Ṣifat Jazīrat al-^cArab.* Leiden.
al-Ḥanafi, Shaikh Jalāl (1964). *Mu^cjam al-Alfāẓ al-Kuwaitiyyah.* Baghdad.
A Handbook of the Spoken Arabic of Baḥrain. Published by Section for Arabic Studies (BAPCO)
Hansen, H.H. (1961). *"The Pattern of Women's Seclusion and Veiling in a Shī^ca Village", Folk* (Copenhagen), III, 23–42.
———. (1965). *Investigations in a Shī^ca Village in Baḥrain.* *Publications of the National Museum* (Copenhagen), *Ethnographical Series*, vol. XII.
Al-Ḥāzmy, A.M. (1975). *A Critical and Comparative Study of the Spoken Dialect of Ḥarb Tribe in Sa^cūdi Arabia. Ph.D.* thesis, Leeds University, Dept. of Semitic Studies.
Hess, J.J. (1938). *Von den Beduinen des inneren Arabiens.* Leipzig.
Hitti, Philip. (1966). *The Origins of the Islamic State, being a translation of al-Balādhuri, Futūḥ al-Buldān.* Beirut.

Ibn Durayd. (1345 A.H.). *Jamharat al-Luġah* (3 vols.). Haydarabad.
———. (1958). *Al-Ishtiqāq.* Cairo.
Ibn al-Faqīh. (1885). *Kitāb al-Buldān.* Leiden.
Ibn Ḥazm. (1962). *Jamharat Ansāb al-^cArab.* Cairo.
Ibn Jinni. (1954). *Sirr Ṣinā^ca t al-I^crāb.* Cairo.
Ibn Manẓūr. (1955). *Lisān al-^cArab.* Beirut.

Jayakar, A.S.G. (1889). *"The ^cOmani Dialect of Arabic," JRAS*, XXI.
Johnstone, T.M. (1961). *"Some Characteristics of the Dōsiri Dialect of Arabic as Spoken in Kuwait," BSOAS*, XXIV, Part 2.
———. (1963). *"The Affrication of Kāf and Gāf in the Arabic Dialects of the Arabian Peninsula," JSS*, VIII.
———. (1964). *"Further Studies on the Dōsiri Dialect of Arabic as Spoken in Kuwait," BSOAS*, XXVII, Part 2.

———————. (1965). *"The Sound Change j > y in the Arabic dialects of Peninsular Arabia," BSOAS*, XXVIII, Part 2.
———————. (1967). *Eastern Arabian Dialect Studies.* London.
———————. (1968). *"The Verbal Affix -k in Spoken Arabic," JSS*, XIII, No. 2.
———————. and Muir, J. (1962). *"Portuguese Influence on Shipbuilding in the Persian Gulf," The Mariner's Mirror*, XXXXVIII, No. 1.
———————. (1964). *"Nautical Terms in Kuwaiti Dialect of Arabic," BSOAS*, XXVII.

Kaḥḥālah, U.R. (1949). *Mu^{c}jam al-Qabā?il al-^{c}Arabiyyah.* Damascus.

Landberg, C. de. (1901–13). *Études sur les dialectes de l'Arabie meridionale.* (2 vols. in four parts). Leiden.
———————. (1920–42). *Glossaire Daṯīnois* (3 vols.). Leiden.
Lane, E.W. (1863–85). *Arabic-English Lexicon* (4 vols.). London.
Lorimer, J.G. (1915). *Gazetteer of the Persian Gulf, ^{c}Uman and Central Arabia.* Calcutta.
Al-Lughawi, al-Halabi. (1960). *Kitāb al-Ibdāl*, (2 vols). Damascus.

Al-Madani, Ṣalāḥ, and Karīm al-^{c}Urayyiḍ (1972) *Min Turāth al-Baḥrain al-Sha^{c}bi* (Baḥrain's Folklore Heritage) Beirut.
Al-Mas^{c}ūdi. (1965). *At-Tanbīh wal-Ishrāf.* Beirut.
———————. (1966). *Murūj adh-Dhahab.* Beirut.
McLure, H.A. (1971). *The Arabian Peninsula and Prehistoric Populations.* Florida.
Miles, S.B. (1919). *Countries and Tribes of the Persian Gulf.* London.
Al-Muslim, M.S. (1962). *Sāḥil adh-Dhahab al-Aswad.* Beirut.

Al-Nabhāni, M. (1923). *At-Tuḥfah an-Nabhāniyyah fi Tārīkh al-Baḥrain*, Vol. 1. Cairo, 1342 A.H.
Nakhleh, E.A. (1976). *Baḥrain.* London.
Neibuhr, M. (1972). *Travels through Arabia and Other Countries in the East.* Edinburgh.

The Principles of the International Phonetic Association, London, 1975

Qafīsheh, Ḥamdi (1975). *A Basic Course in Gulf Arabic.* University of Arizona Press, Tucson.
al-Qalqashandi. (1959). *Ṣubḥ al-A^{c}sha. Cairo.*
———————. (1959). *Nihāyat al-Arab fi Ma^{c}rifat Ansāb al-^{c}Arab*, Cairo, 1959
al-Quṭb, S.A.R. (1968). *Ansāb al-^{c}Arab.* Beirut.

Rabin, C. (1951). *Ancient West Arabian.* London. 1951.
Rayḥāni, Amīn. (1930). *Around the Coasts of Arabia.* London.
Reinhardt, C. (1894). *Ein arabischer Dialekt gesprochen in ^{c}Umān und Zanzibār.* Stuttgart and Berlin.
Rhodokanakis, N. (1908–11). *Südarabische Expedition. Der Vulgärarabische Dialekt im Ḍofâr* (2 vols). Wien.
Rossi, E. (1938). *"Appunti di dialecttologia del Yemen," RSO*, XVII.
———————. (1939). *L'Arabo parlato a Ṣan^{c}a.* Rome.
Rumaiḥi, M.G. (1976). *Baḥrain: Social and Political change Since the First World War.* Essex.

Sībawayhi. (1967). *Al-Kitāb.* Baghdad.

Sinān, M.B. (1963). *Al-Baḥrain Durrat al-Khalīj al-^{c}Arabi* Baghdad.

Smeaton, B.H. (1973). *Lexical Expansion due to Technical Change.* Indiana University.

Sobleman, H. (1962). *Arabic Dialect Studies.* Washington.

Socin, A. (1900). *Diwan aus Centralarabien,* Leipzig.

Sprenger, Dr. A. (1841). *Meadows of Gold and Mines of Gems, being a translation of al-Mas^{c}ūdi, Murūj adh-Dhahab.*

al-Suwaidi, M.A., ed. (1864). *Sabā?ik adh-Dhahab fi Ma^{c}rifat Qabā?il al-^{c}Arab, Baghdad.*

Al-Suyuti. (1945). *Al-Muzhir fi ^{c}Ulūm al-Lughah,* (2 vols.). Cairo.

Al-Ṭabari. (1960). *Tārīkh al-Rusul wal-Mulūk.* Cairo.

Al-Tājir, Ḥajji Muhammad ^{c}Ali. *^{c}Uqūd al-Āl fi Tārīkh Jazā?ir ?Uwāl* (unpublished).

———. *Muntaẓam ad-Durrayn fi Tarājim ^{c}Ulamā? al-Qaṭīf wal-Aḥsā? wal-Baḥrain* (unpublished).

Al-Toma, S.J. (1969). *The Problem of Diglossia in Arabic.* Cambridge.

Wahba, Shaikh Ḥāfiẓ (1935). *Jazīrat al-^{c}Arab fi l-Qarn al-^{c}Ishrīn.* Cairo.

Wallin, G.A. (1855 & 1858). *"Uber die Laute des Arabischen und ihre Bezeichnung," ZDMG,* IX, XII.

Wilson, A.T. (1928). *The Persian Gulf.* Oxford.

Winder, R.B. (1959). *Education in al-Baḥrain* (Report for the World of Islam). London and New York.

Wuestenfeld, H.F. (1874). *Baḥrain und Jemama.* Göttingen.

al-Zayyāni, A. (1973). *al-Baḥrain 1783–1973.* Beirut.

Zwemer, S.M. (1900). *Arabia the Cradle of Islam.* New York.

General index

Aḥsā? (al-) 12, 15, 17, 21, 25, 29
Āl-Bin ᶜAli 7, 23, 25
Āl-Bu ᶜAynayn 24, 25
Āl-Bu Falāsah 7, 25
Āl-Jalāhimah 7, 23, 25
Āl-Khalīfah 1, 7, 23, 31, 32, 39
Āl-Maᶜāwidah 7, 25
Āl-Manāniᶜah 7, 24, 25
Āl-Muqlah 7
Āl-Muslim 7
Āl-Sādah, 7, 25
Āl-Quṣaibi 7
Āl-Zayyāni 7
Arabian Mission 4
Aramco 12
?Awāl/?Uwāl 2, 15, 16, 20, 22, 23, 24, 29, 30, 34, 167
Azd (al-) 16, 19, 20, 24, 167
ᶜAbd al-Qais 2, 16, 17, 18, 19, 20, 21, 22, 23, 24, 29, 167
ᶜAbd al-Qais (Bani ᶜĀmir of) 21, 23, 24
ᶜAbd al-Qais (Jadhīmah b. ᶜAwf of) 16, 17, 20, 21
ᶜAbd al-Qais (Bani Mismār of) 20, 24
ᶜAbd al-Qais (Bani Muḥārib of) 21, 23, 24
ᶜAbd al-Qais (Lukayz ibn Afṣa of) 16, 19
ᶜAbd al-Qais (Shann ibn Afṣa of) 16, 18

ᶜAjᶜajah 22
ᶜAlawiyyah (al-) School 4
ᶜĀi 2, 8, 24, 28, 31
ᶜanᶜanah 36, 42, 143, 166
ᶜAnazah 1, 2, 9, 20, 30
ᶜArād 22, 24
ᶜish-she 28
ᶜUmān 10, 15, 16, 20, 22, 24, 28, 30, 167
ᶜUqair (al-) 21
ᶜUrayyiḍ (Ibrāhīm al-) 12
ᶜUtūb (al-) 15, 23, 24, 25, 26, 30, 31

Baḥārnah 1, 2, 3, 7, 8, 9, 10, 12, 15, 23, 24, 25, 26, 31, 32, 39, 40, 166, 167

Baḥrain Petroleum Company (BAPCO) 2, 4, 10, 11, 27, 28, 133, 134
Bakr ibn Wā?il 16, 17, 29, 35
Bani Jamrah 2, 24, 129
Budayyiᶜ (al-) 2, 5, 9, 23, 24
Carmathians 19, 20, 29, 33, 34
Committee of National Union 32
Dawāsir (al-) 9, 23, 24, 25, 31
Dirāz 1, 2, 34, 43
Dutch Reformed Church 4

Hajar 15, 16, 17
Ḥanbali 7
Hidāyah (al-) School 4
Huwalah 7, 8, 25, 30, 38
Imāla 41, 55, 57-9, 152-3, 164, 166
Iyād 16, 19, 21
Jaᶜfariyyah (al-) School 4
Jid Ḥafṣ 1
Jufair (al-) 1, 23, 24
Juwātha 21, 22
Kashkashah 146, 166
Khaṭṭ (al-) 15, 16, 18, 21
Koine (forms) 3, 5, 10, 40, 47, 128, 131, 167
Kuwait 2, 11, 12, 30, 31
Māliki 7
Manāmah 1, 2, 4, 6, 9, 10, 23, 25, 27, 40
Maᶜn (Bani) 20
Muḥarraq 1, 4, 22, 24, 25, 27
Nabīh Ṣāliḥ 1, 22
Pearls (cultured) 9
Qaṭīf (al-) 1, 5, 17, 20, 23, 30
Rabīᶜah (Bani) 16

Sacred Heart School 4
Samāhīj 22, 24, 134
Shāfiᶜi 7
Shamāl 27
Shīᶜi/Shīᶜah 1, 4, 6, 8, 25, 26, 31, 32
Shīᶜism 7, 33, 34
Sihlah (Sihle) (al-) 23, 24, 116, 131, 141
Sitrah 1, 2, 25, 27, 37, 166
Stressed -é? 41, 55, 108, 114, 151, 163, 166
Sunni 1, 7, 8, 25, 26, 31, 32

Tājir (Ḥajji Muḥammad ᶜAli al-) 22, 24, 35, 36
taltalah 106, 156, 166
Tamīm (Bani) 16, 17, 21, 22, 24, 25, 29

Tihāmah 16, 17, 18, 167

Urdu School 4
Velar ḷ 40, 50-1, 149
Wahba, Ḥāfiẓ 4, 24

Zallāq 4, 9, 24

Zubārah 2, 30, 31, 32, 39

Index of lexical items

?abaaruuḥ 80
?adnaat 131
?adoobiš 3
?ajaawiid 93, 129
?alḥiin 51, 63, 103, 110, 114, 122
?anaajir 140
?ane (1m.s.) 55, 99, 151, 162
?ani (1 f.s.) 59, 99
?anwaaṭ 135
?araaḍiin 92
?astaad 129
?ašraab 138
?aṣmax 40, 53, 150
?iḥmarr 83
?iḥtarr 83
?intiin/e 56, 59, 70, 98-9, 51-2, 164, 166
?intuun/e 56, 70, 98-9, 151-2, 164, 166
?inxaraṭ 133

^{c}adan 131
^{c}afse 131
^{c}ajaan 90

^{c}akaarwa 64, 94
^{c}akkaar 85, 90, 139
^{c}alašaan 110
^{c}ammar 83
^{c}anuud 85
^{c}irbiid 90
^{c}aṣriyye 91
^{c}aṭaay 79, 88
^{c}eeb 65
^{c}eeš 117, 119, 130, 131, 134
^{c}idg 89
^{c}indčem 45, 146
^{c}išrig 141

^{c}luuč 44, 145

^{c}ood/e 62, 113, 116, 118, 128, 129, 133, 160
^{c}ubri 85
^{c}uum 42, 138, 143

baa^{c} 139
baačir 44, 113
baaluul 129
baarḥa 90, 104, 160
baariḥ 27
baaṣug 63
bagaagiil 56, 85, 91
bagil 85, 89, 147
baġa 105
baġle 129
baḥaaḥiir 88
baḥḥaar/a 88, 90
bančar/fančar 135
bandar 137, 161
bannad 83
baraaḥa 90
baraax 140
barastaj 28
barṭam 162
baṭin 85, 131
baṭiin 85
bazz 162
bazzaaz 90, 161
beelajaani 86
beezaat 66, 136, 153
biibaan 93, 166
biiḍaan 117, 161
bilbile 5
binč 131
bištaxte 137
bitt 112
bleelaj 141
bnayye 86, 87
booš 138
bsur 89
bugše 132, 138
buuk 138
buuṣta 5
buuz 135, 162
buxnug 47, 131

čafan 130
čarx 137
čawa 145
čeef čaan 106, 112, 127, 167
čeele 44, 87
čidaak 101
čidi/e 59, 101, 113
čill 46, 146
čitti 137

čuu^{c} 44, 145

daar 115, 162
da^{c}am 42
da^{c}me 5
dalu 131, 161
daraawze 86
dariiše 137
dawaaliib 94
dayyiin 139
de(e) laač 46
de(e) laak 55
deen 63
dibs 131
diira 5, 129
diiwaaniyye 133
dfaaf 140
doošag 137
dreewliyye 136
duulaab 132

ḍakar 44
ḍane 131
ḍruuf 139
faatḥa 90
faatir 131
fahwa 89
falam 53
falla^{c} 68
falag 131
famiin 54
fannaš 83, 135
faraš 129
fariid 53, 90
fašt 137
fatiile 138
faṭas 131
fawaḥaan 88
fčuuč 44, 145
fijje 140
filga 89
foogaani 85
foošar 65, 83
furḍa 161, 162
fuṣṣ 131
fuum 52, 150
gaduu^{c} 90
gaffaḍ 129
gafiif 139
gahwači 86
gaḥamaat 140
galaaliif 91, 157, 166
gal^{c}a 48, 57
gallaaf 91, 131
galaay 90
garaagiir 139
gaṣaaṣiib 91, 157
gašaṭ 131
gatt 49, 138
gaṭaafa 86
gawalaan 78, 88
gdur 132
geeḍ 49
geeṭaan 47
glaafe 90
gaaṣa 88
ġabba 59
ġabba/t 131, 161
ġalyuun 162
ġarše 48, 132
ġasaal 88
ġawaawiiṣ 88
ġawaazi 138, 161
ġazil 140
ġeeṣ 139
ġitra 89
ġru(u) baat 115, 129
ġubba 139
ġubše 109, 131
ġurb 5, 131

haab riiḥ 116, 131, 160
ha(a) daak 101, 121, 127, 144
haade 101, 121, 127, 151
haadi 101, 121, 127
ha(a) diik 101, 121, 127
haak/a 101, 122, 158-9, 166
hadawlaak 101
hadawle 101
hade(e)leen 55, 101, 121, 127, 151
hamza 40, 41-2, 75-6, 143-4, 163
hanaadwa 86, 97
hast 135
hawwas 83
hay 101
heek/a 101, 122, 158-9, 166
hinč 46, 136
hooše 131
hooz/-aat 11, 136
ḥaadi 96, 98

ḥaafi 131
ḥaamuḍ 61, 63
ḥawi 132
ḥabbe 130
ḥadaj 141
ḥaḍḍaar 85
ḥalaab 90
ḥalaayil 8, 86, 129
ḥamaal 88
ḥamaamiil 85, 160
ḥamase 160
ḥammaaliyye 87
ḥammaara 87, 97
ḥasaawiyye 86, 87
ḥaṣiir 133
ḥazze 131
ḥdaade 90
ḥḍuur 139
ḥilbe 141, 162
ḥirš 140
ḥisbaan 85
ḥooba 131
ḥooṭa 57, 152
ḥṣur 139
ḥumraan 94, 161
ḥurma 89, 94
ḥuwwaal 94
ḥyaače 65

iji 55, 110
irsi 137

jaahil 90, 130, 160, 162
jaalbuut 136
jadaḥaat 129
jafiir/gafiir 40, 50, 94, 149
jafur 132
jamaara 64, 68, 86
jariid 50, 139, 149, 160
jayabaan 88
jaziri 63
jazzaaf/yazzaaf 50, 90, 139
jduu^c 139
jid^c 89
jiib 140
jins 128
jookam 136
jraab 139, 161, 162
jufraan 94
juuniyye 133, 134, 161, 162
jzaafe 64

kačče 45, 46
kamče 132
kankari 136
karab 133, 161, 162
kariib 140
karr 131, 139, 162
karraani 161, 162
karwa 131
kašma 132
kašte 137
kawwad 131
killiš 108
koos 27, 46

lagan 138, 161, 162
lanjaat 136
laṭma/h 58, 131
leečem 45, 46, 56, 146
leewaan 137
ličče 131
liiḥaan 93, 166
liiṭa 140
looz 64
looga 133

ma(a)hi 108, 111, 118-9, 158, 165
ma(a)hu 108, 111, 118-9, 158, 165
maay il-hindibaan 141
maay il-ḥilwa 141
maay iš-šaatirra 140
maay iz-zamuute 140
maay l-igruuf 140
maazaḥ 68
ma^{c}ṣuuma 133
madaawis 94, 140
magaaliṭ 139
maḥaaḥ 131
maḥaamil 94
maḥaariir 133
maḥḥaar 139
maḥmuul 84, 130
malaali 4
maluul 85
mamša(a)/e 79, 85, 133
margaduuš 140
maṭaaw^{c}a 4
maxaaruf 60
mawaa^{c}iin 94, 131, 162

m^{c}aabal 64
m^{c}allim 4, 5
m^{c}alme 4
mbaašar 56, 61, 64, 66, 88, 91, 138, 166
mbarṭum 84
mbaġġal 57
mbooyuḍ 56, 65
meewa 137
mḥassin 133
mḥašš 138
mḥoomur 86, 117
middooliġ 84
middoorma 65
milfa^{c} 90
millaale 90
minwar 136
mistaansiin 119
mit^{c}ammim 84
mitbarriz 84
mitbarje 131, 133
mit beexil 63, 84
mit keesil 59, 63
mit labbis 84
mit xoobil 84
miẓraab 162
mkaafaḥ 61, 88, 91, 129, 166
mnazz 66, 131
msaalam 75
msoowid/msoowde 65, 117
mšajjar 86
mṭoowil 86
mu^{c}ḍaḍ 59
mxamma 131
mzayyin 133
mzimne 133
naas 115
načab 44
načaf 129, 145
nadab 131
naḍar 54, 125, 129, 132, 151
nafs 100
nafye 53, 150
nagaay 90
naġde 137
nahhaam 140
naknuuk 129
namuune 136
nasaaje 64, 90
nasaal 131
nasiib 68, 129
nawwax 160
naxaal 90, 131
naxaalwa 64, 94
naxaayil 43
naxlaawi 139
naxle 67
neešaan 137
nfattit 60
nḥammil 60
ni^{c}le 92
ni^{c}me 58, 89, 152
niswaan 112, 117
nṣe(e)fiyye 133
nteefe 87
nxaṭṭur 60

Particles:
?eeš 113
?ida(a) 123
?ileen 55, 126-7, 124
?illi 102, 111, 125-6
?in 124
?inčaan 105, 124
^{c}aad 104
^{c}ajal 104
^{c}ind 101
^{c}ugub 101

čam 112, 113, 127, 145

ḥagg 95, 100, 106, 108, 112, 147, 162, 167
ḥaggweeš 106, 114
-iyya 100, 122-3, 166

kill 103-4, 118, 120-1
laa 77, 114-5, 118
lakid 48, 108, 109, 161, 162, 167
lamma 126-7
leeš 114
lo(o) 109, 123-4
maa (interjective) 105
maa (interrogative) 106
maa (negative) 77, 100, 114-5, 118
maaku 118
maal/at 100
minhi 113
minhu 113

raa^{c}i 95

taali 105
taba^{c} 95
taww 104

weeš 105, 106, 108, 112-3, 114, 120, 129, 132, 137, 160

yaa 116, 125
yoom 126
raas 104, 131
raḍii^{c}a 131
rakba 140
ramaay 79, 88
rassal 82, 154, 166
raziil 53
rde 129, 140
roozane 137
ruuḥ 100
saalye 139
saamaan 136
sačaačiin 56
sadaat 140
sadur 140
saffaaf 85
sagaay 88
sajam 161
samaad 138
samaamiič 68, 88, 166
sammaač 85
sammaače 45, 88, 97, 159
sanaaniir 160
saniin 131
sannuur/a 132, 161
sataarwa 86

sawaagi 138
seeb 139
sheel 130
siibaan 93
siif 85, 139
sirj 133
sluum 85, 131, 160, 161
snaan 139
sooj 140
soolaf 82
sufra 161
suffixes:
- -aat 87
- -čem 99, 166
- -eč (2 m.s.) 99
- -(e) š /-eč (2 f.s.) 99
- -hem 99, 166
- -hum 99
- -iin 86
- -inne 84, 156, 166
- -kum 99
- -n (2 f.s. / 2 c.pl.) 99, 151
- -óo (diminutive) 65
- -óon (plural) 80
- -š (2 f.s.) 41, 44, 59, 66, 99, 146-7, 163
- -tinne 84, 156, 166

šaaġuul 85
šahwa 89
šakaawi 94
šarayaan 88, 91
šarye 85
šayalaan 78, 91
šeex/z 116
šiime 130

ṣabuur 85
ṣaduug 85
ṣarwal 82
ṣaṭwa 139
ṣawaab^{c}a 64, 86
ṣaxle 53, 66
ṣaxxa 131
ṣfaara 90
ṣidgaan 93
ṣixxaam 53, 150
ṣoob 105
ṣooban 56
ṣooġa/at 138, 161, 162
ṣubḥiyye 91
ṣurwaal 135

taali 105
ta^{c}luum 74, 88, 91
tafur 140
tagḍiib 91, 133, 138
taḥdiir 91, 131
taḥtaani 85
taliil 133
tamšiiṭ 91
tanbiit 91, 131
tarbaat 64, 88
tarwiis 139
tasbuuḥ 74, 88

tasluum 70, 75, 88, 91
taswaat 70, 79, 90, 166
tawaali 96, 104, 131
tawdaat 64, 79, 88, 90, 131
taxlaat 79, 88, 91
tfinnin 75, 88
tḥassan 83
tḥeeraṣ 166
tjooram 82
tkeesal 82
tlibbis 75

tmiddin 88
tnabbur 133
trinj 137
tsoolaf 82
tṣirwil 61, 89, 91
tṣooban 166
twaffa 129
tyassar 129

ṭaagah 162
ṭab^{c}aan/e 138
ṭal^{c} 89, 139
ṭamar 133
ṭaraḥ 140
ṭašt 135
ṭawaawiiš 9, 14
ṭooše 130
ṭuus 56
ṭwaaše 64, 90

waadye 129
waafeet 63
waḍaḥ 138
wajbe 89, 131
waniin 131
wardi 86
ward ilsaan it-toor 140
wzaar 129, 140

xaafuur 138
xabaabiiz 157
xabbar 82, 83, 154, 166
xabiiṣ/a 57, 90
xalaal 51, 57, 149
xalaga 90, 132
xalg 115
xammaama 87, 95
xaraaba 90
xašab 129
xayaayiiṭ 88
xayaayṭa 88
xeer 65, 119, 124, 153
xoor 135
xooš 120, 135
xoozar 65, 82
xuuṣ 133
yifriz 60
yiġruf 60
yiġṣub 61
yilṭum 61
yiṣxi 53
yit ġattar 133
yitḥačče 58, 152
yitmašše 152
yitraffas 130
yitris 60
yitšable 58

zaad 130, 140
za^{c}ag 53, 122, 131
zabar 161
zabiil 162
zabrah 131, 161
zaḥme 58
zaffe 160
zalaal 90, 131
zari 137
zariibe 160
zataat 131
zawaali 92
zeen 62, 94, 109, 119, 129
zfur 53
ziblaan 139
zraar 90

MAP I

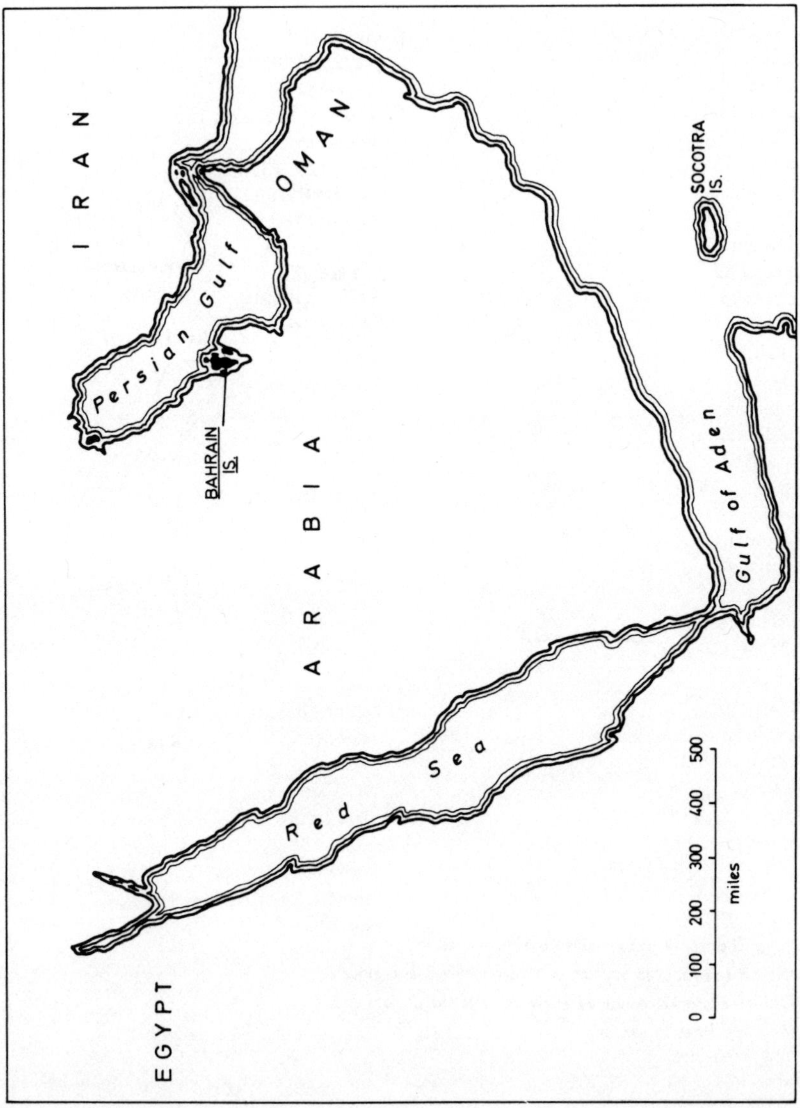
IRAN
OMAN
Persian Gulf
BAHRAIN IS.
ARABIA
SOCOTRA IS.
Gulf of Aden
Red Sea
EGYPT
0 100 200 300 400 500
miles

MAP II

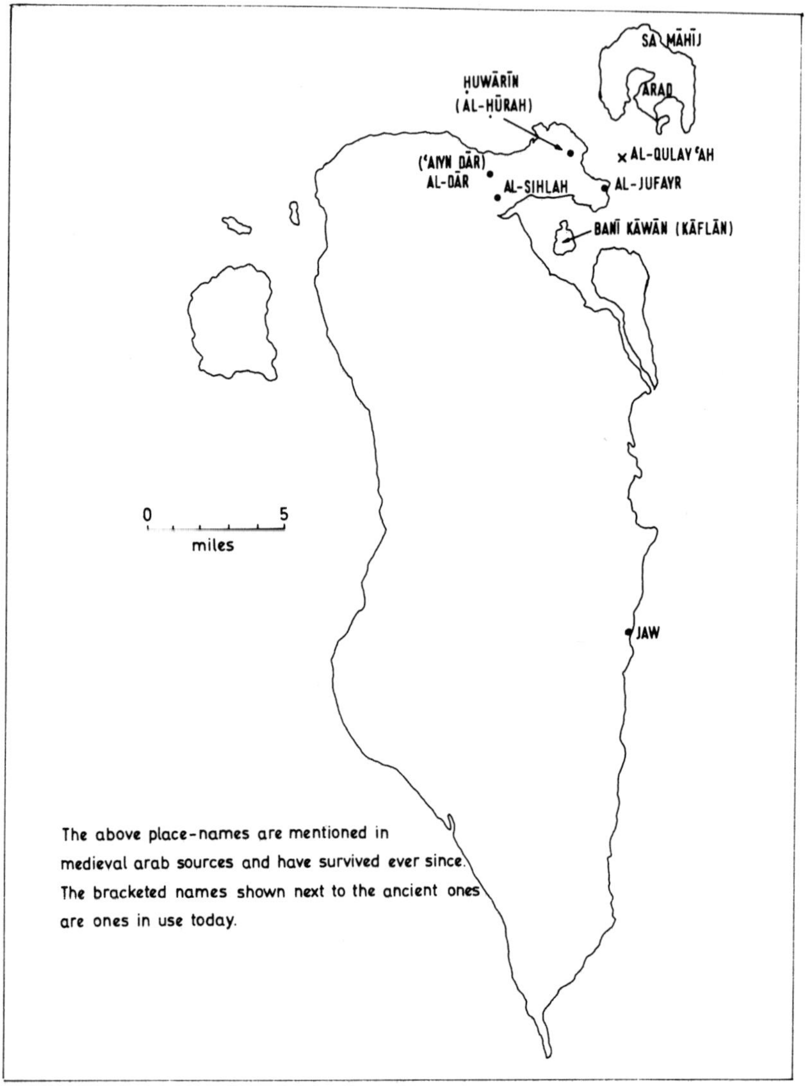
SAMĀHĪJ
ḤUWĀRĪN
(AL-ḤŪRAH)
ʿARAḌ
× AL-QULAYʿAH
(ʿAIYN DĀR)
AL-DĀR
AL-SIHLAH
AL-JUFAYR
BANĪ KĀWĀN (KĀFLĀN)
0 5
miles
JAW
The above place-names are mentioned in medieval arab sources and have survived ever since. The bracketed names shown next to the ancient ones are ones in use today.

MAP III

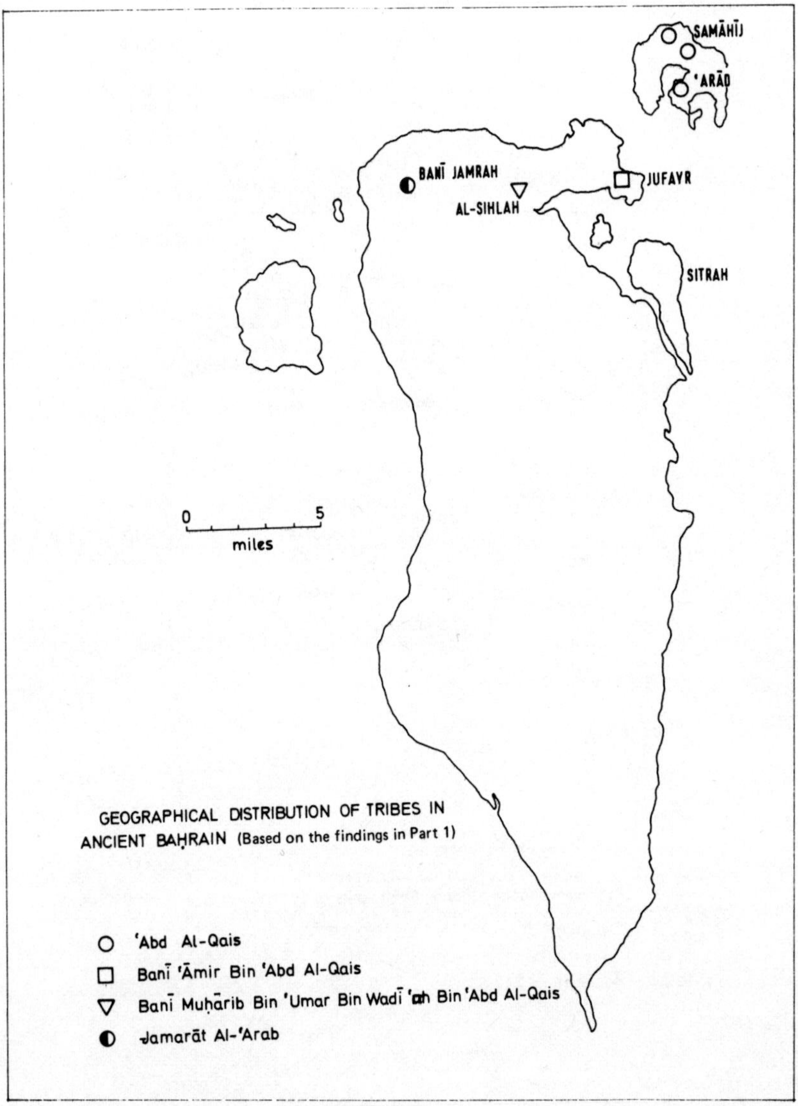
SAMĀHĪJ
'ARĀD
BANĪ JAMRAH
JUFAYR
AL-SIHLAH
SITRAH
0
5
miles
GEOGRAPHICAL DISTRIBUTION OF TRIBES IN ANCIENT BAḤRAIN (Based on the findings in Part 1)
'Abd Al-Qais
Banī 'Āmir Bin 'Abd Al-Qais
Banī Muḥārib Bin 'Umar Bin Wadī 'ah Bin 'Abd Al-Qais
Jamarāt Al-'Arab

MAP IV

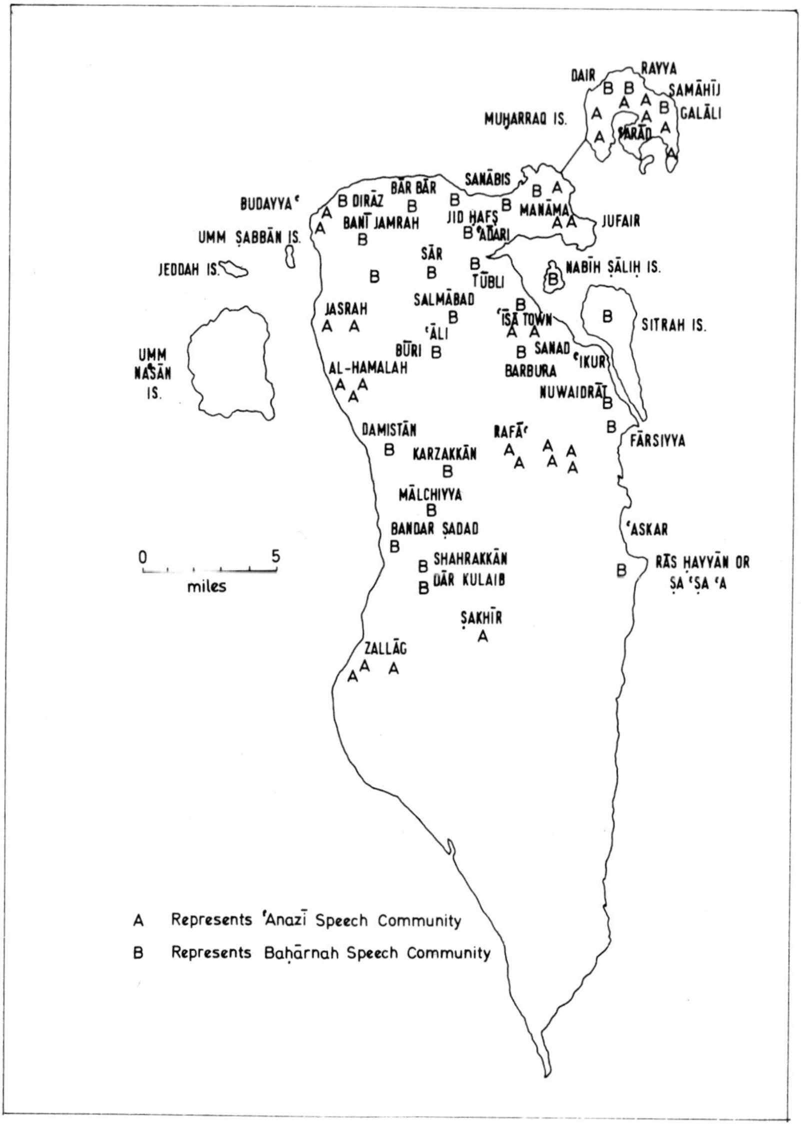
DAIR
RAYYA
SAMĀHĪJ
GALĀLI
MUḤARRAQ IS.
ARĀD
SANĀBIS
BĀR BĀR
DIRĀZ
BUDAYYAʿ
BANĪ JAMRAH
JID ḤAFṢ
MANĀMA
JUFAIR
UMM ṢABBĀN IS.
ʿADARI
JEDDAH IS.
SĀR
NABĪH ṢĀLIḤ IS.
TŪBLI
SALMĀBAD
JASRAH
ʿISĀ TOWN
SITRAH IS.
ʿĀLI
UMM NAʿSĀN IS.
BŪRI
SANAD
ʿIKUR
AL-HAMALAH
BARBURA
NUWAIDRĀT
DAMISTĀN
RAFĀʿ
FĀRSIYYA
KARZAKKĀN
MĀLCHIYYA
ʿASKAR
BANDAR ṢADAD
0 5
miles
SHAHRAKKĀN
DĀR KULAIB
RĀS ḤAYYĀN OR ṢAʿṢAʿA
ṢAKHĪR
ZALLĀG
A Represents ʿAnazī Speech Community
B Represents Baḥārnah Speech Community

MAP V

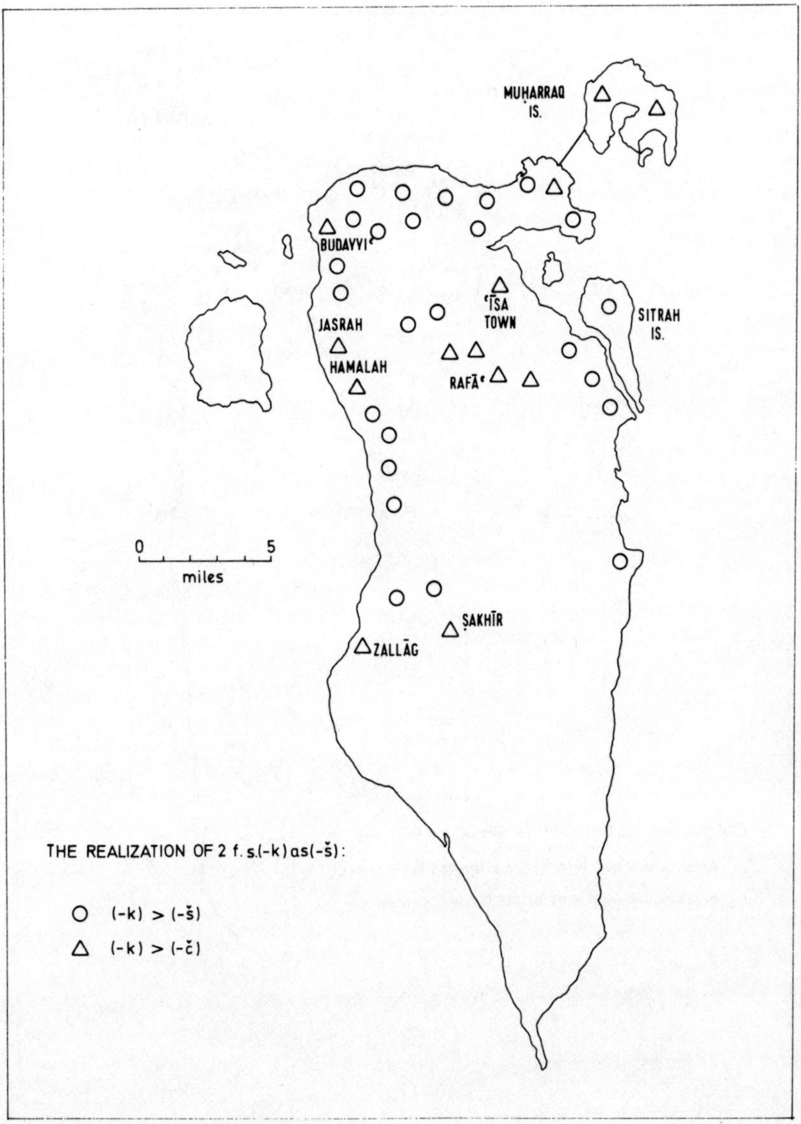
MUHARRAQ IS.
BUDAYYI'
'ĪSA TOWN
SITRAH IS.
JASRAH
HAMALAH
RAFĀ'
0 5
miles
ṢAKHĪR
ZALLĀG
THE REALIZATION OF 2 f. s.(-k) as(-š):
(-k) > (-š)
(-k) > (-č)

MAP VI

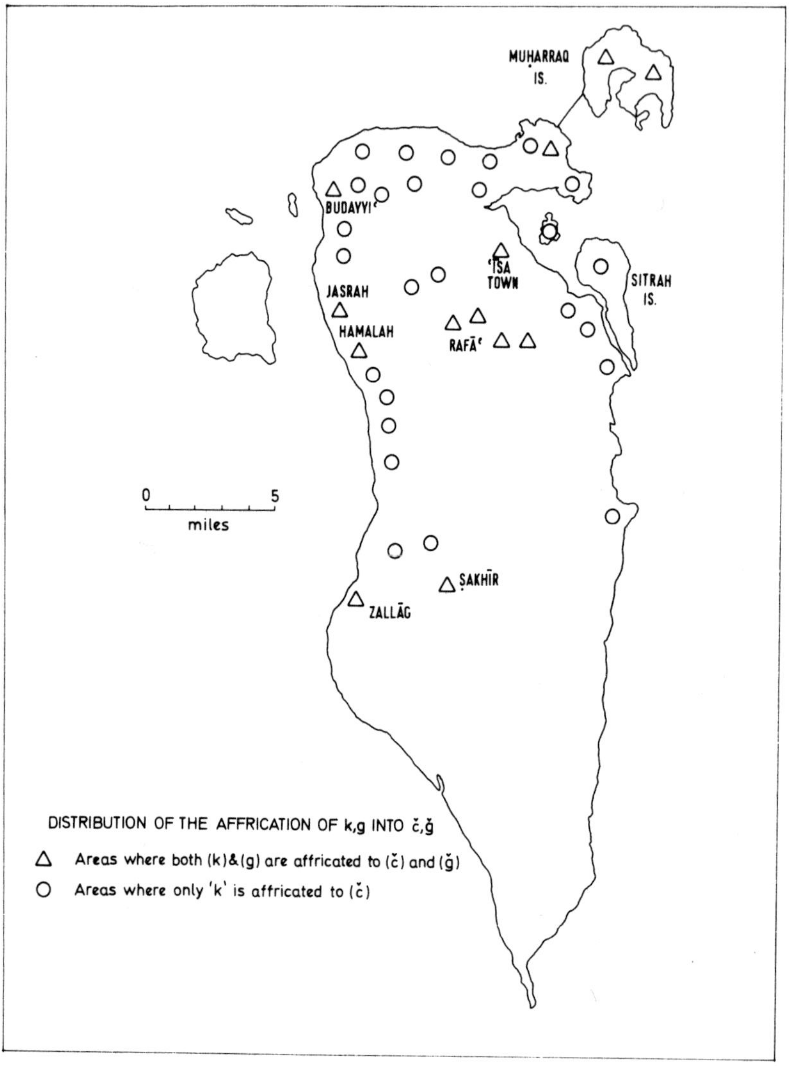
MUḤARRAQ IS.
BUDAYYIʿ
ʿĪSA TOWN
SITRAH IS.
JASRAH
HAMALAH
RAFĀʿ
0 5
miles
ṢAKHĪR
ZALLĀG
DISTRIBUTION OF THE AFFRICATION OF k,g INTO č,ǧ
△ Areas where both (k)&(g) are affricated to (č) and (ǧ)
○ Areas where only 'k' is affricated to (č)

MAP VII

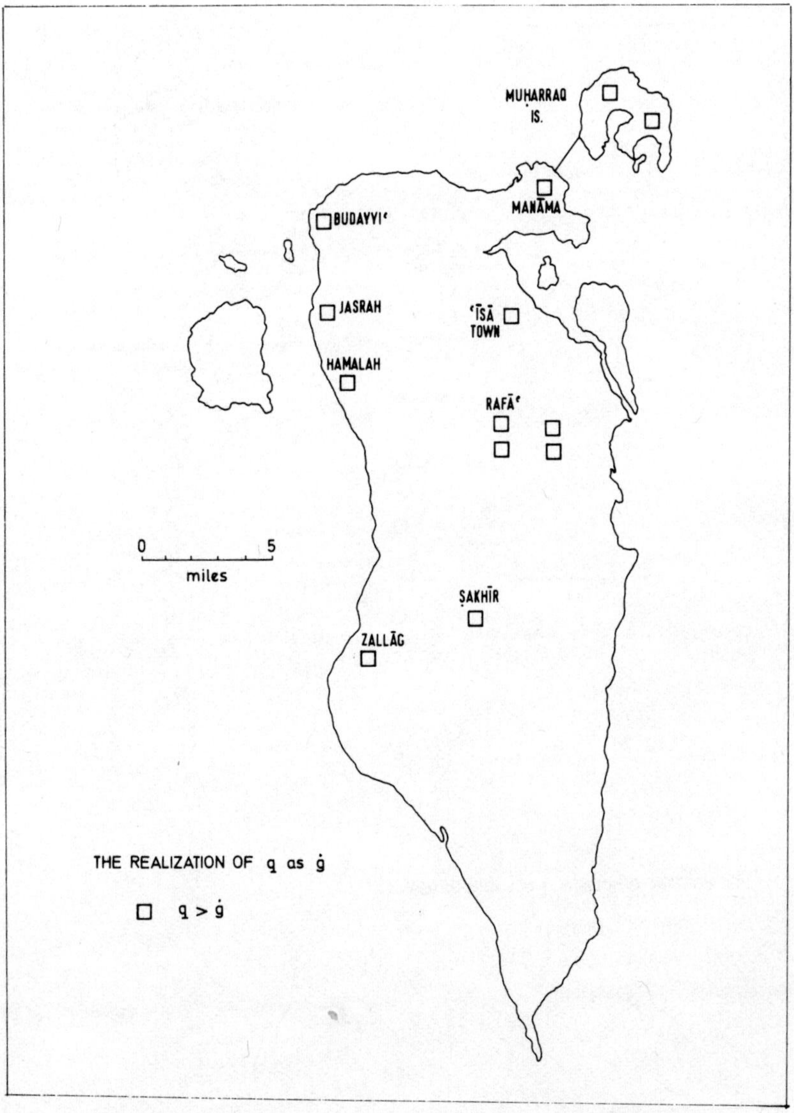
MUḤARRAQ IS.
MANĀMA
BUDAYYIʿ
JASRAH
ʿĪSĀ TOWN
HAMALAH
RAFĀʿ
0
5
miles
ṢAKHĪR
ZALLĀG
THE REALIZATION OF q as ġ
q > ġ

MAP VIII

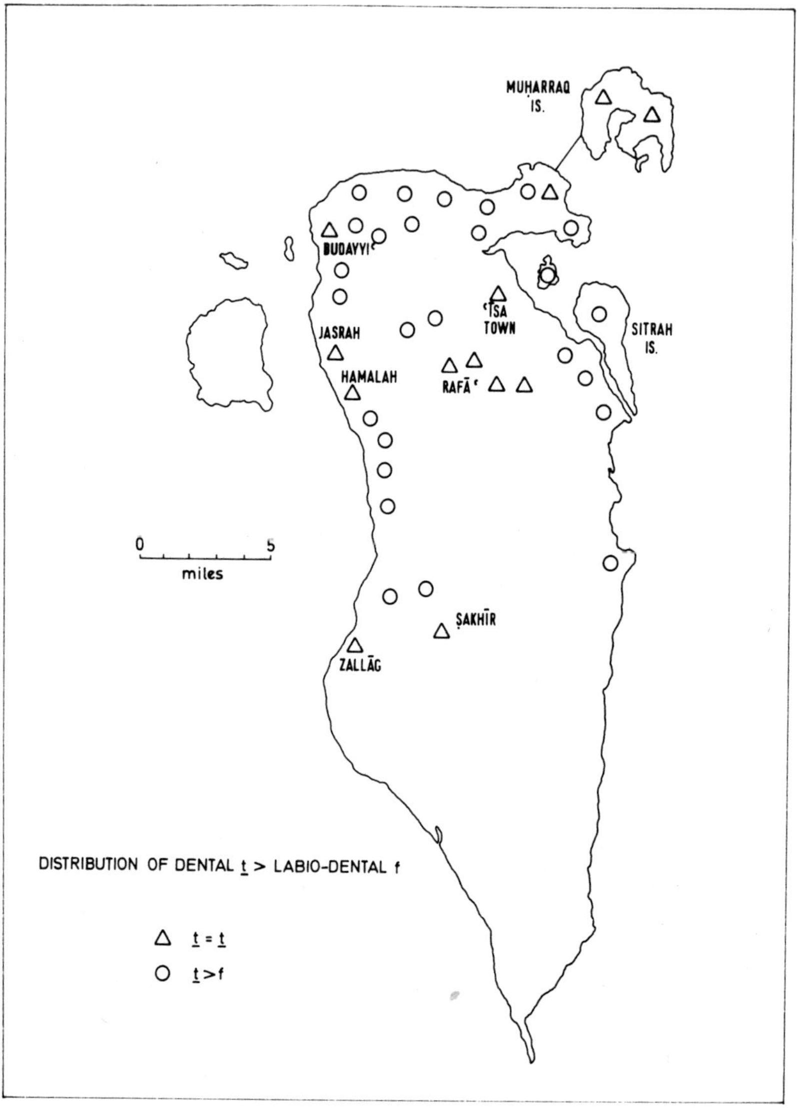
MUḤARRAQ IS.
BUDAYYIʿ
ʿĪSA TOWN
JASRAH
SITRAH IS.
HAMALAH
RAFĀʿ
ṢAKHĪR
ZALLĀG
0 5
miles
DISTRIBUTION OF DENTAL ṯ > LABIO-DENTAL f
ṯ = ṯ
ṯ > f

MAP IX

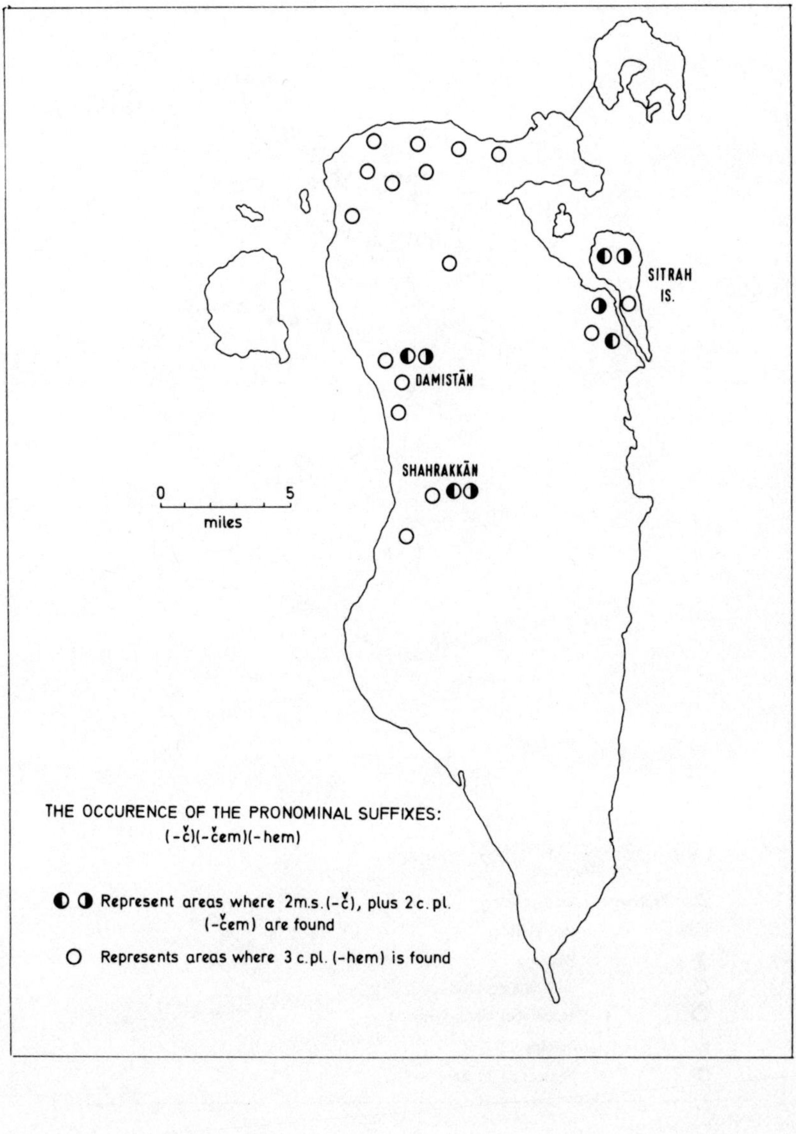
SITRAH
IS.
DAMISTĀN
SHAHRAKKĀN
0
5
miles
THE OCCURENCE OF THE PRONOMINAL SUFFIXES:
(-č)(-čem)(-hem)
Represent areas where 2m.s.(-č), plus 2c.pl. (-čem) are found
Represents areas where 3 c.pl. (-hem) is found

MAP X

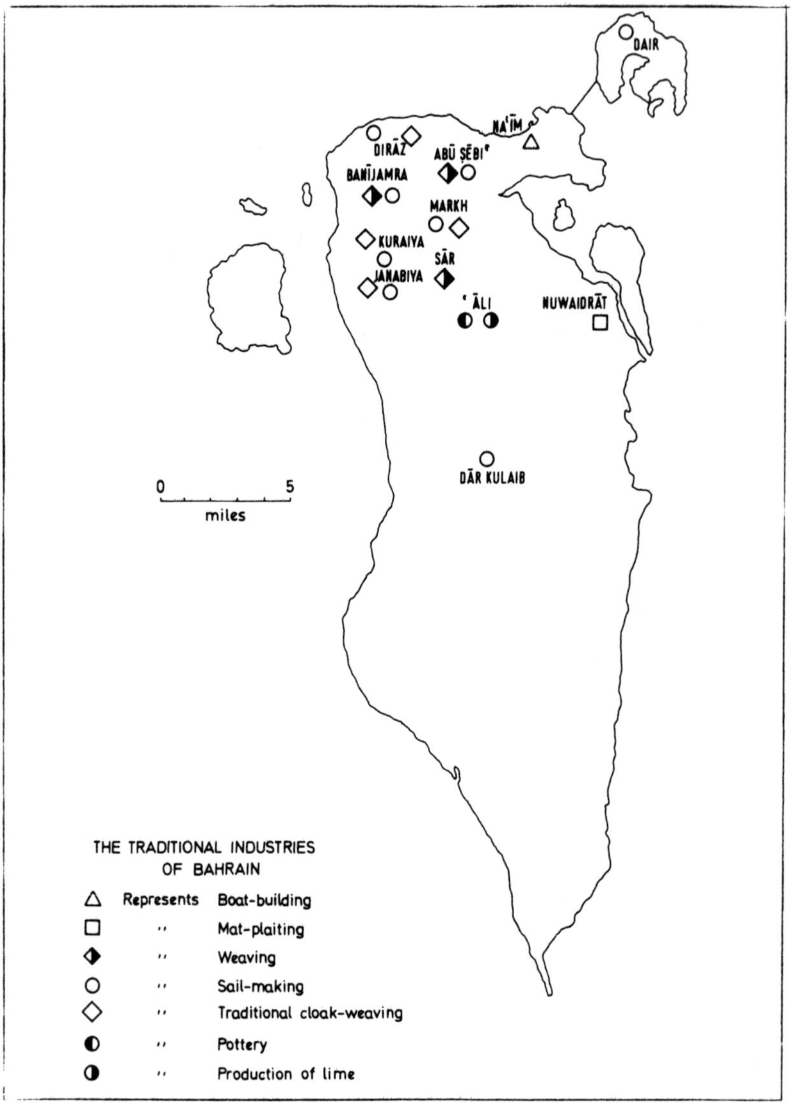
DAIR
NAʿĪM
DIRĀZ
ABŪ ṢĒBIʿ
BANĪJAMRA
MARKH
KURAIYA
SĀR
JANABIYA
ʿĀLI
NUWAIDRĀT
DĀR KULAIB
0
5
miles
THE TRADITIONAL INDUSTRIES OF BAHRAIN
Represents Boat-building
" Mat-plaiting
" Weaving
" Sail-making
" Traditional cloak-weaving
" Pottery
" Production of lime

مكتبة اللسانيات العربية
رئيس التحرير : د. محمد حسن باكلا
جامعة الملك سعود (جامعة الرياض سابقا)
الرياض - المملكة العربية السعودية

الكتاب الخامس

اللغة والأصول اللغوية في البحرين
دراسة في لهجة البحارنة العربية

تأليف

د. مهدى عبدالله التاجر

مؤسسة كيغان بول العالمية
لندن - هنلي - بوستن
١٤٠٢ هـ / ١٩٨٢ م

بسم الله الرحمن الرحيم

تقديم

يعد علم اللهجات العام أحد فروع علم اللغة الاجتماعي إذ أنه يتناول العلاقات بين لغة ما (أو لهجة ما) والمجتمع الذي يستعملها . فكما أن اللغة (أو اللهجة) تعكس لنا جوانب اجتماعية مختلفة للبيئات والطبقات الاجتماعية فان المجتمع كذلك له دور فعال في التطور اللغوي واللهجي . ولعل خير دليل على تأثر اللغة بالمجتمع هو تحرك الموجات البشرية مدا أو جزرا في بيئات جغرافية متنوعة وما يتبع ذلك من الاختلاط أو " المخالطة " أو " تداخل الشعوب " والسكان على حد تعبير العلامة ابن خلدون (المقدمة ، دار القلم ببيروت ١٩٧٨ م ، ص ١٣٠) مما يؤدي إلى ما كان يسمى عند علماء اللغة الأوائل ب " اللحن " أو " فساد الألسن " (مقدمة ابن خلدون، ص ٥٥٨) .

وقد تطورت مناهج علم اللهجات العام وأساليبه تطورا ملحوظا في العقدين الأخيرين وظهرت دراسات وأبحاث جديدة ومجددة في أوربا وأمريكا والهند . ومع ذلك فإن علم اللهجات العربية لا يزال في مراحله الأولى على المستوين النظري والتطبيقي على الرغم من أن هذا العلم قد أصبح مادة تدرس في بعض الجامعات العربية ، كما أن هناك عدة رسائل وأطروحات كتبت عن اللهجات العربية في القديم والحديث (انظر في ذلك كتابنا " اللسانيات العربية : مقدمة وببليوغرافية ، لندن : مانسل ، ١٩٨٢ م) . وقد أُلف عدد كبير من الكتب عن اللهجات العربية شمل أكثرها منطقة الهلال الخصيب ومصر والسودان والشمال الافريقي من الوطن العربي . أما الجزيرة العربية فلم تلق – من قبل – الأهمية والاهتمام اللذين حظيت بهما تلك البلدان على الرغم من الجهود الفردية التي بذلها كل من لاندبرغ ورودوكاناكيس وروسي وغيرهم . فلا يزال هناك العديد من لهجات الجزيرة التي لم تدرس دراسة علمية كافية بعد . كما أن الجزيرة العربية – أكثر من أيّ وقت مضى – في حاجة ماسة إلى أطلس لغوي ولهجي لتشخيص الظواهر الحديثة في المنطقة وجعلها أساسا لمنطلق أبعد وهو وضع الأطلس اللغوي واللهجي للوطن العربي الكبير .

ومن الغريب حقا أن نجد أنه على الرغم من الاهتمام المتزايد بمنطقة الخليج العربي الإسلامي إلاّ أن هذا الاهتمام يكاد يكون جلّه - إن لم يكن كله - منصبا على الدراسات الاقتصادية والتجارية وما إلى ذلك . أما الدراسات اللغوية لهذه المنطقة فلا تزال قليلة جدا . وهناك جهود قيمة بذلها عدد من الدارسين المحدثين لهذه المنطقة ومنهم البروفيسور جونستون (لندن) والبروفيسور سميتون (امريكا) والأستاذ الدكتور حمدي قفيشة (المملكة العربية السعودية) والدكتور كلايف هولز (كيمبردج ، انجلترا) والاستاذ الدكتور عبدالعزيز مطر (جامعة عين شمس) . ومن بين هؤلاء الباحثين يعد الأخيران من أوائل من كتبوا عن لهجة البحرين وخصّوها بأبحاث مستقلة .

فقد نشر الدكتور هولز مقالا بعنوان " التغير الفونولوجي في لهجة البحرين : إبدال الجيم والياء من الفونيم (ج) في "مجلة لدراسات اللغة العربية" التي تصدر في ڤايسبادن بألمانيا الغربية (العدد الرابع ، عام ١٩٨٠ م ، صص ٧٢ - ٨٩) . وقد أشار هولز هنا إلى العوامل الاجتماعية والجغرافية والثقافية التي قد ساعدت على إيجاد هذه التغيرات الصوتية في اللهجة البحرانية . وفي عام ١٩٨١ م انتهى هولز من أطروحته التي نال بها الدكتوراه من جامعة كيمبردج عن لهجة البحرين أيضا .

أما الأستاذ الدكتور عبدالعزيز مطر فقد نشر كتابا بعنوان " دراسة صوتية في لهجة البحرين : بحث ميداني" في مطبعة جامعة عين شمس بالقاهرة عام ١٩٨٠ م تناول فيه المؤلف موضوعات مختلفة وهي : الأصوات الأسنانية ، وصوت الضاد ، صوت الجيم ، وفونيم القاف ، وصوت الكاف في الضمائر . وهذا الكتاب دراسة مقارنة بين لهجات البحرين وبخاصة لهجتي المحرق وسترة . ويشير المؤلف إلى " أن هذه هي المرة الأولى التي يقارن فيها بين هاتين اللهجتين " .

وعلى كل فان البحرين منطقة غنية بلهجاتها وظواهرها اللغوية الجديرة بالاهتمام والدراسة .

هذا الكتاب :

والكتاب الذي أمام القارىء الآن هو أول دراسة علمية مطوّلة تنشر عن اللهجة البحرانية . أما عن منهجه فهو ملتزم بالأسلوب التقليدي في وصف اللهجات ومقارنتها . والكتاب في مجمله دراسة وصفية مقارنة للهجة البحرين . فهو يصف اللهجات البحرانية المتعددة في مختلف مناطق البحرين ويركز على لهجتين هامتين منهما هما : لهجة البحارنة ولهجة قبائل عنزة المستقرة في البحرين . ويؤكد المؤلف على أن هناك عوامل جغرافية وثقافية واجتماعية ساعدت على وجود الاختلاف اللهجي . إلاّ أن هناك عوامل أخرى جديدة بدأت تقرب فيما بين اللهجات العربية في البحرين بسبب تأثير العربية الفصحى ووسائل الاعلام وانتشار التعليم وما إلى ذلك . وما من شك أن هذه العوامل نفسها قد بدأت تقرب بين اللهجات العربية على مستوى الوطن العربي الكبير. وهي ظاهرة ملحوظة واتجاه عام في اللغات الأخرى أيضا .

وهذا الكتاب مبني على دراسات ميدانية قام بها المؤلف في بلده البحرين فاستفاد من عدد كبير من المخبرين اللغويين الذين يمثلون بيئات اجتماعية متنوعة ومختلفة في السن والحرفة وما إلى ذلك . أما المادة اللغوية فقد قام المؤلف بتحليلها بدءاً بالدراسات الصوتية أو الفونولوجية ومرورا بالدراسات الصرفية والنحوية وانتهاءً بالدراسات المفرداتية والمعجمية للهجات البحرين .

يضم الكتاب مقدمة وستة أجزاء مع ملاحق ووسائل إيضاحية متنوعة . يرسم المؤلف في مقدمته الخطوط العريضة لمسار دراسته والخطة التي اتبعها في تنفيذها ويشمل **الجزء** الأول دراسات قيمة عن القبائل التي نزحت إلى البحرين في القديم والحديث . وفي هذا الجزء يرد المؤلف على عدد من الأفكار الخاطئة عن أصول سكان البحرين . كما يشمل هذا الجزء دراسة تاريخية وحضارية عن البحرين أو جزيرة أوال (بفتح الهمزة وضمها) وقد اعتمد المؤلف هنا على المصادر العربية القديمة والحديثة .

أما الجزء الثاني فخاص بالدراسات الفونولوجية والخصائص الصوتية التي تميز لهجات البحرين . ويدرس الجزء الثالث الخصائص الصرفية للهجة البحرانية فيبين خصائص الأفعال والأسماء

وغير ذلك . ويركز الجزء الرابع على الخصائص النحوية للّهجة البحرانية فيتناول بعض الظواهر النحوية كالزمن والاستفهام والنفي والمطابقة وما إلى ذلك . ويتناول الجزء الخامس دراسة الكلمات من حيث علاقاتها الدلالية وتمييز الفصيح من الكلمات عن غيره ، ومن حيث استعارة الكلمات من اللغات الأخرى كالانجليزية والفارسية والهندية . أما الجزء السادس والأخير فهو دراسة مقارنة بين لهجات البحرين من جهة وبين لهجات البحرين وبعض لهجات الجزيرة العربية من جهة أخرى . ويختتم المؤلف متن الكتاب بملاحق متنوعة إحصائية ولغوية . وتمثل الملاحق اللغوية عينات من النصوص اللهجية التي اعتمد عليها مع ترجمتها إلى الانجليزية . يلي ذلك معلومات قيمة عن المخبرين اللغويين .

وتميز هذه الدراسة بين لهجات المدن ولهجات البدو والريف والقرى . وهنا تجدر الإشارة الى أن ابن خلدون كان قد أشار في مقدمته إلى هذه الظاهرة في معرض حديثه عن لغات أهل الأمصار (مقدمة ابن خلدون ، ص ٣٧٩) بقوله :

" اعلم ان لغات أهل الامصار إنما تكون بلسان الأمّة أو الجيل الغالبين عليها أو المختطّين لها ولذلك كانت لغات أهل الأمصار الإسلامية كلها بالمشرق والمغرب لهذا العهد عربية وإن كان اللسان العربي المضري قد فسدت ملكته وتغير إعرابه ..... وسمي لسانا حضريا في جميع أمصار الإسلام ..... واللغات متوارثة فبقيت لغة الأعقاب على حيال لغة الآباء وإن فسدت أحكامها بمخالفة الأعجام شيئا فشيئا وسميت لغتهم حضرية منسوبة إلى أهل الحواضر والأمصار بخلاف لغة البدو من العرب فإنها كانت أعرق في العروبيّة . "

ويشير ابن خلدون أيضا إلى الاختلاف بين اللهجات العربية على مستوى الوطن الإسلامي الكبير بقوله (مقدمة ابن خلدون ، ص ٥٥٨) :

" اعلم أن عُرف التخاطب في الأمصار وبين الحضر ليس بلغة مضر القديمة ولا بلغة أهل الجيل بل هي لغة أخرى قائمة بنفسها بعيدة عن لغة مضر وعن لغة هذا الجيل العربي الذي لعهدنا وهي عن لغة مضر أبعد

فأما إنها لغة قائمة بنفسها فهو ظاهر يشهد له ما فيها من التغاير الذي يُعَدّ عند صناعة أهل النحو لحنا . وهي مع ذلك تختلف باختلاف الأمصار في اصطلاحاتهم . فلغة أهل المشرق مباينة بعض الشيء للغة أهل المغرب . وكذا أهل الأندلس معهما . وكل منهم متوصّل بلغته إلى تأدية مقصوده والإبانة عما في نفسه وهذا معنى اللسان واللغة . وفقدان الإعراب ليس بضائر لهم كما قلناه في لغة العرب لهذا العهد . وأما إنها أبعد عن اللسان الأول من لغة هذا الجيل فلأنّ البعد عن اللسان إنما هو بمخالطة العجمة فمن خالط العجم أكثر كانت لغته عن ذلك اللسان الأصلي أبعد . "

والدراسة التي بين أيدينا الآن تتميز بما يلي :

أولا : أنها تهدف إلى البحث عن الأصول اللغوية للهجة البحرين كما يدل على ذلك عنوان الكتاب . وقد رد المؤلف كثيرا من الأصول إلى تأثيرات لغوية بعضها من جنوبي الجزيرة العربية وبعضها من شمالي الجزيرة ووسطها والمؤلف هنا إذ يقدم أدلة لغوية على انتماء لهجة البحرين إلى لهجات الجزيرة العربية إنما يؤكد بذلك أصالة عروبة البحرين وأنها جزء لا يتجزأ من الجزيرة .

ثانيا : تربط هذه الدراسة بين لهجة البحرين قديما وحديثا بالظواهر اللهجية التي أشار اليها اللغويون العرب القدامى في كتبهم وسجلوها كملاحظات عابرة عن اللهجات التي كانت موجودة في عصورهم . ومن هذه الظواهر : العنعنة (نطق الهمزة عينا) ، والكشكشة (نطق كاف المخاطبة شينا) ، والإمالة ، وإبدال القاف كافا ، والذال دالا والتاء طاء ، والثاء فاء ، والجيم ياء . وقد رجع المؤلف إلى المصادر العربية القديمة لتتبع هذه الظواهر اللهجية العربية ومقارنتها وتأصيلها .

ثالثا : تتميز هذه الدراسة بالتركيز على توزيع اللهجات في المنطقة المدروسة على أسس ديموغرافية وجغرافية واجتماعية فهو يحدد الظواهر الرئيسية التي تميز كل بيئة فيها

وأوضح المؤلف بعض هذه الظواهر بالوسائل البصرية التي اعتمد عليها كالجداول ، والخرائط (أو الخارطات) الجغرافية اللغوية التي وزعت عليها مواقع وجود الظواهر المختلفة في المنطقة . وتقدم لنا هذه الدراسة كذلك نتائج إحصائية قيمة للظواهر اللهجية في الجنوب العربي وشرقي الجزيرة العربية وشمالها الشرقي (انظر في ذلك الجزء السادس وبخاصة الجداول التي وزعت عليها الظواهر للمقارنة بين لهجات هذه المناطق) .

والدراسة في مجملها متكاملة الأجزاء متماسكة الأعضاء واضحة المعالم ، كيف لا وقد قام بها أحد أبناء البحرين الشقيق . وهي إضافة جديدة إلى الدراسات اللسانية العربية بوجه عام ولبنة هامة في دراسة منطقة البحرين لغويا . فهي منطقة جديرة بالاهتمام والدراسة اللغوية وبخاصة في هذا الوقت الذي يتزايد فيه الاهتمام بدول منطقة الخليج في جميع المجالات وعلى جميع المستويات إقليميا وعالميا .

كلمة عن المؤلف :

أتمّ دراسته الثانوية بمدارس البحرين عام ١٩٥٩ م . وحصل على التوجيهية من المدرسة السعيدية الثانوية في مصر عام ١٩٦١ م . ثم واصل دراسته الجامعية بقسم آداب اللغة الانجليزية – جامعة القاهرة – حيث نال درجة الليسانس عام ١٩٦٥ م والتحق بعدها بسلك التعليم بمديرية التربية والتعليم بالبحرين وفي عام ١٩٦٧ م ابتعثته المديريّة إلى انجلترا حيث نال دبلوم الدراسات العليا في اللغويات من جامعة ليدز .

ساهم في أعمال بعض مؤتمرات تدريس اللغة الانجليزية في العالم العربي كان آخرها المؤتمر الذي انعقد في دمشق صيف عام ١٩٧٣ م تحت رعاية المنظمة العربية للتربية والثقافة والعلوم .

نال درجة الدكتوراه في الدراسات الساميّة عام ١٩٧٩ م من جامعة ليدز حيث قدّم أطروحة عن اللهجة البحرانية .

وفي صيف عام ١٩٧٩ م ساهم الدكتور مهدي عبد الله التاجر ببحث عن الأصول القبلية والمنشأ اللغوي لعرب البحارنة وذلك في

ملتقى (سيمينار) الدراسات العربية الذي انعقد بجامعة كيمبردج . وبعد ذلك التحق بمدرسة الدراسات الشرقية والافريقية بجامعة لندن حيث نال درجة الماجستير في التاريخ وهو يتابع الآن دراساته العليا بقسم التاريخ بجامعة لندن .

وهو من مواليد عام ١٩٤٠ م ومتزوج .

والله الموفق لما فيه الخير والصواب ،

رئيس التحرير
محمد حسن باكلا
قسم اللغة العربية
جامعة الملك سعود (جامعة الرياض سابقا)
الرياض ـ المملكة العربية السعودية

تمهيد

تهتم هذه الدراسة - أساسا - بلهجة البحارنة والتي يتخاطب بها عرب جزيرة البحرين الأقدمون الذين يقطنون معظم قُرى البحرين الشمالية والشرقية وكذلك مدينة المنامة حاضرة البحرين اليوم . وتهتم هذه الدراسة أيضا - وبدرجة أقل - بما سمي باللهجة العَنَزِيَّة - والتسمية لأحد المستشرقين - قاصدا بذلك لهجة الرفاع والمحرّق في البحرين المعاصرة . وقد اتبعنا التسمية ذاتها في هذا البحث وذلك توخيا للتبسيط علما بأنه باستثناء البيت الحاكم في البحرين والذي ينحدر أفراده من قبائل عَنَزَة فإن العدد الأكبر من متكلمي اللهجة العنزية ليسوا من أصول عنزية .

تتسم المجتمعات اللغوية المتجانسة بوجود روابط ثقافية عامة وخصائص لغوية مشتركة تميز أفراد المجتمع اللغوي الواحد عن دونه من المجتمعات . وهذا الأمر ينطبق لحد ما على الوضع اللغوي في البحرين . فمن الناحية التاريخية فإن الناطقين باللهجة البحرانية - كما تستنتج هذه الدراسة - تنحدر غالبيتهم من قبائل عبد القيس التي نزحت أصلا من سهول تهامة واستقرت بإقليم البحرين وجزيرة أوال بعد أن تغلبت على قبائل إياد وأجبرتها على الرحيل . (انظر كتاب معجم ما استعجم ... البكري الأندلسي : ج١ الصفحات ٥٢ - ٥٧) .

أما أبناء اللهجة الثانية أو كما سميناهم - تبسيطا - باللهجة العَنَزِيَّة فينحدرون من أصول عربية متعددة نزحت غالبيتها من شمال ووسط جزيرة العرب في أعقاب الحكم الخليفي للجزيرة عام ١٧٨٣ م .

ونظرا لرواج معلومات غير دقيقة عن أصل البحارنة - في الكتابات الأوروبية الحديثة منها والقديمة - فقد خصصنا فصلا كاملا للبحث في الأصول القبلية للبحارنة معتمدين في استقاء

معلوماتنا على المصادر العربية الموثوقة والتي تحدثت عن جزيرة أوال وسكانها الأوائل .

وإذاً فالهدف الأول لهذا البحث هو تقديم دراسة تحليلية عن اللهجة البحرانية ، ليس فقط لأنها تشكل إحدى لهجات شرقي الجزيرة العربية فحسب ، بل لاعتقادنا أن طبقاتها اللغوية تحوي الكثير من الخصائص والسمات التي ميزت لهجات شرقي الجزيرة منذ القدم . والهدف الآخر هو إلقاء الضوء على الأصول القبلية والمنشأ اللغوي لعرب البحارنة وذلك تصحيحا للمعلومات الخاطئة التي روجت ولازالت تروج بقصد أو دون قصد في بعض الكتابات الأوروبية والتي يشار إليها حتي هذه الساعة . من هذه الكتابات التي تفتقر الى الدقة وإلى ذكر مصدر الخبر ما كتبه أستاذ الدراسات الشرقية ر. ب سرجنت عام ١٩٦٨ م ، حيث افترض دون أن يقيم الدليل بأن البحارنة هم من بقايا إما الآراميين أو اليهود أو النصارى الذين كانوا في المنطقة ثم اعتنقوا الإسلام . (انظر BSOAS جزء ٣١ الصفحات (٤٨٨ – ٤٨٩) – ١٩٦٨ م ، المقالة بعنوان "Fisher-Folk and Fish Traps in al-Baḥrain".

المنهج ومحتويات البحث :

أ – المنهج :

إن المادة اللغوية الأُساسية لهذه الدراسة جُمعت من قرابة الثلاثين من الرواة والذين ساهموا في البحث الميداني الذي قمت به خلال الأعوام ١٩٧٥ – ١٩٧٧ م . واعتمدت هذه الدراسة طريقة الوصف التحليلي والمقارن منهاجا للبحث .

فمن حيث علم وظائف الأصوات (Phonology) فإن وصف أصوات اللهجة البحرانية اتخذ التحليل الواسع Broad Transcription طريقةً له ، أي تَمَّ وصف أصوات اللهجة من حيث موضع وهيئة النطق وكذلك مقارنة الخصائص الصوتية للّهجة ذاتها بمثيلاتها من اللهجات المجاورة في المنطقة وقد شملت الدراسة الوصفية وكذلك المقارنة جوانب اللهجة الأربع : الصفات الصوتية Phonology

النظام الصرفي Morphology والنظام النحوي Syntax والمفـــردات Lexis.

والمقصود بالمقارنة هنا هو مقارنة خصائص اللهجـــة البحرانية مع اللهجات الأخرى التي تم نشر دراسات جـادة عنها باللغات الأوروبية بالذات وكما يعلم القارئ الكريم فبان المنهج الوصفي يهتم بدراسة المادة العلمية ـ المادة اللغوية هنا ـ كما هي كائنة وليس كما ينبغي أن تكون .

ب ـ محتويات البحث :

تنقسم هذه الدراسة إلى مقدمة وستة أجزاء وخلاصة . تتناول المقدمة إيضاحات متعلقة بمنهج البحث ، الكتابة الصوتية وماهية الرموز المستخدمة في هذا البحث وبالإضافة فهناك نبذة عن العوامل التي أثرت حديثا فـــي مفردات اللغة المحكية كاستبدال مفردات كانت شائعة فـي اللهجة بأخرى من الفصحى ، ثم مواضع التعامل اللغوي بين العناصر العربية وغير العربية لما له من أثر في مجـــال استعارة المفردات الأجنبية ، وكذلك موجز كرونولوجي عــن الدراسات الجادة التيتناولت لهجات شرقي الجزيرة سواء ما نشر منها بالعربية أو باللغات الأوروبيـــة .

وينقسم الجزء الاول إلى قسمين : أحدهما يعنى بالقبائـــل التي قطنت المنطقة وبالذات قبائل عبد القيس وفروعها التي انتشرت في إقليم البحرين وجزيرة أوال قبل مجيء الاســـلام أما الجزء الآخر فيتناول موجز تاريخ البحرين منذ القــدم مبرزا بعض الأحداث الرئيسية التيأثّرت في سكان الجزيـــرة ـ البحارنة ـ والذين تشكل لهجتهم العربية مادة هـــذه الدراســـة .

وقد استقينا معلوماتنا أساسا من كتب المؤرخـــين والجغرافيين العرب . وكما ذكرت سابقا كان الداعي لكتابة هذا الجزء هو رواج معلومات غير دقيقة عن البحارنـــة ـ لغتهم وأصلهم ـ في الكتابات الأوروبية التي لم تعتمـــد المراجع مصدرا لمعلوماتهـــا .

ومثال بسيط أسوقه هنا وهو مقولة J.G. Lorimer في دليله التاريخي والجغرافي عن دول الخليج والذي نشر فـــي كلكتّه عام ١٩١٥ م ، حيث قال في صفحة ٢٠٨ "بأن التشيـــع

قد بدأ في البحرين قبل ثلاثمائة سنة " . وهذا عكس ما يذكره مؤرخو العرب عن تشيع قبائل عبد القيس للخليفة علي بن أبي طالب ونصرتهم له في حرب الجمل عام ٣٦ هجرية (انظر المسعودي / مروج الذهب - طبعة بيروت - عام ١٩٧٠ تحقيق ش . بيلا الصفحات ١١٤-١١٥. وكذلك ابن خلدون : من كتاب العبر ديوان المبتدأ والخبر - ج٢ الصفحات ١٥٠ - ١٥٩) .

ويتناول الجزء الثاني من الدراسة وصف أُصوات اللهجة البحرانية مبتدئا بالصوامت المجهورة والمهموسة ومنها على سبيل التخصيص الأصوات الانفجارية Plosives ، ثم الاحتكاكية Fricatives ، ثم الانفجارية / الاحتكاكية Affricates ثم الذلقية Liquids ، وأخيرا الأنفية Nasals ... الخ

وكذلك يتناول هذا الجزء وصف الأصوات الصائتة أو الحركات - الطويلة منها والقصيرة - ثم ظاهرة الإمالة وهي بارزة في هذه اللهجة - ثم الحركات الزائدة لتسهيل النطق بالأصوات الساكنة في اللهجة مثل Prosthetic and Anaptyctic والحركات المركبة Diphthongs والتشديد وأخيرا التراكيب المقطعية للكلمات Syllabic Structures الخ.

أمّا الجزء الثالث فيتناول بالدراسة والتحليل النهج الصرفي الذي تسلكه اللهجة وهذا يشمل دراسة سلوك الأفعال الصحيحة والمعتلة - اسم الفعل واسم المفعول - ثم الأسماء بأنواعها - وكذلك استخدام السوابق واللواحق Prefixes and Suffixes مع الأسماء - المثنى والجمع - صيغة التصغير - التنوين - الإضافة - صيغة أفعل للتفضيل والمبالغة - بنية الأعداد الأصلية والترتيبية - الضمائر - أسماء الإشارة - حروف الجر الشائعة في اللهجة - وأدوات الاستفهام ... الخ.

ثم يليه الجزء الرابع وبه دراسة لبعض الخصائص النحوية التي تنفرد بها هذه اللهجة وبالذات المطابقة (Concord) بين المعرّف وغير المعرّف - كذلك المطابقة بين الجنس (النحوي) والعدد . ثم بنية الجملة في هذه اللهجة وسلوك بعض الأدوات والحروف فيها .

اما الجزء الخامس فيدرس الصفات الدلالية حيث يعرض للمفردات الفنية وغير الفنية الشائعة في البحرانية . ومن محتويات هذا الجزء قوائم بمفردات تتعلق بنشاطات أهل اللهجة مثل : صيد السمك الزراعة - النساجة ... الخ . وبه أيضا قوائم بمفردات عربية قديمة لازالت متداولة ونماذج لمفردات مُعَرَّبَة أو مستعارة من لهجات أخرى .

ويهتم الجزء السادس والأخير بالتحليل المقارن . وبه دراسة مقارنة لجوانب اللغة الأربعة التي شملتها الدراسة : نظام الأصوات - التصريف - النحو - المفردات . ويعرض الوصف المقارن لأبرز الخصائص والسمات اللغوية في اللهجة ويقارن بين تلك الخصائص بنظيراتها في اللهجات المحلية المجاورة خصوصا تلك التي نشرت دراسات جادة عنها . ويتناول التحليل المقارن - من ضمن أمور أخرى - ضمير المخاطبة المؤنثة كما في : كتابِش ، ثم يقدم دراسة مقارنة للظاهرة ذاتها في اللهجات العربية الأخرى في المنطقة ثم ظاهرة نطق الثاء فاء أو كما يعتبرها اللغويون العرب من إحدى ظواهر الإبدال . ثم ظاهرة الحفاظ على النون في ضمير المخاطبة المؤنثة : إنتين و في ضمير الجمع : إنتون وتتناول الدراسة المقارنة أيضا النظام الصرفي للهجة كدراسة التفعيلات - الضمائر - الأعداد - والتركيبات المقطعية للكلمات ... الخ وبالإضافة تشمل الدراسة المقارنة المفردات العربية القديمة والتي ظلت متداولة في البحرانية لهذا اليوم ، ثم المُعَرَّبَة والمستعارة . وفي نهاية الجزء السادس جداول بتوزيع خصائص اللهجة الصوتية والصرفية والدلالية ومثيلاتها في اللهجات العربية الأخرى .

ويلي هذا الجزء خلاصة واستنتاجات

النتائج

إن دراسة اللهجة البحرانية تترك انطباعا لدى الباحث بأن مفرداتها المتداولة تشكل طبقة لغوية قديمة انقطع استعمالها في لهجات شمال الجزيرة ولكنها بقيت في لهجات شرقي الجزيرة العربية . إن تحقيق نطق الأصوات الأسنانية أو الأسنانية اللثوية Dentals و Denti-alveolars مثل الثاء والذال والظاء

في لهجة القرى بالذات مرجعه ربما هو نطق الأشهر العربية بالفصحى لافرق في ذلك بين المتكلم المتعلم وغير المتعلم . وسبب آخر ربما ساعد أيضا على إبقاء تلك الأصوات هو تأثير التعليم الديني الذي كان يتلقاه الطلبة الصغار في مدارس تحفيظ القرآن الخاصة. أما تحقيق تلك الأصوات نفسها في البحرانية المتداولة في المدينة فيعكس مدى تأثير أصوات الفصحى خصوصا بعد ازدياد المدارس الحكومية .

ومن نتائج هذا البحث ما يتعلق بظاهرة الإبدال والتي تصيب الصوامت دون الحركات فقد وجدنا أن القاف اللهوية لا تتعرض للإبدال عندما تأتي في سياق قرآني أو عندما تكون الإشارة إلى مفردة من مفردات اللغة الفصحى كما في اسم " الشهر العربي " ذي القعدة " . أما من أمثلة نطق القاف كافا - نطقا غير مشروط - في لهجة القرى . هو :

كوم بدلا من گوم (قم)
بَكِل بدلا من بَگِل (بقل)
حَكّ بدلا من حَگّ (حقّ)

ومن ضمن اللغويين العرب الذين تناولوا ظاهرة الإبدال بالدرس والتحليل أبوالطيب عبدالواحد بن علي اللغوي - من علماء القرن الرابع الهجري - في كتابه المسمى "الإبدال" (من مطبوعات المجمع العلمي العربي - دمشق ١٩٦٠ م) فأورد بالتفصيل أمثلة لإبدال القاف بالكاف . وقد استقى أمثلته هذه من كلام العرب نورد هنا بعضا منها :

نقيب و نكيب
أقحب و أكحب
أعرابيون قُحّ و أعرابيون كُحّ ...الخ

وقد لاحظ حدوث هذه الظاهرة اللغوية المستشرق الايطالي روسّي Rossi في دراسته عن لهجات اليمن فأورد هذه الأمثلة من لهجة صنعاء:

وكت بدلا من وقت
يكفض بدلا من يقفض
بكشه بدلا من بقشه

وكذلك سجل لاندبرغ Landberg أمثلة للظاهرة السابقة في دراسته عن اللهجة الحضرمية ، نورد منها :

كام و تكوم

ومن الظواهر اللغوية القديمة التي أسماها اللغويون العرب بالعنعنه والمقصود بها نطق الهمزة عينا بقيت أمثلة منها متداولة في اللهجة البحرانية ، مثل :

دَعَم	بدلا من	دَأَم
عوم	بدلا من	أوم
عضافير	بدلا من	أظافر
عَفَر	بدلا من	أَثَر

وقد اورد أبو الطيب اللغوي أمثلة عديدة تثبت وجود هذه الظاهرة القديمة لدى العرب ، مثل :

كَثَأَ اللَبَنُ أو كَثَعَ اللَبَنُ

مَوتٌ زُؤاف أو مَوتٌ زُعاف ... الخ

اما ابن جني فقد أخص هذه الظاهرة بلهجة بني تميم ، وأوردها اللغوى الالماني C. Reinhardt في دراسته عن لهجة بني خروص (عُمان) في الأمثلة الآتية :

عصل	بدلا من	أصل
عرنب	بدلا من	أرنب

وكذلك سجلها Rhodokanakis في دراسته عن اللهجة الظفارية .
أما ظاهرة تفخيم التاء أي تحقيقها طاء بجوار الحركة الطويلة في الأعداد من ١٣ إلى ١٩ في اللهجة البحرانية فقد لحظها رينهارت في دراسته للعُمانية دون أن يجد أيّ تفسير صوتي يشترط حدوثها . ويورد أبو الطيب اللغوي تفاصيل هذه الظاهرة في اللغة العربية في كتابه السابق - ج١ - الصفحات ١٢٦ - ١٣٤ .
وظاهرة أخرى تتصف بها معظم لهجات الجزيرة العربية بما فيها البحرانية ما يعرف بالانجليزية ب Affrication أي الانفجار الاحتكاكي والمقصود به نطق الكاف اللهوية / چ / فارسيّة أي تحويل الصوت الانفجاري ك إلى صوت انفجاري / احتكاكي هو / چ / .
وشروط حدوث هذه الظاهرة في اللهجة البحرانية وكذلك العنزية واردة في البحث ولا مجال لحصرها هنا . إلاّ أنه بالامكان أن نبين هنا بأن توزيع هذه الظاهرة / ك / > / چ / في لهجة جزيرة سترة لهو أوسع من توزيعه في باقي مناطق اللهجة البحرانية . وهذا يشمل أيضا ضمير المخاطب في لهجة سترة . كتابچ للمذكر والمؤنث ومن الظواهر اللغوية القديمة والتي مازالت آثارها باقية في البحرانية هي الظاهرة التي يسميها سيبويه بالكشكشة . ومن

أمثلتها : كتابِش و منديلش حيث تُنطق كاف ضمير المخاطبة شينــا ومن الأمثلة التي أوردها سيبويه من كلام العرب في هذا الصدد :

رأيتُ غلامش و دخلتُ دارش

ومن ابن جني عليش و مِنّش

كذلك لاحظها Jayakar في دراسته للعمانية ورينهارت فــي دراسته للهجة بني خروص . وأوردها Cantineau في دراسته للجهة بني صخر ، وسجلها روسّي في دراسته للهجة صنعاء فــي هذه الأمثلــة :

بيتِش – حَكِّش ... الخ

وذكرها أيضا Diem في دراسته عن لهجات ظفار والدامغـة وبينون من اليمــن .

ومن الخصائص البارزة في اللهجة البحرانية هو نطق الثاء فـاء وهذه الظاهرة غير المشروطة في البحرانية أوردها أبو الطيــب اللغوي في هذه الأمثلة المختارة من كتاب الابدال :

الثاء في مقدمة الكلمة :	ثروة	و	فروة
	ثالج	و	فالج
الثاء في وسط الكلمـة :	حثالة	و	حفالة
	انثجر	و	انفجر
الثاء في نهاية الكلمة :	جدث	و	جدف
	تحنث الرسول	و	تحنف ... الخ

وقد لاحظ لاندبرغ حدوث هذه الظاهرة في اللهجة الحضرمية ولاحظهـا كذلك رودوكناكس في الظفارية وروسّي في معظم لهجات صنعاء وتعز والحديدة وأشار إليها Smeaton في دراسته عن لهجة الأحساء.

ومن الظواهر الصوتية أيضا تخفيف نطق النون في لهجة القرى عندما تكون النون في نهاية الكلمة ومسبوقة بحركة طويلة ، مثل :

إنچان او عَلَشان

وأخيرا – في مجال الخصائص الصوتية – نذكر حركة الفتحة الممالة نحو الكسرة اللاحقة المشددة / اِ / والتي لحظناها في اللهجتين البحرانية والعمانية . هذه الظاهرة هي نوع من التنغيم الصاعد الدال على الاستفهام كما في :

أكَلتِ ؟ كَتَبتِ ؟

أما في مجال الصرف – وكما ذكرنا سابقا – فاللهجة البحرانيـة تُبقي على صوت النون في ضمير المخاطبة المؤنثة إنتين و ضمير المخاطب الجمع إنتـون .

وقد سجل جايكار حدوث هذه الظاهرة في ضمير المخاطبة المؤنثة في العمانية وأوردها كانتينو في لهجات سباعة والرس في شمال الجزيرة وأوردها كذلك روسّي في دراسته للهجة صنعاء ودونها H. Blanc في دراسته للّهجة البغدادية في الأفعال - وليس في الضمائر - كما في الأمثلة الآتية :

تِكتبين تِكتبون يِكتبون

وكذلك أوردها T.M. Johnstone في دراسته لبعض لهجات شرقي الجزيرة وذكرها Diem في دراسته عن لهجات اليمن .

ومن الظواهر الصرفية في اللهجة البحرانية التمييز القائم بين ضمير المتكلم المفرد أنا ونظيره المؤنث أني . وقد لحظ روسّي ودييم حدوث هذه الظاهرة في بعض لهجات اليمن ، إلاّ انه لم يأت ذكر هذه الظاهرة في الدراسات المنشورة عن لهجات عمان ودثينة والعراق وصنعاء .

وظاهرة صرفية أخرى هي استعمال ضمير المخاطب الجمع - چم وكذلك الجمع الغائب - هِم في لهجة القرى بالبحرين . هذه الظاهرة لا تحصل في البحرانية المحكيّة في المنامة .

ومن خصائص البحرانية المحكيّة في القرى - في مجال الصرف - استخدام أسماء الإشارة هاك وهاكه وهيك وهيكه في لغة الحريم خصوصا بقرية الدراز البحرانية إلاّ أن هذه الظاهرة لا وجود لها في لهجة المنامة .

ومن الظواهر الصرفية ايضا نطق ياء الفعل المضارع كما لو كانت حركة مكسورة / إِ / في الأفعال المعتلة كما في هذه الأمثلة:

الفعل الأجوف	إِصوم	بدلا من	يصوم
الفعل المعتلّ	إِجي	بدلا من	يجيء
الفعل المشدّد	إِمرّ	بدلا من	يمرّ

وقد ذكر الظاهرة السابقة أيضا كانتينو في دراسته للهجة شُمّر وأوردها روسّي في دراسته للهجات الحديدة وتهامة .

وفرق آخر بين لهجات شمال الجزيرة واللهجة البحرانية وهو كسر الصوت الأول للأفعال الصحيحة في لهجات شمال الجزيرة كما في : كِتَب و شِرَب وبقائها مفتوحة الكاف والشين في البحرانية .

ويلاحظ أيضا أن بعض الافعال التامة من صيغة أَفعَل تُحَقّق على

وزن فَعَّل في كل من اللهجة البحرانية ولهجات الجزيرة الأخرى في الأمثلة :

خَبَّر ورَسَّل بدلا من أخبر وأرسل

ومن الخصائص الصرفية البارزة في اللهجة البحرانية بعض التفعيلات التي تشذ صيغتها عن اللغة الفصحى ومن أمثلتها اسم الفعل المشتق من الفعل الثلاثي كما في :

تِفعال في تِسواه وتِرباة وليس تَفعِلَة أي تسوية و تربية

تِفعول في تِعلوم وتِسلوم وليس تفعيل أي تعليم و تسليم

وقد لوحظ ان التفعيلتين الواردتين في البحرانية توجد أيضا في اللغة الآرامية وفي بعض اللهجات العربية الأخرى في الجزيرة ٠

أما اسم الفعل الذي يُبنى على صيغة مُفاعلة في الفصحى فيتحقق على وزن مْفاعَل في اللهجة كما في :

مْباشر و مْكافح وليس مباشرة و مكافحة

وخاصيّة صرفية أخرى تشترك فيها اللهجتان البحرانية والعمانية هي تحقيق صيغة الجمع فعّالون على وزن فعاعيل كما في :

تلاليف – حماميل – خبابيز

وقد أورد كل من جايكار ورينهارت أمثلة لتلك الظاهرة من العُمانية ، وأوردها روسّي من الصنعانية ورودوكاناكيس من الظفارية وذكرها سميتون في الأحسائية ٠

لقد تكشف لنا من دراستنا للجانب الدلالي للهجة البحرانية أن كثيرا من مفرداتها الشائعة عربي الأصل وهذه المفردات تلاشت في بعض اللهجات إلّا أنها ظلت مستعملة في البحرانية ٠ ومن أمثلة المفردات العربية القديمة التي لا زالت متداولة في البحرانية نسوق الأمثلة الآتية :

مواعين – مَحاح – فاتر – غُبْشة – عَفْسة – زَبَرَة – لَطمَة – حوبة – زتات – بِنج (بُنك) – حَزّة – سلوم الشمس راس السنة – توالي الشهر – هاب ريح (كهبّة الريح – متبرجة الخ ٠٠٠

ومن المفردات الخاصة بالحرف والمهن التي يمارسها أهل اللهجة نورد الأمثلة الآتية :

بحّار – نسّاج – گلّاف – عكّار – صفّار – سگّاي – حَمّار الخ ٠٠٠٠

ومن المفردات الخاصة بصناعة النسيج المحلي نسوق هذه النماذج

من مقابلة مع أحد العاملين بالحياكة :
الليطة - المداوس - الغزل - القفول - السدّات - الخ...
إن التسميات المذكورة أعلاه تدل على الأصل العربي لهذه الصناعة الشعبية . (انظر المقال الذي كتبه صالح العلي في مجلة " الأبحاث " رقم ٤ - مجلد ١٤ - الصفحات ٥٧٤ - ٥٧٨ - ١٩٦١م تحت عنوان : الأنسجة في القرنين الأول والثاني الهجريين) .

ومن أمثلة المفردات الخاصة بالنشاط الزراعي في القرى :
الجزّ - التنبيت - الترويس - التحدير - التقضيب - دِبْس - دَلو - الكرّ ... الخ..

ومن أمثلة المُعَرَّب والمتداول في هذه اللهجة كما في معظم لهجات شرقي الجزيرة نورد هذه الأمثلة :
سروال - خور - ديباج - بزّاز - فتيلة - طشت - دارسين - زنجبيل مِنقلة - جَصّ ... الخ ..
(للاستزادة انظر السيوطي : المزهر في علوم اللغة - ج١ الصفحات ١٢٢ - ١٢٣)
ومن المفردات المستعارة من الفارسية والشائعة في البحرانية والعمانية واليمانية نورد الأمثلة الآتية :
خوش - هَست - قَند - سماور - باغشه - بوز - قنديل - كرّاني - دريشة - جونيّة - غوازي - خاشوگه - مزراب - غليون - لگن - بندر زبيل - صوغة ... الخ ..
(انظر التفاصيل في بحثنا في الجزء المعنون : " المفردات - دراسة مقارنة " الصفحات ١٦٠ - ١٦٣) .

خلاصة وخاتمة :
يتضح من دراستنا للهجة البحرانية أن طبقاتها اللغوية تضم كثيرا من المفردات العربية القديمة التي تلاشت في بعض اللهجات ولكن ظلت مستخدمة في البحرانية ، وهذا ينطبق أيضا على التفعيلات التي تشذ في البحرانية في بنائها عن باقي اللهجات . إن اللهجة البحرانية تلتقي كثيرا في مفرداتها ونظامها الصرفي مع القطيفية والأحسائية ولدرجة ما مع العمانية وهذا ليس بغريب لأن هذه اللهجات هي لهجات شرقي الجزيرة القديمة أما اللهجة العنزية - كما عرّفتها في بداية هذا السرد الموجز - والتي هي أقرب ما تكون إلى لهجات وسط وشمال الجزيرة العربية - فهي

تمثل الامتداد الشرقي للهجات شمال ووسط الجزيرة العربية .

إن وجود شبه في الخصائص الصرفية لكل من البحرانية والعمانية لهو دليل على أن أوجه التقارب والشبه بينهما هي من سمات لهجات شرقي الجزيرة الموغلة في القدم . وبالرغم من التقارب الصوتي النسبي بين البحرانية والعراقية إلاّ أن الخصائص الصرفية والدلالية للّهجة البحرانية تجعلها أُقرب إلى العُمانية واليَمانية منها للعراقية .

والشواهد التاريخية لا تتعارض مع النتائج اللغوية التي توصلنا إليها في هذا البحث . بل إن الدلائل اللغوية تؤكد الصلات اللغوية بين لهجات شرق الجزيرة وجنوبها . فأزد عمان نزحوا من اليمن بعد انهيار سد مأرب وبالمثل فإن قبائل عبد القيس - كما رأينا في هذه الدراسة - نزحت من سهول تهامة باليمن قبل أن تتخذ البحرين مقرا لها . وربما فسر هذا التقارب التاريخي وجود خصائص صرفية موغلة في القدم في كل من البحرانية والعمانية واليمانية ، هذه الخصائص تميز اللهجات التي يتكلمها الحضر من سكان شرقي وجنوبي الجزيرة الذين استوطنوا المنطقة قبل مجيء الإسلام .

اما بالنسبة للكلمات المُعَرَّبَة أو المستعارة من الفارسية فقد وجدنا أنها ليست شائعة في البحرانية فحسب بل هي متداولة حتى هذا اليوم في لهجات شرق وجنوب الجزيرة كالعُمانية والظفارية واليمانية . (انظر الجزء السادس من الدراسة) ومرد هذا هو :

١- الصلات التجارية القديمة بين فارس والهند وشرقي الجزيرة وجنوبها .

٢- الحكم الفارسي لإقليم البحرين وجنوب الجزيرة قبل الإسلام

إن انتشار التعليم وكذلك وسائل الاعلام من إذاعة وتلفزيون قد ترك أثره في السلوك اللغوي لدى الناس . وكذلك نلاحظ اليوم أن كثيرا من مفردات اللهجة استبدلت بأخرى من الفصحى . هذا النوع من التغيير لم يصب المفردات فقط بل تجاوزها فشمل الأصوات والجوانب الصرفية أيضا .

وأخيرا إن النزر اليسير الذي نشر عن اللهجات القطيفية والأحسائية يجعل من المحال الدخول في تفاصيل تلك اللهجتين

على الرغم من أن هذه الدراسة كشفت عن وجود روابط عرقية وقبلية بين بحارنة البحرين المنحدرين من قبائل عبد القيس وفروعها التي لا زالت باقية في شرق الجزيرة والتي ذكرتها المراجع العربية وأهمها بنو مسمار بجزيرة أوال ونظراؤهم في القطيف . وبنو مسمار هم فرع من جذيمة بن عوف من عبد القيس . (انظر مروج الذهب للمسعودي ج١ - ص ١١٠ طبعة القاهرة ١٩٥٨ م - تحقيق محمد محيي الدين عبد الحميد - كذلك انظر التنبيه والاشراف للمسعودي الصفحات ٣٣٩ - ٣٤٠) .

د . مهدي عبد الله التاجر

محتويات القسم الانجليزي

الصفحة

تمهيد وكلمة شكر xxiii
ملاحظات حول الكتابة الصوتية والرموز المستخدمة في الكتاب xxv
الرموز المختصرة xxvii
مقدمة ١
حول البحث الميداني والذين ساهموا فيه ٢
تسجيل المادة اللغوية على الأشرطة ثم كتابتها بالرموز الصوتية ٣
ترتيب المادّة العلمية ٣
أثر المدارس في نشر وتوحيد المفردات التي يشيع استعمالها
في العالم العربي ٣
أسبق المدارس التبشيرية في البحرين ٤
مدرسة الهداية الخليفية ٤
مدارس البحارنة التقليدية ٤
مدرسة با بكو في الزلاق ٤
مدرسة الأردو (الإسلامية) ٤
وصول أول دفعة من المدرسين المغتربين إلى البحرين ٤
استخدام مفردات جديدة في الحقل الزراعي ٥
تأثير وسائل الاعلام ٥
العناصر غير المحلّية في التركيبة السكّانية ٦
العرب المحلّيون ٧
العرب الهولة (حولة) ٧
عرب البحارنة ٧
روايات غير دقيقة عن أصل البحارنة ٨
التوزيع الجغرافي للبحارنة ٨
مواضع التعامل اللغوي بين العناصر المحلية وغير المحلية ٩
الوضع اللغوي في القرى ١٠
موجز عن الدراسات السابقة التي تناولت لهجات شرقي
الجزيرة العربية ١٠

قسم الدراسات العربية بشركة بابكو ١٠
العربية المحكيّة ورأى محلي(من مقابلة مع الاستاذ الكبير
ابراهيم العريّض) ١٣
الجزء الاول ـ قسم أ ١٥
اقليم البحرين قديما ١٥
حول تسمية البحرين ١٥
البحرين وعمان ١٦
جزيرة أوال وإقليم البحرين ١٦
المستوطنون الأوائل ١٦
ظهور قبائل عبد القيس ١٦
فروع عبد القيس : عِجل بن عمرو بن وديعة بن لُكَيز ١٨
شَنّ بن أفصى بن عبد القيس ١٨
هِنْب بن أفصى بن دُعْمِيّ ١٨
النمربن قاسط بن أفصى بن دُعْمِيّ بن جديلة ١٨
سكان جزيرة أوال الأقدمون ١٩
عناصر عربية متعددة في البحرين المعاصرة ٢٣
آل خليفة ٠ الأسرة الحاكمة بالبحرين ٢٣
سكان الجزيرة الأقدمون ـ موجز ٢٤
سكان سماهيج الأوائل ٢٤
سكان قرية بني جمرة ٢٤
١٧٨٣ وبعده ٢٥
قسم ب ملاحظات حول جغرافية جزر البحرين ٢٧
أهمية الجزر جغرافيا واقتصاديا ٢٧
صناعة الغوص القديمة ٢٨
ظهور الزيت وسياسة تنويع مصادر الدخل ٢٨
موجز تاريخ البحرين ٢٨
الفينيقيون ـ البحرين قبل الإسلام وبعده ٢٨
البحرين في العهد الاموي ٢٩
البحرين في العهد العباسي ٢٩
استيلاء صاحب الزنج على البحرين ٢٩
القرامطة في إقليم البحرين ٢٩
حكم أبو البهلول العوام على البحرين ٢٩
البحرين في القرن الثاني عشر الميلادي ٣٠

البحرين تحت الحكم البرتغالي ٣٠
مجيء العتوب إلى البحرين سنة ١٧٨٣م ٣٠
أحوال البحارنة في العشرينات ٣١
تظلمات البحارنة في الثلاثينات ٣١
الجزء الثاني : النظام الصوتي للهجة البحارنة ٤٠
الصوامت ٤١
الأصوات الانفجارية ـ تحقيق وتخفيف الهمزة ٤١
حذف الهمزة ٤٢
الباء ـ التاء ـ الطاء ـ الدال ٤٣
نطق الدال تاء ـ الضاد ـ الكاف ـ نطق الكاف /چ/فارسية ٤٤
الإبقاء على الكاف ٤٥
الصوت / چ / في الكلمات المستعارة ٤٦
القاف ـ نطق القاف ـ ݣاف ـ فارسية ٤٦
نطق القاف كافا ـ نطق القاف غينا في اللهجة أ ٤٧
نطق الكاف جيما في اللهجة ب ٤٨
نطق الكاف جيما في اللهجة أ ٤٩
نطق الجيم ݣافا في اللهجة ب ٥٠
نطق الجيم ياءً ٥٠
اللام المفخمة ٥٠
الراء ـ الاصوات الاحتكاكية : الغين ٥١
الخاء والهاء والواو ٥٢
نطق الثاء فاء ـ الذال ـ السين ٥٢
الزاي ـ النون ـ إدغام الأصوات الصامتة ٥٣
اختصار الأصوات ٥٤
الاصوات الصائتة أي الحركات : ٥٥
الفتحة ٥٦
حذف الفتحة ـ الفتحة المضافة ـ تحقيق الفتحة الأمامية
كفتحة خلفيـــة ٥٦
الإمالة ٥٧
الكسرة ٥٩
الضمة الناتجة عن الكسرة ٥٩
حركة (بادئة) لتسهيل النطق بالساكن Prosthetic Vowel ٦١
حركة لتسهيل النطق بالساكنين المتتاليين Anaptyctic Vowel ٦١

حركة الضمة القصيرة ـ الكسرة الطويلة ـ الحركة
الطويلة / ee / كما في بيت ٦٢
الفتحة الأمامية الطويلة ٦٣
الفتحة الخلفية الطويلة ٦٤
الضمة الطويلة ٦٥
الحركات المركبة ٦٥
اجتماع الصوامت ٦٦
التشديد ٦٧
البنية المقطعية لبعض الأسماء والأفعال ٦٧
النبر في اللهجة ب ٦٨
الجزء الثالث : النهج الصرفي في اللهجة البحرانية ٧٠
الفعل الصحيح ـ الفعل التام ٧٢
الفعل المضارع ٧٢
فعل الأمر ٧٢
نماذج من الأفعال الشائعة في اللهجة ب وتفعيلاتها ٧٤
الفعل المعتل ـ الفعل المهموز ٧٥
همزة الوسط ٧٦
همزة النهاية ٧٦
الأفعال التي تبدأ بحرف الواو وتفعيلاتها ٧٧
الافعال التي تبدأ بحرف الياء وتفعيلاتها ٧٧
الفعل الأجوف ٧٨
تفعيلات الفعل الاجوف ٧٨
الفعل الناقص ٧٨
فعل معتل الحرفين ٨٠
الأفعال المشدّدة ٨٠
المبني للمجهول ٨١
الأفعال المهموزة ٨١
الفعل الأجوف ٨٢
الأفعال الناقصة ٨٢
الأفعال المشددة ٨٢
الفعل الرباعي ٨٢
تفعيلات الفعل الرباعي ٨٢
اسم الفاعل واسم المفعول ٨٣

استخدام اسم الفاعل كفعل ـ نماذج شائعة من اسم الفاعل ٨٤
الصيغ الاسمية ٨٥
استخدام اللواحق ..... لتشكيل الأسماء والصفات ـ المفرد ٨٦
المثنى ـ الجمع السالم ـ صيغة التصغير ٨٦
الجمع ٨٧
اسم الفعل ـ وتفعيلاته ٨٨
تراكيب شائعة من الأسماء وأسماء الأفعال ٨٩
صيغة الجمع المكسور ٩١
نماذج شائعة من صيغة الجمع المكسور في ب ٩٢
التنوين ٩٤
الإضافة ٩٥
مقارنة الصفات ـ صيغة المبالغة ٩٥
الأعداد: الأعداد الأصلية من واحد إلى عشرة ٩٦
من ثلاثة إلى تسعة ـ من إحدى عشر إلى تسعة عشر ٩٦
من عشرين إلى تسعين ـ الأعداد بعد المائة ٩٧
الأعداد الترتيبية من الأول إلى العاشر ٩٨
الضمائر الشخصية ٩٨
الضمائر المتصلة ٩٩
الأداة إيّا مع الضمائر المتصلة ١٠٠
الضمائر الانعكاسية نفس ـ روح ١٠٠
ضمائر الملكية : مال ـ و مالت ١٠٠
أسماء الاشارة ١٠١
اسم الإشارة للدلالة على المكان ـ استعمال أسماء الاشارة
مع الضمائر المتصلة ١٠٢
اسم الموصول ـ اللي ـ الأدوات ـ حروف الجر ١٠٢
حذف حروف الجر ـ الظروف ١٠٢
حروف العطف ـ استخدام حروف العطف كظروف ـ التعجب ١٠٥
الاستفهام ١٠٦
الجزء الرابع : بعض الملامح النحوية ١٠٨
الفعل ـ الفعل التام ١٠٨
الفعل الناقص ١٠٩
استخدام الفعل ـ اجي ـ كظرف ـ الأمر ـ اسم الفاعل ١١٠
استخدام رايح و جاي للدلالة على زمن المستقبل ١١١

المبني للمجهول ١١٢
مطابقة الفعل مع الفاعل ـ الاستفهام ١١٢
نفي الافعال ١١٤
النفي المزدوج ١١٤
الاسم ـ الاسم غير المُعَرَّف ١١٥
المطابقة بين المُعَرَّف وغير المُعَرَّف ١١٦
المطابقة بين الجنس (النحوي) والعدد ١١٦
صفات الألوان ١١٧
نفي الجملة الاسمية ١١٨
نفي الضمائر الشخصية ١١٨
بنية الجملة ١١٩
الجملة الاسمية ـ الجملة الفعلية ـ تأثير التوكيد على
موقع الكلمات من الجملة ١١٩
عندما يتبع الاسم الصفة ـ الصفة : خوش ـ الأداة : ويش ١٢٠
الاداة : كِلّ ـ أسماء الاشارة ـ استخدامها للدلالة على
الأشياء القريبة والبعيدة ١٢٠
أسماء الإشارة مع الضمائر المتصلة ١٢٢
الاداة ـ إيّا ـ الجمل الشرطية ١٢٢
الاسم الموصول ١٢٥
الجمل الزمنية ١٢٦
الجزء الخامس : المفردات ١٢٨
الجزء أ ـ نماذج للتجاور Collocation بين الكلمات ١٢٨
نماذج لجمل فعلية ـ ونماذج لكلمات محلّيّة ١٢٩
بعض الأمثال الشائعة ١٣٠
كلمات عربية قديمة شائعة في اللهجة ب ١٣١
مفردات من الفصحى ـ تغاير المفردات في اللهجتين أ و ب ١٣١
تغاير بعض مفردات اللهجة البحرانية ١٣٢
الجزء ب ـ ملاحظات حول المفردات الانجليزية السائدة
في اللهجة البحرانية ١٣٣
ملاحظات حول المفردات الهندية Hindustani في اللهجة
البحرانية ١٣٤
ملاحظات حول المفردات الفارسية في اللهجة البحرانية ١٣٤
ملاحظات أخرى حول المفردات الهندية والفارسية السائدة
في اللهجة ١٣٥

نماذج من الكلمات المُعَرَّبَة ١٣٥
نماذج من الاستعارات من اللغة الانجليزية ١٣٥
نماذج من الاستعارات من اللغة الهندية ١٣٦
نماذج من الاستعارات من اللغة الفارسية ١٣٧
نماذج من الاستعارات من اللغة التركية ١٣٨
الجزء ج المفردات الخاصة ـ مفردات خاصة بالزراعة ١٣٨
مفردات منتقاة من نص المقابلة مع زارع نخل ١٣٩
نماذج لمفردات من كلام البحارة ١٣٩
نماذج لمفردات من حديث مع حائك نسيج ١٤٠
نماذج لكلمات من الطب الشعبي ١٤٠
الجزء السادس : التحليل المقارن ـ الفونولوجيا ـ الأصوات
الانفجارية ١٤٣
حول نطق صوت الكاف / چ / فارسية ١٤٥
حول استخدام الضمير / ش / للمخاطبة المؤنثة ١٤٦
حول نطق القاف كافا في القرى ١٤٧
حول نطق القاف گافا فارسيّة ـ حول نطق القاف غينا في اللهجة أ ١٤٨
حول نطق الغين قافا في اللهجة أ ـ حول نطق القاف جيما
في اللهجة أ ١٤٨
حول نطق الجيم ياء ١٤٩
اللام المفخمة ـ الأصوات الاحتكاكية ١٤٩
نطق الثاء فاء في اللهجة ب ١٥٠
إبقاء النون في ضمير المخاطبة المؤنثة وضمير الجمع في
اللهجة ب ١٥٠
الإمالة في اللهجة ب ١٥٢
أنصاف الحركات ١٥٣
علم الصرف : التراكيب الفعلية ١٥٤
الياء ـ بادئة الفعل المضارع ١٥٤
اللواحق : -نِّ و تِنّ كما في : شارِنّه و شارِتِنّه ١٥٦
فعاعيل بدلا من فعّالون ـ أفعل > فعل في اللهجة أ ١٥٧
التنوين ـ عَشْ و عَشَر مع الأُعداد ١٥٧
الضمائر الشخصية ١٥٨
أسماء الإشارة ـ تحقيق مقاطع قصيرة متتالية في اللهجة ب ١٥٩
تأثير الأصوات الحلقية على التركيب المقطعي للهجة أ ١٥٩

المفردات ـ دراسة مقارنة ـ ملاحظات حول المفردات ١٦٠
جدول بتوزيع المفردات المقارنة ـ من حيث النظام الصوتي ١٦٣
جدول بتوزيع السمات الصرفية ١٦٤
خلاصة واستنتاج ١٦٥
الملاحق والنصوص ١٧٤
توزيع السكان من حيث الجنسيات ـ إحصاءات ١٧٤
الزيادة السكانية تبعا للجنسيات ١٧٤
التوزيع حسب الديانات ١٧٥
توزيع من هم دون المسلمين ١٧٥
توزيع السكان حسب المدن والقرى ١٧٥
تعداد منازل السكن ١٧٦
مجموع السكان حسب الجنس والسكن (مدينة / قرية) ١٧٧
نماذج من نصوص المقابلات مع أفراد يتكلمون اللهجة البحرانية ١٧٨
قائمة بأسماء الرواة وقراهم ١٩٥
قائمة بأسماء الكتب والمصادر ٢٠٠
الخرائط
خريطة رقم ١ البحرين بالنسبة لباقي المنطقة المجاورة لها ٢١٣
خريطة رقم ٢ الأماكن القديمة التي ذكرها المؤرخون أو الجغرافيون العرب ٢١٤
خريطة رقم ٣ التوزيع الجغرافي لأسماء القبائل حسب ماورد في التحليل المقدم في الجزء الأول قسم أ ٢١٥
خريطة رقم ٤ التوزيع الجغرافي للهجتي البحرين الرئيسيتين ٢١٦
خريطة رقم ٥ توزيع ضمير المخاطبة المؤنثة ش ٢١٧
خريطة رقم ٦ توزيع نطق الكاف گافا فارسية ٢١٨
خريطة رقم ٧ توزيع نطق القاف غينا ٢١٩
خريطة رقم ٨ توزيع نطق الثاء فاء ٢٢٠
خريطة رقم ٩ توزيع الضمائر المتصلة -چ -چم - هِم ٢٢١
خريطة رقم ١٠ توزيع صناعات البحارنة التقليدية ٢٢٢

صورفوتوغرافيــــة

١- قروي بحراني
٢- مزارع يستعرض أدواته الزراعية
٣- الحاج علي عبدالله نجم **ومنسجه** في بني جمرة
٤- صياد سمك
٥- **صيادون من قرية الدراز**
٦- المنازل القديمة في البحرين
٧- بيوت بحرينية قديمة

القسم العربــي

تقديم بقلم رئيس التحرير	١
تمهيد بقلم المؤلف	٨
مسرد بالمصطلحات اللغوية انجليزي - عربي	٣٠

Glossary of linguistic terms: English-Arabic

Affricates	الأصوات الانفجارية الاحتكاكية
Affrication	الانفجار الاحتكاكي
Alveo-Dental	لثوى/ أسناني
Alveolars	الأصوات اللثوية
Articulation	النطق
Manner of ———	هيئة النطق
Point of ———	موضع النطق
Broad Transcription	كتابة صوتية واسعة
Concord	(قوانين)المطابقة
Consonants	الأصوات الصامتة /الساكنة
Context of Situation	الموقف اللغوي
Dental	أسناني
Dento-Alveolars	أسناني لثوي
Descriptive or Synchronic Approach	المنهج الوصفي
Diachronic or Historical Approach	المنهج التاريخي
Diacritical Marks	علامات مميزة
Diphthong	حركة مركبة
Duality of Speech	الثنائية في الكلام الانساني
Epiglottis	لسان المزمار
Etymology	علم تاريخ الكلمات

Formal Characteristics	خواص أومميزات شكلية
Fricatives	الأصوات الاحتكاكية
Gender	النوع (تذكير ـ تأنيث)
Glottal Stop	الوقفة الحنجرية (صوت الهمزة في العربية)
Glottis	فتحة المزمار
Grammar	قواعد اللغة
Grammatical Categories	الأجناس النحوية
Gutturals	الأصوات الحلقية
Intonation	التنغيم
Labials	الأصوات الشفوية / الشفهية
Larynx	الحنجرة وبها الوتران الصوتيان
Lexicography	الدراسات المعجمية
Linguistics	علم اللغة
Liquids	الأصوات الذُلقِيّة
Morpheme	وحدة صرفية / المورفيم
Bound ————	المورفيم المقيَّد
Free ————	المورفيم الحرّ
Inflecting ———	المورفيم المتعلق بالصرف والنحو
Morphological Categories	الأجناس الصرفية
Morphology	علم الصرف
Mutual Intelligibility	الفهم المتبادل
Narrow Transcription	كتابة صوتية ضيقة
Nasal Cavity	تجويف الأنف
Normative or Prescriptive Approach	المنهج المعياري
Oral Cavity	تجويف الفم
Orthography	الأبجدية / الألف والباء
Palatals	الأصوات النطعية

Palate	الحنك
At the Phonetic Level	على مستوى الفوناتيك / على المستوى الصوتي المحض
Phonetic Realization	التحقيق الصوتي
Phonetic System	النظام الصوتي
Phonetic Transcription	الكتابة الصوتية
Phonetics	علم الأصوات/دراسة نطق الأصوات
Phonological Feature	ظاهرة صوتية فونولوجية
At the Phonological Level	من الناحية الصوتية الوظيفية / على المستوى الصوتي الوظيفي
Phonology	دراسة وظيفة الأصوات في الكلام
Plosive	صوت انفجاري
Prefix(es)	سابقة / سوابق
Prominence	الضغط / الارتفاع
Semantics	علم الدلالة /علم المعنى
Sound Units, Phonemes	وحدات صوتية
Speech Souns	الأصوات الكلامية
Stop	وقفة
Stress	النبر
Prefix(es)	لاحقة / لواحق
Syllabic Structure	التركيب المقطعي
Syntax	علم النحو / علم التراكيب
Uvula	اللهاة
Uvular	صوت لَهَوي
Vocal Apparatus	الجهاز الصوتي
Vocal Cords	الوترين الصوتيين
Voiced Sound	صوت مهجور
Voiceless Sound	صوت مهموس
Vowel Glides	حركات انزلاقيّة

Vowels	الحركات / الصوائت
Anaptyctic	حركات لتسهيل النطق بالساكنين المتتاليين
Back	حركات خلفيّة
Central	حركات مركزيّة
Front	حركات أماميّة
Long	حركات طويلة
Prosthetic	حركات (بادئة) لتسهيل النطق بالساكن
Semi-	أنصاف حركات
Short	حركات قصيرة